The Afterlife
and the
True Nature of Reality

The Quest for Answers
to the
Great Questions of Existence

John T. Mennella

The Afterlife and the True Nature of Reality

Copyright © 2015 by John T. Mennella

Disclaimer

It is not the intention of the author to advise on health care. The information in this book is provided as an information resource only, and is not to be used or relied on for any diagnostic or treatment purposes. This information is not intended to be patient education and should not be used as a substitute for professional diagnosis and treatment. Please see a medical professional about any health concerns you have.

To contact the author, to read articles and discussions regarding topics covered in this book, and to access free downloads of relevant materials, please visit the author's web site at:

www.reality-revealed.com

ISBN-13: 978-1507613030

ISBN-10: 1507613032

THE AFTERLIFE AND THE TRUE NATURE OF REALITY

To my wife Sally and my son Tom:
While under hypnosis I learned that you both are
my closest soulmates in the Afterlife.
(But, of course, I already knew that!)
Our family has been my greatest source of peace and joy.
Thank you both *so much*.

– and –

To Amy Benesch and Mira Kelley,
who guided me with great skill and care
through the other-realities of the subconscious.
I could not have chosen better guides for these incredible journeys.

THE AFTERLIFE AND THE TRUE NATURE OF REALITY

Contents

The earlier period [the Middle Ages] was the age of faith, based upon reason. In the later period [the eighteenth century] ... it was the age of reason, based upon faith. ... In comparing these epochs it is well to remember that reason can err, and that faith may be misplaced.

– Alfred North Whitehead, mathematician and philosopher

The suppression of uncomfortable ideas may be common in religion or in politics, but it is not the path to knowledge, and there's no place for it in the endeavor of science.

– Carl Sagan, astrophysicist

Science doesn't deal – as it's always at pains to point out – with what's called "subjective experience." Well, that's really too bad, because that's all any of us ever have – is subjective experience.

– Terence McKenna, author

The greatest ignorance is to reject something you know nothing about.

– Derek Bok, lawyer and educator

Alone, of all human beings in human history, Thomas the doubter touched the incorporeal resurrected body of Christ. *Only the doubter* was allowed *that* privilege.

– Terence McKenna, author

The Afterlife and the True Nature of Reality

Introduction

An important theme that arises repeatedly throughout the latter part of this book is a cornerstone principle of the Hermetic tradition: "As above, so below." One common interpretation of this phrase is the notion that the earth plane is patterned after the heavenly realms, and I personally believe there is some degree of truth to that idea. But there is another interpretation that harbors a much more profound implication: namely, that the structure of reality at any given level bears a correspondence to its structure at every other level. This ancient Hermetic concept has cropped up, quite unexpectedly, in the modern-day discoveries of holography and fractal geometry.

A hologram is a virtual 3D image created by shining a laser through a holographic plate. A fascinating property of holograms is that, if you break up the holographic plate into pieces, then each piece contains all the information necessary to produce the entire holographic image; that is, the whole is contained within each of its parts – "as above, so below."

A Fractal is a geometric figure that exhibits the same repeating pattern at every level of scale; this property, wherein an object's overall structure is similar to that of its parts, is called self-similarity – again, "as above, so below." Holograms, fractals, and self-similarity play important roles in topics covered later in this book.

In keeping with the "as above, so below" theme, this book's title is in self-similar correspondence with the book itself, in the sense that the totality of the book's content is encapsulated within its brief title. As such, a deconstruction of the book's title affords an excellent opportunity for presenting an overview of the book's subject matter. Let's begin, then, by looking more closely at the title ...

Deconstructing the Book's Title

The Afterlife and the True Nature of Reality

Disassembled, the title reveals the two most important topics to be covered: *The Afterlife* and *The Nature of Reality*. Use of these phrases in the title implies that there is something meaningful and, presumably, *new* to be said about them; furthermore, qualifying *The Nature of Reality* with the adjective *True* suggests that the commonly held notions about Reality are false. Finally, combining those two phrases together into a single title implies that there is some connection between the two. And there you have the essence of this book. Specifically, what we find beneath the surface of this book's title are three deceptively simple, yet staggeringly profound, implications. Namely, that:

1. There actually *is* an afterlife, and we actually *know* something concrete and specific about the afterlife.

2. The reality in which we exist is different from that which we experience it to be.

3. The afterlife and our living reality are somehow interrelated.

These are three rather bold assertions, yet I suggest that they are all true. Further, I propose that an awareness of the truth of these assertions, and of the facts and evidence which underlie them, can have a positive transformative effect on our lives, both individually and collectively.

Let me briefly elaborate further on each of these points before we explore them in depth throughout the remainder of this book.

ASSERTION #1: There actually *is* an afterlife, and we actually *know* something concrete and specific about the afterlife.

For most of us, our beliefs and conceptualizations regarding the afterlife – if we believe in one at all – are an outgrowth of our religious convictions and upbringing. And these convictions, while sharing some basic tenets, can vary dramatically from one religion to the next (or even among sub-factions within a single religious system). Most importantly, these religions offer no proof whatsoever that the afterlife is what they claim it to be; religious adherents are asked to accept the unsubstantiated claims regarding the afterlife on faith alone. Mainstream science, on the other hand, does not acknowledge the existence of an afterlife at all, nor does it acknowledge its necessary precursor, the soul. Yet most people are not aware that there exists a surprisingly voluminous and detailed body of knowledge about the afterlife that derives from sources other than religion, speculation, or myth. These more modern examinations into the hereafter have produced an amazingly elaborate model of the afterlife's structure, function, and process. Furthermore, the model that emerges from these diverse sources boasts a high level of credibility due to rigorous methods of investigation and analysis, repeated replication of results, corroborative consistency among sources, and, in some cases, verifiable data. Additionally, and perhaps more importantly, this model possesses a logical coherency and an elegance which leave one with a powerful, gut-level sense that it simply must be so.

Parts I and II of this book will cover the subject of the afterlife in depth, beginning with a brief discussion of some of the sources of information about the hereafter, followed by a thorough examination of recent findings, and, ultimately, a discussion of the surprisingly elaborate afterlife model that emerges therefrom.

ASSERTION #2: The reality in which we exist is different from that which we experience it to be.

My inclusion of the word "True" in this book's title – "The Afterlife and the *True* Nature of Reality" – implies that our perceived reality is somehow different from a presumably objective, "genuine" reality. Strange as it may seem, this appears to actually be the case. Findings from the fields of physics, mathematics, and neuroscience, as well as studies of human perception, offer tantalizing evidence that our "reality" is not the concrete, mechanistic system we heretofore thought it to be. Indeed, indications are that the reality which we experience is not a fundamental, objective reality but, rather, the product of our perception of a more complex reality as it is received through our sensory organs and decoded/interpreted by our brains. If the implications of these findings prove true, then a whole flurry of vitally important questions is unleashed; to wit: *What is the raw, un-encoded reality that underlies our perceived reality? Why are we programmed to interpret that raw reality into the reality that we experience? Is our programming the result of natural processes (e.g., evolution) or is it artificially imposed?* I intend to provide very specific answers to each of these questions.

ASSERTION #3: The afterlife and our living reality are somehow interrelated.

Most religions and ancient belief systems espouse the doctrine that our experiences after we die are a direct result of how we live our lives here on Earth: If we live our lives in accordance with specific moral precepts, then our after-life (or after-death) experiences will be positive; if, however, we succumb to worldly temptations and live amoral lives, then our after-life experiences will be unpleasant. Presuming, for the moment, that this widely held belief is true, it follows logically that the reality we perceive here on Earth has been specifically designed for that purpose; that is, to facilitate a system of evaluating our conduct and then holding us accountable accordingly. In other words, the question that arises is this: Is our perceived reality a purpose-made construct designed specifically to provide us a setting, with attendant circumstances, to serve as a method of testing and evaluation for determining where we will find ourselves in a consequent afterlife?

The modern-day, secular model of the afterlife that we will explore in this book suggests very strongly that this is precisely the case. Our earthy existences and concomitant experiences appear to be intimately intertwined with, and dictated by, the larger life we live on the spiritual plane. Thus the reality in which we live out our earthly lives seems to have been specifically created and designed to serve as the stage upon which these living dramas are carried out. If this is indeed so, then it is of supreme importance that we develop an understanding of what the afterlife is, how it relates to our earthly lives, and how our experience of reality fits into this overall scheme. That is precisely the purpose of this book. For these reasons, Part III will focus on a discussion of *The Nature of Reality*.

Part IV of this book proposes an alternative theory of the nature and origin of reality that incorporates points discussed in Part III of this book, while also postulating a possible relationship between this reality model and the model of the afterlife introduced in Part II. Part IV will also introduce a new theory that planet Earth is in the process of undergoing a dimensional shift in conjunction with a corresponding evolutionary leap of the human race. I've included a discussion of this purported dimensional shift because it is intimately intertwined with both our experience of reality and with the modern model of the afterlife.

Each one of us appears to be uniquely different from the billions of other human beings living upon this planet; our physical appearances, attitudes, beliefs, talents, life circumstances, and experiences vary dramatically from one person to another. Yet there are at least three points of commonality that we all indisputably share: we are all born, we all experience an existence in this reality, and we all die. It seems a matter of obvious common sense that we would want to know as much as possible about these three fundamental common denominators of human existence: Where do we come from before we are born? What is the nature and purpose of existence? And where do we go when it ends? These are *huge* questions, pregnant with complexity and mystery. Yet they are of profound and primal importance if we are to truly understand *what* we are and *why* we are. How can we dare *not* ask these questions?

Theses Overview

While the main title of this book highlights the broad topics to be covered, the book's subtitle – "The Quest for Answers to the Great Questions of Existence" – alludes to the major theses to be presented and the motivating factors that led to their development. The motivating factors – the sources of incentive and inspiration for me – are these "Great Questions of Existence," which I take to be the following:

- Where do we come from before we are born?
- Where do we go after we die?
- Why are we here?
- What is the true nature of the reality in which we exist?
- Where are we headed?

These questions have both intrigued and haunted me since my youth. In my early years I considered them to be unanswerable philosophical mysteries, but as I grew older and acquired more knowledge I began to suspect that the answers to these questions were not inherently elusive but, rather, tangible and fathomable. The theses that will be set forth in these pages arose out of discoveries I've made during my own journey of research and personal exploration in pursuit of the answers to these questions. Those theses are as follows:

- There is an afterlife.
- Research has led to the establishment of a detailed model of the afterlife.
- The essential nature of human beings is spiritual and eternal.
- Karma and reincarnation are fundamental features of our spiritual existence.
- Our reality is not a physical reality.
- The true reality is an energy-information construct.
- Our reality is a perceived reality that is decoded by our senses and brain.
- We decode the energy-information construct into a holographic reality.
- The holographic illusion of reality serves as a school for spiritual growth.
- The Earth will soon undergo a dimensional shift.
- This dimensional shift will be accompanied by an evolutionary leap for humanity.

The model of the afterlife I will explore arose primarily out of research in the areas of near-death experiences, past-life and life-between-lives hypnotic regression, and spontaneous past-life recall – most particularly from the life-between-lives research of Michael Newton, PhD. The information regarding the nature of reality derives mostly from quantum physics, chaos theory, mathematics, and the holographic model of reality; most notable in this regard is the work of Michael Talbot.

As for myself, an intense personal interest in all of these areas led to a great deal of reading over many, many years. A diagnosis of prostate cancer in 2003 made the relevancy of these topics even more acutely personal and significant for me, and inspired me to experience hypnotic regression first-hand for the purposes of healing, past-life and life-between-lives exploration, and the discovery of deeper revelations regarding life and reality. This book is the product of the discoveries and insights that resulted from my many years of research and personal exploration.

Truth

So, then, what of the "truth" of the premises presented herein? As to the Model of the Afterlife, I strongly feel that it is an extremely accurate representation of what lies on the other side of the veil: it is logical, it is elegant, and the evidence is compelling. Other than the possibility of minor refinements or additions to the model, I would be shocked to learn that it was seriously flawed. So I, personally, accept this model of the Afterlife as accurate with a high degree of confidence and a modicum of skepticism. The model of Reality presented in these pages, however, is another story. Obviously, I accept it as the best model currently available, or I would not have included it in this book. But the level of confidence I ascribe to it is not as strong as that which I ascribe to the Afterlife Model. This lower level of confidence is not due to any perceived flaw in the Reality Model, but rather is due to the complexity and elusiveness inherent in the very concept of the nature of reality itself. We are, each of us, after all, intricately enmeshed *within* this reality: how can we study and analyze something from within? An eye cannot see itself, and a hand cannot touch itself. As Marshall McLuhan has noted, "Whoever discovered water, it certainly wasn't a fish." Nevertheless, I strongly believe that – via a systems approach incorporating physics, neuroscience, and spirituality – we will someday acquire a very accurate picture of the true nature of reality. I just don't think we're there yet. That being said, I am reservedly confident that the Holographic Model is pointing us in the right direction.

Intent

A word about the *intent* of this book: By no means am I attempting to convince you that the theses presented in this book represent a "true" state of affairs. I, myself, make it a point to always maintain a degree of skepticism about any premise to which I'm exposed, no matter how tempting and convincing it may seem. I do this for two reasons: (1) the premise might be false; (2) if not entirely false, it might merely represent a limiting case of the whole picture… a *quasi-truth*, as it were. One never knows what new discoveries might come along and supersede, or refine, the existing consensus on a particular idea. For centuries Newton's model of physics reigned supreme, only to be supplanted by Einstein's insights, which, in turn, succumbed to quantum physics. Knowledge and understanding are ever-expanding, and one should, I believe, always make allowances for the possibility that a prevailing theory might not, well, "prevail" indefinitely. Therefore, I offer the ideas presented in this book as concepts to be mentally played with – as playthings for the intellect. My hope is that you will approach these concepts with an open mind tempered with skepticism and a sense of reasonableness, as well as with your personal gut feelings regarding their plausibility; and also that you will afford them due consideration consistent with the evidence presented. Furthermore, and perhaps more importantly, I offer them as seeds for the germination of new ideas – rudimentary yet interesting and enticing notions which, after personal contemplation, might evolve into yet more accurate models of reality and the afterlife.

But by far and most importantly, I've written this book with the hope that those who read it will experience the amazing and uplifting transformation that I, and many others, have experienced when exposed to this information. Profound personal changes, such as: a diminished fear of death; increased feelings of love, empathy, and compassion; reduced concern for material possessions; increased happiness and optimism; and reduced stress and worry – just to highlight a few – routinely result from exposure to, and contemplation of, details about the afterlife. The extraordinarily positive changes I have undergone as a result of my research and hypnosis experiences have improved my life, attitudes, and sense of wellbeing immeasurably. It is my sincere hope that readers of this book will enjoy a similar transformative experience.

Part I

Karma, Reincarnation and the Afterlife

We are, in fact, hyper-dimensional objects of some sort which cast a shadow into matter, and the shadow in matter is the body. And at death ... the thing that casts the shadow withdraws.

– Terence McKenna, author

The body is the placenta of the soul.

– Thomas Vaughan, philosopher

Chapter 1

Reincarnation and Karma

For you to be *always you* would be an insufferable bore, and therefore it is arranged that you stop being you after awhile and then come back as someone else altogether.

– Alan Watts, philosopher

As mentioned in the introduction, most peoples' conception of an afterlife derives from their religious beliefs and upbringing. While the details of these varying doctrines can differ dramatically, there is nevertheless a core of suppositions that is common to virtually all spiritual belief systems, namely: (a) that our true essence is of a spiritual nature; (b) that our spiritual essence assumes material form for the purpose of experiencing a brief physical existence; (c) that our behavior throughout our earthly lives is evaluated against a system of moral precepts; and (d) the resulting verdict determines the subsequent quality of whatever mode of existence awaits us after physical death.

To illustrate how such a system might operate in a specific case, let me use my own religious upbringing as an example. I was raised as a Catholic. While my parents were also both brought up Catholic – my mother being of Italian descent and my father Italian-Irish – neither was a practicing Catholic: they did not attend mass on Sundays or other holy days, they did not abstain from eating meat on Fridays, and, in general, they did not abide by any of the rules or rituals of the Catholic religion. Indeed, my father, for reasons I can only guess at, had at some point in his life completely abandoned the notion of a God, as well as a hereafter, and had become an atheist who firmly believed that after we die there is nothing. Nevertheless, their limited enthusiasm for Catholicism notwithstanding, they both insisted that I follow a Catholic path: I was made to attend church, receive the holy sacraments, etc. (I attended public school however), all of which I abandoned (without any apparent realization on their part) when I was about fourteen years old. My understanding of the Catholic view on the subject of the afterlife, as it was relayed to me by priests, nuns, and "religious instruction" laypersons, is as follows: We experience exactly one lifetime in physical form on Earth; after we die we are judged against a system of rules rooted in the ten commandments; then, depending upon how we measure up, our soul will experience either an eternal life in heaven (a place of unimaginable bliss) or in hell (a place of unimaginable suffering and horror), with a possible temporary respite in a place called "purgatory" where the soul may be sent for limited punishment and cleansing if one's earthly sins were not severe enough to qualify for an eternity in hell yet not minor enough to permit immediate access to heaven (once a soul in purgatory is sufficiently cleansed it is then allowed to ascend to heaven). As can clearly be seen, the Catholic scenario possesses all the basic elements constituting the core of common religious beliefs which were discussed earlier: we are a soul which temporarily inhabits a physical body to experience a lifetime on Earth, we are judged, and then, based upon that judgment, we are either rewarded or punished with an afterlife in either heaven or hell. But it was precisely this belief system that caused me to question the Catholic philosophy and, ultimately, to abandon it entirely. The reasons for my "crisis of faith" are highly relevant to the main concepts to be established in this chapter, and they provide a perfect segue into a discussion of those concepts.

For me, the major problem with the Catholic model lay in what I would call its inherent unfairness and illogicality. Given that, within this model, each person is afforded one and only one opportunity (i.e., one and only one lifetime on Earth) to demonstrate his or her deservedness of an eternity in heaven versus an eternity in hell, it seems outrageously unjust that the life circumstances of each individual can vary so wildly. For example, one person can be born into the nurturing and encouraging circumstance of a loving family that enjoys economic prosperity, while another can be born into a dysfunctional family mired in the ravages of poverty and ignorance. Add to this the disparate possibilities with regard to personal qualities and talents, physical appearance, physical handicaps, etc., and one has to ask: "How is it determined who wins the 'birth lotto'?", "How can a person born with multiple advantages be judged against one born into a setting with multiple disadvantages?", and "How can such a system possibly be considered fair and reasonable?" Also, is it really reasonable to give a person "one shot" at *anything*, let alone something as critically important as one's eternal salvation? These conundrums, which grew out of my religious upbringing, plagued me from a very young age. I have always firmly believed that logic is the fundamental standard against which any theory, system, or model must be judged. I found the Catholic model not only grossly unfair and imbalanced, but also implausibly illogical. To me, this model was akin to a situation where two people are to participate in a race and one is given a supped-up sports car while the other is given a bicycle. This scenario is unreasonable to the point of being absurd, yet this is precisely the life/afterlife model that I was asked to accept by the adherents of the religion into which I was born.

Well, this scheme was so against what I considered just and sensible that it (along with some other factors) ultimately led me away from Catholicism. But I continued to ponder the enigma, and I often wondered if there might be a model to replace it that was fair, logical, and tenable. Ruminating over this question, I proceeded to analyze it by breaking it down into smaller parts and attempting to identify precisely *where* the model was weakest. To my way of thinking, the core of the problem lay in the "one and only one lifetime" aspect of the model: It seemed to me that, if we were each given multiple opportunities (i.e., multiple lifetimes) to demonstrate our spiritual qualities, then we would in effect be getting multiple "second chances", something I considered fair and reasonable. Also, this new "multiple lifetimes" model also solved the problem of the inequitableness of varied life circumstances – i.e., with the opportunity for multiple lifetimes we could all get to experience the wide range of possibilities available: prince or pauper, sage or simpleton, etc. Furthermore, with multiple lifetimes I could easily envision this new model incorporating *learning* into its design: we could learn from our mistakes – from one lifetime to the next – and thus be afforded the opportunity to improve and advance along a path of spiritual evolution. I can barely describe the elation I felt when this new model first occurred to me – it was so logical and so *elegant.* Being a person with a mathematical background, this appealed to me greatly. I'm embarrassed to admit, however, that I thought this idea was original and that I had brilliantly and single-handedly solved the problem of the life-afterlife conundrum. It wasn't until I was in my late 20's when I learned that, not only was my great idea far from being original, but *it was over two thousand years old.*

As I alluded to above, one of my preferred areas of interest has always been mathematics. I had been a strong math student throughout my public school years, and I went on to major in mathematics in college. Stemming from my interest in math, I was also very interested in physics. However, unlike my situation with math, I did not have any formal training in physics, so I sought to satisfy my curiosity in this area by reading popular physics books geared to the layperson. One of these books exposed me to a longstanding life-afterlife model that was shockingly like the model I had naively thought I had originated, and it did so through a discussion of a philosophy of life that ultimately filled the void left by my abandonment of Catholicism. Moreover, it opened my mind to such a degree that I do not exaggerate when I say that I consider my reading of this book to be one of the pivotal experiences in my personal intellectual and spiritual development. The book was "The Tao of Physics," by Fritjof Capra; the philosophy it discussed (and which I adopted) was Buddhism, and the life-afterlife model it described was reincarnation.

In his book *The Tao of Physics*, Fritjof Capra examines the fascinating parallels that exist between cutting edge physics and the Eastern philosophies of Buddhism and Taoism. Capra develops his thesis in a logically structured three-part exposition: part one is a sort of primer of modern physics, part two offers a similar presentation of eastern mysticism, and part three then presents his thesis by describing the parallels between the two. I bought the book solely for the purpose of reading part one – the physics section – but it was part two which had a profound impact on my thinking, my personal philosophy, and my worldview. Mr. Capra's book was my very first exposure to eastern mysticism, so the concepts and philosophies of Buddhism, Taoism, and Zen were entirely new to me. To say the least, my mind was blown by the revelations contained in these age-old wisdom traditions. I found virtually every aspect of these philosophies highly appealing to my personality and my way of thinking, and I embraced them as a replacement of my since-abandoned Catholicism. Not only did these philosophies fill a spiritual and ideological void within me, but they also made me aware, for the very first time, of the doctrine of reincarnation, a formalized life-afterlife model – thousands of years old – that eerily coincided with the model I had envisioned as a replacement for the one-and-only-one-lifetime belief espoused by Catholicism.

The clearest definition I have found of reincarnation, or metempsychosis, is by W.R. Alger: "…the notion that when the soul leaves the body it is born anew in another body, its rank, character, circumstances, and experience in each successive existence depending on its qualities, deeds and attainments in preceding lives." [1]
Metempsychosis in its strictest sense refers to the transmigration of the soul, that is, the passage of the soul, after death, from one body to another body – the soul being "born anew in another body." The second part of Alger's description of reincarnation – the part mentioning "…its rank, character, circumstances, and experience in each successive existence depending on its qualities, deeds and attainments in preceding lives" – suggests reincarnation's complementary concept of *karma*.
Karma is a Sanskrit term denoting "action" or "deed" and is the governing force driving the principle of Hinduism known as *samara* – the circle of cause and effect. This "Wheel of Karma," as it is often described, is a system governed by: an act, the quality of the act, and the resulting consequence. The system works as follows: a person's acts or deeds performed in a given lifetime are judged as being good or evil (often referred to as "good karma" or "bad karma"); that person's fortune or misfortune in subsequent lives is then a result of the qualitative assessment of the deeds they performed in previous lives. [2] This is the message implicit in the well-known Bible adage "as ye sow, so shall ye reap." As Mr. Alger so succinctly noted, the character and circumstances of each successive existence depend upon the caliber of the deeds performed in previous lives.
It's easy to make the mistake of viewing the karmic system as one of "reward and punishment," but an in-depth study of the philosophy underlying karma makes it clear that punishment is *not* the intention behind the process. Rather, it is one of balance, justice, and learning. Souls redeem or "pay off" their bad-karma debts by experiencing the very acts of wrongdoing which they themselves had perpetrated in previous incarnations. But, more significant is the idea that a soul can best acknowledge and comprehend the dreadful effects of his/her evil acts if he/she experiences such acts from the receiving end. This is something that I think we can all relate to from personal experience, especially if we think back to our childhood. Who of us cannot recall an occasion where we had made fun of someone, without the slightest degree of empathy for the pain we had caused them, only to later find that when *we* are the victims of such abuse, we suddenly

and shamefully comprehend the suffering we had caused when we had been the perpetrator? And, if you can recall such an experience, was it not at precisely that moment that you experienced a crystal clear understanding and appreciation of why doing such hurtful acts is *wrong*? There is no better teacher than personal experience, and that is the key philosophy underlying the law of karma and the way it is played out via the process of reincarnation. The purpose of the system of reincarnation is to afford the soul the opportunity for spiritual growth, the ultimate goal of which is reunification with the Godhead.

I think you can now see why I found the doctrine of reincarnation and karma to be more intellectually and morally satisfying than the Catholic-inspired belief system under which I was brought up. The fairness, the logic, and the opportunity for growth inherent in the concept of reincarnation are totally lacking in the Catholic one-life doctrine. The Catholic system affords us one and only one opportunity to prove ourselves worthy – if we blow it, we're doomed to suffer eternity in hell. Under the system of reincarnation and karma, however, we are given the possibility of multiple lifetimes; if we commit sins in a given lifetime, then we experience the effects of those sins from the receiving end in subsequent lifetimes, thereby "learning our lesson" by developing an understanding, via empathy, of the wrongfulness of those acts and (hopefully) never committing them again. Hence through the system of reincarnation we pay off our karmic debts, we grow spiritually as we learn from our mistakes, and, as our soul is repeatedly cleansed through recurring incarnations, we eventually reach a point of spiritual perfection (and thus liberation from earthly incarnations and reunification with God). Which system seems more logical and reasonable to you?

The concepts of reincarnation and karma lie at the very core of the model of the afterlife that will be presented in Part II, and which I believe is the most accurate representation of what happens after we die. An important fact that is often overlooked is that the joint doctrines of reincarnation and karma *themselves* presuppose the existence of an afterlife as well as the concept of the soul. Thus, before we can get into the specifics of the Afterlife Model, the most logical approach would be to first establish, to the extent possible, the actuality of both the soul and the afterlife realm. This endeavor is undertaken in the next three chapters; specifically, Chapter 2 presents a discussion of the Near-Death Experience as evidence for the reality of an afterlife and the soul, while Chapters 3 and 4 amplify the argument by offering an analysis of Childhood Past Life Memories and Past-Life Hypnotic Regression as evidence for the truth of reincarnation.

Chapter 2

Evidence for the Afterlife: The Near-Death Experience

The world is a living mystery: our birth, our death, our being in the moment – these are mysteries. They are doorways opening on to unimaginable vistas of self-exploration, empowerment and hope for the human enterprise. And our culture has killed that, taken it away from us, made us consumers of shoddy products and shoddier ideals. We have to get away from that.

Terence McKenna, author

2.1 Overview of the Near-Death Experience

Quite probably the first scientifically-grounded and formally researched evidence for the existence of an afterlife derives from the extraordinary experiences recalled by people who were clinically dead but subsequently resuscitated.

The term "Near-Death Experience" (NDE) was first coined in 1975 by Raymond Moody, M.D., in his book "Life After Life," and refers to a collection of reported personal experiences associated with a near-death episode during which a person is either clinically dead, near death, or in a situation where death is likely or expected. After resuscitation, individuals who have undergone an NDE typically describe an experience of detachment from their physical body and subsequent travel to the Afterlife/Spirit Realm. Near-death episodes can result from illness, injury, or complications during surgery. It should be noted that many near-death experiencers (NDErs) take issue with the phrase "near-death," as they believe that they were truly dead rather than merely *near*-death.

One of the most fascinating aspects of the near-death experience – and also one of the most powerful arguments for its validity – is the set of core characteristics which are common to the majority of NDEs; these include: [3]

- A perceived out-of-body experience (OBE)
- A sense of passing through a dark tunnel toward a light source

- Arrival at a realm of light, spirit, or non-material otherness
- A sense of alteration of time and/or space
- Encountering a deceased loved-one, religious figure, or spirit guide
- Heightened senses and emotions
- The experience of a panoramic review of the life just lived
- An infusion of profound cosmological knowledge and understanding
- A reluctance to return to the earth plane
- Disappointment at finding oneself revived

Let's take a closer look at several of these features to acquire a better understanding of exactly what transpires during an NDE from the point of view of the NDEr.

NDErs often have a sense of floating out of their bodies, initially "seeing" (and "hearing") events in their immediate environment from a point above. For example, during NDEs that occur as a result of surgical complications NDErs will generally find themselves looking down upon their lifeless body from a location up near the ceiling, while seeing and hearing medical personnel frantically employing resuscitation efforts. The NDE literature abounds with cases of patients accurately reporting specific details of the environment in which their NDE occurred – activities, conversations, furniture and equipment – including technical details of resuscitation efforts by hospital personnel. Recall of these observed or overheard activities by NDErs is unexplained insofar as these events transpired while the NDEr was clinically dead, unconscious or under general anesthesia.

Generally, after a period of time viewing events occurring at or near their physical body, the NDEr will undergo the sensation of travelling through a tunnel toward a particularly brilliant point of light. Passage through this cylindrical corridor is involuntary, with the NDEr feeling as though he/she is being drawn or pulled through the passageway by an unknown source and at a high rate of speed.

The journey through the tunnel ends in an ethereal realm of blinding, dazzling light where the NDEr experiences an overwhelming sense of peace and love. Also noteworthy is a complete absence of pain or fear, even if the individual had been in a state of extreme pain or fear just prior to the onset of the NDE. Intensely beautiful music and/or vividly resplendent scenes and landscapes are also sometimes reported. These sensations, coupled with a perception that time and space are somehow different or totally absent, lead the NDEr to conclude that the tunnel was a means of conveyance to the Afterlife.

The conclusion that the NDEr has reached the Afterlife is further affirmed by their being greeted by a "being of light" who is usually recognized as a deceased relative, friend or loved one, or a spirit guide or established religious figure. This light-being emanates feelings of love and compassion, and is communicated with telepathically; the being also serves to facilitate the NDEr's transition from the physical to the spiritual, and accompanies them during the most fascinating and profound component of the near death experience – the Life Review.

During the Life Review component of the Near Death Experience the NDEr participates in a very detailed and emotionally involving replay of his/her entire life. It is described as a complete recall involving the subtlest minutia – even down to the thoughts and emotions associated with each event – yet, incongruously, the entire review seems to last for only an instant. Researchers and near death experiencers have used the terms three-dimensional, panoramic, and holographic to describe the Life Review [4] (the "holographic" aspect being of particular importance in the second part of this book during our discussion of the nature of reality).

Some NDErs describe the review as involving only major events of their lives, while others say that every detail of their life was "viewed." But the term "viewed" is, in truth, inadequate to describe the full depth of the experience, because during this review the NDEr experiences all of the emotions he/she had felt during the actual events and – this is the most fascinating aspect – he/she also experiences the emotions that their words or actions evoked in the people with whom they had interacted. So, for example, while reviewing an event in your life where you had said something cruel to someone, you would not only re-experience *your* emotions at that time, but you would also experience the emotional pain felt by *the person you had hurt*. Likewise, you would also experience the joy you caused in people as a result of kindness on your part. Thus the Life Review becomes something more than a mere rehashing of one's life: the profound empathic experience of the effect our words and actions had upon others leads to an inevitable judgment of the moral quality of our life, a judgment where *we* sit in judgment of *ourselves*. NDErs repeatedly affirm that it is not the light-being that passes judgment upon them, but rather the NDEr himself who makes a moral assessment of his conduct. NDErs describe feeling sadness and shame for the times when they hurt others, while feeling joy and satisfaction as a result of their acts of kindness and compassion. Needless to say, NDErs report undergoing significant changes in attitude and outlook as a result of the lessons learned so dramatically during the Life Review. Particularly relevant is the fact that the Life Review emerges as an important element in the model of the afterlife we will later examine.

Yet another fascinating component of the near death experience is the claim on the part of many NDErs that they received a "flash of universal insight" during which all knowledge – *complete* knowledge – was revealed to them. Expressions such as "All the secrets of the universe were revealed to me," "I know how everything works," and "I knew everything there was to know" are commonly employed to convey this remarkable occasion of insight and omniscience.

Although the NDEr can recall a sense of having had this consummate revelatory experience, she does not "bring back" any memory of the specific details of the all-encompassing knowledge to which she was exposed. That being said, there are, however, cases in which the NDEr *does* exhibit, upon returning, knowledge – e.g., of a scientific or mathematical nature – which he did not possess prior to the NDE, as well as incidents of increased overall intelligence and psychic abilities. Another relevant after-effect of the near death experience is the fact that many NDErs return with a tremendous thirst for knowledge; that this craving might be a direct result of the previously experienced, but later forgotten, exposure to all knowledge is a distinct possibility. A final intriguing point in this regard is the fact that many NDErs return from their experience with the strong conviction that loving others and *accumulating knowledge* are of primary importance during our lifetimes on earth.

As the near death experience draws to a close, the NDEr is either given a choice as to whether he wants to remain in the afterlife or return to his earth life, or he is told unequivocally that it is "not his time" and therefore he *must* return to his earth life. In either case, most NDErs exhibit a strong reluctance at returning. The feelings of unconditional love and lightness of being experienced in the afterlife, when contrasted with the hardships and "heaviness" of physical life, make the decision a "no-brainer": they do not want to return to the earth plane (one individual, upon returning to his body after successful resuscitation, likened the feeling to putting on wet, muddy overalls). The lure of the afterlife is so strong that even happily married women with young children will often express the desire to remain in spirit rather than return to their families on earth. As we will see in our later discussion of the afterlife model, a similar reluctance is expressed when the time comes for a soul to leave the spirit realm and return to earth for another incarnation.

At this point, I think it will be beneficial to summarize the common features of a typical near death experience with the following representative scenario: A person "dies" as a result of a serious accident, severe illness, or medical mishap, and finds herself out of her body and floating above it, observing the efforts to resuscitate her; she may remain in that immediate locale or float off some distance; at some point she is drawn into a tunnel through which she is pulled at a high rate of speed toward a distant light source; she emerges from the tunnel into an ethereal realm of bright light and experiences a profound sense of peace and love; she is greeted by a being of light who may be a deceased relative or friend, a spirit guide, or a religious figure; the light-being accompanies her to a Life Review, where she undergoes an extremely detailed three-dimensional review of her entire life, replete with the emotions and thoughts she experienced at the time, as well as an empathic experiencing of the feelings her words and actions elicited in others; this moving and supercharged replay of one's life's impact upon others inevitably results in a self-judgment from which important lessons are learned and significant life-changing decisions are made; aside from matters of a personal nature, she may also be provided with an elucidating apprehension of all knowledge and understanding, the details of which are forgotten but which nevertheless later manifest as a thirst for knowledge, an increase in overall intelligence, and/or a heretofore nonexistent facility in a particular area; as the near death experience draws to a close, she is either given the option to return to her life or told she must return – in either case, she expresses a reluctance to return and a preference to remain in the afterlife.

2.2 A Specific NDE: The Pam Reynolds Case

One of the most well-known and oft-cited near-death experiences is that of Pam Reynolds, a singer-songwriter who had an NDE in 1991 while undergoing brain surgery. Although her NDE itself was quite typical, exhibiting many of the common core characteristics noted earlier, it was the circumstances of her surgery that make her case particularly impressive and persuasive.

Ms. Reynolds was diagnosed with having a large aneurism (a saclike widening of an artery resulting from weakening of the artery wall) in her brain. The positioning of the aneurism at the base of her brain stem made her chances of survival virtually nil. Fortunately, a rare surgical procedure known as hypothermic cardiac arrest was successfully performed by neurosurgeon Dr. Robert F. Spetzler and Ms. Reynolds had a complete recovery. Ms. Reynolds died approximately 19 years later, in May of 2010, from heart failure. [5]

As implied by its name – *hypothermic cardiac arrest* – the procedure involved lowering Reynolds' body temperature to 60° F, stopping her heartbeat and breathing, and draining the blood from her head. Additionally, her eyes were taped shut and her ears were fitted with small ear plugs containing clicking devices (the purpose of which was to ensure she had a flat EEG, i.e., a non-responsive brain, before the surgery was begun). And therein lies the astounding enigma of the Pam Reynolds case, for, although Ms. Reynolds was clinically dead during the procedure – with *no brain-wave activity* and *no blood flowing to her brain* – she nevertheless had an NDE in which she: (1) observed specific actions performed, and specific statements made, by members of the surgical team (later confirmed as accurate); and (2) was drawn to a bright light and met, among others, her deceased uncle whose insistence that she must return to her body she willfully resisted. Additionally, Ms. Reynolds also later experienced several transformative aftereffects commonly reported by NDErs (and which will be discussed later). [6]

As you can see, this was a classic NDE – accurate reportage of activities of medical personnel, being pulled to a bright light, meeting deceased relatives, unwillingness to return to the body – but it was all experienced while Ms. Reynolds' brain exhibited no brain-wave activity and was drained of blood, her eyes taped shut, and her ears plugged with a device that made clicking sounds.

Such factors render as spurious the attempts of skeptics to "explain away" the NDE phenomenon.

The volume of evidence that has been assembled in support of the reality of the near death experience is literally staggering; any attempt to present all the evidence here would be an overwhelming undertaking. It would also be pointless since, with the ubiquity of internet access, the information is readily available – just a Google search away – to anyone who is interested. Nevertheless, I would be remiss if I did not address some of the arguments offered by skeptics in their attempt to present a more mundane explanation for NDEs. For the counter-arguments, I'll simply highlight some the more significant evidentiary findings and occurrences.

2.3 Responding to the Skeptics

As described in the previous section, the sheer commonality and consistency of the core components of the NDE, reported by thousands of people, provide powerful evidence for the reality and actuality of the experience, and, by consequence, for the reality and actuality of the existence of an afterlife. Further evidence derives from the fact that, in the decades since Dr. Moody first brought this phenomenon to light, many other investigators have confirmed his findings through similar research and via scientifically rigorous controlled studies. Nonetheless, skeptics abound. Their alternative interpretations of NDEs – i.e., that the phenomenon can be rationalized via recourse to explanations more mundane than the afterlife scenario – are worth considering for the sake of completeness, fairness, and meaningful elucidation.

As mentioned earlier, NDErs frequently are able to describe in striking detail the events and setting amid which their NDE occurred, even when they are in coma or clinically dead. Skeptics often attempt to explain away such cases by claiming that the patient "unconsciously overheard" selected elements of the activities transpiring around them, whereupon the patient's brain then pieced together a mental representation of a likely scenario. However, the particulars which some NDErs relate are often too specific and detailed to be explainable in such a manner. For example, NDErs have described the *color* of pieces of furniture in the room, or have offered precise physical descriptions of medical instruments or equipment. Skeptics also claim that some of the elements of the NDE phenomenon are attributable to hallucinations, possibly caused by biological factors such as loss of oxygen to the brain. A strong argument against this claim is the fact that some patients have had NDEs while registering a flat EEG: hallucinating involves brain activity and, just as with thinking and dreaming, would thus register on an EEG. Also, hallucinations cannot explain the cases of children who have undergone an NDE and reported meeting deceased relatives whom they had never met and of whom they were not even aware. In a similar vein, some people have met a known relative during their NDE who, as far as they knew, was alive and healthy before the NDE, only to later discover that the relative had, unbeknownst to them, passed in the interim.

Two particularly inexplicable NDE occurrences were related by Kenneth Ring, Ph.D., in his book, "Lessons from the Light." The first case involved a man who had become friendly with one of his nurses while being hospitalized with double pneumonia. Later, while in a coma, the patient met this nurse on the "Other Side" and learned that she had died in an automobile accident. After coming out of the coma, the other nurses in the hospital were astounded to learn that this man was aware of the deceased nurse's death and its circumstances, including the type of automobile involved, a detail known only to her parents. The second case involved a woman who suffered cardiac arrest while in a hospital coronary care unit. During the OBE portion of her NDE she found herself not only floating above her body but also outside the hospital where she noticed a tennis shoe on a third floor ledge of the hospital building. The patient described her NDE to her critical care social worker, including the bizarre tennis shoe episode. The social worker was skeptical, but at the patient's request went up to the third floor and was shocked to discover the tennis shoe on the ledge, exactly as described by the patient.[7]

While such individual anecdotal accounts make the case for the NDE in a dramatic and personal way, and also provide the necessary and important particulars, it is ultimately analyses of aggregations of these accounts that offer a powerful "strength-in-numbers" statistical argument; though admittedly more prosaic and less fascinating, this approach provides a big-picture overview of the consistency and similarity of specific details arising from the multitude of cases reported, and thus argues against coincidence, subjective fantasy, religious or cultural predispositions, etc., as explanations. It is also more appealing to those with an inclination toward the scientific and quantitative.

One of the largest and best-known of the organizations studying the NDE phenomenon is NDERF, the Near Death Experience Research Foundation (www.nderf.org), started in 1998 by Jeffrey Long, M.D., a radiation oncologist. In his book "Evidence of the Afterlife: The Science of Near Death Experiences," Dr. Long presents the results of a study involving data from over 1300 near death experiencers accumulated over a period of ten years. Nine specific areas of evidence are discussed and analyzed in detail, and Dr. Long is quite unambiguous as to his conclusion: "My research convinces me that near-death experiences are the exit from this life and the entrance to another life." [8] In particular, the findings resulting from this study confirm, in the aggregate, the credibility of the details presented in individual cases. For example:

- The events experienced during the Life Review phase of an NDE are genuine events from the NDEr's life.
- Friends and relatives encountered by the NDEr during the experience are virtually always deceased.

- The events and settings "seen and heard" by NDErs during their out-of-body state are often verified later as being realistic and accurate.

What I find uniquely impressive and persuasive, however, are the study's findings with regard to NDEs involving children, NDEs involving the blind, and cross-cultural NDEs.

The relevance of an analysis of children's NDEs to the assertions of skeptics lies in the fact that the skeptics will often attempt to explain away the content of the NDE as being nothing more than the result of cultural and/or media influences, belief systems, or other life experiences. The conclusion reached as a result of Dr. Long's NDERF study, which did include NDEs experienced by children as well as adults, offers strong evidence in opposition to those skeptics' claims. The study found that the NDEs of very young children (who Dr. Long defines as five years of age and under) possess every NDE element that is present in the NDEs of older children and adults. Dr. Long also points out that a review of the literature covering thirty years of research on childhood NDEs fully supports the NDERF study findings. As Dr. Long so succinctly puts it, "The NDEs of children, even very young children, have the same content as adult NDEs. This strongly suggests that NDEs are not significantly influenced by preexisting cultural influences, beliefs, or life experiences." [9]

The cognitive content of the NDEs of blind people offers yet more tantalizing evidence that whatever is occurring during an NDE is much more complex than the mundane rationalizations posited by the skeptics. People who have been blind from birth cannot "imagine" what a true visual experience entails; rather, they would have to extrapolate an analogy of vision from their four remaining senses. Indeed, a study conducted by Dr. Craig Hurovitz at the University of Hartford "revealed that those blind since birth or very early childhood had (1) no visual imagery and (2) a very high percentage of gustatory, olfactory, and tactual sensory references." [10] Yet Dr. Long's findings indicate that, astonishingly, "Normal or supernormal vision occurs in near-death experiences among those with significantly impaired vision or even legal blindness. Several NDErs who were blind from birth have reported highly visual near-death experiences." [11] This determination is supported by a two-year study of NDEs and OBEs of the blind conducted by Kenneth Ring and Sharon Cooper, wherein they found that these experiences were often described in visual terms and involved visual imagery. [12]

The cross-cultural component of the NDERF study convincingly dispels (along with the portion involving childhood NDEs) cultural influences as a causative factor of the NDE phenomenon. The results suggest that NDEs "are remarkably consistent around the world," [13] including the same elements occurring in the same order. A fascinating and relevant study that further corroborates this particular feature of the NDE phenomenon is discussed in the Wikipedia article "Near-Death Experience": "Recent research into afterlife conceptions across cultures by religious studies scholar Gregory Shushan analyzes the afterlife beliefs of five ancient civilizations (Old and Middle Kingdom Egypt, Sumerian and Old

Babylonian Mesopotamia, Vedic India, pre-Buddhist China, and pre-Columbian Mesoamerica) in light of historical and contemporary reports of near-death experiences, and shamanic afterlife 'journeys'. It was found that despite numerous culture-specific differences, the nine most frequently recurring NDE elements also recur on a general structural level cross-culturally..."[14] What is particularly intriguing about the universality of the near-death experience is the fact that it transcends not only cultural boundaries, but also virtually every other demographic parameter one can imagine. Kenneth Ring, Professor Emeritus of psychology at the University of Connecticut, is a researcher within the field of near-death studies and is also the co-founder and past president of the International Association for Near-Death Studies (IANDS), and is the founding editor of the Journal of Near-Death Studies. In an interview in The New York Times from August 28, 1988, Dr. Ring addressed the all-encompassing nature of the NDE phenomenon by noting that, as a result of his research, he has discovered that "atheists were just as likely to have a near-death experience as religious people," and that "factors such as race, gender, social class, education, and age didn't affect the experience either. It also doesn't vary because of personality traits or whether you know about this kind of experience."[15] When one considers this universal character of the NDE in conjunction with the vast number of people having this experience (Dr. Ring again, from the same article: "Roughly one out of every three people who come close to death will have transcendental experiences. According to a 1981 survey, 23 million adult Americans have come close to death, so we're talking about something that is not rare."), the implications regarding the genuine and non-subjective nature of the phenomenon are staggering.

In the documentary video "Watchers 4" Dr. Long states that there are more than twenty divers explanations offered by skeptics for the near-death experience, and he goes on to note that, "The reason that there are so many skeptical explanations is that there's no one, or several, explanations that makes sense, even to the skeptics."[16] This is an excellent point, for the fact is that a theory's strength lies in how much of a phenomenon it can explain; if one needs many individual theories to account for each aspect of a particular phenomenon, then one is merely grasping at straws.

2.4 Skeptic Turned Believer: Dr. Eben Alexander

And yet, while these thousands of NDE cases and the corresponding studies make a powerful argument for the inadequacy of skeptics' specious explanations, probably the most compelling single case is that of Eben Alexander, M.D. Dr. Alexander is a neurosurgeon who, at age fifty-four, was struck by *E. coli* meningitis, a rare disease that affects the brain. Due to this illness Dr. Alexander was in a coma for seven days during which time, as he describes it, "...my entire neocortex – the outer surface of the brain, the part that makes us human – was shut down. Inoperative. In essence, absent." [17] It is this rare combination of Dr.

Alexander's credentials as a neurosurgeon (i.e., a *brain* surgeon), coupled with the closing down of his neocortex, that led to a situation wherein this NDEr was uniquely qualified to evaluate the near-death experience from a personal as well as a medical and scientific perspective. As Dr. Alexander himself explains: "[I]n my case, the neocortex was out of the picture. I was encountering the reality of a world of consciousness that existed *completely free of the limitations of my physical brain*."[18] He also notes that bacterial meningitis is a disease that can most closely "mimic human death without actually bringing it about" (and which it often does),[19] and he refers to his NDE as being "in some ways a perfect storm of near-death experiences."[20] Dr. Alexander's professional stance is that his case of having had gram negative bacterial meningitis while undergoing an NDE completely discredits the simplistic alternative explanations typically offered by skeptics.[21] The amazing experiences undergone by Dr. Alexander during his otherworldly journey are brilliantly and poignantly conveyed in his book *Proof of Heaven: A Neurosurgeon's Journey into the Afterlife*. I urge anyone interested in this topic to read his book – the details of precisely what Dr. Alexander's NDE entailed are absolutely fascinating; indeed, the experience was so deeply profound and moving that it completely altered his worldview. Dr. Alexander freely admits that, prior to his coma experience, he was a skeptic on spiritual matters as well as NDEs.[22] All that changed, however, after Dr. Alexander's NDE: "My experience showed me that the death of the body and the brain are not the end of consciousness, that the human experience continues beyond the grave ... The place I went was real. Real in a way that makes the life we're living here and now completely dreamlike by comparison."[23] Indeed, Dr. Alexander was so moved by his near-death experience that he founded an organization – Eternea – whose "...mission is to advance research, education, and applied programs concerning spiritually transforming experiences, as well as the physics of consciousness and the interactive relationship between consciousness and physical reality (e.g., matter and energy)."[24] You can visit Eternea's web site at: www.Eternea.org

So what we have is a phenomenon – the near-death experience – experienced by tens of thousands of people who, regardless of age, societal beliefs, cultural backgrounds, or visual ability, perceive the experience in a remarkably similar way. And we have an enormous volume of individual reports rich with common detail, and supported by rigorous statistical studies of aggregates of these reports, confirming the consistency and similarity of their mutually corroboratory content. To say that this mass of evidence is "compelling" is an understatement in the most restrained and moderate sense of the word. But the really big elephant in the room here is this: If the near-death experience and its coincident content are genuine and real, then the unavoidable implication is that there is indeed an afterlife. That is the singular and significant deductive hypothesis to which all the evidence points.

2.5 What We Learn from the Near-Death Experience

The near-death experience, in addition to offering an irresistible argument for the existence of an afterlife, is also rich with wisdom and transformational possibilities.   Recall from our earlier discussion that one of the core characteristics of a typical near-death experience is "an infusion of profound cosmological knowledge and understanding." During the near-death experience, NDErs are frequently presented with insights and revelations that relate to the most fundamental aspects of the nature and workings of life, existence, and reality. Often, these received insights, combined with the powerful emotional impact of the Life Review, result in a striking and transcendent spiritual awakening characterized by a re-forming of the NDEr's personal values and the adoption of a radically different outlook on life – so much so that friends and relatives of the NDEr often observe that he or she has become an entirely different person.[25] Furthermore, evidence indicates that the personal transformation experienced by NDErs is available to *anyone*; all that is required is an honest consideration and contemplation of the insights imparted and the attendant shift in consciousness that results.[26]

Let's begin, then, by taking a detailed look at the wisdom revealed to near-death experiencers. Some of the most important and affecting messages conveyed during the NDE include the following:[27]

- The primacy of love
- Everything is one
- God is everything and everything is God
- The importance of acquiring knowledge
- Everything happens for a reason
- Live life fearlessly

A detailed exploration of the above points will reveal the tremendous latent power inherent in each gem of wisdom, and will help us to comprehend and appreciate how they can cause NDErs (and us) to undergo a cogent life-altering shift in personal attitudes and beliefs.

Without doubt, the most fundamental piece of knowledge that NDErs return with from their brief visit to the afterlife realm is the firm conviction that love is of momentous significance and importance in life on earth. "What matters most in life is love," is the sentiment reiterated over and over again by NDErs. Specifically, the importance of loving others, as well as oneself, is expressed – unconditional and empathic love, acceptance, and concern for others. As one NDEr so clearly put it: "One thing I [learned] was that we are ALL here to do an 'assignment of love'."[28] Now, we may think: *Well, duh! – Of course love is the most important thing!* But what is uniquely interesting in the case of the NDE experience is that NDErs learn that love is one of only two things we can take with us after we die (the other is knowledge). This realization raises the importance of love to an entirely new level in that love becomes not merely a source of joy and peace in *this* lifetime, but it also has an eternal value and currency; it is, in a sense, an investment that promises *future* applicability and rewards. So many of us devote so much time and energy in the pursuit and acquisition of material wealth, even though we all readily acknowledge that "you can't take it with you." Love, however, is a treasure that we apparently *can* take with us.

Another unique characteristic of love mentioned by NDErs is that "everything is love." This observation raises the importance of love to even astronomically higher levels, especially when considered with two of the other pieces of NDE wisdom noted above; namely, that "Everything is one" and "God is everything." Considered in conjunction with these two points, the idea that "everything is love" leads to the portentous conclusion that all the seemingly distinct things that make up reality are, in actuality, mere manifestations of one single thing, which is composed of love, and which is God. This is a realization the awesomeness of which cannot be overstressed. And, as we will later see, it is a fundamental concept in the model of the afterlife we will study; in addition, it possesses an eerie correspondence to ideas arising out of quantum physics regarding the nature of reality.

NDErs often remark that, after experiencing the infusion of far-reaching knowledge and understanding discussed earlier, they come to an understanding that "Everything happens for a reason." By means of the broader perspective of awareness resulting from his newly acquired knowledge, the NDEr perceives that all the experiences of life, even the suffering and unfairness, derive from a logical framework and system which, when viewed in its entirety, results in an apprehension that it all "makes sense" and that there is an acceptable and plausible reason for everything. This realization is another component of the NDE phenomenon that has specific relevance to the model of the afterlife we will soon explore, particularly with regard to reincarnation and karma.

It doesn't require a great leap of insight to surmise that these profound concepts – love is of primary and eternal importance, everyone and everything is one thing, and everything happens for good reason as part of a logical cosmic plan – when acquired in the powerful and affecting setting of the NDE can result in dramatic changes in an NDEr's personality, world view, and value system. And this is precisely what occurs. As a direct consequence of their near-death experience, NDErs typically undergo a momentous personal transformation which the vast majority describes as positive and life-enhancing. Indeed, in his book "Evidence of the Afterlife," author and medical doctor Jeffrey Long notes that he is often told by NDErs that they consider the aftereffects to be the most important part of their near-death experiences.[29] Of particular import to those of us who have *not* had an NDE is the fact that these positive, life-enhancing NDE aftereffects offer benefits and rewards of immense potential; for it has been discovered that merely becoming *exposed to* the concepts and wisdom inherent in the near-death experience is sufficient to result in a transformation similar to that experienced by the NDEr himself. Thus, by simply reading about or otherwise studying the NDE phenomenon and considering its content with an open mind, each one of us can have an opportunity to undergo a similarly life-transforming, life-enhancing metamorphosis.[30] The implications of this possibility are nothing short of profound. I can personally attest to having undergone precisely such a life-altering transformation after reading several books about NDEs (and the afterlife model), and I assure you it has improved the quality of my life significantly.

Let's start with an itemized listing of some of the common aftereffects reported by NDErs, followed by a more detailed discussion and analysis. As you note the bulleted items on the list below[31], I think it will become immediately obvious how and why they serve as the seeds for a rich and advantageous life transition.

1. Diminished fear of death
2. Less judgmental/more tolerant and forgiving
3. Major changes in life situations (relationships, career)
4. Increased love, compassion and empathy for all life forms
5. Religious orientation replaced by spirituality
6. Increased appreciation for nature and ecological concerns
7. Less concerned with material possessions
8. Newfound interest in reincarnation, psychic phenomena, and the "new physics"
9. Increased zest for life
10. Increased happiness and optimism
11. Decreased stress and worry
12. Belief in God
13. Hunger for knowledge
14. Importance of service-to-others

I think it is very important to consider the points in the above list in conjunction with the Life Review component of the NDE. It seems rather obvious that many of these life changes can be attributed not only to specific items of imparted wisdom, but even more so to the deeply moving and emotional experiences that characterize the Life Review. Recall that, during the Life Review component, the NDEr experiences all the emotions, both painful and pleasurable, that their words and actions evoked in the people with whom they had interacted throughout their life. It goes without saying that having such an experience inevitably must result in some degree of "increased compassion and empathy for others" (item 4 on the above list), not to mention the fostering of a more tolerant and less judgmental attitude (item 2) and an increased sense of the importance and value of service to others (item 14). Likewise, the overall nature of the near-death experience itself clearly can be seen as the incentive behind items 1, 5, 8, 9, and 12. Let's explore these transformative effects further in order to see what we can learn from them.

As a result of their experiences, NDErs typically report having less death anxiety than prior to their NDE. [32] While the vast majority of us might not go about our lives in a state of trembling terror due to a morbid anxiety over death, I think it is fair to say that a subtle, repressed fear of death lurks in the background of our thoughts and quite likely exerts a delicate though insidious effect on us psychologically and emotionally. In their paper "The Universal Fear of Death and the Cultural Response," authors Calvin Moore and John Williamson quote anthropologist Ernest Becker's belief that "the idea of death, the fear of it, haunts the human animal like nothing else;" They go on to note that, "because of its seeming finality, death presents one of the most formidable challenges to the idea that human life has meaning and purpose."[33] And *that*, I believe, is the key point: if death represents the primary obstacle to human beings possessing a sense of purpose and meaning to their lives, then it is no surprise that something which results in a loss or reduction in death anxiety would evoke an increase in zest for life (item 9), increased happiness and optimism (item 10), and decreased stress and worry (item 11). Now, think a moment about these three changes, and consider the myriad ways in which people strive to achieve them: psychiatric care, drugs and/or alcohol, participation in cults … you get the idea. The near-death experience appears to bestow upon its participants, as aftereffects, qualities of life that are deeply desired and actively sought after by the bulk of humanity. I, personally, can attest to the fact that I underwent a dramatic reduction in death anxiety after merely *reading* books about the near-death experience phenomenon. And as I noted earlier, my experience is far from unique. This fact has profound implications for humanity as a whole, for it suggests that each of us can enjoy the positive, life-enhancing transformative effects experienced by NDErs merely by *reading about* the subject and giving meaningful thought and consideration to its content. This represents a practical application of this subject with the potential to change all our lives, individually and collectively, for the better. The personal and societal ramifications of this possibility are enormous and difficult to overstate.

In addition to the Life Review, another aspect of the near-death experience to which many of the above-listed aftereffects can be attributed is the received wisdom that "everything happens for a reason." Contrast this concept with what science tells us about our lives, namely, that we live in a fatalistic Newtonian clockwork universe in which everything is the result of mechanistic determinism and that *we ourselves* are the result of nothing more than a Darwinian cascade of mutations and random accidents. Add to those cold and callous notions science's explanation that human emotions are little more than chemical processes and neuronal discharges, and it becomes strikingly clear how the alternative conjectures that "everything happens for a reason" and "what matters most in life is love" would result in the encouraging and uplifting transformations undergone by NDErs. Truly, whether or not the NDE is an actual "visit" to the afterlife becomes almost irrelevant in light of the life-affirming, heartening, and life-altering impact it has on those who experience it. Terence McKenna, a brilliant thinker and philosopher to whom I will refer frequently throughout this book, said, "Western civilization can be thought of as an accumulated series of misunderstandings." Many of those misunderstandings derive from science, particularly the Newtonian and Darwinian concepts noted above. Other western misunderstandings derive from religion. These limited and limiting scientific and religious presumptions form the foundation of our personal perceptions of life and reality, and unquestionably lie behind the debilitating existential angst suffered by so many of us. The lessons imparted by the near-death experience, and their accompanying aftereffects, offer a refreshing, hopeful, and inspiring alternative life-view. Let's face it: any unique and interesting new theory, no matter how fascinating and exciting it may be, is no more than a curious exercise in intellectual musings unless it can be shown to have some useful and meaningful application to real, everyday life. The fact that any of us can experience the aftereffects of a near-death experience by merely exposing ourselves to information about NDEs offers a practical application of this knowledge that is readily available and easily employed, and which provides a payoff of enormous life-enriching potential. Read through the list again: now consider the state of the world today, and then imagine how different it would be if everyone – or even most people – assimilated and lived by the life-altering precepts intrinsic to the near-death experience. There is an ironically serviceable, pragmatic aspect to this highly spiritual phenomenon that offers benefits of incalculable worth. To ignore it would be a regrettable lack of good judgment.

Chapter 3

Evidence for Reincarnation

Having hopefully established at least the plausibility of the existence of an afterlife (and, by implication, the soul) through our examination of the near-death experience phenomenon, let us now go about establishing the credibility of the concept of reincarnation. As discussed in Chapter 1, reincarnation refers to the transmigration of the soul, after death, from one body to another body. People from the modern western world are usually surprised to learn that reincarnation as a religious doctrine is the norm throughout most of the world's religions, and was actually part of Christianity until the 5th century.[34] While religious belief does not even remotely satisfy the empirical rigor required by the scientific method, one must nevertheless acknowledge that the ubiquity and ancientness of the reincarnation belief system should earn it, at the very least, the courtesy of serious consideration. Certainly, it is entirely conceivable, as the skeptics argue, that the idea of reincarnation sprung from early man's observance of cycles in nature – the seasons, day and night (with the sun "born anew" each day), etc. But, as I discussed in Chapter 1, the logic and reasonableness inherent in the concept of reincarnation make it just as *intellectually* appealing as it is morally appealing. I cannot help but suspect that there has to be some degree of substantial worth to a doctrine that is so widespread and has been around for so long, and that is also so satisfyingly rational and coherent. It is interesting to note that René Descartes, who established the framework for the scientific method in his treatise, *Discourse on Method*, claimed that he was told *by an angel* that understanding of the world should be pursued through mathematics and logic.[35] Thus the gulf between science and religious mysticism may not be as wide as we are often led to believe; Isaac Newton was a practicing alchemist and was deeply religious, and both Plato and Pythagoras fervently believed in reincarnation. Albert Einstein and Stephen Hawking, however, are among the non-believers.

Religious beliefs aside, the question of the credibility of reincarnation has a more immediate and personal relevance, for, as the historian H.T. Buckle said, "If immortality be untrue, it matters little whether anything else be true or not."[36] Fortunately, we are not limited to religion in our efforts to establish the truth of reincarnation: two particularly convincing approaches to this study are Past Life Hypnotic Regression and Early Childhood Past Life Memories. Both of these avenues of investigation offer a more scientific and objective analysis of this phenomenon than that available from religious sources. Also, the evidence amassed via these modern approaches is voluminous, available, and current.

Therefore it is these two methods of investigation upon which I will focus in this chapter.

Before we delve into these two topics, however, I would be remiss if I did not at least mention that there are other sources of evidence for the existence of an afterlife, souls, and reincarnation aside from near-death experiences, religious beliefs, past-life hypnotic regression, and childhood past life memories. Most prominent among these other sources is supposed communication with deceased individuals via psychics, mediums, and channelers. I, personally, do not necessarily dismiss the validity of this approach, but its value as evidence is problematic because of the very subjective nature of the process and the unfortunate tainting it has endured due to exploitation by charlatans and con artists. These are not reasons to reject it outright, but they do render an objective and scientific analysis difficult. That being said, there is one notable investigation into this phenomenon known as "The Scole Experiment" which deserves mention. Referencing the book "The Scole Experiment, Scientific Evidence for Life After Death", by Grant & Jane Solomon, the web site afterlife101.com quotes, from the back cover, a thoroughly concise and informative summary of this remarkable investigation:

> The Scole Experiment chronicles the extraordinary results of a five-year investigation into life after death. At the beginning of 1993 four psychic researchers embarked on a series of experiments in the Norfolk village of Scole. The subsequent events were so astounding that senior members of the prestigious Society for Psychical Research asked to observe, test and record what took place. Those who attended the sessions at Scole came away convinced that discarnate intelligences were making direct contact with them. The incontrovertible evidence they witnessed included:
>
> - Handwriting, symbols and messages which appeared on factory-sealed, unopened photographic film
> - Objects, lights and solid beings which materialized before previously skeptical observers
> - Spirits who communicated instructions for the building of complex instruments and communication devices
> - Personal information about those present which was revealed to the group by discarnate intelligences [37]

From the Author Update of 2006 for that same book we read the following: "*The Scole Experiment* is now widely regarded as the most important scientific investigation of evidence for life after death in history. Highly qualified and objective scientists, and a whole range of other people who attended the Scole Group's sessions, came away convinced that (mostly) invisible, discarnate intelligences were making direct contact with those present." [38]

I first became aware of the Scole Experiment when I watched the video *The Afterlife Investigations* and I must say that it was this video that made me reconsider my previously held attitude of extreme skepticism toward this type of psychical phenomena. To my mind, the Scole Experiment represents about as scientific and objective an analysis of this phenomenon as one could have expected at that time, and I think its findings are persuasive enough to warrant a modern investigation using the more sophisticated tools and technology available today. With that I will leave the topic of psychic/medium communication with the dead and return to the discussion concerning Past Life Hypnotic Regression and Early Childhood Past Life Memories.

A well-known law of physics – The Law of Conservation of Energy – states that energy can neither be created nor destroyed. If our souls are comprised of energy, then their obligatory obeisance to this scientific law necessitates their immortality, and thus, *ipso facto*, the soul "lives on" after the physical death of the body; *where it goes* and *what it does* are the big questions screaming for answers. One widely held belief, as we've seen, is that it reincarnates – i.e., it returns to physical reality in the vessel of another human body. The most intriguing evidence for this belief, in my opinion, can be found in the research conducted by Dr. Ian Stevenson.

3.1 Childhood Past-Life Memories: Dr. Ian Stevenson

The late Dr. Ian Stevenson was a professor of psychiatry, and former chairman of the Department of Psychiatry, at the University of Virginia, where he was also the founder and head of the Division of Perceptual Studies until his retirement in 2002. For approximately forty years and throughout the world, including North and South America, Europe, Africa and Asia, Dr. Stevenson investigated reports of young children who described unprompted memories of previous lives, ultimately conducting more than 2,500 case studies and publishing twelve books over the course of his lifetime.[39] In a review of one of Dr. Stevenson's books, Lester S. King, the Book Review editor of *JAMA: The Journal of the American Medical Association*, wrote that, "in regard to reincarnation [Stevenson] has painstakingly and unemotionally collected a detailed series of cases from India, cases in which the evidence is difficult to explain on any other grounds."[40] Dr. Stevenson was described by one of his colleagues in the field of psychiatry as "a methodical, careful, even cautious investigator whose personality is on the obsessive side."[41] His work is continued by another respected name in the field, Jim B. Tucker, M.D., a child psychiatrist at the University of Virginia and author of the book, *Life Before Life: Children's Memories of Previous Lives*.

Unlike cases of past life memories recalled by means of hypnotic regression (which will be discussed in the next section), cases of childhood past-life recall do not involve hypnosis, but rather rely upon spontaneous recall on the part of the subject. This is an important point in that it nullifies the objections made by detractors of hypnotic past-life regression who claim that the very process of hypnosis itself might in some way be responsible for generating the information that is revealed by the hypnosis subject (e.g., because of "leading questions" posed by the hypnotist). By relying solely on the spontaneous recollections of the subjects, Dr. Stevenson's studies remove this potential source of contamination. The purity, if you will, of Dr. Stevenson's data is further preserved by the fact that his subjects are children mostly in the age range of two to four years, and generally not beyond seven years of age. This factor obviates possible contamination of the data by cultural and media influences, as the children are too young to have been so affected. As you will see, the individual stories are so rich with specific details and obscure facts that it is simply inconceivable how a young child could have come upon the information by any means. But before we get into the specific cases, let's first get an overview of what Drs. Stevenson and Tucker have found.

As mentioned above, the children typically make statements about a past life at a very early age, generally between the ages of two and four. By the age of six or seven the past life seems to have been forgotten as the child ceases discussing it. In recalling their past lives, the children talk about people, places, events, and circumstances of those lives – for example, they will make statements about friends and relatives, their home town or village, the cause of their death, and their occupation. They make these statements in a very serious and matter-of-fact manner, saying things such as, "My other father…", "When I died…", "My wife…" – much to the befuddlement of their parents. Most commonly, the people and events described by the child are from a point in time near the end of their past life. The mode of death, when discussed, is frequently violent or sudden. The past lives themselves are generally recent to their current life, with the median time between the past-life death and the current-life birth being fifteen to sixteen months. Most describe ordinary, unremarkable lives; claims of "famous personalities" are rare. Some children are able to speak a language they could not possibly have learned. Frequently, strong emotions accompany the memories. The child's manner of play will often reflect the occupation of the previous personality, and some children will act out the death scene from the previous life. Preferences for certain foods – and even alcohol and tobacco – are carried forth from the previous life, and phobias related to the mode of death sometimes manifest: for example, a child may demonstrate a fear of water or bathing if death in the previous life was by drowning. Many of these children are born with birthmarks or birth defects that match wounds, usually fatal, on the body of the previous personality. The children will often insist upon being taken to the town or village where they claim to have lived the past life. When their parents abide this wish, the facts uncovered during the visit corroborate the claims made by the child: names and descriptions of people, locations and descriptions of homes, details about the claimed previous personality, cause of death – all or most of these are found to be precisely as the child claimed. Needless to say, the child had not had the opportunity to visit the location and had no reason to be in possession of any of the information relayed; the same can typically be said of the parents as well.[42]

One classic case discussed in Dr. Stevenson's book, *Twenty Cases Suggestive of Reincarnation*, is that of Swarnlata Mishra, a girl born in Pradesh, India in 1948. At the age of three she began relating details of a past life in Katni, a town more than 100 miles from her home; the information recounted by Swarnlata was rife with specifics, and her father began to make a written record of her narration. Swarnlata said that her name in her previous life was Biya Pathak and she lived in Zhurkutia, a district of Katni; she had two sons, and she resided in a white house with black doors fitted with iron bars, behind which was a girl's school and with lime furnaces nearby; her family owned an automobile, a rarity in India in the 1950's; she said that Biya died of a "pain in her throat" in 1939, and she gave the name of the doctor who treated her. Professor Sri H. N. Banerjee, an Indian researcher of paranormal phenomenon and colleague of Dr. Stevenson, became aware of the case in 1959, when Swarnlata was ten years old. He travelled to Katni, with Swarnlata's father's notes in hand, to see if he could confirm the accuracy of Swarnlata's recollections. What Professor Banerjee discovered is nothing short of astonishing. From Swarnlata's description alone he was able to locate the house and learned that it did indeed belong to a wealthy family named Pathak; there was indeed a girl's school behind the property and lime furnaces on land adjoining the property; an interview with family members affirmed that a Biya Pathak had died there in 1939 leaving behind a husband and two sons – the Pathaks and the Mishras had no knowledge of one another and, as stated above, lived one hundred miles apart. As if these revelations were not fantastic enough, later developments proved even more amazing. In 1959, Biya's husband, son, and eldest brother paid an unannounced visit to Swarnlata; they did not reveal who they were, and they brought along nine unrelated local residents. Swarnlata correctly identified her (i.e., Biya's) brother (whom she called "Babu," which was Biya's pet name for him), her husband, and her son, despite the fact that her son falsely denied the relationship to test her. Several weeks later Swarnlata's father took her to Biya's home in Katni, where she accurately identified changes to the house and grounds. She correctly recognized relatives and friends of Biya's, as well as a former servant, using pet names and identifying marriage relationships accurately. Even subtleties such as her behavior towards the males were consistent with their relationship to Biya: she was reserved towards Biya's elders yet relaxed and playful with Biya's sons. Finally, her knowledge of the Pathak family was limited to the period up to 1939, the year Biya died – she knew nothing of the family thereafter. Recall that Swarnlata was a mere ten years when this "reunion" occurred.[43]

Another fascinating case (*not* from Dr. Stevenson's research) was highlighted in a segment by Suzanne Stratford of Fox 8 News out of Cleveland, Ohio. The case involves an eleven year old boy named James Leininger. Beginning when he was a toddler, James demonstrated an avid interest in World War II fighter planes and seemed to be inexplicably familiar with such aircraft. He made many drawings of airplanes in dogfights, planes shooting at (and being shot at from) naval vessels, and planes dropping bombs. Additionally, he had night terrors – starting at age 2 – where he would cry out statements like, "Airplane crash, on fire, little man can't get out!" When his mother asked him who "little man" was, he would reply, "I'm little man." Understandably mystified by these behaviors, James' parents began to ask him specific questions, which he answered:

- What kind of plane?   *Corsair*
- Why did your plane crash?   *It was shot down*
- Who shot down your plane?   *The Japanese!*
- Where did you take off from?   *A boat*
- What was the name of the boat?   *Natoma*
- What was your name then?   *James* (also his current name)

His parents tracked down and interviewed veterans from the U.S.S. Natoma Bay and determined that their son was a WWII pilot named James Huston. When young James Leininger later met with a group of Natoma veterans, he recognized and greeted them *by name*. During a subsequent meeting with James Huston's sister, he exhibited knowledge of specific personal details regarding James Huston and his two sisters that he, Leininger, could not possibly have known. During a visit to Japan with his parents, the boy was able to identify, without help, the exact location where James Huston's plane went down. At that site the young boy became very emotional, crying in his mother's arms in what was clearly a cathartic release of deeply repressed feelings.[44] The details of this story were published in the book *Soul Survivor: The Reincarnation of a World War II Fighter Pilot*, by Bruce and Andrea Leininger; the video of the Fox 8 News segment is viewable on YouTube and other web sites.

As the two stories related above illustrate, individual accounts of Childhood Past-Life Memories are replete with absorbing human drama and explicit detail, and when the truth of those details is independently confirmed one is hard-pressed to come up with an explanation, other than reincarnation, that is not ludicrous or far-fetched. Books, web sites, and videos presenting such accounts are legion – the sheer volume is staggering. I urge anyone who doubts the veracity of reincarnation to research the topic of Childhood Past-Life Memories; the stories are fascinating, and the evidence is plentiful and persuasive.

3.2 Past-Life Hypnotic Regression

Another area of research that offers strong evidence for the reality of reincarnation is that of Past-Life Hypnotic Regression. While perhaps not as immune to reproof as Childhood Past-Life Memories, the field of Past-Life Regression is richer with detail and information. Past life regression is a technique that uses hypnosis to recover purported memories of past lives or incarnations.

Skeptics, however, regard the "memories" as fantasies or delusions. What is particularly interesting about this discipline is that it is typically used in, and in a sense grew out of, a psychotherapeutic setting. To my knowledge, one of the first mental health professionals to employ past-life hypnotic regression therapeutically was psychiatrist Denys Kelsey. Dr. Kelsey had employed hypnosis to regress patients to their childhood as a means of resolving psychological problems. However, after meeting and ultimately marrying author Joan Grant and becoming exposed to her interest in past lives, he adapted his use of regressive hypnosis to explore the past lives of his patients. In so doing he was able to resolve patients' problems that had hitherto been resistant to childhood regression and other therapies, and he thereby ascertained that these problems were somehow connected with incidents from the patients' previous lives.[45] To this day, psychologists and psychiatrists – many of whom do not believe in reincarnation – have found past-life hypnotic regression to often provide an effective means of resolving a wide range of phobias and ailments in their patients.

One of the leading experts in the field of past-life regression therapy, and probably the most well-known, is Brian Weiss, M.D., a psychiatrist and graduate of Columbia University and Yale Medical School. Dr. Weiss' interest in reincarnation began in 1980 when a patient by the name of "Catherine" began discussing past-life experiences under hypnosis. Although Weiss was not a believer in reincarnation at that time, he changed his opinion after confirming elements of Catherine's stories through public records. Dr. Weiss has since regressed over 4,000 patients and he believes that some part of the human personality survives death. He is an advocate of hypnotic regression as a therapy capable of curing certain phobias and ailments by getting patients to recognize their connections to past-life experiences. [46]

Many other mental health professionals would concur with the curative effect of past-life regression therapy, and they routinely use it for precisely that purpose. The literature abounds with case studies of people who have been cured of persistent ailments after exposure of the causative factor via past-life regression. The mechanism at work here suggests that an extremely traumatic experience from a past life – particularly at the time of death – will leave an imprint on the current life in the form of repressed emotions that manifest as a psychosomatic ailment, a phobia, or a negative behavior. A particular case that stands out in my mind involved a man who suffered from severe abdominal pain. After consulting several medical doctors who could find no physiological cause for his pain, the man was referred to a psychiatrist, through whom, via hypnotic regression, it was discovered that the patient had, in a previous life, died a painful death from a bayonet wound in the belly as a soldier in World War I. Once the cause of the man's abdominal pain was brought forward from the subconscious to the conscious mind the associated repressed emotions were released and his pain ceased. This scenario is typical of the application of past-life hypnotic regression for the treatment of psychosomatic conditions. In his book *Past Lives, Future Lives*, Dr. Bruce Goldberg references a wide variety of examples of this type of therapeutic utilization of hypnotic regression, such as: an overweight man who had starved to death in a previous life; a workaholic whose family in a past lifetime died because of his inability to provide for them; and an insomniac who, as a soldier in the Civil War, had fallen asleep on guard duty and thereby caused the death of himself and his fellow soldiers at the hands of the enemy. [47] While these cases do not represent as strong an argument for the reality of reincarnation as the spontaneously recalled childhood past-life memories discussed earlier, they nevertheless offer logical and plausible explanations for ailments whose causes would otherwise be inexplicable.

Aside from its therapeutic value, past-life hypnotic regression is sought by people who simply want to gain a deeper insight into themselves and their current life circumstances. A few years ago I became acquainted with a woman who shared my interest in spirituality and other esoteric subjects. We had many interesting and enjoyable conversations about these topics, mostly sharing information from books we had read. One day I remarked that I had always wanted to try past-life hypnosis, to which she matter-of-factly replied that she had actually undergone several sessions. After getting over my initial amazement, I excitedly asked her, "So, what was it like?" I fully expected her to respond by describing the details of one of her past lives; after all, it was precisely such detailed accounts in the books I had read that I had found so utterly fascinating. But, instead of regaling me with a dramatic narrative of one of her previous incarnations, she completely surprised me by saying, "It explained a lot about my life now." *That was it?* I wondered. I expressed my bewilderment that she had not launched directly into a description of a particular lifetime, and she said, "Oh, the specifics were very interesting; but the really fascinating thing was how my past situations explain so much about my life, and who I am, *now*." At that time, having not yet undergone hypnotic regression myself, I really couldn't comprehend the significance of what she was saying. And when she then went on to relate some details of one of her past lives – which was truly captivating – I was even more perplexed by her claim that the details of her past lives were of only secondary importance. However, when I did finally experience past-life hypnotic regression, I understood – and appreciated – firsthand just how accurate her assessment was.

I am going to end Book I with a detailed account of my own personal experience with past-life regressive hypnosis, but before I do I would first like to devote a short chapter to a discussion of the question "Are Other Lives Recalled via Hypnosis 'Real'?" Hypnosis is not only an important tool in uncovering details of past lives, but, as we will later see, it also plays a key role in the development of the Afterlife model we will examine in Part II of this book; thus I believe it is important and necessary to present a case for the credibility of information revealed by means of hypnosis.

Chapter 4

Are Other Lives Recalled via Hypnosis "Real"?

Science has become a tyrant; it's become the arbiter of all truth. That's ridiculous. Most of what's interesting doesn't fall under the purview of science.

- Terence McKenna, author

Just as it did in past-life regression, hypnosis also plays a critical role in obtaining information about the afterlife (as you will see in Part II of this book). Critics of hypnotic regression as a tool for extracting information claim that the past-life memories recalled during hypnotic regression are "false memories" that derive from: (a) fantasies or products of the subject's imagination; (b) memories, possibly forgotten, of experiences in *this* life; or (c) intentional or unintentional suggestions from the hypnotist. The importance of hypnosis as a tool for accessing past-life and after-life memories demands that these claims be addressed. An honest assessment of the use of hypnosis and the results obtained will, I feel confident, reveal the claims of critics as meritless.

First, and most compelling to me, is the consistency and universality of the information revealed. At the risk of jumping the gun, let me simply note here that, in the model of the afterlife we will examine in Part II of this book, you will see that hundreds of people from all walks of life describe, while under hypnosis, a remarkably consistent picture of the afterlife realm, replete with highly similar descriptions of design, experience, entities, and processes. The idea that individual fantasies or imaginings would share such a high level of congruity is simply preposterous. The suggestion that it is the result of memories of present-life experiences is equally ridiculous insofar as the experiences described are exceedingly *unworldly* and unique. Fantasies and memories are highly personal experiences, intimately entwined with the personality and history of the person having them. We should thus expect that the *content* of the fantasies and memories of large numbers of people would vary wildly – indeed, they should be almost as diverse as the number of individual people who are having them; yet with regard to hypnotically regressed recall of the spirit realm this is not the case: the consistency of reported details is conspicuous and dramatic. Finally, the implication that the hypnotist is "leading" the subject, intentionally or not, can easily be disproved by reading the verbatim transcripts of the sessions: knowledgeable and professional researchers are well aware of this potential pitfall and they take great care to avoid it by formulating their instructions and questions with discernment, caution, and prudence.

In the case of past-life regressive hypnosis, subjects often relate obscure historical facts and details which, in their current life experience, they could not possibly have known yet which are often verified as true after subsequent research. That such knowledge could derive from fantasy or the imagination is unlikely in the extreme. In line with unexplained historical knowledge is the phenomenon of xenoglossy, which refers to a person's ability to speak a previously-unknown foreign language. This incredible ability has been demonstrated by some past-life hypnosis subjects when recalling a previous life in a country where a language different from their current-life language was spoken. In such cases the subject typically claims no facility with the foreign language, nor is there anything in their current-life experience to explain how they could have developed such a facility. In some rare documented cases the person not only can speak in a language hitherto unknown to them, but they speak in obscure dialects or in archaic languages that are no longer used and are known only to a handful of experts.[48] Dr. Ian Stevenson described two cases of xenoglossy in detail in his book *Unlearned Language: New Studies in Xenoglossy*, and he brought to the subject the same degree of scientific rigor and objectivity that characterized his studies of childhood past-life memories. In a discussion of this book on the web site afterlife101.com it was noted that, "Transcripts of tape recordings provide evidence that the subjects could speak the foreign language intelligently and were not just repeating a few phrases of a language that they may have learned casually in some other way. The results of extensive inquiries into the possibility that either subject might have learned normally in early life the foreign language he spoke in adulthood were negative in each case."[49] Of particular interest, I would also note that in cases of early-life regression, where a subject is regressed to an earlier part of their current life, the subject will often adopt the speech patterns and voice of a child appropriate to the youthful age to which they are regressed. To my mind this suggests a definite, and expected, correspondence between the time period to which a subject is regressed and the characteristics of speech which he/she employs... exactly as is found in the cases of xenoglossy. Now, I think it is very important to point out that the phenomenon of xenoglossy does not provide absolute proof of the reality of reincarnation; it does, however, strongly suggest that whatever hypnosis is tapping into is independent of the subject's mind, thus ruling out fantasy, imagination, or forgotten memories as explanations for the past-life memories uncovered. Also, the coherency of manner of speech with geographic location and/or time period is a solid indication that scenarios uncovered via hypnosis possess an internal consistency that is both logical and accurate with respect to the real-world counterpart of the past-life that is uncovered.

This concordance between past-lives revealed via hypnosis and their related real-world setting offers very persuasive evidence that these recollections are, in fact, honest and accurate memories of actual past lives. The case being made along these lines becomes even stronger when we consider the work done by psychologist Dr. Helen Wambach. Rather than simply looking at individual accounts of past-life regression, Dr. Wambach's study involved a statistical analysis of large numbers of hypnotically regressed subjects with the goal of investigating, among other things, possible discrepancies between details reported by the hypnosis subjects versus the actual facts for a given historical period and geographic location. With regard to particulars related to things such as architecture, climate, landscape, and clothing, serious discrepancies were found in only 11 of 1088 responses. In an interesting coincidence regarding this particular study, I was recently watching a series of lectures about ancient history when the lecturer, a professor of history, made a statement to the effect that: *People who claim to remember past lives always remember a life of great fame and wealth; this proves that their claims are false, since it is statistically inconsistent with the historical fact that the vast majority of people who lived in the ancient past were extremely poor.* At which point I began to curse at the TV screen, because I knew the truth of the matter to be otherwise. This history professor was clearly not familiar with the literature of past life memories and regression: the vast majority of the past-life recollections that I have read about were of poor lives from the lowest economic and social classes of their respective time periods. As it turns out, Dr. Wambach's study confirms statistically, in the aggregate, what I had ascertained from my acquaintance with individual accounts; namely, Dr. Wambach's subjects mostly reported humble lives, with 70 per cent belonging to the lower class, 23 per cent to the middle class, and a mere 7 percent to the upper class. Furthermore, regardless of their class, most subjects reported lives that were bleak and unhappy, and, significantly, no one reported being a historically famous or important person.[50] Surely, if past-lives recalled via hypnotic regression were fantasies or imaginings – as the skeptics claim – then one would expect the lives recalled to be, well, *fantastical* – unusual in a positive, desirable, exciting way. Yet the reality of the hypnotic past-life regression experience is quite the opposite: the majority of people recall unhappy lives of poverty lived in unpleasant circumstances – precisely in accordance with the reality of life for the majority of the population in those past time periods. Yet another area in which Dr. Wambach's subjects' recollections demonstrated agreement with historical reality is with regard to population density. Dr. Wambach's subjects had been given the choice to regress to one of ten time periods from the past four-thousand years. Tellingly, there was a faithful correlation between the time periods selected by the study's subjects and the known historical populations, viz.: more subjects regressed to periods of high population than to periods when population was known to be low. With regard to gender, the numbers of Dr. Wambach's subjects reporting lives as males versus lives as females closely approximated the actual male-female ratios (even though, in many cases, current males reported past lives as females and vice versa).[51] This is especially striking when one considers the commonly known reality that life – particularly in the past – was much harder for females than it was for males.

Let's pause for a moment and really consider what all this research is telling us. From an examination of individual cases of past-life regression, as well as collective studies, we find that: subjects' recollections of specific details of their past lives are consistent with historical reality; amalgamate analyses indicate accurate statistical consistency with regard to a variety of demographic parameters such as population distribution and socio-economic status; and some subjects demonstrate the ability to converse in a language of which, in their current life, they have no knowledge. If looked at with reasonable objectivity, these findings are astounding. I will be the first to say that this evidence does not unequivocally *prove* the reality of reincarnation, but I do maintain that reincarnation is currently the most rational and sensible theory available to explain it; certainly much more so than the specious theories offered by the skeptics and naysayers.

The last two arguments I would like to offer, in support of the claim that past-life memories recalled via hypnosis are real, derive from my own personal experiences with regressive hypnosis. As of this writing, I have had four hypnosis sessions – one was a past-life regression, one was an attempt to deal with my prostate cancer, one was a life-between-lives (i.e., spirit realm) regression, and the last was a very long session that delved into my subconscious and super-conscious minds. The first three sessions were all done with the same hypnotist, while the last long session was done with a different hypnotist. I will discuss each of these experiences in depth elsewhere within this book, but since we are currently engaged in a discussion of reincarnation, the next and final chapter of Part I will look at my past-life session. However, before I go into that session in detail, I want to note two particular aspects of my experience that struck me as being powerful proof of the reality of the past-life I recalled. One was the potency of the emotions I experienced while recalling the event and the other was how the particular lifetime I recalled was very different from what I expected it to be. It would be pointless to go into the specifics of these points now, as they can only be adequately appreciated after you have read the detailed description of the session. Suffice it to say that at one point during the session I became extremely emotional, to the point of crying and feeling choked up with heartbreaking sadness. The emotions I felt were exceedingly potent, painful, and real. I simply cannot accept that they grew out of a fantasy or imagined creation of my mind. The other convincing aspect of the experience was that I had gone into it with an expectation, and in possession of some very persuasive "evidence", of what that particular lifetime would be; in fact, I was virtually certain, because of my "evidence", that that particular life experience was exactly what would be uncovered. Yet, astonishingly, a completely different life emerged. If past-life memories are merely a product of the subject's fantasies or imaginings, then the lifetime that I had fully expected to discover should have been the one that was revealed; yet what happened was that I recalled a life that was totally counter to my expectations. Furthermore, the particular event recalled was neither exciting nor desirable, and the lifetime as a whole appeared to be a rather sad one. Let's look at my experience more closely; I believe a personal account offers insights that are not possible from clinical, second-hand analyses of the experiences of others.

Chapter 5

My Past-Life Regressive Hypnosis Experience

5.1 Background

I had been passionately interested in the subject of past-life regression for a very long time and I have read extensively in that area. I often thought of trying it myself, but for a variety of reasons – primarily lack of funds and fear – I continually postponed making any serious attempt to pursue what was, for me, an almost lifelong dream.

My reasons for finally deciding to take the plunge and actually undergo hypnotic regression were three-fold:

First, I was diagnosed with prostate cancer in 2003. I underwent radiation therapy and the cancer was in remission for several years. However, at some point my PSA began rising and two of the doctors I had been seeing thought the cancer had returned (two other doctors disagreed). After much frustration and unpleasantness resulting from my experiences with the medical establishment I decided to give hypnotic regression a try in the hope that it would enable me to: (a) give my body subconscious suggestions to boost my immune system and work extra hard to rid me of the cancer, and (b) see if the source of the cancer might lie in a traumatic experience from one of my past lives; a reading of the past life regression literature (as noted in Chapter 3) shows this is often the case – physical ailments in one's current life frequently have their cause in a negative experience from a past life, and when that experience is faced via hypnotic regression the ailment often disappears due to the release of the pent-up negative energy.

Second, just out of curiosity and an interest in the subject, I had wanted to try this for myself. I thought it would be extremely interesting to learn about my experiences in past lives, and to see how these experiences had impacted on my current live. The books I had read on this subject were indescribably fascinating, entertaining and informative. I very much wanted to experience this for myself.

Finally, I ultimately wanted to use hypnosis to be regressed to the spirit realm. This has been done by several professionals, most notably Michael Newton as documented in his books *Journey of Souls* and *Destiny of Souls*. I have read these books several times and I am not exaggerating when I say that they are the most amazing books I have ever read (and I read a lot). I will discuss this afterlife model in detail in Part II, but for now let me simply state that this model provides the answers to the three most fundamental questions of existence: *Where do we come from before we are born?*, *Where do we go after we die?*, and *Why are we here?* I had long hoped to experience this for myself.

My first hypnotic regression session was in September, 2009. The hypnotist was a woman named Amy Benesch (Amy's web site: http://www.inner-journeys.org/) who made me feel very comfortable and at ease. We had previously discussed, via e-mail, my situation with prostate cancer and my desire to use hypnosis to help rid my body of the cancer, as well as my personal desire to explore past lives. Amy suggested we begin the session with some healing work to address the prostate cancer, and then if time permitted move on to a past life regression. I, however, had some definite thoughts on what my most recent past life had been and I had some pretty convincing circumstantial evidence to support my suspicion; I also believed that certain aspects of this presumed past life might have a direct causative bearing on my cancer situation. For these reasons I wanted to get right to the regression work. After hearing me out, Amy agreed and we started right in with the regression.

5.2 A Word about the Hypnosis Experience

Although my past life regression hypnosis session was the very first time I had ever been hypnotized, the fact is that I knew quite a lot about hypnosis from the types of books I read; specifically, I had read a great number of books dealing with past-life regression and also books dealing with alien abduction – both of these fields use hypnosis to explore the experiences of their subjects. So I was a bit more aware of what to expect than would be a person with absolutely no exposure to hypnosis. Probably the thing people find most surprising about being hypnotized is that you are fully aware of your surroundings while you are under hypnosis. The general belief is that you are in some kind of unconscious, sleep-like state, but that is absolutely not the case. Nevertheless, it is not the same as a normal waking state either. I felt unusually calm while under hypnosis, and, although I was fully aware of my surroundings, I felt that my mental focus was more inward-directed than outward. Also, as particular portions of an episode grew more intense, my focus grew correspondingly more inward; at those times my awareness of my surroundings was minimal.

One phase of my first hypnotic session that I'd like to specifically address involved going into my mother's womb. This experience was in some ways more profound and more intense than the visit to my past life. At the start of the hypnosis process, the hypnotist talks you through a series of stages that gently brings you into the hypnotic state. One of these stages involves being inside your mother's womb. When Amy (my hypnotist) told me I'd be going to the womb I thought the effect would be that I would feel like I was floating in a warm liquid; however, when Amy brought me to this point and said "OK, you're now in your mother's womb," what I felt instead was an incredibly intense, almost overpowering sense of my mother. It was really overwhelming – I was instantaneously overcome with powerful emotions, and the sense I had of my mother was truly uncanny. It was a totally positive feeling, beautiful really to an almost magical degree. My mother had been dead for 17 years, so my memory of her and the corresponding feelings associated with her had diminished considerably with time. Nevertheless, the very second Amy said "You're now in the womb," it was like I had been hit by a lightning bolt of joy and peace and love. I mean, it was really *POW!* I felt choked up and my eyes got a bit teary from the sudden and powerful emotions. I'm being totally serious when I say that my sense of my mother when she was alive was not even remotely as acute as what I felt during this phase of the hypnosis session. If this were all I had experienced in this session, I would have felt that I had gotten my money's worth. I recall this part of my hypnosis experience with just as much pleasure and fascination as I do the portions dealing with the actual past life regression.

The aftereffects of having undergone hypnosis are amazing as well. Since my hypnosis sessions I've felt lighter, calmer, and more centered. These feelings do diminish over time, but, for me, I still feel pleasant reverberations. I would imagine that these effects are in part due to the ultra-calm state you enter when under hypnosis – it's like going on an internal vacation, very refreshing and rejuvenating – and also in part due to the resolution of subconscious conflicts brought about by re-experiencing an important episode from one's past life. I believe you release a negative energy, or tension, when you face and re-live moments from a past life. Indeed, that is usually why people seek out Past Life Hypnotic Regression – to find and eliminate the unconscious underlying cause of some present-day physical or psychological dis-ease. As noted previously, many psychiatrists and psychologists use hypnotic regression for precisely this reason, and very often they have tremendous success with it (interestingly, even mental health professionals who do not believe in reincarnation have used this technique successfully in treating their patients – they accept that it is an effective treatment strategy, but they simply refuse to believe that the past life memories recalled by the patient are real memories).

5.3 My Past-Life Regression Hypnosis Session

Amy skillfully eased me into a hypnotic state by guiding me from a self-created peaceful setting to a pleasant childhood memory, then on to my mother's womb before I was born, and finally to a past life episode. As I noted above, when hypnotized you are, surprisingly, fully aware of your present surroundings; it is not an unconscious dream-like state. It is really quite hard to explain: You "see" or "experience" the past life episode in your mind in a very real way, yet you are still present in – and fully aware of – the here-and-now. It is a strange but very, very amazing feeling. I should also mention that you are not directed to a specific past life by the hypnotist; rather, your psyche or inner spirit (or something else, internal or external) guides you to the past life that you need to see at that moment. So, when you "step out" into this particular lifetime you have no idea where you are going to arrive. For me, it was very different from what I had suspected it would be.

At first I "saw" nothing. But slowly a setting emerged that was quite disturbing. I was standing in a street of a town where it appeared all the buildings were severely damaged. Smoking rubble and partially or fully collapsed buildings were everywhere. Amy had me look down at my feet and describe what I was wearing (this must be a common technique used to help the hypnosis subject orient himself to his surroundings, as hypnotist Mira Kelley also employed this method during my session with her). I immediately said "boots," and when she asked what color they were I said without hesitation "black." Further inspection revealed that I was wearing a uniform, and ultimately I realized that I was an American soldier in Europe (France or Germany I thought, but I couldn't decide which) during World War II. I somehow knew that I had gotten here as part of the D-Day invasion and that I was part of an army unit that was moving inland clearing out and securing towns for further occupation by allied forces. Amy asked about the cause of the damage to the buildings and I realized it was the result of bombings by American forces.

Amy asked me if I was in any danger. My immediate response was "No," but I then qualified this by adding, "Either I'm not in any danger or I just don't care. I know I feel no fear." When Amy asked me if I saw any other people, I said "Civilians, hiding." And this is where I became extremely emotional, ultimately crying and indeed almost sobbing. I was overcome with sadness and pity for these people. I described, through a voice cracking with emotion, how terribly I felt for these people whose "lives were ruined" and who had "lost everything." "And all for nothing," I bemoaned, "A waste. So stupid." I will tell you (the reader of this book) that the emotions and the anguish I was feeling while lying on Amy's couch were very real and very painful. This part of the session was probably the most convincing evidence to me that I was truly re-experiencing an episode from a past life. I honestly cannot remember ever before feeling such deep despair. And I simply cannot believe that an "invented episode" or a "fantasy" could possibly generate such a raw and extreme emotional response. The other evidence, for me, was the vivid detail of my surroundings. I saw the boots I was wearing, I felt the weight of the rifle in my hand, I sensed the fear of the civilians as they peeked from their hiding places. The experience of reliving this under hypnosis was truly awe-inspiring.

After giving me some time to deal with the emotions I was feeling, Amy asked me if I had continued on with my mission; my reply was that I did continue, but only to the extent that I was attempting to keep myself safe and alive. Basically I had lost my enthusiasm for "the cause" and conveyed the feeling that my heart was no longer in it. I expressed great outrage against the people in power whose decisions had led to this deplorable state of affairs (i.e., the destruction of townspeople's lives and homes). I emphatically stated that I would gladly kill those people in power without any sense of remorse or guilt. My emotions were a mixed storm of great sadness and livid anger. As I mentioned earlier, I was openly crying during this phase of the session.

Amy attempted to prompt me further along in this memory, but I appeared to be stuck in that moment and I could not "see" what happened next. Amy then had me jump slightly ahead in time, and I found myself in some type of "vehicle, maybe a truck or...a boat, a ship." Gradually my sense of the setting became clearer: I seemed to be in the hold of a ship at sea, sitting on the floor with other soldiers. Amy asked me if we were now going home and I replied that it was possible we were. She asked if anyone was talking and I replied "No, everyone is quiet. All the joy has been sucked out of us." I was sitting with my elbows on my knees, my head hanging down. The other soldiers' heads were hanging down too. There was a feeling of great sadness in the air. It was deadly quiet. No joking, no bravado – "Nothing like the movies," I said to Amy, in a voice cracking with bitter laughter.

Amy then asked me if I get a job when I get home. "That's the plan," I replied, "A simple job." I expressed the desire to get a simple job and live a life of solitude. My reasons were that I did not want to get myself in a situation where people could control my life or put me in a predicament where I was forced to do something I felt was wrong. "That's how I got in this mess," I said angrily, referring to my involvement in the war. "I guess there's no wife or girlfriend waiting to greet you with a hug and a kiss when you get home," Amy said. "I don't see it," I replied coldly. And that was pretty much the end of my hypnosis session.

5.4 Analysis of My Past-Life Hypnosis Session

It was very obvious to me that my experience standing amid the rubble and devastation of that town and its frightened residents was a major turning point in my personal outlook on life and in my view of the world. It was truly a life-changing event in that it was a revelation which resulted in me developing: (a) a deep level of distrust in people and institutions, (b) a loathing of authority and the people who wield it, and (c) a bitter, doleful and tragic outlook on life. It's surely not difficult to see why such an experience would generate such feelings and views in someone who has witnessed it firsthand – peoples' homes demolished, their loved ones killed or injured, their lives ruined ... and for what purpose? To what end? And then multiply that town and those people by thousands and thousands more. That was how I viewed the war, after having stood amidst the horror of that town. I don't know what my views and beliefs were before that day (since that information did not materialize in this session), but I imagine that I felt like virtually every other soldier in that war – I was probably consumed with patriotic fervor, wanting to defeat the enemy and knowing with certainty that I was on the side of "good" and they were on the side of "evil." Well, after my heart-wrenching and illuminating experience in that town (and, presumably, other war-related experiences) my views became different. I felt I had received a jolting wake-up call, a slap in the face telling me to pull my head out of my ass and start to see past the bullshit.

I had mentioned earlier that an acquaintance of mine who had undergone past-life hypnotic regression surprised me by suggesting that the highlight of her experience was *what it told her about her life now*. Well, that was precisely my experience as well: What I found most fascinating about this regressive hypnosis session is what it has to say about my current life and the person I am today. First, and quite interestingly, I am (in my present life) an Army veteran. I served almost four years on active duty in the United States Army, both as an enlisted man and a commissioned officer. I am extremely proud of my military service and in many ways it was one of the best experiences of my life. Throughout my entire early life I felt compelled to be a soldier. When I graduated high school I planned to enlist in the Army but, much to my surprise, my father forbade it. He insisted I go to college. I said, "Fine. I'll go to college for you, but after I graduate I'm going right into the Army." I can still remember him laughing and saying, "When you graduate college you won't be stupid anymore and you won't want to go in the Army." Much to my father's surprise, several months after I got my Bachelor's degree I enlisted in the United States Army. I excelled in the Army and I was particularly amazed at the fact that I was a first-class officer; I was very good at what I did and I had an excellent rapport with my men. Nothing in my life prior to that point suggested that this would be the case; in fact, if anything, my life prior to my military service would have predicted that I should have utterly failed as a military officer. But I didn't fail. Far from it.

Having said all that about my military service, what I find particularly fascinating about my current life as it relates to what I learned from my regression session is that my personality in *this* life was clearly formed from my experiences in *that* life. In my current life: I loathe authority and authority figures; I am extremely distrustful of people; I am very much a loner, shunning friendships and relationships; I feel empathy in the extreme when I hear or see reports of human tragedy such as airplane crashes, earthquakes, etc.; and I am very conspiracy-minded – what others see as paranoia I see as prudent awareness.

It doesn't require a giant leap to see the similarities between the feelings I expressed as a result of my experience in that town in my past life and the personality traits I possess in my current life. It's clear to me now that a large part of who I am today was formulated as I stood in that war-torn town in my previous lifetime. And this is, to me at least, a monumental discovery about myself. It's interesting that, on the train ride home after the hypnosis session ended, I was wondering why the episode of that past life to which I regressed was so seemingly unspectacular. One would think a person would recall something much more dramatic or sensational. But after much reflection I now see that this episode was in fact pivotal and critically important to both that lifetime as well as my current lifetime. My psyche/spirit/whatever did, in fact, bring me to an event of extraordinary significance. And I continue to discover – or uncover – new relevancies and connections between that past-life moment and my current life. It is an awesome and humbling experience… and very, very enlightening.

Since I earlier offered the data derived from hypnotic past-life regression as part of the evidence in support of the reality of reincarnation, the question "How valid are these hypnotically induced memories?" is of critical importance, and was therefore addressed in detail in Chapter 4: Are Other Lives Recalled via Hypnosis "Real"? At this point I'd like to use my personal experience with hypnotic regression to delve a little deeper into that question.

Skeptics claim that what is "recalled" under hypnosis is not a real memory of a past life but rather an artificial memory, or fantasy, created by the subject's brain. In Chapter 4 I presented some very credible and persuasive objective evidence against this claim, but there also exists very compelling subjective evidence to support the validity of memories uncovered during Past Life Regression, and I would like to address these from my own personal experience.

One such piece of evidence is the potent emotions I felt during the session when I began crying due to the heartbreaking circumstances of the civilians in the town. I find it inconceivable that anyone could experience such realistic and forceful emotions merely because of an imagined or made-up event. The feelings I felt were so intense, ran so deep, and possessed such a personal quality, that I simply cannot accept that they were prompted by a made-up experience.

Another compelling piece of evidence in favor of the reality of these memories lies in the recalled experience itself. I briefly mentioned previously that I was initially surprised at the mundane nature of the event that I recalled. Granted that it happening during World War II is no trivial matter, but the fact is that it was by and large a relatively tame situation – I was standing in a bombed-out town after the "action" had transpired. While my feelings may have been intense, the activity around me was minimal. One would think that if your mind was going to make up a memory of a past life episode it would create one that was a bit more exciting and awe-inspiring, especially if it was going to use World War II as the setting. I think the absence of any movie-like action or drama speaks heavily in favor of this being a true memory of a real past life event. All the more so due to the fact that I grew up watching countless World War II movies that promoted a pro-war theme and were filled with the gunfire and explosions typical of action-filled combat scenes.

My final item of evidence for the reality of this past life regression memory lies in the discrepancy between what I had *thought* my most recent past life had been compared with what *actually was reported* under hypnosis. I have already mentioned that I arrived at Amy's home with some very definite thoughts regarding the circumstances my most recent past life. Let me now explain exactly what my belief about my past was, and why I believed as I did.

For a long time, prior to my first hypnosis session, I was quite convinced that in my most recent past life I had been a Nazi SS officer. I was sickened by this possibility and in fact had considered not undergoing hypnotic regression because I did not want to learn that I might have played a role in the atrocities committed by the Nazi SS during the war. My reasons for believing I was an SS officer are compelling:

First, as a young boy I was inexplicably fascinated by the entire Nazi episode of German history. I had no feelings of anti-Semitism nor did I revel in the barbarity of the Nazi reign. I was merely intrigued by their ideology, philosophy, psychology, and military exploits. I remember writing a paper on Hitler in the seventh grade and the history teacher asking me "What're you – a Nazi?" My fascination with Nazism was extreme, and I could not find any explanation for it.

Secondly, during my military service in the U.S. Army (in my current life) I had the opportunity to attend the Army's language school to learn the German language (this was necessary to prepare me for an upcoming assignment in Germany where I would have to work very closely with the German military). In spite of the fact that I had never in my life exhibited any facility with foreign languages whatsoever, it turned out that I did extraordinarily well in the Army's German language course – so much so that I was chosen to receive the top award (which I turned down). Also, at the end of the oral portion of my final exam (where we had to converse one-on-one with one of our instructors completely in German), my instructor told me, "The other instructor and I are both of the opinion that after you have lived in Germany for about six months your German will be indistinguishable from that of a native German." Needless to say, I was floored by her assessment. Her prediction later proved to be true when, while traveling in Southern Germany while on vacation after having lived in Northern Germany for about a year, my wife and I stopped at a small hotel for the night. The owner and I conducted our business exclusively in German. After a while the hotel owner asked me (in German), "Where are you from?" I answered her by naming the area of Germany where we were living and where I was stationed. She replied that she couldn't believe that I was from that part of Germany, and when I asked her why she said, "Your accent sounds like a Berlin accent." It was only then that I realized that she thought I was a German citizen! I told her (in German), "No, no – I'm an American soldier stationed in Germany." She absolutely would not believe me. My wife and I had a good laugh over it later, but then my wife recalled the prediction my language instructor had made back in America, and we both exclaimed, "Wow, that's exactly what she said would happen."

Finally, and this was the one experience that *really* made me think I had been a Nazi in a previous life, several years ago I had a very, very vivid dream that I was standing in a street in what I somehow knew was Germany; there was snow on the ground and it was getting on to dusk. I was standing across the street from a building in which I knew a concert or performance of some type was about to begin. Well-dressed people were milling about in front of the theater or making their way inside. I knew I was an officer of the Nazi SS, and I was dressed accordingly: black uniform, black boots, long black leather coat. I remember very distinctly feeling the power and authority that went with having such a position in Germany at that time. As I watched the people in front of the theater I noticed a man walk along the side of the theater and then duck into a side door. For some reason I felt that something suspicious was afoot, and I quickly ran down the side street to the side entrance, drew my pistol, and entered the building. The performance had not yet started and people were standing and talking or moving about trying to find their seats. I remember holding the pistol down at my side so as not to alarm the theater-goers. That is all I remember of that dream. But what was so fascinating to me, when I awoke, was how real the dream felt. Everything about it felt like a real experience – the cold air, my sense of who I was, the other people – there was no sense of surrealism as one usually gets in most dreams. Everything felt accurate and normal. It was eerie. I remember wondering, "Why did I dream that?" I had not recently seen a movie about the Nazis, had not recently read anything about them, and I was not thinking about them at all in the days leading up to that dream. The sheer unlikelihood of having such a dream, combined with the stark realism of the dream itself, made me feel that it might not have been a dream at all but rather a recollection of some event from a past life. Later, after I had made arrangements with Amy via e-mail to do past-life regression with her, I had been thinking about my belief that I had been a Nazi SS Officer, and the reasons for that belief, and I had also been thinking of how I wanted to do some type of healing hypnosis for my prostate cancer... and then an idea hit me like a truck: What if I really had been an SS Officer, and what if I, in that capacity, had participated in the horrific experiments that the Nazis performed on concentration camp inmates? Many of these acts of barbaric cruelty involved doing damage to the inmates' sex organs – e.g., irradiating men's testicles. And then it occurred to me that not only do I have prostate cancer now, but I also have a history of prostatitis and kidney stones. I began to formulate the theory that I had indeed been an SS Officer who had participated in these experiments, and that now, either due to extreme subconscious guilt or by means of karmic retribution, I was experiencing in my present life the manifestation of that guilt or karma in these many groin-located ailments with which I've suffered. It all made so much sense that I became virtually certain this was the case.

OK, so what's the point of all this? Well, just think about it: I am almost totally convinced, through some pretty good circumstantial evidence, that I was a Nazi SS Officer in my last past life. And some medical issues I've suffered tie in perfectly with that scenario, making me even more convinced. I get hypnotized, have a past life regression which leads to WWII, and ... I discover I'm an *American* soldier! If my mind was making up a past life for me, then doesn't it stand to reason that it would have created a fictitious life that mirrored my very strongly held belief about a previous Nazi lifetime? In fact, when I had gotten to that point during the hypnosis session and Amy asked me "Where are you?" I remember thinking "I bet I'm going to see myself as a Nazi." --- I even expected this to come out *while I was under hypnosis*! Yet, in spite of my pre-conceived notions and my expectations, the lifetime that emerged was quite different from what I had imagined it would be. This, to me, is very compelling evidence that my mind did not create this memory but, rather, that it was an honest and factual recollection of an actual past lifetime.

So, those are my arguments in favor of the validity of past lives that are recalled via past life regressive hypnosis, based upon my personal experience of the process.

Part II

A Model of the Afterlife

There is some kind of controlling, minded, integrative thing behind nature.

– Terence McKenna, author

Entertain all possibilities, but never commit to belief – belief always being seen as a kind of trap; because if you believe something, you are forever precluded from believing its opposite.

– Terence McKenna, author

A story is told of a wealthy businessman who, while passing through Radin, Poland, decided to take the opportunity to visit Rabbi Yisrael Meir Kagan, a famous rabbi in Eastern Europe at the time. Upon entering the rabbi's modest home the tourist was surprised by the lack of furniture and asked, "Rabbi, where is your furniture?" To which the rabbi responded, "Where's *yours*?" The tourist, taken aback, replied, "I have no furniture – I'm just passing through." "Well," said the rabbi, "So am I."

Chapter 6

Karma, Free Will, and the Spirit Realm

A healthy science is a science that seeks the truth and lets the evidence speak for itself.

- Paul Nelson, philosopher of biology

6.1 Reluctance, Resistance and Skepticism

In many ways, I came to the topic of the Afterlife kicking and screaming. In the early years of my life I was very much a left-brain person. My education and my interests were almost exclusively geared to reductionist, materialist concepts, and this is attested to by my education background which includes a B.S. degree with a major in Mathematics and an M.S. degree in Computers in Education. I greatly admired the structure, formality, logic, and exactness inherent in mathematics, and I also found it beautiful and fascinating for those very same reasons. I found that in math – as in no other field of knowledge – concepts could be *proved* with absolute certainty; there was little conjecture and no guesswork or opinion. I derived a sense of comfort and security from math's stable concreteness and mechanistic precision. When the personal computer revolution kicked off in the early 80's, I jumped right in. For eleven years I worked as a high school mathematics and computer teacher. I generally scoffed at all matters spiritual or psychic in nature. My interest in the paranormal was strictly limited to flying saucers, which I believed (at that time) were solid aircraft piloted by beings from other star systems, and thus this particular area of the supernatural did not conflict with my nuts-and-bolts outlook on reality. Other paranormal topics held no interest or validity for me, and I actively shunned them. Nevertheless, and quite interestingly and importantly, it was my interest in flying saucers that led me, via a very circuitous route, to a broader awareness and acceptance of the more spiritual aspects of the paranormal. How this happened is telling in its own right, and I believe it has something significant to say about the flying saucer phenomenon in general.

Browsing through the "occult" section of a bookstore one day I came across a book entitled *Aliens Among Us* by Ruth Montgomery. I did not recognize the author, but the title intrigued me as I presumed it referred to UFO occupants. I bought the book and was brimming with anticipation about the possibility of learning some inside scoop regarding the identity and agenda of the beings piloting the saucers. Well, after I began reading the book my initial enthusiasm quickly diminished: it turned out that the book was not so much about flying saucer "aliens" but rather it dealt with matters of a more spiritual nature, including a discussion of "aliens" which Ms. Montgomery identified as 'walk-ins" – souls who for various reasons switch places with a soul currently occupying a human body during an in-progress physical incarnation. Although I was terribly disappointed that the book did not deal with the type of aliens in which I was interested, I found myself intrigued by the spiritual and philosophical insights discussed in the book, inexplicably so since, as I mentioned above, I was, at that time in my life, a total non-believer in any paranormal topics other than nuts-and-bolts flying saucers. In all honesty, I didn't believe that the information presented in *Aliens Among Us* was true; nevertheless, I was captivated by the doctrines put forward. This book most probably constituted the initial breakdown of my resistance to spiritual subjects – I still didn't believe any of it, but I found the information comforting and fascinating, so much so that I proceeded to read other books by Ms. Montgomery. Two of her books that particularly accelerated the dismantling of my rejection of spiritual ideas, and actually caused me to accept and embrace such concepts, were *Here and Hereafter*, which dealt primarily with reincarnation and karma[52], and *A World Beyond* which represented my very first exposure to the spirit realm as a real and actual place. In *A World Beyond* Ms. Montgomery recounts the results of her communication with an old friend who had "passed on to the other side." He conveys to her a surprising amount of detail regarding life in the spirit realm and what souls experience while "residing" there.[53] When I read that book many years ago I didn't accept it as being the truth. I found the information fascinating, interesting, and astoundingly logical – so much so that I remember thinking "I wish it really was like that" and "That's how the afterlife *should* be" because it made sense and also because it explained a great deal about our lives in the physical world. But ultimately I decided it was implausible, so I merely accepted it as an interesting work of fiction being passed off as fact. Many years later I bought a copy of Michael Newton's book *Journey of Souls*, and my attitude about the subject of the Afterlife (and towards Ms. Montgomery's book) changed completely.

6.2 Dr. Michael Newton: Our Life Between Lives

Dr. Michael Newton is a psychologist who had been using hypnosis to regress his patients to past lives in order to treat problems in their current lives. During one of these sessions, as a result of some vague directions and unintentional prompting, it became clear to Dr. Newton that his patient had not regressed to a typical past life setting. Upon further questioning Newton discovered that his patient had indeed gone back to "a time before" her current life, but rather than going to a past life she had regressed to the time she spent in the spirit realm *before* being born into her current life – a period Dr. Newton refers to as our "Life Between Lives" (LBL).[54] Dr. Newton went on to intentionally regress other patients to the spirit realm, and after amassing a huge collection of data from these hypnosis sessions he sifted through the data, organized them, and presented his findings in a series of books. What resulted is a very clear, concise, and structured representation of what "life" is like in the Spirit Realm, with very precise descriptions of what souls experience while there. What I found most convincing about Dr. Newton's patients' revelations about the spirit realm was the consistency of their descriptions. The extent of agreement among the descriptions given by Dr. Newton's patients is nothing short of amazing. And because of this high degree of consistency Dr. Newton was able to assemble, from the amassed transcripts of his clients, a very detailed model of the afterlife.

6.3 The Three Great Questions

I honestly consider Michael Newton's book *Journey of Souls* and his follow-up book *Destiny of Souls* to be the two most important and personally influential books I have ever read. If you accept the information presented in those books as being true and accurate (and I most definitely do), then it is no exaggeration to claim that those two books provide very specific and conclusive answers to the three great mysteries of life: "Where do we come from before we're born?", "Where do we go after we die?", and "Why are we here?" I kid you not – these three questions are answered quite definitively by Dr. Newton's books. I have read each book several times and with each reading I continue to find them enlightening, uplifting, and utterly fascinating. I highly recommend these books to anyone who has even the slightest interest in the answers to those three huge and important questions.

But there are yet richer treasures to be mined from Dr. Newton's books, richer even than the answers to those three great questions. I discovered, much to my surprise, that in the months after I first read those books, the information presented began to have a very subtle and inconspicuous effect on my psyche, my way of thinking, and the way I interpreted and evaluated my day-to-day experiences. Initially the effect was so subtle that I was completely unaware of it, but its influence and impact slowly and continually increased until one day I realized that I had been profoundly changed at a very fundamental level and in a very significant way. I found that I had undergone a transformation that was in many ways similar to the aftereffects experienced by NDErs as discussed in Chapter 2; but the transformation I experienced as a result of reading Dr. Newton's books was more powerful and more deeply penetrating, so much so that it ultimately resulted in significant behavioral and personality changes, as well as a total restructuring of my core beliefs and moral philosophy. This change was momentous and incredible, and it was totally positive: what emerged was a much happier person, a much more content person and, in my opinion, a much better person. I will discuss the Transformative Effects of LBL Awareness in a later chapter and you will see, I believe, that this transformation has the potential to be much more powerful and effecting than the aftereffects produced by a near death experience.

6.4 The Spirit Realm and Karma

The Spirit Realm is the place we come from before we're born, and the place we go to after we die – it is our "Life Between Lives." In his books *Journey of Souls* and *Destiny of Souls* Michael Newton offers an amazingly detailed description of how the Spirit Realm is structured, the things experienced by souls there, and the reasons why we do what we do there. Ultimately, most of what we as souls experience in the Spirit Realm revolves around the concepts of "karma" and "reincarnation" which, as we saw in Chapter 1, exist together in an association of correlative interdependency. Simply put, *karma* is a universal law of cause-and-effect whereby our acts and deeds in any given lifetime become determining factors of aspects and events experienced by us in future lives; and *reincarnation* refers to the belief that upon biological death the human soul leaves the deceased body and is later born anew in another physical body, the life circumstances of which are dependent upon the degree of moral quality exemplified in that soul's previous lives. The purpose of karma appears to be two-fold: spiritual evolution and balance. Our ultimate goal as souls is to evolve to a state of spiritual perfection so that we can reunite with the Source/Creator/Godhead from which we all originally sprung.[55] By eliminating "negative" karma we cleanse our souls and thus make progress in our pursuit of spiritual perfection. We eliminate "negative" karma – or, more accurately, we *balance* our karma – by living lives where we experience the effects of negative deeds similar to those we had committed in earlier lives; for example, if you lived a life where you were a large, strong male and you used your physical attributes to bully smaller men, then in a subsequent life you might be born small and frail and find yourself being *victimized* by bullies. Or, if you lived a life where you sold wood alcohol as a drink during the prohibition era you might find yourself being born blind in a later life. It is important to understand that karma is *not* punishment; it is balance. It is not until we personally and directly experience the *effects* of horrible acts that we can truly perceive the damage and devastation *caused* by such acts and hopefully appreciate and fully comprehend the wrongness of those acts, and thus be moved to no longer commit such acts. In this way we will learn from our experiences, make the appropriate adjustments, and purge our souls of any dark tendencies. We undergo these experiences by living a variety of different lives; this cycle of recurring lives – birth-death-rebirth-etc. – is reincarnation. Our souls incarnate (i.e., "take on flesh") into an earthly life with the express purpose of living a life involving specific experiences and characteristics that will enable us to address our karmic issues.[56] If we are successful in dealing with these karmic issues, then through a series of lives lived in the physical we can ultimately wipe the karmic slate clean and achieve our goal of spiritual perfection. As the Buddha said: "Do you want to know what your past lives were like? Then look at your life now. Do you want to know what your next life will be like? Then look at your life now."

6.5 Free Will

The idea that our actions in one lifetime are a determining factor of our experiences in a subsequent lifetime – which really is the gist of karma and reincarnation – seems to imply that our lives are governed by predestination and fate. The truth, however, is quite the opposite. As you will shortly see, one of the most fascinating aspects of the Spirit Realm is the fact that we, as souls, have much to say about the details and circumstances of our upcoming lives; in the Spirit Realm, with the assistance of other souls, we formulate a plan for how we can best address our karmic issues, and then *we choose* a particular life experience that will offer us the situations and circumstances necessary to carry out the life plan that we devised.[57] The one great caveat to all this in-depth planning is this: We, as human beings, have *free will*. When we plan our next life we are *not* setting up a rigid script that is guaranteed to be followed to a "T". What we are doing is devising an outline where the players are free to ad lib. Lives in the flesh are not always lived according to the plans made in the Spirit Realm. It is hoped that we will adhere to the plan closely, but, ultimately, there are no guarantees. So, far from having a pre-fabricated lifetime dumped upon us, the truth is that we play an active and contributory role in the development of our life plan and, further, while we are actually *living* that life we are free to act as we wish, and thus deviate from our life plan, without constraint. From the perspective of spiritual growth and advancement such deviation from the plan is usually imprudent, but the point is that we are free to do so if we choose.[58]

The system in place in the Spirit Realm that assists us in formulating the strategies necessary to address our karma and advance spiritually is as fascinating and beautiful as it is ingenious and logical. Let's have a look at exactly how the Spirit Realm is structured and how its design offers us the means to work out our karma and evolve spiritually.

Chapter 7

The Newton Model of the Spirit Realm

Life is a sexually transmitted disease and the mortality rate is one hundred percent.

– R. D. Laing, psychiatrist

Western society is in denial about death. The medical profession views death as a failure; governmental agencies view death as a statistic; the entertainment industry views death as lurid, slapstick camp; and the average person views death as an uncomfortable and awkward subject. Our attitude and approach toward death is to either avoid the subject altogether or to trivialize it to the point of mockery. But rarely do we deal with death in a serious and mature manner. Yet death is an entirely normal and natural process, and it is quite probably the most profound experience any of us will ever have. So, then, why the denial and the trivialization? The main reason is that we *fear* death, and our fear of death is so great that we have a difficult time facing the subject rationally and maturely. *Why* do we fear death so? The answer, it turns out, is surprisingly simple: we fear death because it is unpredictable and unknowable; we fear what we don't understand, and death is the ultimate mystery.

Well, not anymore …

7.1 A Note Regarding Source Material and Terminology

Throughout this book I will frequently make reference to what I call "The Newton Model of the Spirit Realm." I decided to attribute the Spirit Realm model to Dr. Newton for three reasons: (1) He, more than any other researcher in this field (at least to my knowledge), has painstakingly and laboriously sifted through a mind-bogglingly huge amount of disparate data extracted from reams of transcribed recorded hypnosis sessions and miraculously organized and assembled it all into a coherent, meaningful and useable model of the Afterlife; (2) His model is a masterwork of systematization, structure, assessment and classification; and (3) His presentation of the fruits of his labor, specifically in his books *Journey of Souls* and *Destiny of Souls*, is as forthright, clear and concise an exposition as one could hope for.

There are, however, other researchers who have also explored the Spirit Realm via regressive hypnosis and published the results of their findings. Their reports are fascinating in their own right, and their findings both confirm and expand upon the findings of Dr. Newton; for those reasons I consider their work to be of tremendous value and interest, and they provide an important contribution to the field of Life Between Lives research. So I ask the reader to realize that, while I am referring to this model of the Spirit Realm as the "Newton Model", and while I am drawing much of my information from Dr. Newton's books, I am nevertheless utilizing other sources in addition to Dr. Newton's work, and those sources do in very large measure agree with and confirm Dr. Newton's findings and model. If I reference something that I believe is unique to another researcher I will generally note that in the text of my book; also, see the footnoted references for citing of specific source material. In addition to Dr. Newton's two books mentioned above, my other primary sources regarding details about the Afterlife are the following: *From Birth to Rebirth: Gnostic Healing for the 21ˢᵗ Century*, by C.V. Tramont, M.D., *Beyond Reincarnation: Experience Your Past Lives & Lives Between Lives*, by Joe H. Slate, Ph.D., *Between Death and Life*, by Dolores Cannon, and *Courageous Souls: Do We Plan Our Life Challenges Before Birth?* by Robert Schwartz (this last book relies upon information derived from mediums and channels rather than regressive hypnosis, but the description of the Afterlife that emerges is remarkably consistent with Dr. Newton's model and with the information reported by other authors). I also draw heavily from information obtained from my own personal experience of a Life-Between-Lives hypnosis session, which involved most of the components of a classic LBL experience (my LBL session is covered in detail in Chapter 12).

In the *An Overview of the Spirit Realm* section which follows I will include footnote citations to all relevant source material, but in the *In-Depth Look at the Spirit Realm* section I will limit my citations almost exclusively to Dr. Newton's books; nevertheless, please realize that the *In-Depth* section is in large part an expansion of the topics from the *Overview* section and therefore citations from non-Newton sources in the *Overview* section should be applicable and relevant to related portions in the *In-Depth* section.

7.2 An Overview of the Spirit Realm

The Spirit Realm is the place where we (a) review our past lives with a focus on our karmic successes and failures, and (b) plan our future lives so as to have opportunities to address karmic issues that are as yet unresolved. Before I discuss various aspects of the Spirit Realm in depth, I thought it would be wise to present a broad overview of the design and features of the Spirit Realm that enable us, as souls, to conduct this review and planning. Some of the key aspects of the Spirit Realm that help us accomplish this are the following:

Soul Groups: We each belong to a soul group consisting of, on average, 15 souls. As souls we study with our fellow group members, analyzing our past lives and preparing for our future lives. During incarnations in the flesh, soul group members will usually, but not always, live lives together marked by very close acquaintanceship – siblings or best friends, for example.[59]

Soul Mates: Our soul mates are souls from our soul group with whom we feel especially bonded and who play important roles in our earthly lives. Our ***Primary Soul Mate***, however, is our "eternal partner" who brightens and enhances our existence immeasurably and who is often in our earth lives in a very close and supportive role such as our spouse, sibling, or dear friend.[60]

Schools and Libraries: These "places of learning" in the Spirit Realm enable souls to study and review their past lives – again with specific focus on the karmic aspects – and decide what karmic issues need to be addressed in future lives, and in what ways these issues can best be addressed.[61]

Spirit Guides: Each soul has at least one Spirit Guide, an advanced soul who acts as a mentor/teacher/advisor/guardian. These guides play a crucial role in our spiritual evolution and development. They assist, support, direct, motivate, encourage, and instruct us... they are our coaches and trainers, and so much more.[62]

Council of Elders: This is a panel of very advanced souls possessing great wisdom and experience who review our past lives with us, and also help us plan out our future lives. Sometimes mistakenly thought of as a tribunal of judges they actually neither judge nor condemn us; ultimately, each soul judges itself. The Council's role appears to be that of providing expert analysis, evaluation, and guidance.[63]

Place of Life Selection: This is a place where we can view, experience and evaluate the options available to us for our next life in the flesh. Amazingly, we have quite a lot of input in choosing both who we will be in our next life as well as what the circumstances of that life will be. These choices are made, of course, based upon the karmic issues we are planning to address in the upcoming life. Will we be born female?, ...to a wealthy family?, ...physically handicapped?, ... possessing a special talent? The choices we make here are in accordance with the karmic issues we identified, and the plans we made, as a result of the studies and learning conducted in the schools and libraries, and the meetings, consultations, and discussions held with our soul group members, spirit guides, and Council members. It all comes together here: If we learned well and planned effectively, then we will make a life selection that affords us an excellent opportunity to make some serious karmic progress.[64]

Soul Auras: Dr. Newton found that souls in the Spirit Realm radiate auras of various colors and that the color of a soul's aura is an indication of that soul's level of spiritual advancement. Beginner souls emit a white aura; then, as a soul's level of spiritual development advances, its aura progresses through various shades of yellow, gold, blue, and, ultimately, purple. Thus souls with a whitish aura are rookies with regard to spiritual development, while souls with blue-to-purple auras are highly advanced and have reached the near-master or master level.[65] How, and at what rate, we advance spiritually is determined by our earthly incarnations and the ways in which we handle and cope with the challenges we face therein.

7.3 A More In-depth Look at the Spirit Realm

Now that you have an idea of some of the characteristics of the Spirit Realm, and the functions they serve, I'd like to put the pieces together by describing, in very condensed form, a general representation of a soul's experience in the afterlife from the moment of arrival in the Spirit Realm, after just completing an earth lifetime, up to the moment just before it returns to earth for a subsequent lifetime. As we follow the soul's movements and activities throughout the Spirit Realm I will take the opportunity, at various points of interest, to expand upon some of the key aspects noted in the overview above. Also, in addition to the material drawn from my source references, I will occasionally intersperse relevant portions of my own LBL hypnosis session (my LBL session will be covered in depth in the last chapter of Part II).

There are three important facts about the nature of the Spirit Realm that should be noted at the outset: (1) *communication* in the Spirit Realm is reported as being telepathic – possibly of a musical nature – or else by "touch" (i.e., conjoining of two souls) for private communication[66]; (2) *time* in the Spirit realm is completely unlike time as we experience it on earth – time in the afterlife is a nonlinear concresence of what we would think of as past, present and future; it is an eternal *Now*, if you will, where (if a comparison is even possible) tiny durations equate to years passing on Earth.[67] (So, throughout the remainder of this book, wherever I use a phrase such as "she said" or "shortly after" in regard to the Spirit Realm I am using such phrases figuratively to convey that communication is occurring – "she said" – or to relate a sense of relative duration – "shortly after"); (3) it could easily go unrealized that the souls with whom Dr. Newton (and others doing similar research) communicate are, of necessity, souls that are still reincarnating and are therefore limited to the sub-group of souls at or below the purple-aura level; thus these souls have limited experience and access in the Spirit Realm and are subsequently limited in the information they can provide regarding that realm. There are hints and indications in Dr. Newton's findings that there are potentially many levels of the afterlife existing beyond the restricted portion to which Dr. Newton has access.[68] The situation is analogous to asking an American high school student about the American educational system – he/she could give you very specific, first-hand information about elementary school through high school, but could not provide any meaningful information about college other than hearsay. The point is that the reader must remember that any statements made about "the Spirit Realm" are, in fact, limited to that portion of the afterlife to which Dr. Newton and other researchers are privy by virtue of the limited range of souls available on Earth.

Those caveats having been established, let's now take a more in-depth look at the Spirit Realm.

Crossing Over

Access to the Spirit Realm during a Life Between Lives hypnosis session typically involves having the subject go to a past lifetime and then moving him/her to the moment of death in that lifetime. As the subject passes over, the episode they describe is remarkably similar to that of a near-death experience, including the out-of-body experience, an inability to communicate with those still living, a sensation of being pulled away from the scene, an absence of fear, and a bright white light at the far end of a tunnel of darkness. The "tunnel effect" appears to depict the gateway from physical existence to the Spirit Realm.[69] During my hypnosis session I first experienced myself floating through the sky among clouds, and then shortly after surrounded by fog with flashes of light visible in the fog.

Arrival

Upon leaving the tunnel the soul feels a strong sensation of love, peace, harmony, relaxing sounds (music, chimes, a humming or vibration), and a sense of being "home." Some perceive buildings and/or cities (often seemingly made of ice or crystals) or pastoral scenes such as fields of flowers.[70] Most souls are then met by one or more other souls who assist them with the transition from physical life to the afterlife. This welcoming soul is usually a spirit guide or soul mate, or a close relative or friend (not necessarily deceased).[71] (At this point in my LBL regressive hypnosis session I was met by one of my spirit guides). The transition from physical life to the Spirit Realm appears to go easier and quicker for the more advanced souls, so much so that some of them do not require a supportive soul to assist in the passage from one state to another.

Reunion with Soul Group

After the soul has sufficiently recovered from the shock and disorientation of physical death and transport to a new reality, the next step in the re-acclimation process is a kind of "welcome home" reception where the soul is reunited with members of its soul group and other souls of importance to them. Seeing familiar "faces" and reuniting with beloved soul mates is a very comforting and uplifting experience for the newly arrived soul, and this homecoming experience is often described as having a festive, party-like quality.[72] During my session I described it as a "party atmosphere" and, feeling strong emotions, stated, "It feels good. It really *is* coming home."

Place of Healing

After the homecoming the soul may go to a place of healing for further readjustment to the spiritual environment; this phase, if needed, helps to cleanse the soul of unpleasant aftereffects or residual negative energy from the recent physical life.[73]

Session with Spirit Guide

At this point the soul should be fully re-acclimatized to their true home, and now work on karmic matters can begin. This phase is generally initiated by an in-depth "counseling session" with our spirit guide: this session amounts to a kind of debriefing of the life just lived where we review (alone with our guide) our behavior, decisions, missed opportunities, etc., to include an analysis of our attendant mind-sets and emotions. This phase marks the beginning of the soul's self-evaluation and helps to prepare the soul for its upcoming session with the Council of Elders.[74]

As mentioned in the "Overview of the Spirit Realm" section above, each soul has at least one Spirit Guide, an advanced soul who acts as a mentor/teacher/advisor/guardian. In the cases where a soul has two guides, one guide is the senior or primary guide while the other is usually a junior guide-in-training. During my LBL hypnosis session I learned that I had two guides: one, Kayla, who met me as I crossed over from the physical, was the junior guide; my senior guide, I was surprised to learn, was someone I know in my current life (an in-depth account of my LBL session is presented later in this book, at the end of Part II). These guides play a crucial role in our spiritual evolution and development. They assist, support, direct, motivate, encourage, and instruct us, both in the afterlife as well as during incarnations. In addition to their obvious role in the Spirit Realm, guides can also provide us helpful guidance and support while we are living in the physical, usually via dreams, inspiration and intuition[75], and even, as I personally discovered, meditation. As with all good teachers, guides do not solve our problems for us but rather help us to solve our problems ourselves. Their individual approaches toward this end can vary, and appear to be determined by the personality of the guide. In my case, my primary guide is very knowledgeable but also tough and sarcastic, whereas my junior guide is gentler and more sensitive. Just as with the Elders, our guides are patient and compassionate but not judgmental. However, while souls feel great reverence towards the Elders they do not enjoy what one would call a "close" relationship with them; our relationship with our guides, however, is very close and often involves feelings of deep affection. We, as souls, do not choose our guides but, rather, they choose us.

Council of Elders

A soul typically meets with its Council once or twice between lives: once shortly after returning to the Spirit Realm, and possibly once again just before beginning a new life. The Council is composed of highly advanced souls (Elders) who are extremely knowledgeable and who possess and exemplify the qualities of discernment, sagacity, and diplomacy. These Elders represent the most advanced level of being that reincarnating souls ever meet in the Spirit Realm (although an even higher level entity or "divine energy" – referred to as "the Presence" – is sometimes *sensed* by souls when they appear before their Council, almost as if it is overseeing the proceedings). A Council typically has 3 to 7 members (but can be more if the subject is an advanced soul) with one member, seated in the center, serving as moderator and primary questioner.

The Council is not a tribunal in the earth-sense and it is meant to be neither judgmental nor accusatory. The main purpose of the Council is to assist the soul in reviewing and evaluating its most recent life (to include relevant factors and patterns from any and all past lives) with regard to the soul's choices and behaviors and, through objective analysis reinforced by experience and wisdom, guide the soul in making meaningful choices and plans regarding their next lifetime. All of this advisement is, of course, pertinent to that soul's particular karmic history and issues. The goal is spiritual development and advancement, and it is accomplished by addressing karma via the opportunities and challenges offered by physical incarnations. Our success is determined by how we employ our free will to take advantage of those opportunities and to overcome those challenges. The Council of Elders, and our Spirit Guides, thus function much like expert advisors and coaches who assist us in formulating effective plans and strategies based upon an evaluation of our past successes and failures. The Elders do not *direct* us, they *guide* us: they want to hear how *we* feel about the progress we've made. It is a process of self-discovery in which they help us learn from our experiences and then apply that learning when making choices for, and in, subsequent lives.

As stated above, the Council Elders does not sit in judgment and they do not condemn. If any judgment occurs, it is the soul judging itself. The Elders are generally described as being patient, kindly, and respectful, and the subject soul is free to voice his/her feelings and frustrations. Souls *are* held accountable by the Council for how they lived their recent life, but the entire process is tempered by a sense of forgiving and fairness. That being said, some souls do admit to feeling a degree of trepidation or apprehension when going before their Council.[76] In my case, during my LBL hypnosis I felt a bit intimidated just prior to my session with my Council, and I asked my guide Kayla, who accompanied me, to "Stay close!" I had a very acute awareness of what I was feeling at that time and, upon later contemplation and analysis, I concluded that the feelings of apprehension and intimidation that souls sometimes experience can be attributed to: (1) The extremely advanced spiritual standing of the Elders; (2) The austere setting in which we appear before our Council (usually in a domed chamber with the Council members sitting behind a table on a raised dais); (3) Our own cultural preconceptions regarding trial courts, the roles of authority figures, punishment, judgment, etc.; and (4) Our personal feelings of guilt and/or shame at the mistakes and bad decisions we made in our previous life.

Although our guides usually accompany us during our session with the Council, their role is primarily passive; they may on occasion clarify or offer explanations to facilitate understanding, and they also provide moral support for the soul under their care, but, on the whole, they are usually a quiet presence in the background. For souls who are apprehensive about appearing before the Council, their guide's supportive presence seems to alleviate some of their anxiety.[77] When I asked my guide Kayla to "Stay close!" during my LBL session, my hypnotist remarked, "Sounds a little intimidating." "Oh, it is," I said, "I'm not going to face this alone." Although my guide did accompany me before the Council, no further involvement on her part was apparent throughout my entire hypnosis session.

A final point regarding the Council of Elders, for those who might be wondering: members of the same soul group do not typically appear before the same Council. [78]

Schools and Libraries

After the returning soul has completed its initial review and evaluation, with its Spirit Guide and Council, of its most recent incarnation it then devotes itself to much study, contemplation, and planning at schools and libraries, usually in the company of its soul group members. In these "places of learning" souls study from multidimensional "books" that contain "live pictures" wherein they can review their past actions, choices, and mistakes, as well as get glimpses of "future possibilities." The souls collectively reexamine and critique, with occasional assistance from teachers, these past decisions and choices. The recurring point throughout the entire Spirit Realm/earthly incarnation process appears to be that we, as souls, continually pursue spiritual perfection by means of schooling which involves both a practical phase – physical incarnations on Earth – and an abstract, theoretical phase – study and contemplation in the Spirit Realm.[79] The process is circular, not only in the sense of cycles of reincarnation, but also in so far as it is a recurring sequence of: physical experience on Earth – study and evaluation of that experience – planning of the next physical experience based upon lessons learned

– application of the new plan in another physical experience – reevaluation – revised/refined planning – application of the refined plan … etc., until spiritual perfection is ultimately achieved. Thus our lives on Earth represent the empirical phase of the process where we acquire hands-on experience, while our activities in the Spirit Realm constitute the academic phase where we examine the data from the field, as it were, and through study and analysis refine the design details for our next field trip.

Lest I unintentionally mislead the reader, I want to point out that a soul's schooling is not limited to matters of its personal spiritual development and earthly incarnations (for example, there are schools where souls learn the art of creation)[80]; I am merely focusing on that particular aspect of Spirit Realm learning because it is directly relevant to the theses presented in this book. It is important for the reader to realize that what I am presenting here, with regard to Dr. Newton's work, is simply a brief synopsis of a subset of the material he presents in his books *Journey of Souls* and *Destiny of Souls*. Those books delve into these topics so much more, and they also present a wealth of material upon which I have not even touched. Firstly, Dr. Newton's books are rich with verbatim transcript excerpts from his hypnosis sessions, and I, personally, found each and every one of those excerpts to be fascinating and extraordinary. Short of undergoing LBL hypnosis oneself, there is nothing like reading first-hand what these people experienced *in their own words.* Secondly, Dr. Newton's commentary and reflections are erudite, insightful, and often poignant; his analysis of his findings provides a critical dimension to a meaningful interpretation and understanding of this complex and fertile subject. Thirdly, there are many aspects to the Spirit Realm discussed in Dr. Newton's books which I only mention in passing or do not address at all; to note just a few: levels of souls, advanced souls, souls that create, incarnations on worlds other than Earth, soul isolation and cleansing ("evil souls"), soul birthing/creation, Spirit Realm games and recreation... and much more. I have said it previously in this book, and I will most certainly say it again: I strongly urge you to read Dr. Michael Newton's books *Journey of Souls* and *Destiny of Souls*. I cannot say this more sincerely or directly: I consider those books to be the most important, most fascinating, and most interesting books I have ever read. I have read them each several times, and I fully intend to read them again. They have changed my life in ways both positive and profound. In my opinion, one of the most effective ways of bringing about such changes is by reading verbatim transcript excerpts from LBL hypnosis sessions and, as I noted above, Dr. Newton's books *Journey of Souls* and *Destiny of Souls* are replete with many such excerpts.

The Place of Life Selection

At some point in this process of study, contemplation, and preparation the unperfected soul makes the decision that the time has come to leave the Spirit

Realm and return to the physical for another incarnation. For reasons that I think are at this point obvious, many souls are reluctant to leave the idyllic existence in the Spirit Realm for the less-than-perfect experiences offered by an earthly incarnation.[81] Souls have the option to choose *not* to incarnate, but they note that spiritual progress is much, much faster via the path of direct experience attained by living a life in a human body on Earth. Souls may not be forced to incarnate, but they are "encouraged" to do so.[82] (The only exception I've found to this was in the book *From Birth to Rebirth*, by C.V. Tramont, wherein a subject was quoted as saying that the Elders give souls their life assignments and also decide when they reincarnate).[83] During my own LBL hypnosis session my hypnotist specifically addressed the question of what makes a soul decide to reincarnate , and I think the answer I provided is interesting and relevant:

> **Amy** (hypnotist): How do you know when it's time to incarnate? Does someone tell you?
>
> **John**: You begin to get restless. You can't fully enjoy the pleasures of the Spirit Realm. At first it's like an annoyance in the background that goes buzz, buzz in your ear. But it gets bigger, and it starts to impede your enjoyment, and eventually you realize that you've got to deal with it, that you won't be comfortable there if you don't deal with it. There's a tremendous resistance to knowing that – at least to me – but the discomfort there gets so great that it tips the balance. And in order to recoup the pleasurable feelings there, you have to come back here and deal with the issues. And that's what motivates you.

(An interesting question here is: Is that "annoying buzz, buzz" the result of our own personal guilt, or is it an inherent, preprogrammed aspect of the Spirit Realm designed to give us the boot in the ass we need to finally give in and agree to make a return trip to the physical?).

When we, as souls, finally decide it is time to reincarnate, we pay an important visit to the Place of Life Selection; there we are given the means to assist us in choosing the details of our next life, to include: who we will be; who our parents will be; and the time, place, setting, and circumstances of our new life. Options for our next life are presented to us, and we evaluate those options with regard to how each scenario might help us address our karmic issues and facilitate our spiritual progress. It also seems that part of our evaluation is influenced by more subjective concerns, such as how hard or easy a particular option might be, or simply for the sake of having new experiences. Also, our choices may be based upon a desire to experience both the dark and the light aspects of life, not for the purpose of balancing past karma but rather as an aid in our learning and understanding and our pursuit of balance. Our decision is ours to make, but it is influenced by input from our Guides and Council Elders, and also from members of our soul group.[84] The Place of Life Selection, also known as the Ring of

Destiny, is often described as a kind of 360° holographic movie theater where the soul can actually scan through selected portions of the life options offered; the soul not only is able to *view* the action but can also *enter into* particular scenes and *experience* them. As one might expect, the soul is not permitted to view all moments of these lifetimes, thus some portions are obscured.[85]

During my LBL hypnosis session I re-experienced my visit to the Place of Life Selection prior to embarking on my current lifetime, and I learned that the other life options that were presented to me were less difficult than the life I ultimately chose. I briefly lamented not having taken an easier path, but then I was made to see that if I had chosen one of those easier lives I would *not* have made the karmic and spiritual progress which I have accomplished. I noted that this was precisely *why* I had chosen the most difficult option presented to me, even though I was apprehensive about facing the challenges it offered.

After the soul decides upon one of the several alternatives of life situations presented in the Place of Life Selection there usually follows a final "dress rehearsal" – involving their Guide, specialist souls called "prompters," and the soul mates who will play major roles in that lifetime – to review particular important aspects of that lifetime and to go over the circumstances under which the souls will meet, as well as certain cues that will aid them in recognizing one another.[86] (when, during my hypnosis session, I described my final meeting with my wife in the Spirit Realm I alluded to such "cues" by describing us saying to one another: "Make sure we hook up. Make sure we hook up. Don't want to miss it.").

Upon mutual consent between reincarnating souls and their advisors, an amnesiac state is imposed so that we will not remember our past lives (with some exceptions).[87]

Dr. Newton likens souls preparing for their return to Earth to "... battle-hardened veterans girding themselves for combat."[88] Indeed, returning to Earth for another lifetime can be a difficult and anxiety-ridden prospect, especially when the rigors of physical existence are contrasted with the idyllically beautiful and peaceful experience of the Spirit Realm. One of Dr. Newton's subjects, while describing how she passes the time in her mother's womb just prior to birth, notes that it is her last opportunity for "quiet contemplation" because, as she so affectingly put it, "When I come out – I'll be running."[89]

Chapter 8

Is There a "God" and/or a "Hell"?

I prefer not to think about the Newton Model of the Afterlife in religious terms, and I think it's safe to presume that Dr. Newton feels likewise. Nonetheless, religious implications and associations are unavoidable given the nature of the topic. Thus it is inevitable that virtually everyone, at some point during their initial acquaintance with Life Between Lives research, is struck with curiosity concerning whether such research has anything to say about the existence of God. And, while one is in such a mindset, the question of the existence of Hell generally follows.

Interestingly, these topics do come up during some LBL hypnosis sessions and, although they are typically addressed rather obliquely by the hypnosis subject, enough information is revealed to leave one with a tantalizing, albeit frustratingly incomplete, solution to the mystery. This is particularly true in the case of "God."

8.1 Is There a "God"?

LBL hypnosis subjects never claim to have "seen" God, but many do sense a powerful presence that they feel is somehow directing and coordinating events in the Spirit Realm.[90] This supreme intelligence, or "Oversoul", is often referred to as the Source, and some souls suggest that it may actually be an aggregate of extremely advanced souls (the "Old Ones"),[91] or else that the Source and the Spirit Realm (and, indeed, possibly *everything*) are one and the same.[92]

Interestingly, Newton notes that some of his more advanced subjects imply that this Oversoul is not the "absolute God" but merely one member of a divine pantheon of Gods in which each God is not infallible but is learning, progressing, and advancing in much the same way that we souls do. Under this scheme our imperfect world can be seen as the result of an imperfect God-Creator who is in the process of learning from Its mistakes. This system does not obviate the existence of a single ultimate God, but simply suggests the possibility that *our God* is not *The God*.[93]

Whatever it is, this divine Presence or Oversoul is most often sensed by Dr. Newton's subjects when they appear before their Council of Elders, where they report a distinct impression that this Presence is overseeing their session with the Elders. While these subjects do not specifically identify this Presence as being

"God", they do sense that it represents the closest thing to God in their Spirit Realm experience.[94]

I, personally, find the "God as everything" scenario most appealing from both a scientific as well as a metaphysical/ontological point of view, and it is intriguingly consistent with the model of reality we will examine in Part III of this book.

8.2 Is There a "Hell"?

Whether or not there is a single, supreme God (in the sense claimed by the major monotheistic religions), it is nevertheless not much of a stretch to accept the Spirit Realm of Newton, et al., as a reasonable representation of heaven: the Spirit Realm is, after all, a place of peace and serenity, enveloped in love, and devoid of any and all of the negative attributes associated with an earthly existence; its inhabitants are ethereal and are imbued with limitless patience, compassion, and kindness. If that isn't *exactly* heaven, then it is surely the next best thing. But what, then, of heaven's counterpart? For those of us burdened with religion-inspired notions of what awaits us after death, the BIG FEAR is the prospect of having to spend eternity in the agonizing throes of hell. But does "hell" really exist? Is there truly a place of unimaginable suffering and horror reserved for the more sinful among us?

I, personally, was very happy – and *relieved* – to learn that LBL hypnosis subjects appear unanimous in their assertion that neither hell nor Satan, in the archetypal sense, exist.[95] And the same assertion is made by Near-Death Experiencers.[96] Although some NDErs have reported an initial experience that is highly suggestive of hell – replete with demons, fire, and torment – most such experiences are temporary, and the experience quickly transforms itself into a typical positive NDE scenario.[97] Interestingly, one of Dolores Cannon's subjects reported that the very concept of hell was borne out of reports of precisely such negative NDEs in years past.[98]

The existence of "evil" – as an independent force or entity – is also denied by LBL hypnosis subjects. To the extent that something approximating evil exists, it is described as a form of negative energy, created by *people*, and fueled by fear and hate.[99]

What we call "evil" appears to be the result of an innate corruption associated with the personality that inhabits human bodies independent of the soul; if the soul merging with a human host body cannot gain effective control over that innate personality and tame it (if you will) then the corrupt aspects of the host personality will "contaminate" the soul, with the result that the body-soul hybrid will indulge in what we would call "evil" acts. It seems that one of the primary missions and responsibilities of a soul incarnating on Earth is to master or subjugate the intrinsic body personality and establish a degree of control by creating a situation where the soul's positive qualities of morality, ethics, and love will offset the more base tendencies of the physical body and thus deter it from engaging in aberrant, destructive behavior. When a soul fails in this mission, it not only is held responsible (from a karma perspective) for the destructive acts committed by the body, but also the soul's energy can literally be damaged or contaminated by those actions. In such cases, depending upon the degree of damage or contamination, the soul returning to the Spirit Realm might require a period of quarantine or isolation during which time the soul's energy undergoes special restorative treatment.[100] So, while the general consensus of LBL subjects and NDErs is that there is no afterlife version of hell, one might interpret the quarantine procedure discussed above as being in some sense analogous to the Christian concept of purgatory.

Ultimately, the closest approximation to a hell, by all NDE and LBL accounts, is Earth.[101] The pain, suffering, violence, hatred, etc., that is endemic of earth life, together with the ravages of disease and aging, all combine to make physical incarnations on Earth a hell-like experience.[102]

8.3 My View Regarding Evil

Although I was relieved to learn that LBL hypnosis subjects deny the existence of "hell," I've nevertheless had great difficulty in accepting their assertion that "evil" does not exist as an independent abstraction or entity (other aspects of the Afterlife model that cause me concern are discussed in Chapter 10: The Elephants in the Room). One reason I'm troubled by this claim is the simple fact that there are clear examples of evil acts being committed on a routine basis in this world; the other reason is that virtually every religious belief system discusses its own version of evil entities, be they called "demons" or "archons" or "jinn"... the list is almost endless. As noted earlier in this chapter, what we consider "evil" may be simply a label for certain despicable acts committed by people. Thus it appears that we might very well be creating the notion of a malign "force" or "energy" simply as a means to categorize, in one grouping, the various deplorable actions which humans can, and often do, carry out. Evil acts on the part of humans are a reality; whether or not there is an actual invisible agency *inspiring* these acts is the real question at hand.

After considering the LBL view regarding evil, and giving the subject a great deal of thought, I've arrived at a possible explanation for what "evil" may be. Evil acts can range from the trivial – a white lie or petty theft – to the horrific – torture, rape, murder. Frequently it is thought that such people do such things because they have been possessed by a demon or evil entity of some sort. Even educated and sophisticated people tend to lean towards a variation of this notion as a way of explaining what is, in truth, inexplicable behavior. We do this because we cannot conceive of how or why a human being could do such things; we even use the phrase "capable of" as in "How can someone be *capable of* such acts?" Extremely evil behavior is so foreign to most of us that we have a real problem comprehending how it can even be possible, let alone carried out. We often describe the kind of person who commits these more extreme acts of evil as being "soul-less," for it clearly seems to be the case that such people possess no conscience, no sense of right and wrong, no compassion or empathy, and no sense of guilt or shame. They truly appear to be without a soul. In a way, I think the "soul-less" theory is very close to the truth.

Recall that the LBL literature suggests that there is a "host personality" already present in the human body before a soul from the Spirit Realm takes up residence beside it, and it is the responsibility of the soul to merge with that preexisting personality and gain control over it. The host personality represents the more base aspects of behavior such as hatred and greed, while the soul brings with it the purer traits of love, kindness, compassion and the like. I think what we call "evil" may come about as follows: Consider a situation in which a soul enters a body and is incapable of exerting sufficient control over the host personality. Eventually the host personality subjugates the soul and gains full control over the human being. At that point the soul is either ejected from the body, or else it is fully suppressed within the body – a kind of *reverse exorcism* takes place: evil does not possess the person but, rather, the soul is exorcised (or suppressed) and the host personality is given full, unimpeded reign over the person. This person is now completely susceptible to the seduction of the pleasures of materialism and the flesh – power, wealth, sex – and has no internal mechanism (i.e., no soul) capable of controlling its wanton pursuit of such pleasures. Thus this individual will do *anything* to satisfy its urges and is fully "capable of" committing acts that "normal people" (i.e., people whose souls *have* gained effective control over the host personality) find reprehensible and inconceivable.

I'm not yet ready to say that I'm totally convinced the above theory explains evil, but I think it is a plausible thesis that deserves consideration.

Chapter 9

Similarities Between the NDE and the Afterlife Model

9.1 Common Features of the NDE and the Afterlife Model

In Chapter 2 I presented the case for the reality of the Near-Death Experience with the intention that, if we can establish the claims of Near-Death Experiencers as being honest and accurate, then, ipso facto, we have established the existence of the soul and the afterlife. Having thus used the NDE to confirm the existence of an afterlife, it is of critical importance that both the afterlife model and the NDErs' descriptions of the afterlife be consistent and mutually corroborative. And this is precisely what we find: a comparison of the narratives of NDErs with those of LBL hypnosis subjects reveals details that are so precisely similar as to be virtually interchangeable. But even more than a congruity of detail, the two experiences share subtler qualities of emotional content and personal impact that speak powerfully of their truth and interrelatedness.

Some of the more basic details common to the near-death and life-between-lives experiences derive from the "crossing over" phase, and both Michael Newton and Dolores Cannon make note of some of these similarities.[103] NDErs and LBL subjects both report: an out-of-body experience (OBE); a sense of peace and an absence of fear; a pulling away from their physical body through a tunnel and towards a distant light; being greeted by a relative, loved one, or spirit guide; and arrival in an ethereal realm.

But aside from these rather elementary particulars, the NDE and LBL share other common ground that is deeply revealing and significant. Both groups indicate that "time" in the hereafter is profoundly different than our earthly experience of it.[104] They also concur in a reluctance to return to earth and a preference to remain in the Spirit Realm,[105] and both groups note a distinct feeling that the Spirit Realm is their true "home";[106] indeed, both groups make the point that earth life is an illusion and that the Spirit Realm is the true reality.[107] Each group proclaims a divinely inspired awareness that love and learning are of paramount importance during life on Earth.[108]

As intriguing as all these corresponding features may be, the commonality that I find particularly interesting is the amazing similarity between the Life Review experienced by NDErs and the initial session before the Council of Elders experienced by LBL subjects. In both situations the soul in question undergoes a review of the life just lived; in the case of the NDE it is a rather fast, almost kaleidoscopic recapitulation of the subject's life up to the point of the NDE, whereas in the LBL it is a more leisurely and focused examination of select events and episodes, subject to greater scrutiny and evaluation. But they are both life reviews, and they clearly are both designed to make an impression upon the subject soul. In the case of the NDEr it may simply be a "wakeup call" to get him/her back on the right track – hence the speed and brevity of the review – whereas in the LBL situation it serves the more important and substantive purpose of evaluating successes and failures with an eye on gaining spiritual insights and making plans for the next incarnation – and thus the longer, more elaborate review session.

9.2 NDE and Afterlife Model Transformative Effects

One final area where the NDE and LBL mirror one another is in the transformative aftereffects they produce. In Chapter 2 I presented a list of 15 transformative effects associated with NDEs, and I'm reproducing the list here for ease of recall and reference:

1. Diminished fear of death
2. Less judgmental/more tolerant and forgiving
3. Major changes in life situations (relationships, career)
4. Increased love and empathy for all life forms
5. Religious orientation replaced by spirituality
6. Increased appreciation for nature and ecological concerns
7. Less concerned with material possessions
8. Newfound interest in reincarnation, psychic phenomena, and the "new physics"
9. Increased zest for life
10. Increased happiness and optimism
11. Decreased stress and worry
12. Belief in God
13. Hunger for knowledge
14. Increased compassion and empathy for others
15. Importance of service-to-others

At this point we've looked at a great deal of information regarding the Newton model of the afterlife, and I think it is fair to say that if you review the list of NDE aftereffects above you will immediately see many correspondences between those listed items and the nature and experience of the afterlife as reported by LBL subjects: items 4, 5, 7, and 12 thru 15 are in many ways direct reflections of the overall tone of the Spirit Realm and the wisdom acquired by souls while residing there. In Chapter 2 we also learned that, in addition to NDErs individually experiencing many of these transformative effects as the result of having had an NDE, there have been formal studies that confirm that these transformations can be realized by merely *acquainting oneself* with the NDE literature. With regard to LBL research, however, I am not aware of any formal exploration into people experiencing qualitative changes in their personality or world view as a result of reading LBL literature. Nevertheless, I wholeheartedly believe that such is the case: for one thing, it is clear at this point that life in the Spirit Realm is in many ways a deeper and much more elaborate extension of the near-death experience, and so it follows logically that any transformative effects elicited by familiarity with NDE literature would also be experienced – likely even more powerfully – by knowledge of LBL literature. Another reason I believe this to be so – and the more important reason – is that I have experienced it myself.

After my first reading of Dr. Newton's books *Journey of Souls* and *Destiny of Souls* – and long before I had personally experienced LBL hypnotic regression – I noticed some very profound changes in my personality, world view, and personal code of morality and ethics. The first change I noticed was the obvious one: my fear of death vanished, utterly and completely. The beatific nature of the Spirit Realm and the opportunities for "second chances" afforded by reincarnation combined to erase any dread I harbored regarding death. I now accepted life on Earth, however painful, as temporary and illusory, and I saw my true existence as ethereal and eternal in a realm of love, beauty and peace. Death now became for me little more than a relocation … and to a better place! I'm not saying I looked happily upon the prospect of death or that I longed for it – absolutely not – but I no longer regarded it with anxiety, apprehension, or horror. And, years later, the proof of this transformation was put to the test in a most dramatic way.

In December of 2003 I found myself sitting in my urologist's office and receiving the unpleasant news that I had prostate cancer. My initial *mental* reaction to this was completely consistent with the way we've been trained to react, namely, I thought, "I'm dead; my life is over." But my *emotional* reaction was quite atypical: I was completely calm and collected, and I asked the doctor in a very matter-of-fact tone, "Is there any indication that the cancer has spread beyond my prostate?" The doctor just stared at me for a long time, a look of incomprehension on his face; and then finally (ignoring my question) he asked, "You're *okay* with this?" To which I replied, "No. I'm absolutely *not* okay with it." He shook his head: "Whenever I tell patients that they have cancer, they always react by screaming or crying or raging," he said. I am certain that, had I not read Dr. Newton's books, I too would have responded in precisely that way. But the fact is that *I felt no fear whatsoever* at the prospect of dying. And I never did in the awful years of testing and treatment and bad test results that followed. I did feel sadness; terrible, debilitating sadness at the thought of having to leave my wife and son. But not once have I experienced even an iota of fear.

Beyond the loss of a fear of death, however, I began to notice, with the passage of time, that more subtle, yet also more prodigious, changes were occurring in my character and makeup; and these changes were slowly beginning to manifest as changes in my behavior and my perception of existence. I became more spiritual and less materialistic; I became ravenous for knowledge, reading a multitude of books at once; my empathy and compassion for others soared to an almost ridiculous level – when I would see news reports of tragedies such as airliner crashes or earthquakes I would experience such sadness for the victims that it became physically painful (much to my wife's consternation); and my previous left-brain dominated mentality began to shift to a much more right-brained outlook. But the most important change that occurred in me was that I began to consider and analyze *everything* through what I call an LBL filter. By way of explanation, let me provide some examples. Firstly, I began to evaluate my own life circumstances in terms of them being the result of *choices I made* while in the Spirit Realm; this resulted in the loss of a "victim mentality" where we commonly wonder why life is screwing us so badly. I now accepted my circumstances, bad as well as good, as being chosen by me as necessary for my spiritual and karmic advancement. I cannot tell you how much *lighter* this made me feel about life and about myself. Secondly, I became less judgmental of others, as I began to see *their* life situations to be the result of choices *they* made in the Spirit Realm; alcoholics, drug addicts, the homeless – no longer did I perceive them as failures or lazy and weak – I now saw them as souls living a life situation chosen by themselves for the purpose of addressing some karmic issue or spiritual matter of which I (and they) could not fathom. Trust me when I say that letting go of judgmental tendencies is a life-enriching attitudinal improvement that feels wonderful. Thirdly, and, I think, the most significant change I experienced, is that I began to pre-evaluate my words and actions by thinking to myself, "How will I feel going before my Council of Elders if I react in such-and-such a way?" This simple proactive, introspective act of self-appraisal – performed before reacting to a situation – has transformed me, as a person, in ways so profound and far-reaching that I can barely recognize the person I am now when compared with the person I used to be. Is it an improvement? You bet it is! I've found that, having researched and accepted the Newton model of the afterlife, I absolutely do not want to find myself standing before my Council, and facing my own self-judgment, trying to understand or explain why I did or said something that caused pain to another living being. I absolutely do not want to be in that situation, so I now reconsider all my words and deeds – before committing them – in that light. The result is nothing short of miraculous. It is such a simple, easy technique to employ, and yet its payoff is a monumental improvement in one's personal character and humaneness. In many ways I consider this to be one of the greatest gifts ever bestowed upon me. And it's blatantly obvious that practicing this on a massive scale would solve so many of the problems in our world. It really is a formula for fixing what is broken in us, and it is a compass for helping us to find our way back onto a safe and proper path.

9.3 The "Fairness" Aspect of Reincarnation Revisited

Much earlier in this book I mentioned that a major factor in my abandonment of Catholicism was what I considered to be the unfairness inherent in a system that permits each person only one chance to pass the test and achieve an eternity of bliss in heaven over an eternity of suffering in hell. The doctrine of reincarnation, on the other hand, is, to my way of thinking, a much fairer system because it affords each individual, via repeated lifetimes, a more reasonable opportunity to gradually learn from their mistakes and "get it right" as they pursue spiritual perfection. But this is only part of the "fairness" aspect of reincarnation – namely, as it relates to individuals. The fairness of reincarnation actually extends in scope far beyond individuals to encompass all of humanity, for the fact is that *as each one of us is reborn into a new life we become the inheritors of the world we helped fashion during our previous lifetimes.*

Nowadays we hear a lot of talk about "what kind of world are we leaving to our children?" with regards to resource depletion, the failing economy and debt, ecological destruction, etc. Well, under the Newton model, these are all legacies that we are leaving to *ourselves* – *we* are going to have to live with the ramifications of the choices we are making now. What could be fairer, or more just, than that?

Chapter 10

The Elephants in the Room

As much as I've come to accept the Newton model of the afterlife as being *the best model* I've seen, the fact is that there are a few aspects of the model which trouble me. As far as I can tell, these troubling aspects are not due to any flaw in the model; rather they appear to be matters that were not sufficiently addressed either by the LBL subjects or else by the LBL researchers, and the possible reasons for this are many. An intentionally imposed amnesia regarding our past lives and our Spirit Realm existence appears to be status quo upon entering into each new life on Earth, and, while regressive hypnosis obviously breaks through that amnesia, there appear to be situations where a hypnosis subject resists addressing a particular matter, either because he/she does not know about it or has been blocked from providing relevant information in that area.[109] There is also the possibility that researchers may be withholding certain information for reasons known only to themselves. One of the topics I will be discussing in this chapter has the potential to be very disturbing, and for that reason I can easily see a researcher deciding to omit certain findings that might allude to a particularly troubling facet of the phenomenon. More mundane reasons could simply be that the soul has no knowledge of a particular feature of the afterlife, or else that a particular topic just never came up. Whatever the reasons, there are three specific implications of the model that appear to me to be unresolved, and they have caused me no end of contemplation and speculation.

10.1 Is "Evil" a Necessary Component of Karma?

Consider our discussion of the system of karma: we balance the bad deeds we performed in a given lifetime by finding ourselves on the receiving end, if you will, of similar negative acts in a subsequent lifetime. By being in a position where we experience *first-hand* the pain we had caused others we will realize the terrible wrongness of our actions and thus mature and grow spiritually. All well and good; it's a sensible system, logical in design and commendably fair. Recall also that sometimes a soul will choose to have unpleasant experiences in an earthly lifetime not to pay off bad karma, but simply for the spiritual growth value inherent in that experience. But there's one feature of this system that has always bothered me: in both of these situations there is the need for a perpetrator of bad deeds. For example, if I was a rapist in one of my lifetimes, then I might very well find myself the victim of rape in a subsequent life. Clearly, nothing would impress on my soul more the awfulness of subjecting another human being to forcible sexual violation than suffering the very experience myself. That's the very point of the karmic process. But in that later lifetime where I am the victim, the system *requires the participation of a rapist* in order for me to learn my karmic lesson and redeem my karmic debt. There's the contradiction: the karma system requires the very kinds of behavior that it is seeking to eliminate. In order for me to experience the effects of some terrible act I committed in a previous lifetime, I will at some point need someone to commit a similarly terrible act against me. Is this person who brutalizes me doing a good thing because they are helping me to pay off my bad karma and grow spiritually? Or are they themselves accumulating bad karma by committing the brutality against me (and thus perpetuating a vicious cycle of endless generation of bad karma and brutal acts)? I think this is an important question and a troubling issue. In my contemplation of this dilemma I've come up with a possible scenario that would make this whole state of affairs acceptable, at least to my mind: I've toyed with the idea that our incarnations on Earth might not be true "physical" experiences involving other people, but rather I've considered the possibility that for each of us the lifetime we live is a sort of virtual reality illusion where *we* are the only real entity, while everything and everyone else are nothing more than simulations designed to present us with various situations to which we must respond. This particular model of reality has two very appealing features: (1) Any bad things done to us in order to help us karma-wise are *not* being performed by other actual souls; and (2) Any bad acts *we* perform are not causing real harm to another actual soul. There are other appealing aspects to this model, but a more involved discussion will have to wait until Part III of this book where we will talk about the nature of reality.

10.2 Do Souls Co-opt a Preexisting Human Personality?

This second problematic aspect of the afterlife model is the one I alluded to earlier as being "potentially disturbing"; at least, I find it to be so. The issue here is that there is much evidence in the LBL literature that there is a personality of sorts already existing in the human fetus before a soul enters into the picture. Apparently the soul somehow melds with this preexistent identity – often referred to as the "host" – and, supposedly, enhances it. There are suggestions that souls and their human hosts were created precisely for the purpose of being joined together, and also that one of the soul's most important tasks is to gain control or mastery over the indigenous personality. There is an admission on some souls' parts that the preexisting personality has no say with regard to accepting the incoming soul, and, furthermore, the soul sometimes experiences resistance from the preexisting personality.[110] I find this entire state of affairs alarming. Why does the "host" personality not enjoy a right to freedom and independence? What gives us the right, as souls, to enter this mind and impose our will and control over it? A living entity's right to freedom and independence goes to the very core of what we as humans consider moral, ethical and just. I cannot overstate how appalled I was when I first read about this aspect of the afterlife model; and, for me, it calls into question the righteousness and legitimacy of the entire system. This is the one feature of the model that causes me great concern and discomfort; I think it is a very big deal and I desperately would like to hear a reasonable and acceptable explanation for it. To his credit, Dr. Newton has on more than one occasion called a soul to task over this matter, but the explanations provided by the souls were, to me, weak and vague.[111]

Personally, I find the most appealing thing about the afterlife realm to be its predominating atmosphere of love, kindness and fairness. This business of souls co-opting a host personality, possibly against its will, reeks of a kind of spiritual rape that I find repugnant, and it casts a dark shadow over the entire design and conduct of the Spirit Realm enterprise. Now, granted, the mere fact of discussing something like the nature of the afterlife automatically takes us way outside of our normal experience, and therefore it is entirely plausible that there is a much bigger picture here than we can possibly see, and perhaps from that broader perspective this whole co-opting business is perfectly ethical and acceptable. But from my limited frame of reference I find it deeply, deeply troubling.

10.3 Why Are Physical Incarnations Necessary?

By all accounts, "life" in the Spirit Realm is a beautiful and joyous experience; it is a place of oneness, harmony, compassion, and humor where each and every soul is accepted and loved without judgment.[112] Indeed, the Spirit Realm appears to be completely devoid of all the negative qualities – hatred, anger, jealousy, stress, worry – so often found on Earth.[113] Thus it follows that souls, being the populace of the Spirit Realm, do not exhibit any of the unsavory characteristics typical of human behavior (hatefulness, envy, etc.) while in residence there. Dr. Newton specifically states that souls shed most of their negative energy when they shed their bodies, and they expel more negative energy during the initial phases of their return to the Spirit Realm.[114] In other words, in the Spirit Realm souls display all the positive qualities that humans are trying to develop, and souls lack all of the negative characteristics that humans are trying to discard. So, then, why the heck are we incarnating? The usual answers are: to achieve spiritual perfection, to purge ourselves of negative traits and desires, to develop love and compassion. Am I missing something, or are we not already *precisely* that way when we are in spiritual form in the afterlife? We are leaving a place of harmony and beauty where we are the epitome of love and compassion, to go to a place (Earth) rampant with hatefulness, dishonesty, selfishness, etc., in order to develop the very qualities we already possess and enjoy in the Spirit Realm. *Why?* If our spiritual nature is our true nature, as is claimed (and as I believe), and if our human nature is false and illusory, as is also claimed, *then what are we doing?* We leave bliss in order to temporarily wallow in a cesspool, the purpose of which is to learn to achieve... bliss. In the vernacular of text messaging: *WTF?!!!* Seriously, this particular conundrum of the afterlife model is very perplexing: in a model that is so elegantly logical and sensible, we have this eerily illogical and nonsensical absurdity. I can't help but think that there is a deeper purpose to the whole reincarnation system than that offered by the evidence available.

I personally ruminated over this enigma for many, many years, and never found a sufficiently satisfactory explanation. Then, during a long hypnosis session with hypnotist Mira Kelley, I was presented with a rationalization for reincarnation that was not only radically different from the standard explanations but also stranger than any explanation I dared imagine. This concept is more related to the nature of reality than it is to the afterlife, and it would make little sense outside the context of that overall hypnosis session, so I will present it all together in Part IV of this book, under the heading of "My Personal Insight Regarding the Nature of Reality." Let me just say at this point that I'm not entirely sure that I accept the reason for reincarnation that was revealed to me, but it is a fascinating and tantalizing theory that greatly expands the canvas upon which our understanding of reality is painted.

These three questions, then, constitute what I refer to as "The Elephants in the Room" with regard to the afterlife model: *Is "evil" a necessary component of karma?*; *Do souls co-opt a preexisting human personality?* and *Why are physical incarnations necessary?* I do not for a moment think that these problems invalidate the afterlife model, but I do think they suggest that the model is incomplete in its present form. As discussed earlier, there are many reasons to suspect that we are not getting the full picture of the afterlife and its purpose from LBL hypnosis subjects: perhaps those souls don't know the whole picture, or perhaps *we humans* are not meant to know it. Whatever the case, I believe there is much more to learn here. And since our earthly existence appears to be intimately intertwined with, and determined by, the Spirit Realm, it is inconceivable that we would not *want* to know the full story.

Chapter 11

Technology and the Afterlife

11.1 Whitley Strieber's "The Key"

The decision to include this chapter in this book was a quandary for me. The idea of using technology to communicate with the afterlife was not something I gave much consideration to – that is, until I read Whitley Strieber's fascinating book *The Key: A True Encounter*. In the book Mr. Strieber relates an experience he had in the wee hours of June 6, 1998, when an elderly man entered his hotel room and proceeded to impart profound gems of wisdom and information regarding the present and future of human life on Earth. Who this man was remains a mystery, but the content of his messages is enthralling, frightening, heartbreaking, and enlightening. Mr. Strieber affirms that the occurrence did happen as he relates it, but, after having read the book several times, I find that the actuality of the episode's occurrence is of minor consequence to me. As far as I'm concerned, the book's content is so rich with wisdom, intelligence, and heart that its real value *is* its content, while the reality of the event itself is, for all practical purposes, of secondary importance. In any event, one of the many intriguing pieces of information offered by the elderly gentleman was to the effect that it will be possible for humanity to develop a "means" that will enable us to communicate with the dead.[115] He also said that, "[T]he science of the soul is just another science. There is no supernatural, only physics."[116] This appears to suggest that the means of communication with the dead will be science-based, and thus, potentially, technological.

When I first read this in "The Key" I found the suggestion of such a technology exciting and disturbingly enticing, but, with no additional evidence to support the possibility of that technology, I ultimately filed the idea away as "remains to be seen."

11.2 Thomas Edison's Device

Then, sometime later, I read an illuminating article in *Atlantis Rising* magazine written by John Chambers and entitled "Machines to Talk to the Dead: Thomas A. Edison, W.B. Yeats, and Instrumental Transcommunication." The article discussed an 80-year-old rumor that the inventor Thomas Edison devoted a significant amount of time attempting to construct a machine that would allow communication with the dead.[117] This was the first I had heard of such a thing regarding Edison, but some online research quickly turned up much information that was in complete agreement with Mr. Chambers' article.[118] While the evidence for the rumor is by no means conclusive, it *is* highly suggestive. And, if true, then given Thomas Edison's stature as a brilliant and inventive genius – he is credited with over 2300 worldwide patents, almost 1100 of which were in the U.S., including the electric light bulb and the phonograph[119] – the idea that such a machine might actually be possible must be taken seriously.

In his article Mr. Chambers references a book and several magazine pieces in which either Mr. Edison himself or acquaintances of his discuss Edison's belief that the human "personality" survives physical death and his interest in the possibility of communicating with the dead. Edison apparently considered paranormal-oriented attempts at contacting the dead (e.g., Ouija Boards) to be "unscientific" and "silly" thus implying (as did Strieber's late-night visitor) that real communication with the hereafter would be of a more mainstream scientific nature, i.e., technological. Indeed, one of Edison's acquaintances is quoted as confirming that the famous inventor did speculate on the possibility of making a "machine" to effect such communication. Also noted was the claim that Edison's parents were spiritualists, and that Edison was a believer in telepathy and may even have possessed some telepathic ability himself. As to the existence of an actual device, the article states that although mentalist Joseph Dunninger claimed to have been shown, by Edison, an apparatus for communicating with the dead, there are no surviving notes, records, or devices to indicate that Edison had actually constructed such an apparatus. However, the article also discusses a device (dubbed the "Metallic Homunculus" by poet W.B. Yeats) which was supposedly "a machine for talking to the dead." The Metallic Homunculus was built by David Wilson, a former assistant to Nobel Prize winner Sir William Crookes; Crookes was aware of Wilson's work with the device and, since Edison and Crookes corresponded with one another, it is quite possible that Edison heard about the device from Crookes. Unfortunately, the device was confiscated by the authorities during World War I due to a fear that it was being used for espionage purposes, Wilson – its inventor – was drafted into the military, and neither the device nor its creator ever resurfaced again.

So we learn from Mr. Chambers' article and the web sites cited that Thomas Edison:

(a) believed in telepathy and the survival of the human personality after death; (b) was exposed to spiritualism as a child; (c) believed that communication with the dead should be possible via scientific means, and; (d) was likely aware of Wilson's work on a device for accomplishing such communication. Considering these points in conjunction with Edison's talent and passion for inventing, it almost seems ridiculous to think that he did *not* attempt to build such a device himself. The absence of notes, records, or relevant hardware certainly does not qualify as evidence against such a device's existence.

When I reconsidered the statements made by Whitley Strieber's elderly visitor in light of the information about Thomas Edison, the idea of a technology to communicate with the dead became much more plausible; in fact, I began to wonder if Edison had actually succeeded in building his device and if Strieber's visitor was hinting at a future unveiling of Edison's (or Wilson's) technology.

Personally, I'm undecided as to whether such a technology truly exists, but I do believe it may be possible (I agree with Strieber's visitor: "There is no supernatural, only physics.") and I also believe that Edison was likely pursuing it. If such a device were to be successfully created, utilized, and made public, then we could put the afterlife model to the ultimate test and see if the Spirit Realm is, in fact, as the model describes it. Conclusive confirmation of Newton's model of the Afterlife would be one of the most momentous discoveries in the entirety of human history.

Chapter 12

My Life Between Lives
Hypnosis Session

On October 3, 2009, I had a hypnosis double-session with hypnotist Amy Benesch for the purpose of exploring my Life Between Lives (i.e., the Spirit Realm as investigated by Michael Newton). Prior to this LBL session I had had two previous hypnosis sessions with Amy, one being the past life session discussed in Chapter 5, and another concerned with the issue of my prostate cancer.

The LBL session was a long one, and I was under hypnosis for about 2 hours and 10 minutes. When it ended it felt to me like I had only been hypnotized for maybe 20 minutes; apparently I had gone into a deeper hypnotic state throughout portions of this session and, unlike my first regression (past-life/World War II), I did not remember every detail of this session. Fortunately both Amy and I had recorded the session so I was able to replay the recording and review what I had experienced. I'm not exaggerating when I say that when I first listened to the recording I was astounded at how profound some of my statements were, and I was shocked that I had not remembered them.

I think the best place to begin this review of my LBL session is with the questions I had prepared. Basically, I had hoped to learn the following:

- What karmic issues am I supposed to be addressing in my current life?
- How successful have I been thus far in addressing these issues?
- Is there something I'm supposed to be doing that I'm not doing?
- Should I write a novel?

Additionally, I wanted to discover if certain people in my current life also play a major part in my spirit life; specifically, I was interested in my wife, my son, and a nurse at one of the medical facilities I visited regarding my prostate cancer.

In order to "travel" to the spirit realm one usually must first experience the death episode from a past life. Thus Amy began by bringing me back to my lifetime from my first regression session, namely that of a soldier in World War II. I have to admit that I was a bit apprehensive about this part as I feared that my death in that lifetime might have been very traumatic. When I first "arrived" I couldn't get a fix on anything. Amy asked me to look down at my feet and see what I was wearing. My first impression was "socks" but eventually I had the sense that I was wearing slippers. That seemed to jar my perceptions and suddenly more impressions began to form. I was in a hospital, in a hallway, and I was wearing pajamas – clearly a patient there. Amy asked if I was injured and my sense was that no, I seemed to be physically OK – I had all my limbs and I could not feel any pain. I felt "tired" and "spent", extremely lackadaisical. Amy asked if it might have been a psychiatric ward, and I replied that I felt as if I was there for psychiatric reasons but that it was not a psychiatric hospital but rather a "normal" hospital. I saw IV bags hanging, and although at first I did not think one was connected to me I later felt that it was and that I was "dragging it around with me" on one of those stands that look like a hat rack. I noted that I wasn't feeling anything – "blasé to the max." Interestingly, during a subsequent discussion with my son about this session he suggested that my lackadaisical and tired state might have been due to the fact that I was drugged. This idea ties in nicely with the possibility that I was there for psychiatric or emotional reasons, which in turn is consistent with what I experienced during my first regression session in a European town during World War II. The logical connectedness of all this was evidence, for me, of the reality and validity of these remembrances.

When the hospital scene from my most recent past life began to stagnate Amy asked me if I was ready to visit my death scene from that life, and I replied that I was ready. After giving me some time to move to that scene, Amy asked me what I was seeing. I was receiving no impressions whatsoever, and I attribute this to the apprehension I felt at visiting this death scene. When I continued to be unable to proceed to my death, Amy stated that she would touch her finger to my forehead and then the scene would become clear (prior to starting this hypnosis session Amy had informed me that she would employ this technique in the event I was unable to focus in on a particular scene or situation – as it turned out, it worked wonderfully!). When Amy again asked me what I was seeing I quickly responded, "Clouds ... the sky." Amy then asked if I had a sense that I had already separated from my physical body, to which I replied, "I think so ... I don't understand, I think so." Apparently my fear of facing my death scene was so strong that my psyche simply skipped the actual death and moved directly to the point after my soul had left my body – at least, that is my interpretation of what happened. In any event, with further guidance from Amy I ultimately found myself surrounded by fog speckled with flashes of light. Just to confirm my situation Amy asked me if I had in fact left my physical body and I immediately answered "Yes" with a very noticeable tone of certainty. Amy then asked me how I felt about my death, and I replied, "I couldn't wait for it ... glad to be gone ... relieved." After offering further direction and guidance, Amy asked me if there was any unfinished business from that lifetime that I wanted to attend to before I moved on, and I replied, "No ... I think I never procreated and I feel bad about that." I then expressed my belief that "It's gone now" and therefore I considered the issue moot.

As I moved on I first noticed it getting darker but I eventually moved into a place where it was a bright "soupiness ... cloudiness." I soon became aware of a presence coming towards me which I sensed as being female, and when Amy asked if I was sensing any messages from this being I replied "'Welcome back.'" This simple statement is actually quite interesting in that people who are regressed to the spirit realm frequently state that it is their true "home," so the *Welcome back* greeting I received is really full of significance. It eventually was revealed that this being was my spirit guide, Kayla. Amy asked if Kayla had anything to say about this last life that I had just left, and I quoted Kayla as saying, "It was rough ... no?" (To which I most emphatically replied "Yes!"). Kayla then said, "You look well. You survived."

I just want to interject a few personal observations at this point. My *feeling* during this meeting with Kayla was indeed that of experiencing a homecoming, and very powerful as well. It reminded me of how I felt after I was discharged from the Army and returned to my parents' home – a feeling of great comfort and relief, of having successfully completed a very trying ordeal and now returning to a place of peace and familiarity. It was a profoundly wonderful and sublime experience.

Kayla then brought me to "see friends" (my soul group) where I experienced a "party atmosphere." I stated, "It feels good. It really is coming home." One member of my soul group jokingly commented, "That was a quick one," referring to my recently completed life. Amy asked me how many were there in my group, and for some reason I could not sense a definite number; "eight ... maybe twelve" was the best I could come up with. Amy then asked if anyone was detaching from the crowd and coming towards me, and I stated, "My wife, from this life." Overcome with very powerful emotions at this point, I continued: "We weren't together in that life and it was lonely." Amy asked if I knew why we had made the decision not to be together in that life. My response (still feeling very emotional) was, "I think I depend on her too much for emotional support – I had to try to go it alone one time. It wasn't easy."

As I experienced the almost unbearable bliss of reuniting with my soul-mate after spending a very lonely and painful lifetime apart, my hypnotist Amy asked me what spirit names I sensed for myself and for my wife/soul-mate. Now this part is actually quite interesting, not because of the names themselves but because of the difficulty I experienced in trying to discern the names. In my readings about the afterlife and reincarnation I'd come across situations where the person under hypnosis was having trouble making out the answer to a relatively simple question posed by the hypnotist, and at the time I was reading those passages I had wondered what the problem was – my attitude was: "you either see it or you don't – what's the big deal?" Now, however, having undergone hypnosis myself and having personally experienced the same problem, I think I understand what is happening. I've given this a great deal of thought and it seems to me that the information we perceive while under hypnosis is not actually "seen" so much as *sensed*. At times it did feel to me like I was visually seeing what I was perceiving, but upon later reflection I now think that my perceptions were conveyed to me as *information* which was then somehow translated into an image or an idea that my human mind could comprehend. The best analogy I can come up with to try to explain this is from the original *Matrix* movie. Specifically, I'm thinking of the scenes where Morpheus' people were sitting in front of computer monitors which showed binary digits running down the screens; what they were looking at was the actual digital representation of the matrix itself, but they were so versed in mentally decoding those ciphers that, even though they were looking only at the matrix's digital representation, in their minds they were "seeing" the physical manifestation of the matrix. Their brains were decoding the binary digits and translating that code into mental images that *seemed* visual but, technically, were not. That is how I believe my perceptions of my past life and of the spirit realm were functioning while I was under hypnosis; I was not really "seeing" any of those scenes but rather my mind was receiving *information* which it then translated into something I could mentally discern and conceptualize. This is my own personal theory of how people perceive the experiences they recall when undergoing past- life or life-between-lives hypnotic regression. I'm curious as to whether other people who've done past-life or LBL hypnosis sessions would describe it similarly. (Also of note is the possibility that our perceptions of everyday "reality" might also function along similar lines – this will be explored in detail in Part III of this book).

In any event, when Amy asked me about the spirit names I struggled at attempts at pronunciation: For my wife I was getting the sense of a word beginning with the letter "S" – "Ssss…sss…Sorna?" I eventually decided tentatively. For myself: "Guh… guh…Gale?...or Gael?" That was the best I could come up with. I should also mention that another reason for having trouble discerning spirit names is the possibility that the actual names may be unpronounceable for humans and thus our brain struggles to find an accurate approximation of those unutterable words.

Now things got really interesting. Amy said to me, "Take a look at your wife. Is she radiating a particular color?" This was a very important question and I am so very grateful that Amy had the presence of mind to ask it. It will be necessary at this point to once again delve into Michael Newton's books for some background on this aspect of the spirit realm. As discussed in Chapter 7, Dr. Newton found that souls in the Spirit Realm radiate auras of various colors, and that these colors have very important meanings. Most importantly, the color of a soul's aura is an indication of that soul's level of spiritual advancement. Beginner souls emit a white aura; then, as a soul's level of spiritual development advances, its aura progresses through various shades of yellow, gold, blue, and, ultimately, purple. Thus souls with a whitish aura are rookies with regard to spiritual development, while souls with blue-to-purple auras are highly advanced and have reached the near-master or master level. How, and at what rate, we advance spiritually is determined by our earthly incarnations and the ways in which we handle and cope with the challenges we face therein. When I looked at my wife's aura in response to Amy's request I noted that it was "light purple." This would place my wife, as a soul, at what Dr. Newton has designated as the Level VI (Highly Advanced) Learning Stage. I have no trouble whatsoever in accepting this as being true as my wife is a very good-hearted and centered person who often displays great wisdom. Interestingly, when I conveyed this information to my wife she deemed it totally implausible – more evidence, I think, that she is indeed an advanced soul.

After asking me about the color of my wife's aura, my hypnotist Amy asked me, "And how about you? What color do you seem to be radiating?" I answered almost immediately, "Blue." According to Michael Newton's "Classification Model for Soul Development Levels" a blue aura would indicate a soul at the Level V (Advanced) level. Now, while I had absolutely no problem accepting that my wife is a Purple/Level VI soul, I did find it inconceivable that I am at the Blue/Level V level. It's both interesting and intriguing to see how some people find it so hard to accept that they might be advanced souls (we will see this reaction yet again when I discuss my nurse's reaction to what I learned about her in the spirit realm). I do not think this reaction is mere humility or self-deprecation; there seems to be a genuine and compelling inability to believe that one might truly be an advanced soul. *Why* this is so is, of course, open to speculation. My own personal feeling is that an advanced soul would, by definition, be a modest and unpretentious person, not caught up in the trappings of materialism and ego. In any event, I later eventually began to accept my "blue status" for two reasons: first, something my son said to me (which I feel is too personal to relate here) began to convince me that it was possible that I really was of blue status; and secondly, the structure of soul groups in the Spirit Realm appears to be such that the souls in a given soul group are all at very similar advancement levels (and this would make perfect sense given the purpose and function of soul groups). So, if my wife is a Purple/Level VI soul, then it is entirely plausible that I (being in the same soul group as my wife) could be a Blue/Level V soul. This was an awesome revelation to me, and something which, once I could accept it, gave me a feeling of great inner harmony and peace. Without getting into any in-depth self-psychoanalysis here, suffice it to say that I've been plagued by intense feelings of low self-esteem and low self-worth for my entire life. To now discover that I might actually have been successful at something – especially something of such scope and importance – is a source of great contentment. Needless to say, I am extremely grateful that Amy thought to ask about my wife's aura as well as my own.

After letting me enjoy the reunion with my wife, Amy asked me to step back, take a look at my soul group, and see if I noticed anyone else who is in my current life. To my great surprise and astonishment I saw my father. I hadn't expected him to be in my soul group, and in all honesty I didn't *want* him to be a member of my group. At the risk of letting this discussion deteriorate into a personal Freudian nightmare, I feel I should briefly explain why I felt this way: my father and I, for the most part, did not have a good relationship; he was a very overbearing, tyrannical, and insensitive person. In all fairness, he did have many good qualities and I did gain much personal benefit from them – for example, my father had a very strong work ethic which he passed on to me by the example he set, and that work ethic has been a source of great pride and practical utility for me throughout my life. But on a personal level he was a difficult man to be around, and especially difficult to have as a father. So I had truly hoped he would not be a member of my soul group for the simple reason that I do not look forward to spending another lifetime with him, in any capacity. Also, in Michael Newton's books it was mentioned that one's parents are generally *not* from one's soul group. Thus it was a great shock and disappointment to me to see him appear before me at that time (I want to mention that, during and immediately after this LBL hypnosis session, I had automatically *assumed* that my father was a member of my soul group because he had appeared while I was with my group; upon later reflection, however, I've come to think that his emergence at that point in time is *not necessarily* an indication that he is a member of my group – he may simply have chosen that moment to greet me and "make his peace with me." In truth, thinking back now, I did not get any real sense of he and I having any strong connection while we met at that moment; indeed, if anything, my sense was of a rather limited or trivial connection – but, then again, perhaps that is only wishful thinking). When Amy asked me how I felt about seeing my father in my soul group I replied, "Shocked. He's so nice! Very different." I also noted my surprise at how non-judgmental he was. I had an image of him smiling broadly, and I had a sense of great warmth coming from him. It was a very, very nice feeling. Amy then asked about the role he played in my current life. I was reluctant to explore this, but the message I received from him, and which I relayed to Amy was, "We both had things to work out, and it was necessary for it to be this way now to each work out the things we needed to work out. I'm not sure what they were but… it was a mutual thing." Amy asked me if I could now feel forgiveness towards him, and my answer was an emphatic "Yes! Definitely. We're laughing and smiling… It's a relief."

And this now brings me to another aspect of hypnotic regression that I'd like to briefly discuss. I don't recall ever having come across this in any of the many books I've read about past life and LBL regression, but as a result of my own experience with my hypnosis sessions I have the very strong sense that regression hypnosis has the potential to function like a very powerful form of psychotherapy. Let me be clear: I have no formal training in psychology or psychiatry, and I've never been to see a psychologist or psychiatrist as a patient, so I'm talking now strictly from a layman's perspective. But the fact is that as a result of my regressive hypnosis sessions I have definitely developed a profound sense of inner peace and well-being, and a healthier and more positive sense of self. I feel better about myself and better about my life, and I am more tolerant of others and of life in general. I would presume that these are also the goals of psychoanalysis; if they are, and if my experience with hypnosis is not unique, then it seems to me that undergoing regressive hypnosis is a quicker, more effective, and less costly way of achieving those goals. I think this would be a great idea for a PhD thesis: Can one achieve the same (or better) results through hypnotic regression as through psychoanalysis?

After having made my peace with my dad, Amy asked, "Is there anyone else coming forward?" My response was, "My son. He's my best friend here." (i.e., in the Spirit Realm). This particular disclosure came as no surprise to me. My son and I are very close in my current life and, in many ways, he's my best friend now as well. What came next, however, was a bit of a shock to both Amy and me. "We get in trouble together," I added. "Over there?" Amy asked, surprised, "Or in your lives together?" "Over there," I replied, but that was quickly followed by a sense that my son and I got "in trouble" both in the Spirit Realm *and* in past lives together. Amy and I both laughed. "I didn't know that was possible," Amy remarked. It was revealed to me that my son and I have been very, very close in past lives, as best friends and as brothers. One particularly interesting observation I made in this regard was to state: "That's probably why I don't have a close friend in this life." This last was a very telling statement for me, as I've often wondered why I don't have any close friends in my current life. I've noted previously that I'm very much a loner and I shun relationships with people (and the reason *why* I'm this way was very clearly explained in the earlier discussion of my regression to my past life as a soldier in WWII – see Chapter 5), so I've kind of attributed my lack of a close friend to this aspect of my personality, but deep down I've always felt a sadness and a void at not having a close friend or a brother; also, having read Michael Newton's books about the Spirit Realm, I knew that members of our soul group often reincarnate with us as close friends or siblings, so I was often wondering, *Where the heck are the members of my soul group in my current life?* Now I finally had my answer: my dearest friend throughout eternity – the soul who would be most likely to be my brother or my best friend – is my *son* in my current life. It may sound like a rather trivial discovery, but to me it was the answer to a question that had been nagging me for most of my adult life.

After meeting my soul group member who is my son in my current life, Amy asked me, "So, taking a look again at the group, would you say that there's a common denominator of talents or interests or goals among you?" My answer was immediate: "Stability." "You're all searching for stability?" Amy asked. "Not searching for it," I replied, "but wanting to provide it, I think. It's what we value."

Now, I think this simple remark deserves some amplification. I've mentioned this previously, but it bears repeating here. A few years back I met a woman who shared my interests in esoteric subjects. During one of our discussions she mentioned that she had twice undergone past life hypnotic regression. Since this was something I had wanted to try myself, and something about which I had read a great deal, I was extremely interested in hearing of her experiences. She surprised me by saying, "But you know, what was *really* fascinating was what it told me about my life, and who I am, *now*." I was astounded at her remark – I couldn't understand or fully appreciate how it could possibly be that the hypnosis session's illumination of her current situation was more interesting than what she learned about her past life. I honestly thought she was being a bit dramatic. But now, having gone through it myself, I fully understand what she was saying. Throughout my hypnosis sessions, both past life and LBL, I have repeatedly found that what the sessions told me about myself and my life *now* was at least as fascinating as what I experienced in that past life or in the Spirit Realm. It's hard to explain exactly how that can be so, but, after giving it some thought, I've come to the conclusion that the explanation lies in the fact that: (a) most of us don't really know *why* we are as we are – we just accept it as a given – so any explanation of why we have the personalities we do is truly a revelation, and (b) regardless of how exciting or interesting a past life might have been, the fact is that it is *our current life* that's most important to us now, so any insight into why we are as we are is found to be utterly enthralling and captivating and, most importantly, is found to be utterly *relevant*. Well, what this discussion is leading up to is the fact that, once again, a simple disclosure from the hypnosis session turns out to speak volumes about who I am today. Without going into too much explanation let me simply say that "stability" is a hallmark of my personality and, indeed, my life now. I place enormous value on stability, I strive for it always, and it is an integral part of virtually every facet of my life. So, when I stated under hypnosis that stability is the common denominator of my soul group … well, let's just say it came as no surprise, yet it was nevertheless astonishing in that it gave me an insight into a core aspect of my personality that I had heretofore taken for granted. I find these unexpected insights into my identity to be extremely illuminating. The effect is similar to what one feels when solving a puzzle or a riddle, except that the personal ramifications of finding *these* puzzle pieces is enormous and thus so much more satisfying. It really is a wondrous feeling.

With regard to my soul group, Amy went on to ask me, "Are there any differences among you?" My reply was, "Some are workaholics and some are laid back. There's some friction there, I think. My wife's in the workaholic group." My entire statement, including the last part about my wife, was said in total seriousness. And, again, the relevancies to my current life are striking. I am, in my current life, very laid back, in the sense that I'd rather read or ruminate or get lost in my imagination. My wife, on the other hand, is just the opposite: she prefers to be *doing* things; sitting around *thinking* is a waste of time to her. Needless to say, this dichotomy leads to a rather fascinating relationship. I often tell her, "I'm a human *being* and you're a human *doing*." I won't bother printing her response. Since Amy has never met my wife, it was with a surprising degree of perceptiveness that she then said, "I'll bet she (i.e., my wife) doesn't call herself 'workaholic'." Laughing, I replied: "No, no. And she doesn't call me 'laid back' either."

Continuing on with my soul group, Amy asked me if there was anyone in the vicinity who seemed to be directing my soul group, and I replied, "It seems that my wife is the leader, but I don't know if that's for the group or just between us." The possibility of my wife being the leader of the group does make sense at least insofar as it had been determined earlier that my wife's aura was light purple – a level VI/Highly Advanced soul according to Michael Newton's "Classification Model for Soul Development Levels"– and therefore, due to her advanced level, quite capable of being a soul group leader.

Amy then asked me, "Is there anything else you want to do or say to your soul group – your friends – before we move on?" I replied, "They want to talk about this last life." When Amy then asked who wanted to talk about it, I responded, "All of them." Amy asked what they wanted to say; I explained that they wanted to know, "Was it worth it? Was it helpful? Did I get what I wanted?" Amy asked, "And what is your answer?" to which I replied: "Yes, very much. I think I did. They say I needed to develop a different perspective on the material world. And this very much did that for me." Amy asked what my perspective had been before that life, and I explained that it had been "Too material, too focused on fun, enjoying the physical. Now I have a disdain, a complete opposite view of it. I see there's a bad side to it, and the good and bad are connected. You can't have one without the other."

Once again I think it would be worthwhile for me to expand upon these statements a bit, particularly with regard to their relevance to my current life. First, my assertion that in my previous lives I was "...too focused on fun, enjoying the physical..." rings disturbingly true when considered in light of the early part of my current life. The fact is that when I was in my late teens and early twenties I excessively pursued physical pleasures and gratification, especially in regards to sex and alcohol. I was crazed in my pursuit of these pleasures, to the point of self-destruction. Now, about forty years later, I look back on those days and wonder, incredulously, exactly what the hell I was thinking. I am seriously aghast at my behavior back then and I look upon it now as if it were not me but some other person living some other life.

Thus, it would seem that the hedonistic nature to which I alluded from my past lives continued to remain a part of my personality into the early part of my current life. And it was only in my current life, as a result of experiences and decisions too involved and complex to enumerate here, that I finally overcame these indulgent tendencies and brought myself under control. I am truly – *now* – an entirely different person than I was some forty years ago, so much so that it is almost uncanny. I have racked my brain on-and-off over the years wondering how such a momentous transformation could have occurred. Now I've learned that it is the main karmic issue I came here to address, and that – thankfully – I seem to be addressing it successfully. So, when during this hypnosis session I then said, "Now I have a disdain, a complete opposite view of it," I want to make it clear that this change of view occurred *during my current life* as a result of intentional actions and decisions on my part to bring precisely such a change about. It is now obvious to me that it is in my *current* lifetime that I was able to effect this transformation. (I make this point because it appeared that, during this part of my hypnosis session, I was initially talking about my previous lifetime – i.e., as a WWII soldier – but at some point I began to answer questions and make statements from the perspective of my current lifetime. It was only after the session had ended, and I was reviewing my recording of it that I became aware of this change in perspective, and at first it had me a bit confused). All of this seems to correlate with the point I made earlier about how past life and LBL hypnotic regression offer us amazing insights into our current lives and personalities. This appears to be a recurring theme of the hypnotic regression experience, and I think it is no accident since, while it may seem like we are engaging in this practice to explore our "other" lives, the fact is we are really looking to learn about *ourselves* – our *eternal selves.* Who am I really? What is my true nature? Why am I having the experiences I'm having? *These* are the questions we are ultimately asking when we delve into our pasts.

Continuing with this thread, Amy asked, "How about compassion? Do you feel that life helped you develop compassion?" Here my answer was referring back to my WWII lifetime: "Yes, very much," I replied. Amy then asked, "So what do your friends think about this?" "They think it was a good life," I said, "They think it was productive. I think so too. It had the desired effect, very much so. They're very pleased." "Good," Amy said. And then I made a statement which, when I later listened to the session recording, nearly broke my heart: "I don't want to be alone again, though."

Having finished, for the time being, with my soul group, Amy asked, "So, is there any place you want to go now?" I replied immediately: "The Learning Place." Amy then directed me to say goodbye to my soul group friends and have my spirit guide Kayla take me to The Learning Place. When I arrived there Amy asked me what it looked and felt like, to which I replied, "Like a schoolroom." I further noted that, "I like to spend a lot of time here. My guide just brought me here to make me feel better." Relating, once again, my Spirit Realm experiences to my current life I find yet more consistencies. In this case, the idea that I like to spend time in the Learning Place and that it makes me feel good to be there are perfectly in tune with the fact that, in my current life, I derive tremendous enjoyment from reading and learning; I feel an almost obsessive mania about acquiring knowledge, and I feel extremely happy and peaceful around books – I can spend hours in a library or bookstore just perusing the shelves. In fact, I have very serious regrets that I did not pursue a career as a Librarian. So it came as no great surprise to me to find that, as a spirit, I obtain much peace and pleasure in The Learning Place. What fascinates me about all the similarities I've discovered between my current self and my spirit self is that we seem to have an eternal personality, if you will, and we bring much (if not all) of it with us when we incarnate. I just find it interesting – and even somewhat touching – that our particular individual traits and quirks run so much deeper than who we are in any single lifetime.

Amy then asked a very insightful question which led to some rather fascinating revelations about my personality, my past lives, and my karmic situation: "Is there anything that you could learn here that would relate to your current life?" To which I replied, "As much as I didn't like being alone in the last life, I liked parts of it, and that carried over into this life. That's why I sought out loneliness in this life, even though I didn't like it in the last life." Amy then continued with the perfect follow-up question: "Is it that it was familiar from the last life, or that you found there was some value in it?" My response, which I found very enlightening and also very perceptive with regard to an issue that's haunted me in my current life, was: "That's what I can't work out. In one sense it seems like it was just a carry-over, but in another sense it does seem like I did partially [find some value in it], and there were some things that I liked, that I wanted to keep, and also that it was a rut, and I couldn't break out of it. And the material thing... people were the cause of my problems in my other lives, not a cause, but being around people brought on temptations, or helped bring them on. It was all part of the bad choices I made. I made better choices when I was alone." Then, realizing how much this observation applies to my current life as well as to my past lives, I added, "I *make* better choices when I'm alone. So it's good for me to be alone, to a certain extent." Amy prompted me further: "So it sounds like, for many of your past lives, you were easily led astray by others?" "Yeah," I replied, "I don't think 'led astray', I think my self-discipline weakens, my tendency to bad things. I know better, and when I'm alone I can control myself and do what's right, but when I'm with others, who do the things I want to do, I let my guard down and go ahead and do it. It's my fault, but ... I'm learning that in this life. I'm learning that well. I'm learning to be among people but still stay in control. I've done well. I feel good. I've done well."

Trust me when I say that the degree to which the above statement accurately describes my current life (and a major personal inner struggle) is nothing short of astounding. In the early part of my current life I had a great deal of trouble resisting the bad influences from others; it took me a very long time to develop a personal sense of self, a strength of character, and a confidence and self-respect strong enough to allow me to resist negative temptations and influences from others. I grew up in a tough urban neighborhood, so this was a very serious issue during my early years. Often, when reflecting back on that period of my life, I'm genuinely amazed that I survived those times intact and was able to go on to live a normal and productive life. I'm not being overly dramatic: things could easily have gone horribly wrong for me back then, and almost did on several occasions. Fortunately, however, I successfully dealt with this karmic issue and was able to make some profound changes for the better. It is indescribably satisfying to be able to look back – especially back over many lifetimes and from a spirit-realm perspective – and realize how one has overcome difficult obstacles, challenges and handicaps, and emerged triumphant. In my mind I can still hear myself speaking those last words from my statement above: "I've done well. I feel good. I've done well." – It leaves me with a lump in my throat.

Amy then asked me if there is a library in this place of learning that I'd like to visit. My response was, "That's in a different place, and I love to go there. Too much." (Recall my previous comments where I mentioned that, in my current life, I love bookstores and libraries, and I seriously regret not pursuing a career as a Librarian). As I was speaking these words while under hypnosis, I actually *wanted* to go to the library right then but felt it wasn't a good idea (hence the "Too much" comment). Amy apparently picked up on this as well because she immediately proceeded to nudge me along to something else by asking, "So is there anything else that you want to do now? Or are you ready to go to your Council now?" "I'm ready for that," I replied.

As discussed in Chapter 7, The Council (also called The Council of Elders, The Old Ones, The Sacred Masters) is a very important aspect of the Spirit Realm: they are a group of highly evolved souls before whom we appear upon completing an incarnation (and sometimes also before beginning a new incarnation) in order to review our actions and choices from the life we have just lived. These advanced souls are more spiritually evolved than our Guides and are "the most advanced identifiable entities" with which Dr. Newton's subjects interact in the Spirit Realm. Although the Councils are, in some sense, a form of authority in the Spirit Realm, they are *not* a trial court and *do not* sit in judgment of us or of our actions, nor are they there to criticize or punish us; rather, they function more in the roles of patient counselors and teachers. In my experience with my Council I found them to be more like interpreters helping us to understand and make sense of our actions from our previous life. They also function in an advisory capacity, offering observations as to the import of specific events or overarching themes from our past lives, as well as suggestions as to how we might improve ourselves and better handle situations. They are truly there to assist and support us in our efforts to advance spiritually.

As I prepared to move on to my session before my Council my hypnotist Amy asked me, "Are you going to go there by yourself?" My answer was an emphatic "No!" causing both Amy and I to laugh aloud. "No, I don't want to," I continued. "OK," Amy said, "So who's going to go with you?" I responded that my spirit guide Kayla was going to accompany me, and then I said (as if to Kayla), "Stay close! Very close!" This reaction on my part prompted Amy to remark, "Sounds a little intimidating." "Oh, it is," I said, "I'm not going to face this alone." This reaction of apprehension on my part at the prospect of facing my Council is fairly common. While it is true that the purpose of our Council is not to criticize, punish, or judge us, it seems that many souls nevertheless do approach their meeting with their Council with a certain degree of anxiousness (I discussed the reasons why I believe this is so in Chapter 7). Council members thus appear to make every effort to put us at ease before and during our life review with them.

Amy asked me to describe the travel route taken to get to my Council. I described "flying through clouds" that "part as you fly through them." Soon I approached a structure and floated up towards it. "There's a high dais. They're all there," I said, noting the presence of five beings awaiting me. As I now went before my Council Amy asked me, "How are you feeling?" "Not as bad as I thought," I replied, "I over-judge myself." This again seems to be a common reaction of souls when they go before their Council: their trepidation is often discovered to be more the result of their own self-judgment (or, more likely, their *anticipation* of their own self-judgment) rather than anything attributable to the Council Elders.

In response to a series of questions from Amy I went on to describe myself standing before a podium with the Council members sitting behind it. I had a definite sense of three or four of the Council members being male, and a vague sense that another was either androgynous or female. I described them as wearing sheer white garments. One Council member – "A very old soul" – appeared to be directing things and he sat, "In the center and a little forward. It's like a semi-circle, or like a half-moon." I can remember seeing very clearly in my mind the shape of the table behind which they sat, but having trouble finding the right word to describe it; when I said "semi-circle" and "half-moon" the word I was actually searching for was *crescent*, but for the life of me I could not bring that term to mind while under hypnosis.

After I had described the setting Amy asked, "Which one of these entities addresses you first?" "One of the males," I replied, "but not the main one."

Amy: And what does he say?

John: He's almost laughing at my apprehension. He finds it amusing.

Amy: So how do they seem to feel about how you lived your last life?

John: Very positive. They say I made a good choice. It went according to plan, pretty much. It was a simple plan, but that's what I wanted, and I got what I wanted from it, in spades.

Amy: Great! What a relief, huh?

John: Yeah.

Amy: Does anyone have anything to say about your current life, the one you're living now?

John: It was another fairly limited life, but my choice. I tend to want that. I'm not willing to go out and take on a lot of big major things. I'm afraid to expose myself to too much. I don't trust myself to handle anything big. I like things limited and contained, manageable. But I did take risks with the little things – a lot of little things, and in that way it was tough. It went against my grain a lot. That was hard, but that was what I was intending.

Amy asked me if any of the Council members had any "constructive criticism or any kind of encouragement" for me in my present lifetime. My reply was, "'Lighten up.' They seem serious about it, almost finger-wagging. It seems to be a serious issue."

I found two things about their response intriguing: first, while the phrase "lighten up" generally has an air of frivolity about it, I immediately clarified the tone of their response as being one of total seriousness; and second, my use of the term "finger-wagging" suggests that I was being scolded by the Council. This last is interesting because in Newton's books the point is often made we are never subjected to judgment or punishment when our lives are reviewed in the Spirit Realm. Nevertheless, I have seen cases in his books – as well as in my situation described here – where the Council or a Spirit Guide do come close to rebuking or chiding a soul for its behavior or shortcomings. I think it is important to note this because one could easily misconstrue the absence of judgment and punishment as meaning that we are not held accountable or held to task for our actions by the more advanced souls; clearly we *are* reprimanded, albeit with compassion and understanding. The fact that we are not punished or coldly berated does not suggest a license to live our lives as we see fit. There are principles and limitations that must be observed and standards of behavior that must be met; when we fail to do this we are made acutely aware of our shortcomings. And this is as it should be, in my opinion, because our karma – and thus the nature of our future lives – is determined by how we've lived our previous lives. Honest feedback is essential if we are to accurately and meaningfully assess the progress we are making (or not making). So I, for one, am glad that the Council members engage in "finger-wagging" when they feel it necessary.

Amy went on to ask, "Do they have any constructive ideas how you can do that (i.e., *lighten up*)?" I responded by saying, while laughing, "They're telling me to listen to my wife. That's why she's here. I know that." Knowing both my own and my wife's personalities, this statement rings completely true. I am a very emotional and excitable person, I fret a great deal, and I take everything to heart. My wife, on the other hand, is usually very calm and cool, and she has an extraordinary ability to detach from her emotions and evaluate circumstances in a dispassionate, aloof manner. (I call her "comatose" but she insists she is merely "stoic").

As I noted at the outset of this chapter, I had prepared a list of four questions that I wanted to address during my LBL session. Amy now directed the session to those questions. The Council's answers are, I feel, some of the most dramatic and illuminating revelations to come out of my entire LBL session. I think it best to provide that portion of the transcript verbatim:

> **Amy:** Do you feel it would be appropriate to present your questions to the Council now?"
>
> **John:** Yes.
>
> **Amy:** Ask them what karmic issues you're supposed to be addressing in this life.
>
> **John:** Fear … selfishness tied in with the fear. I'm aware of this consciously. I feel like I addressed these too late. I feel like I have addressed these pretty successfully, but I'm disappointed that it's only recent, but they say that's the way it works. Everything else had to happen to lead up to this. That's the way it happens. I'm not late. It took all the other stuff to get to this point … that I should realize that.
>
> **Amy:** Can you take a moment to realize that and let that sink in?
>
> **John:** Yes, I realize that intellectually, but I guess not emotionally. I want things to happen too quickly, they say. I know that too. I don't allow for development. I have to slow down and accept that it takes time.
>
> **Amy:** You're next question is, "How successful have I been?", but I think we just answered that. (*my third question*) Is there something that you should be doing that you're not doing?"
>
> **John:** Helping others more. I'm still too selfish. My desire to be alone is impeding that.
>
> **Amy:** Do they have any specific ideas about how you can help others more?
>
> **John:** I'm not supposed to be afraid of people hurting me. If they hurt me, they hurt me. I shouldn't let the fear of that isolate me. They say too much caution is not good for you. It's limiting. But, at the same time they say I'm right about the influences of others (*i.e., the fact that I was easily*

swayed by the negative influences of others, and that I make better personal choices when I'm left to myself). It's almost like there's a disagreement on the Council: some feel like I should open up more to people, others think I'm right, that I would have exposed myself to making the same mistakes I made in other lives, and the only way I could succeed in the things I wanted to succeed in, in this life, I *had* to limit myself, they say. I wasn't wrong. But I wanted to play it cautious. That was my plan in the beginning. My plan for this life. I wanted to do that. So I am living according to my plan, more or less. I foresaw the problems and tendencies I'd get into and tried to prevent that from happening.

I want to interject an interesting observation here: My statement above that "It's almost like there's a disagreement on the Council" truly amazed me. In all my readings about the Spirit Realm I cannot recall ever once reading about a situation where Council members disagreed over their assessment of the correctness of a soul's actions in a given lifetime. I find this fascinating because it would seem to suggest that the criteria by which we are evaluated are not cut-and-dried; apparently even very advanced and wise souls base their evaluations of us on their personal opinions, and, even more incredibly, their opinions can differ! The implication, obviously, is that whatever principles and norms govern behavior in the Spirit Realm (and, thus, our lives here on Earth as well) do not represent an exact science. The implication of *that* possibility is extraordinary, and I can't even begin to imagine the complexities and enigmas that would derive from it.

Anyway, to return to the session transcript, Amy once again was remarkably prescient and asked the million dollar question that led to what I consider the most enlightening and important information to come out of all my hypnosis sessions:

Amy: How about now? Do you and the Council feel that you're strong enough now in your identity that you can come out of your shell a little bit more?

John: That's exactly what they're saying: I'm staying in an obsolete mode now. I've learned a lot in this life now and developed some pretty strong personality traits, and am at the point where I can deal with this stuff better. And indeed, that's how I should be testing my success.

Amy then asked, "Is there anything else on this, or can we move on to the next question?" But there was clearly much more that I – or, more likely, the Council – had to say on this matter.

John: I have to trust my own judgment. I was right not to trust my judgment early on, but now I've developed good judgment, very good judgment. And now my judgment is actually better than that of others. I'm not adapting well to the changes.

Amy: Maybe you can now actually help people who are having the same kinds of problems that you used to have.

John: I was worse than I thought, but I'm better than I think, is what they're saying. I'm judging things too much from past perspectives. I can't do it anymore. It's not valid. If we move on, then that's what counts. Where we are is what counts. Where we are *now* is what counts.

I just want to mention something rather interesting … and eerie. Somewhere during the last statement above I noticed a very distinct change in how I was conveying the information I was speaking. It was as though I was no longer relaying the information passed on to me by the Council but rather I was acting as a direct conduit *for* the Council. Although I did not comment on this to Amy after the session, it was obvious that she had nevertheless picked up on it too because she said to me, after the session, "There were some points in the session where it was almost as if you were channeling the information." And that is exactly how it felt to me – like I was *channeling* the information. This "channeling" went on for the remainder of my discussion of this particular topic.

Amy: Is there a sense that you're still carrying judgment of yourself from past lives?

John: Yes! And even from this life, early on, and I'm not supposed to be. None of us are supposed to be. We're not supposed to do that. I find that odd but… Huh! And that's why we're not supposed to be judgmental of others. Anything anyone did doesn't matter. It's what we're doing now. That's everything. I… didn't see things this way. I can't believe it. Hmmm.

Amy: What?

John: (Laughs). I thought we learned from the past by looking at the past, and that's totally wrong. We learn from the past when the past is the present. We're learning *then*, and once we move on, to look back to it to learn is foolish and counter-productive. I do that a lot. That's not right. I don't, uh… The forest and the trees. You learned back then, why do you have to learn now? It's interesting. Too much value on the past. The value of the past is when it's the present. Once it's the past, it has no value; it's nothing. Forget it. Forget about it. They're showing me ropes. I'm tied to my past. My past is like a wagon, a heavy wagon, and I'm like a horse pulling it. And the ropes attached to the wagon are what's holding me back. I should let it go. Untie the ropes, cut the ropes. It's amazing. Wow. Oh, God.

OK. There's A LOT I want to say about this last section:

- First, the emotions I was feeling during this portion of the session, as conveyed by my voice, were quite deep. When I said, "*Anything anyone did doesn't matter,*" my voice had a sense of awe about it, as though this information was a personal revelation to me. Likewise, at the end when I said, "*Wow. Oh, God,*" there was again a sense of being awestruck, but on an even more profound level, conveying a sense of intense wonderment. When I listened to the recording, the *way* I said, "*Wow. Oh, God,*" actually sent chills down my spine. When I said, "*Forget it. Forget about it,*" my voice had a forceful quality to it, as though I were issuing a command. Presumably it actually *was* a command from the Council to me, which I was now conveying directly (recall my earlier comment that some of the statements which I made during this portion of the session appeared to be channeled).

- Second, a point continually made here is that we should not dwell in the past but, rather, it is the present that is important. While this is not a particularly novel idea I was nevertheless rather impressed with the way it was presented here. I particularly liked the imagery of me pulling a heavy wagon as a metaphor for how a too-intense focus on the past can hold us back. I also found interesting the similarities between the wisdom conveyed by my Council and the book *The Power of Now* by Eckhart Tolle. In his wonderful book Mr. Tolle makes the point that living in the present – i.e., the *Now* – is the surest path to happiness and enlightenment; the past is over and the future is uncertain, so any time spent worrying about either is wasted and pointless. The guidance conveyed to me by my Council is amazingly consistent with the premise of Mr. Tolle's book.

- Third, I found especially poignant the observation that the fact that the past should not be dwelled upon is the reason why we should not be judgmental of others: we often, if not always, form judgments about people based upon their past actions, but the point that was quite emphatically made by my Council is that the past is *over*, let it go – "*Forget about it*" … not only with regard to ourselves, but with regard to others as well.

- Finally, as has been the case throughout my entire hypnosis experience, the comments made about me were astonishingly pertinent and accurate. I really *do* place an inordinate amount of value, concern and anxiety on the past. And when I think about it, it is very clear that it is confining and suppressing me. The advice given to me to let go of the past and concentrate on the present affected me deeply and really has had an immensely positive transformative effect on me. It might seem obvious and silly to some – hell, it seems ridiculously obvious to me, *now* – but I guess that's what I meant when I said, *"The forest and the trees."* All that being said, I think it is very important to note that the wisdom offered by my Council, while directed at me and my particular circumstances, is not exclusive to me alone. I think it is made quite clear that the advice and admonishments offered are valid for all people. These are fundamental truisms, applicable to everyone. As I note in my next statement below, *"There are laws that guide this stuff."*

Returning to the transcript, Amy asked me, "Can you do that right now? (*i.e., cut the ropes, let go of the past*)." My response, while introducing the caveat *that the past is not completely without value*, finally brings the concept's disparate pieces together in a nice, neat package.

John: Yeah! Once I see it, it's like insane… oh, oh, God! No, no, no. Don't devalue the past. The past is not without value. Just keep it in the right place. You can think about it; you can recall things from it, but only that – only informational. There should be no emotional attachment to the past – that's the point. *That's* the point. I'm getting it now. That's the point. That's where I got confused. I knew I needed to look into the past, but only mentally. All emotional attachment should be in the *present*. There are laws – I knew it! – there are laws that guide this stuff. We know them, but we forget them. Very definite laws. (Big sigh).

At that point Amy moved the session on to other areas of interest, one of which was the roles played by some of the important people in my current life. Earlier I mentioned the questions and points I had wanted to address during my LBL session and I noted: "I also wanted to discover if certain people in my current life also play a major part in my spirit life; specifically I was interested in my wife, my son, and a nurse at one of the medical facilities I visited regarding my prostate cancer." It is the addressing of these points where we now pick up in my LBL session:

Amy: So how about the people in your life? Starting with your wife.

John: My soul mate, definitely. More advanced soul. I'm here to bring out her emotions. That's her weakness. I may be a little too flippant or carefree, but she's too much the other way. She's an anchor to me, and I'm wings to her. I need to be held down, she needs to be brought up. It's a good mix.

Amy: And how about your son?

John: He's like me. She's holding us both down. She's keeping us more centered, a lot more sane.

I want to break away from the transcript here and discuss some of the points that were made during that last exchange. First, my comments about my wife here are totally consistent with my remarks regarding her from earlier in the hypnosis session, as well as being consistent with the relationship she and I have together in the present. Particularly with regard to our lives now, my wife is a very serious and "stoic" (her word) person while I am extremely emotional. And I do feel that, because of these disparate personalities, we complement each other quite well – as I said under hypnosis, "She's an anchor to me, and I'm wings to her. I need to be held down, she needs to be brought up. It's a good mix." We really do have exactly those effects on one another.

Second, regarding my son in my current life, again my comments under hypnosis here are fully consistent with my earlier comments as well as with the relationship my son and I have in our current life together. Earlier in the session it had been revealed that my son is my best friend in the Spirit Realm and that we have had many lifetimes together where we were very close, and also that we've had a tendency to get into trouble together in past lives as well as in the Spirit Realm. This ties in nicely with my comment above – that my wife keeps both me and my son centered and sane. I think it is also interesting to note that the relationship between me and my wife (and my son) is in full agreement with the aspect of the karmic scheme whereby particular souls incarnate with one another for the express purpose of providing mutual assistance in developing and maturing both spiritually and with regard to karma. This, to me, provides a degree of validation of the truth of the karmic system: we are paired up with people who possess certain traits and qualities which interact with *our* unique personalities in such a way as to enable us both to advance and grow. It is quite an impressive and efficient system.

I want to note that, as you might expect, the desire to explore the potentially broader roles played by people in one's current life is very common among people undergoing LBL hypnosis. This would stand to reason not only because it would be an obvious point of interest but also because the work of Michael Newton and others in the LBL field clearly indicates that the key people in our lives often incarnate with us in various capacities from lifetime to lifetime and are also often members of our soul group; thus it's no surprise that we would be curious to discover the extent to which this might be true about the people we consider important to us, and particularly in our current life.

In the previous paragraphs I covered the exploration into the roles played by my wife and son (which was actually begun earlier in the session when I first encountered them as I initially crossed over, and then continued at this latter part of the session). There was only one other person whom I wanted to investigate in this regard and that was the nurse at one of the facilities where I received care for my prostate cancer. I've already alluded to the fact that I'm not a very social person and that I prefer to keep to myself, so it shouldn't be a surprise that the number of people I was interested in looking into was quite small; but what is probably a bit shocking is that one of the people on that very short list would be a nurse at a medical facility where I received care. This requires some explanation, and that explanation turns out to be very relevant to the amazing information about this nurse that was revealed during this part of the session. So let me give you a little background:

I received forty-one radiation treatments over a period of nine weeks during the summer of 2004. The treatments were done daily, Monday through Friday, and on one day each week I also sat with the nurse at the facility to afford her the opportunity to see how I was holding up and to allow me to bring up any problems or concerns I was having. Initially my meetings with that nurse, who I will call Megan (not her real name), were very formal and business-like, but over time we fell into a more casual relationship and I began to feel very comfortable and relaxed when in her presence. Megan initially struck me as a tough woman but I quickly learned that beneath her business-like exterior there was a very caring person who felt genuine concern for her patients, much more so than any other doctor or nurse I'd ever dealt with. Also, she would do anything to help her patients in any way possible, and on more than one occasion I benefited greatly from her generous assistance. But, most importantly, Megan has the wildest and craziest sense of humor of anyone I've ever known. I can't count the times she had me laughing so hard that I had tears in my eyes. The nine weeks of radiation treatments were a living hell in more ways than one, and I honestly don't know how I would have gotten through it with my sanity intact if it were not for Megan's kindness, help, and comical antics. After the treatments ended I continued to have follow-up appointments at this facility for several years. Over that long period of time I had begun to realize that the feeling that came over me each time I'd meet with Megan was highly unusual, especially for me: I had a feeling of extreme comfort and security, and a very strong sense of "Ahhh, I'm home now." This baffled me immensely; yes, I'd obviously grown very fond of Megan for all the reasons discussed above, but the feelings I was experiencing went far beyond that. It was also obvious to me that they were not romantic feelings – it was something much, much deeper and infinitely more profound. It was particularly uncharacteristic of me to feel this way since I generally don't like people, even a little bit, and I never, ever put anyone (except my wife) on a pedestal, yet I was having this profound sense of familiarity and comfort every time I was in Megan's presence. I began to explore these feelings more and more and I came to realize that I had a strong sense that I had known Megan a long time and that there was a very, very powerful connection between us, far beyond what could be explained by the very limited interaction which was occurring between us (what ultimately became, for the follow-up visits, about 15 or 20 minutes once a year). Since I was a firm believer in reincarnation, I eventually came to the conclusion that Megan and I had probably known each other in a previous lifetime; that would account for the strong feeling of familiarity I had with regard to Megan, and the feelings of comfort and security could be attributed to the probability that our relationship in that previous life had been a positive one. This theory seemed to explain all the unusual feelings I was experiencing while in Megan's presence so I accepted it as being the most plausible explanation; once I'd come to that conclusion, I no longer gave my feelings about Megan much thought and the great mystery had been put to rest as far as I was concerned.

Approximately six to twelve months later I had been thinking a lot about the afterlife (for reasons completely unrelated to Megan) and I decided to reread Michael Newton's first two books, *Journey of Souls* and *Destiny of Souls*. One day I found myself rereading a section which discussed the possible roles played by members of a person's soul group in that person's lifetimes. As I've mentioned previously, if a member of our soul group incarnates with us it is usually in a role that is very close to us, generally as a good friend or a sibling. However, Dr. Newton went on to note that occasionally two members of a soul group may incarnate together in a very limited and temporary capacity, their life paths crossing only briefly and superficially. This happens, he explained, when one of them is going through a particularly difficult time in his or her life, and the other person temporarily comes into their life to help them through this challenging situation. When I read this part the book literally fell out of my hands. I remember sitting there with the book in my lap and saying out loud in an empty room, "Megan." It then all became clear to me: Megan and I did not simply know each other in a past life – *we were members of the same soul group!* The more I thought about it, the more sense it made; Megan came into my life at precisely the time I was going through the worst ordeal of my life – prostate cancer – and she absolutely was almost single-handedly responsible for helping me to deal with it and get through it. Also, this explained (much better than my previous theory) why I had such a strong impression of familiarity and comfort when I was with Megan – members of the same soul group are very close to one another and have an eternal connection that runs very, very deep. I'm not exaggerating when I say that I sat there in awe, utterly amazed and astounded at this unexpected turn of events.

With all of that as background, let's pick up in the session where Amy (my hypnotist) addresses this point (this occurs immediately after I talked about my relationship with my wife and son):

Amy: And how about your nurse friend?

John: I sense she's an old soul too.

Amy: Is she in your soul group?

John: I don't sense that, but I do sense that she's someone I know there. But she's too advanced to be in my group, I think.

Let's stop a moment to really consider this – two amazing facts were just revealed here:

First, Megan is *not* a member of my soul group, in spite of the fact that I was convinced that she was (this situation of having information disclosed via LBL which is at odds with the hypnosis subject's conscious beliefs and expectations offers, I believe, some very strong confirmation of the validity and credibility of the LBL experience).

Second, Megan is "too advanced to be in my soul group" – this is of staggering importance in that it indicates that Megan must be an *extremely* advanced soul. Recall my discussion of the auras radiated by souls in the Spirit Realm, covered previously, where it was revealed that my wife's aura is light purple while my aura is blue; according to Dr. Newton's findings this would identify my wife as being at the "highly advanced" spiritual development stage and me at the "advanced" stage. Since my wife and I are in the same soul group, and since members of a particular soul group are all at, or very close to, the same development level, the fact that Megan is "too advanced to be in my soul group" indicates that *she is at an amazingly advanced level of spiritual development*. I have to wonder: Exactly what color is Megan's aura? But, as astonishing as this revelation regarding Megan is, the bombshell that follows was even more awesome to me, and yet it is perfectly consistent with this discovery of Megan's extremely advanced spiritual level.

Since (under hypnosis) I was having difficulty ascertaining the connection between me and Megan in the Spirit Realm, Amy thought up a brilliant way around the blockage:

Amy: Can you ask someone on the Council?

John: I sense she's [i.e., Megan] like a Guide, but I can't tell if she's Kayla [i.e., my Spirit Guide who met me as I crossed over] or not. Or another Guide. Can there be two Guides?

Amy: Sure.

John: Yes. Oh, I think Kayla is a young Guide in training, that's what it is. So Megan has removed herself a bit from as direct involvement with me as she would have, and Kayla has stepped into that role. Megan is still my Guide and came to help me through the cancer, as I thought. There was no mistake.

So there's the mind-blowing revelation: Megan, my cancer nurse in my current Earth life, *is my Spirit Guide*! I cannot even begin to describe how awesome, incredible and emotional a discovery this was for me.

Dr. Newton specifically refers to this as "the emotional intoxication a subject feels when an in-life contact is made with their guide."[120] To know one's Guide while living a life on Earth is amazing and wonderful and, as far as I know, rare. In fact, one of my first reactions to this revelation was disbelief because I didn't think it was *possible* for a soul and his/her Guide to have any interaction in an earthly life, but then I recalled the story (from Michael Newton's book *Journey of Souls*) of a woman who, while undergoing LBL hypnosis, discovered that her son in her current life was her Spirit Guide. Once I recalled that story, I accepted what I learned about Megan being my Guide.

There are several things I want to elaborate on regarding this discovery. First, it is odd that as I began to get the "message" that Megan is my Guide I asked, "Can there be two Guides?" In Dr. Newton's books it is made very clear that a person can, in fact, have two Guides, and I was well aware of this since I did read his books. Yet I can clearly recall being momentarily mystified by this realization, and I can also recall why: I had already identified Kayla as my Guide, and I also found it hard to believe that someone I knew in my current life would be my Guide. But even as I asked the question "Can there be two Guides?" I already knew the answer as indicated by my reply of "Yes" as Amy said "Sure."

Secondly, I'd like to comment on my statement that "Megan is still my Guide and came to help me through the cancer, as I thought. There was no mistake." This is referring to what I discussed previously about my belief, after rereading the relevant section in Dr. Newton's book, that Megan came into my life to help me get through the difficult challenges of dealing with cancer – I did not realize that she was doing this in the capacity of my Spirit Guide (I thought she was merely a member of my soul group), but I was correct in my assessment that she came into my life in order to help me in dealing with my cancer ordeal. This is what I meant when I said, "There was no mistake." I think it's interesting that I reasoned this out almost totally accurately on my own, and it's important to realize that I would *not* have figured this out had I never read Dr. Newton's books and been familiar with the details of the afterlife which I learned from them. This suggests an important point, and something I feel very passionately about regarding the whole field of LBL research: I think it is extremely important and beneficial for people to read books about LBL and become familiar with what the research teaches us; I believe it can help us evaluate occurrences and circumstances in our lives in a much more meaningful, accurate and useful way. I can definitely attest to LBL having had such an effect on my life. Indeed, as I've noted previously, I can honestly say that I filter virtually everything I experience through an LBL outlook on life: before I do or say anything I think to myself, "How will I feel going before my Council having handled this situation in such-and-such a manner?" Once I evaluate a situation in this way I find that my handling of it is usually done in a much better way than if I had simply acted spontaneously or thoughtlessly. Because of my familiarity will LBL literature I know I will ultimately be accountable for everything I do and say in this life and therefore I try very hard to handle things in a way *now* so that I won't feel ashamed or guilty *later* when I have to face my actions in the afterlife. Also, I now look upon any challenges that present themselves to me as being put there to assist me in my spiritual or karmic advancement, rather than cursing them as "bad luck" dealt to me by the hands of a cruel and random fate. Trust me, life is much easier when you look at it in this way, and the way you conduct yourself will be much better – at least, that has been the case with me. In my opinion, merely being aware of the facts pertaining to LBL can be a very positive life-transforming experience. Many, many people who have had near death experiences (NDEs) have found their lives transformed in a similar manner (as was noted in previous chapters), and I think we can realize a similar transformation in our lives without having to undergo a traumatic near death experience; we simply have to educate ourselves about the facts and details of our life between lives, and we can do that by reading books such as those by Michael Newton and/or by undergoing LBL regressive hypnosis.

Finally, I'd like to comment upon the situation of a soul having two Guides. Let me begin by quoting a pertinent section from Dr. Newton's *Journey of Souls*: "It is not uncommon to find guides working in pairs with people on Earth, each with their own approaches to teaching. In these cases one is dominant, although the more experienced senior guide may actually be less evident in day-to-day activities of their charges. The reason for this spiritual arrangement in tandem is because one of the pair is either in training (such as a junior guide under a senior), or the association is so long-standing between the two guides (as with a senior to a master) that a permanent relationship has evolved." [121]

Comparing the above statement to my own personal LBL experience I find it interesting that I noted that Kayla is a young guide-in-training under the tutelage of the more advanced soul Megan. Even more relevant, I specifically mentioned that "Megan has removed herself a bit from as direct involvement with me as she would have, and Kayla has stepped into that role." This corresponds exactly to Newton's remark that the "senior guide may actually be less evident in day-to-day activities of their charges." While these similarities are compelling it must nevertheless be noted that they might very well be the result of my having read that information in Dr. Newton's book and then recalling it while under hypnosis. If that is the case then I can honestly say that I had no *conscious* recollection of having read that information (other than knowing that two guides are possible) and also that my sense while under hypnosis was that I was honestly relating the truth as it pertained to me and my Guides. But I'll be the first to admit that it ultimately is a case of *which came first, the chicken or the egg?* I obviously cannot say for certain whether the similarities between my LBL experience and the information contained in *Journey of Souls* indicates a validation of the reality of my experience, or was merely an unconscious recall of information stored in my subconscious and falsely interpreted by my mind as a spiritual experience. Again, all I can say is that the LBL experience felt quite "real" to me and I did not have any conscious recollection of having been previously exposed to similar information from Dr. Newton's book.

Of course I have no way of proving to you, the reader – nor to myself, for that matter – that Megan is truly my Spirit Guide. The circumstantial evidence discussed above – regarding my feelings in her presence and the way she came into my life and helped me through my cancer situation – are intriguing and suggestive, but they are by no means proof. Two additional pieces of information which are, again, circumstantial but which nevertheless strengthen the case, are the following: (1) It is commonly noted throughout virtually all spiritual literature that advanced souls who choose to incarnate on earth usually work in a public service field, most often in the medical field – this makes perfect sense, as one would expect an advanced soul to be strongly driven to help people in some capacity; that Megan is an oncology nurse fits in nicely with that fact; (2) Unbeknownst to either me or Megan, we learned from a chance remark that she and I had grown up in the same city, literally walking distance from one another; I find that "coincidence" astounding.

All that being said, the bottom line for me is that I have a very strong intuitive sense that Megan truly is my Spirit Guide. I feel the reality of this very powerfully, and on a level that is beyond the rational and intellectual levels. It is difficult to describe this type of knowing – it is like an instinctive awareness of the truth of the matter. For me, that is reason enough to accept it – the circumstantial evidence is merely icing on the cake.

(I saw and interacted with Megan often during the early phase of my cancer, and then once or twice a year later on. A few years ago the doctor at the facility decided there was no longer any need for me to return for visits there and so, sadly, my personal interactions with the individual whom I believe is my Spirit Guide came to an abrupt end. Nevertheless, I feel privileged and blessed to have had the unique opportunity to have met and known my Spirit Guide while living a life on Earth).

Immediately after I identified my oncology nurse Megan as being my Spirit Guide, Amy (my hypnotist) directed the discussion towards my cancer.

> **Amy**: This wasn't one of your questions, but do you want to ask anything about the cancer?

> **John**: Yeah, I do. (Long pause, as I received the information). Necessary, as I thought. I have to accept it, and I pretty much do. It has a purpose. I'm afraid to ask where it's going to lead. I don't think I'm going to ask that.

Amy: OK.

John: I don't even know if they would tell me.

Amy: OK. Do you want to ask if there's something you can do that will change the outcome?

John: Live a cleaner life. Eat better. Treat my body better. Let go of the past, let go of the worries. Lighten up. That will be a big help. Worry makes the body denser. It compresses it. And density is bad. The more dense, the more poisoned or decayed or malfunctioning or corrupt things are. Worrying is like a pressure that makes everything denser. I have to ease the pressure, then things will get better. It's like squashing a fruit. If you squeeze the juice out of it, it's not good.

Amy: Great! I'm glad we asked, huh?

John: (Laughs) I'm glad *you* asked. I didn't want to think about it.

I'd like to make some commentary on the above exchange. First, God bless Amy for deciding to take the session in this direction. As I think back now, it seems incredible to me that I hadn't included my cancer situation on the list of things to be explored during the LBL session. Yet, when I consider my final remark – "I didn't want to think about it" – and my earlier statements – "I'm afraid to ask where it's going to lead. I don't think I'm going to ask that" – it becomes pretty obvious that the omission was not an oversight but rather an intentional (albeit unconscious or subconscious) attempt to avoid the topic due to fear of learning something unpleasant. Thinking about it now, it seems fairly unlikely to me that my Council would have permitted me any foreknowledge if my cancer situation is destined to end horribly. I even alluded to that during the session when I said, "I don't even know if they would tell me." I have to admit that I become very sad now whenever I read or listen to the part where I say that I'm afraid to ask where it's going to lead. It really drives home the reality of the mental and emotional anguish that cancer patients suffer – often alone in the depths of their own minds so as not to upset loved ones – and also the degree to which we must cultivate a state of denial in order to be able to somehow cope with this horror and, to the extent possible, get on with our lives. It's a very depressing realization, yet that is the truth of the situation.

I'd also like to comment on my statement that the cancer is, "Necessary, as I thought. I have to accept it, and I pretty much do. It has a purpose." This is true; from the very beginning of this nightmare I've always had the attitude that it was necessary – I've never felt that I was cursed or the victim of bad luck – and I have accepted it as being part of my karma, an unpleasant learning situation to help me to overcome some negative acts or tendencies from either a past life or my current life. But let me be clear: When I say I feel it is "necessary" and that I "accept it" I sure as hell am not saying I like it, or that I don't want to get rid of it. Trust me, I pray constantly to God to rid this blight from my body, even going so far as to ask that I be forgiven the karmic debt that made the cancer necessary. That, to me, is a sign of how desperate I feel about the cancer, since I doubt karmic debts would be forgiven so easily (although I really don't know) and it is against the whole point of karma to even request such a thing, yet I want to be free of this disease so desperately that I'm willing to make requests that I think are unrealistic and unlikely to be honored. Also, I'm personally doing everything I can to try and rid myself of this disease – I've made drastic changes in my diet, have sought medical intervention, do guided imagery, exercise, and generally do anything that I think might help in removing the cancer from my body. So when I say I "accept" it what I mean is I recognize it as being necessary from the perspective of karma. My wife often says to me, "I'm furious that you have cancer! It's so unfair. Aren't you angry?" And my answer is always, "No, I'm not angry. I'm extremely sad and depressed about it, but I don't feel anger over it." I just hope and pray that merely contracting cancer and dealing with the horrors of the early stages will be enough to balance whatever karmic debt caused it to be necessary, and that it will *not* be necessary for me to see this nightmare through to a bitter end.

Finally, I found quite interesting my remarks about how worrying makes the body denser and the corrupting effect this density has on the physical body. We all know that worry and stress are bad for our health, but I never before considered the possibility that worrying makes the body *denser*. I do, however, associate "density" with negative things – i.e., negative emotions are more dense than positive emotions, the physical plane is more dense than the spiritual plane, etc. – but I never applied the concept of denseness to physical health. I think my comments in this regard provide an interesting explanation as to why worrying degrades the immune system and thus results in health problems. After I reviewed this portion of the transcript I thought a lot about what I had said, and the whole thing made sense to me. Worrying and stress really *do* feel like pressure, like we are being squeezed or crushed; indeed, when suffering extreme anxiety it is often hard to breath – we feel suffocated and a tightness in our chest. This was just one of several "unique" ideas which came out of my mouth while under hypnosis and which I do not recall ever previously giving any thought to. I found many of these utterances interesting and fascinating, and upon reviewing the transcript I thought, "Wow, what an intriguing concept!" and I found it hard to believe that these ideas had come out of my mind. They really were like revelations to me, and I consider that to be further evidence of the validity of the LBL hypnotic experience. And even if one presumes that these thoughts simply came from my subconscious rather than from another realm of existence, then I still find it astounding that such relevant and interesting ideas might be floating around in my subconscious.

If nothing else, hypnotic regression has great value as a means by which we can access this buried, subconscious wisdom and employ it to our benefit.

Before I continue on with my LBL session, I want to take a moment to comment upon the importance of the wisdom that the hypnotist brings to a hypnosis session. Obviously, the hypnotist's hypnosis skills and training are critical to the success and comfort level of any endeavor into hypnosis, but I think that goes without saying, so I don't feel the need to add to the obvious. But I think there are some subtle, personal qualities that a hypnotist can bring to this experience which could make a huge difference as to how the session progresses and what results from it. Although I think this point had been illustrated on several occasions by my hypnotist Amy, I believe it was most clearly demonstrated in the way she conducted the portion of the session just discussed. Recall that although I had neglected to include any exploration into my cancer problem in my list of topics to be addressed Amy nevertheless had the wisdom to ask me, while hypnotized, if I wanted to ask my Council about it. Although I had avoided the issue out of fear of receiving unpleasant news, it is obviously a huge problem in my life now and, whether I consciously realized it or not, it was screaming to be addressed. Thankfully, Amy had the wisdom to ask me if I wanted to look into it, despite my unconscious reservations. And, as you saw, some interesting and helpful advice regarding dealing with the cancer was given by the Council. Had Amy not steered the session in that direction then I would never have been exposed to my Council's suggestions. Also, I imagine that, after the fact, I would have had major regrets about not having included it myself in the list of items to be explored. So, I just want to say that not only am I extremely grateful to Amy for the expert way she brought me into the hypnotic state and conducted the sessions, but I am also very, very grateful for the creativity, wisdom, and caring that she brought to the sessions. I consider myself extremely lucky to have conducted my sessions with Amy. I've heard of some very lousy hypnosis experiences that other people have had because of the inadequacies of their hypnotists; thankfully, my experience was totally the opposite – I couldn't have hoped for a better navigator to take me on this remarkable voyage to the Spirit Realm dimension. Amy's sharp, intuitive sense of where to lead things becomes apparent yet again in the next portion of the session where her decision to ask if there is "anything else" leads to some of the most important and profound advice I was to receive from my Council.

After I received guidance on some things I should try to do in dealing with my cancer situation, Amy asked if there was anything else I needed to discuss with my Council:

> **Amy**: Is there any last thing you want to ask, or any last thing they want to tell you?

John: I still have to be careful. This is going to be the hard part. I have to balance the lightening-up with not losing control like I did in other lives. The danger of that is much diminished, because of the progress I've made, but there is still that danger. I have to be careful when I lighten up. They're yelling at me when they say that, because my tendency is to go back to the tightness. I'm too black and white. I have to allow for the gray areas. I have to take a risk. I don't want to take a risk, because I feel like I've made so much progress, I don't want to undo it this late in life. But they say, no, I have to keep going.

Amy: Trust yourself?

John: Yes. Trust myself. Acknowledge the progress I've made. Let that give me strength. Let that give me confidence. If I made this kind of progress, turning out the way I did, with nothing, then I should be able to do this next phase. It's actually easier. It's the hard part, not because it's hard, but because *I* see it as hard. I'm afraid. But it will actually be easier, because I'm equipped to deal with it now. I don't realize that, and I have to realize that. But I do have to be cautious. I have a tendency to… that's it… *that's* the problem. If I allow myself an opening, I dive through it. It's not the way it's supposed to be. But I know myself, and they have faith I can do it. I have to have the faith in me that they have. I have to do it, but I have to be cautious… not the way I define caution. Their definition of caution is not the same as my definition of caution. And I get that they're almost reprimanding me. I have to lighten up on the caution.

Amy: OK, it's time to thank your Council. Is there any way you want to give gratitude for their time and their effort?

John: Tremendous thanks. Thanks for everything, to Kayla. Thanks.

As I said at the outset of this section, I feel that the guidance I received from my Council here was some of the most significant and useful information to come out of the entire LBL session, and there are several observations I'd like to make in that regard. First and foremost, the main theme here clearly revolves around the need for me to "lighten up" while at the same time being careful not to lighten up too much, and the fact that I tend to be a bit too cautious; I need to be bolder and have more confidence in myself and in my ability to lighten up without losing control. Similar sentiments were expressed earlier in the LBL session. Once again, this describes my personality to a "T": I am very much a person of extremes, and because I'm aware of that I tend to be exceedingly cautious in how I conduct myself, fearing that if I allow myself even a little leeway I will get carried away and go totally in the other (wrong) direction. I am definitely "too black and white" – my wife has often told me, "There are no gray areas with you."

I also found very interesting my statements, at two different points in the exchange, that "They're yelling at me when they say that" and later "I get that they're almost reprimanding me." The Council clearly had some very strong feelings about this advice and they apparently didn't hold back in expressing their feelings. In an earlier part of this session, as my Council was (yet again) rebuking me to "lighten up" I noted, "They seem serious about it, almost finger-wagging. It seems to be a serious issue." I have already discussed in depth the distinction – at least as I see it – between *reprimanding* on the part of the Council as opposed to them *being judgmental*. I think those points are pertinent here as well, perhaps even more so since this time I seem to have advanced from being the object of mere "finger-wagging" to being "yelled at" and "reprimanded." I never felt, during either of these "scoldings" that my Council was being in any way judgmental; rather, it seemed quite clear to me that they were simply being emphatic in order to impress upon me the importance of the guidance they were imparting.

Another sense I got from this was that the Council feels that I've made good progress, and I found this very encouraging, but I have to admit that, even after having received their advice and guidance (and believing them to be correct) I *still* feel afraid to "lighten up"; I have lightened up somewhat, but I feel that I could and should do even more, yet I'm fearful of enjoying the feeling and letting go completely. Nevertheless, I have to admit that, when I look back on my current life, I can see that I have made great strides and I am a much more mature and responsible person now, so it does seem to me that, as I said in the session, "…it will actually be easier, because I'm equipped to deal with it now."

I found quite humorous my statement that, "Their definition of caution is not the same as my definition of caution." Their definition of caution, as I perceived it, would be: *Proceed, but just be aware and be careful*; my definition of caution is more along the lines of: *Stay put! If you don't take any chances then you won't risk losing anything!* I truly am not a risk-taker: I never gamble for money, and any investments I've made have been very conservative with low returns and minimal risk. When applied to financial matters my attitude is probably wise and prudent, but obviously when applied to my life situation it is restrictive and stifling. I do believe in the Council's wisdom, and I am determined to incorporate their advice into my life.

Finally, I thought it very intriguing when I said that I have to lighten up without "losing control like I did in other lives." What in the hell was *that* referring to? What exactly did I do in those other "out-of-control" lifetimes? Earlier in the LBL session I had felt that my son and I had been very close in past lifetimes and that we got in trouble a lot together. I also make allusion to the possibility of going astray – "back to my old ways" –later when I visit the Place of Life Selection. I have to presume that those comments are somehow relevant here. Needless to say,

I am VERY curious about these past lives and exactly how I was out of control and exactly what trouble I got into. While we didn't explore any of those lifetimes, I did get some sense that I was a rather carefree and irresponsible person, and, as much as I hate to think it, I feel that I will not like what I will discover should I ever seek to examine those lives in future hypnosis sessions. I do hope to do more past life regression sessions with Amy, but I must admit that I feel quite a bit of trepidation about what I might learn.

After my extremely informative and enlightening meeting with my Council ended, Amy steered me towards the Place of Life Selection. I believe that a broad summary of this aspect of the Spirit Realm would be appropriate as a prelude to a discussion of my particular experiences there. Previously, as part of a general overview of the Spirit Realm, I offered a synopsis of the Place of Life Selection, which I reproduce verbatim here:

Place of Life Selection: This is a place where we can view, experience and evaluate the options available to us for our next life in the flesh. Amazingly, we have quite a lot of input in choosing who we will be in our next life as well as the circumstances of that life. These choices are made, of course, based upon the karmic issues we are planning to address in this upcoming life. *Will I be born female?, ...to a wealthy family?, ...physically handicapped?, ... possessing a special talent?* The choices we make here are in accordance with the karmic issues we identified, and the plans we made, as a result of the studies and learning conducted in the schools and libraries, and the meetings, consultations, and discussions held with our soul group members, spirit guides, and Council members. It all comes together here: If we learned well and planned effectively, then we will make a life selection that affords us an excellent opportunity to make some serious karmic progress.

The one great caveat to all this in-depth planning is this: We, as human beings, have *free will*. When we plan our next life we are *not* setting up a rigid script that is guaranteed to be followed to a "T". What we are doing is devising an outline where the players are free to ad lib. Lives in the flesh are not always lived according to the plans made in the Spirit Realm. It is hoped that we will adhere to the plan closely, but there are no guarantees.

In his book *Journey of Souls* Michael Newton notes that, "...souls do have the freedom to choose when, where, and who they want to be in their physical lives."[122] He also explains that, after our "training sessions" with our "counselors and peer groups" in the Spirit Realm are completed and we thus begin the process of planning a return to a physical lifetime on Earth, "The soul must now assimilate all this information and take purposeful action based upon three primary decisions:

- Am I ready for a new physical life?

- What specific lessons do I want to undertake to advance my learning and development?
- Where should I go, and who shall I be in my next life for the best opportunity to work on my goals?" [123]

Also pertinent here is the fact that most souls are very reluctant to leave the beauty and bliss of the Spirit Realm in order to return to a physical existence on Earth with all its attendant pain, violence, illness, cruelty, etc. (I recall one NDEr stating that when he returned to his physical body after his brief sojourn to the Spirit Realm, the feeling of reentering his body was like donning a pair of dirty, wet overalls). The more accounts one reads of descriptions of life in the Spirit Realm, the more one gets the sense that existence on that other plane is ecstatic and rapturous, whereas life here on Earth, as we all know from personal experience, is often difficult, demanding, and uncomfortable. Interestingly, I've found in my readings that when Near Death Experiencers as well as LBL hypnosis subjects are asked if there such a thing as a "hell" – in the sense of a place of eternal damnation and suffering overseen by the "devil" – they invariably respond that there is no such place, but then they often qualify their answer by stating that life on Earth is the closest thing to a "hell." So it is no surprise that most souls are not particularly eager to return to Earth for a new incarnation. One question that always nagged at me was: *Well, then, why do they do it?* Of course I understand the *reasons* given as to why we need to return for more lifetimes on Earth, but what I never fully understood was why we ultimately agree to take the plunge, given the attractiveness of life in Spirit compared with the unattractiveness of life in the physical (I should note that it is often stated by LBL subjects that although we are encouraged to return to Earth, we are never forced to do so; ultimately we choose to reincarnate of our own free will). Well, finally, in my own LBL session, I received an explanation that made sense to me.

So, with that as background, let me resume my hypnosis session at the point where Amy prompted me to move on to this next phase:

Amy: So let's go now to the Life and Body Selection place. How do you know when it's time to incarnate? Does someone tell you?

John: You begin to get restless. You can't fully enjoy the pleasures of the Spirit Realm. At first it's like an annoyance in the background that goes buzz, buzz in your ear. But it gets bigger, and it starts to impede your enjoyment, and eventually you realize that you've got to deal with it, that you won't be comfortable there if you don't deal with it. There's a tremendous resistance to knowing that, at least to me; but the discomfort there gets so great that it tips the balance. And in order to recoup the pleasurable feelings there, you have to come back here and deal with the issues. And that's what motivates you. It's like going to work here to earn money to buy things to give you pleasure. It's like that, in a way.

(*An interesting question here is: Is that "annoying buzz, buzz" the result of our own personal guilt, or is it an inherent, preprogrammed aspect of the Spirit Realm designed to give us the boot in the ass we need in order to finally give in and agree to make a return trip to the physical?*).

Amy: So in considering your incarnation for this life, how did you feel about incarnating this time around?

John: I dreaded it. I didn't want to come back, period, to this world. And then I knew the things I was going to be faced with in this life, that I had planned, for the reasons that I had, but I knew that it wasn't going to be very pleasant. The early part, much more so. The later part has been good.

Let me take a moment to elaborate on this last statement. As I mentioned earlier, most souls do not look forward to a return to life on Earth. And, obviously, I felt the same – "I dreaded it." But notice that I go on to point out that, while I dreaded the particulars of the specific lifetime I had chosen ("...I knew the things I was going to be faced with in this life, that I had planned...") in order to address whatever karmic issues I needed to address ("...for the reasons that I had..."), I nevertheless stated that, "I didn't want to come back, period, to this world." I think the use of the word "period" in this statement is heavy with meaning, and, frankly, rather chilling: it suggests that I didn't want to return to an earthly life *under any circumstances*. I have to admit that, looking back on my life, it has definitely not been an easy road. And I also have to agree with my statement that the early portion of my life was much more unpleasant than the later part – and consider that for the past ten-plus years (i.e., in the later part of my life) I have been waging a very uncomfortable and stressful battle with prostate cancer: that gives you some idea about how difficult the *early part* of my life was. Given that while in the Spirit Realm we are permitted to see at least some of the details of what awaits us in the next life we've chosen, it's no wonder that I dreaded incarnating into my current lifetime. That "annoying buzz, buzz" must be pretty damn irritating!

Returning now to my LBL session, after that brief exchange regarding reincarnation Amy nudged me on to the Place of Life Selection.

Amy: Do you go to this place of life selection alone, or with your guide?

John: With Kayla. Megan came too, to help. She's a bit sarcastic. I find that amusing, but irritating. Kayla's more loving and warmer, but not as experienced. I'm comforted by Megan's experience – all she knows and all she's learned. She offers a lot from that, but she's also a pain in the ass sometimes. I lean more towards Kayla.

I want to insert a brief commentary here, because I think the above exchange is yet another one of those subtle yet tantalizing pieces of evidence in support of the truth of information recalled via LBL hypnosis. First, as I've noted previously, in my present life my nurse Megan has made a profound impact on me in many ways, and I hold her in the highest regard. One would then think that, having identified her as one of my two Spirit Guides, she would be my favored Guide. Yet, astonishingly, that turns out *not* to be the case: "I lean more towards Kayla," were my exact words. Second, recall that it was Kayla who greeted me upon my return to the Spirit Realm after the end of my previous life (i.e., my life as a soldier in WWII). This is totally consistent with my statement above that I seem to favor Kayla because she's "more loving and warmer" – it would stand to reason that if I do have two Spirit Guides, then the one designated to greet me during my crossover would be the one I felt a greater affinity for. What is interesting is that, although I was totally unaware of Kayla's existence before undergoing hypnosis, and although I think the world of Megan in my present life, it is *Kayla* whom I seem to prefer, and who materialized to greet me upon my return to the Spirit Realm; and it turned out that her being there did, in fact, make more sense once all the details were known about my two guides. Any pronouncements made under LBL hypnosis that fly in the face of the subject's known beliefs and preferences are, to my mind, strong indications that what the LBL subject is saying is *not* a product of his/her imagination or fantasies.

Amy: Describe the surroundings of this place [*i.e., the Place of Life Selection*].

John: I feel like it's an amphitheater, or has a round dome, like a planetarium. You view the scenes on the ceiling, on the round ceiling.

Amy: How many choices were there available to you?

John: I think there were several, or at least a few. I think I'm blocking the others out, because I'm afraid I would have regrets, but those regrets would be ill-founded, because… what I'm getting is that I would have gone astray with those other choices. They were less difficult, would have led me back to my old ways, and I think that is why I chose this one, ultimately. I knew what I needed to do. I was afraid of it, but I went with what I knew I needed to bring me here, but it would have been nice to do it the other way. It would have been fun.

Amy: What would you say was your primary mission in this life?

John: Containment, discipline. *Self*-discipline. And self-awareness. I was very superficial previously. I never went inside. Everything was external. Physical. Material. So limited.

Amy: What did you do just before leaving the Spirit World, before you incarnated?

John: Said goodbye to my friends. Spent a lot of time alone with my wife. We were looking forward to spending a life together after the last one where we didn't. Saying, "Make sure we hook up. Make sure we hook up. Don't want to miss it." Her telling me to behave myself and be careful and think.

Recall the following segment from Chapter 7: *After the soul decides upon one of the several alternatives of life situations presented in the Place of Life Selection there usually follows a final "dress rehearsal" - involving their Guide, specialist souls called "prompters," and the soul mates who will play major roles in that lifetime - to review particular important aspects of that lifetime and to go over the circumstances under which the souls will meet, as well as certain cues that will aid them in recognizing one another.* I find very interesting the degree to which my LBL session followed this pattern: After my visit to the Place of Life Selection and immediately before reincarnating I describe a meeting with my wife – my primary soul mate – where we are clearly going over the importance of recognizing each other during our earth existence.

Amy: Were there any triggers or clues that were given to help you remember what you wanted to do in this life?

John: Yes. And I was aware of them. (Laughs). It's crazy. It's insane!

Amy: What's crazy?

John: Oh, God. It's crazy. I knew this. I knew it consciously, and yet.... seeing it like this is unbelievable. I loved that show as a kid ... and as an adult.

Amy: What show?

John: The Twilight Zone. And it made me want to write. I love Rod Serling. He's my idol. I always say that I learned my morality from that show, and I did. And it was there for that in my life, but also, too, it gave me the desire to write, to create like that, the way he did. God, how could it be? That TV show was so important to my life. And it is to this day. I'm looking for little, subtle clues, and it's this huge thing. And it's been with me all along.

Amy: Before we close and leave the Spirit World, take a look around and tell me if there's anything else you'd like to explore.

John: No.

Amy: As we get ready to leave this high realm of your soul and the beautiful existence in the Spirit World, remember that this loving world is always with you.

I cannot think of a more appropriate way to end this section of my book than with Amy's last statement. Indeed, Amy's remark reflects in many ways what I consider to be one of the most important messages I am trying to relay: namely, that we can derive great comfort, wisdom, guidance, and practical benefits by simply remembering, as Amy says, "that this loving world" – the Spirit Realm – is always with us. But before we can *remember* it, we first must be *aware* of it. That is why books about the Spirit Realm – particularly Michael Newton's *Journey of Souls* and *Destiny of Souls* – are so important. These books provide the means for us to break through the amnesia imposed upon us at birth and allow us to recall our true nature and our true home in that "loving world." Once we are aware of who we really are and why we are here, we will then be better equipped to live our lives in ways that further our spiritual growth, while at the same time enhancing our life experience (as well as that of others) here on Earth. Knowing that we are eternal souls and that our purpose is to love others and acquire knowledge can have a dramatic effect on our priorities and beliefs, and on how we conduct our lives. Learning this – or, more accurately, *relearning it* – is the first step toward awakening.

The second step in the awakening process is to understand the stage on which the drama of our physical lives occurs. What is the *true nature* of our physical reality, and how does it correlate with the Spirit Realm and reincarnation? These are the subjects addressed in Part III of this book.

Part III

A Model of Reality

Something unknown is doing we-don't-know-what.

- Sir Arthur Eddington, astrophysicist

This whole world is a phantasmagoria, an amazing illusion, a weaving of smoke.

- Alan Watts, philosopher

Who is to say what is real and what is not? 'Real' is a distinction of a naïve mind. I think we're getting beyond that.

- Terence McKenna, author

The picture of the universe as a machine, subject to a few laws discovered by a bunch of guys in powdered wigs – that's ridiculous. You've got to be kidding.

- Terence McKenna, author

Chapter 13

Our Perception of Reality

The world which we perceive is a tiny fraction of the world which we can perceive, which is a tiny fraction of the perceivable world.

- Terence McKenna, Author

Perception is a brain-dependent, species-dependent, and often culture- and mythology- dependent experience. It has nothing to do with fundamental reality.

- Deepak Chopra, M.D., Author

The perceiving self is the primary datum.

- Terence McKenna, Author

There are certain things that most of us instinctively and unconsciously take for granted. Whether it is because they are so unquestionably obvious or because they are so conspicuously omnipresent, we accept them without question or thought. Yet it is often the case that these axiomatically accepted "givens" are not the fundamental truths they were assumed to be; furthermore, if we can climb outside the box and look at such suppositions objectively, we frequently discover that questioning these assumptions leads to significant breakthroughs in thinking and understanding. Such is the case, I believe, with the nature of reality.

Reality is all around us, it is the environment in which we exist. It is ever-present, patently detectable by the senses, and so fundamentally basic to our existence that the majority of us barely, if at all, give it a second thought. Speaking for myself, the idea to even contemplate the nature of reality, let alone question it, never crossed my mind until I was well into my 30's. Reality, to me, was so primal, apparent, and self-evident that the very notion of speculating about its nature would have seemed ridiculous. But as my mind began to open as a result of my exposure to new and exotic concepts, I found that challenging fundamental truths was not only acceptable but was, in fact, a necessary activity if one was serious about expanding one's awareness, intellect and reason. My interest in mathematics and physics encouraged this mindset further as I learned of some rather bizarre concepts in these fields that appeared to defy "common sense." (These concepts will be discussed in Chapter 14: Cracks in the Foundation of Our Understanding of Reality).

In Chapter 6 I mentioned three questions which represent, for many, the three great mysteries of life: "Where do we come from before we're born?", "Where do we go after we die?", and "Why are we here?" That last question – "*Why are we here?*" – begs yet a fourth question: "What, precisely, *is* 'here'?" Or, more accurately, "What is the true nature of the reality in which we find ourselves?"

Part III – the current part – of this book, entitled "A Model of Reality", is a musing on the possibility that our external reality might not be the solid, objective reality we have been led to believe. The model of reality that will be discussed and explored here – and which, by the way, is embraced by many scientists – is commonly referred to as the "Holographic Model." But before we can look at the details of this model, some background information will first be necessary.

13.1 Input: The Five Senses

For quite some time, the dominant view regarding the nature of reality has been the materialist view – "Materialism." According to this theory, all of reality is composed of either matter or energy, and all phenomena – including consciousness – is nothing more than the result of material interactions.[124] As mentioned in the introduction, the reality in which we exist, and, more specifically, the materialist view of our reality, is usually taken completely for granted, often to the extent of being accepted without any thought or scrutiny. Yet there are some very reliable reasons to suspect that the materialist view may be inherently flawed. Quantum physics – the branch of physics that studies the behavior of matter and energy at the molecular, atomic and subatomic levels – has produced some rather strange and counterintuitive findings that seriously call into question the materialist doctrine. That aspect will be discussed in detail in later chapters. Yet another, more accessible, reason to question the materialist view is the fact that our *concept* of reality is a direct result of our *perceptions* of reality, and these perceptions are determined by our five senses – what we can see, hear, touch, taste, and smell – and processing performed by our brain.

The simple fact is that we have no way of knowing if our experience of "reality" – as presented to us by those five senses – is an accurate representation of the "true" reality. After all, our sensory input is received through our sensory organs (eyes, ears, etc.) and then that inputted information is processed by our brain. This realization leads to two critically important questions: (1) Do our sensory organs comprehend external reality in a way that is accurate and reliable?; and (2) How much "editing" is our brain performing on the raw data it has input before those data are translated into our experience of reality? Most of us, myself included, have given little, if any, thought to these questions: we see a chair in front of us and we assume that the chair exists "out there" in "reality" exactly as we perceive it. There is good cause, however, to think that the situation might not be quite that simple.

First of all, we know from everyday experience that our perceptions can be unreliable: the earth *appears* flat to us, yet – contrary to what we perceive – we know that the Earth is round; the Sun *appears* to revolve around the earth, yet we know the reverse is true; matter appears solid, but is actually 99.999% empty space, and the piece that is not empty space is itself not solid material; the ground upon which we stand feels stable and stationary, yet we know that it is spinning and flying through space at incredible speed. These examples suggest that "reality" and what we *perceive* as reality may be two totally different things.

Let's start by considering how our perception of reality occurs, from a biological perspective. Our sensory organs contain sensory receptor nerve cells which can detect stimulus energy received through those organs from the external environment. These stimuli can be, for example, light (detected by photoreceptive cells, as in the eyes), pressure (detected by mechanoreceptive cells, as in the ears), or tastes and smells (detected by chemoreceptive cells, as in the tongue and nose). Those stimulus energies are decoded into electrical signals which are then passed to the brain via nerves. The brain processes those signals and, through a process of association, assigns meaning to them. The meaning deduced from that external-environment stimulus energy, by our brain, is our perception of reality.

Consider our sense of sight as an example. Light is the stimulus energy our eyes detect when we "see," and the visual sensory receptors of the eye are located in the retina. Humans can detect light in the roughly 400 - 700 nm range (1 nm = 1 nanometer = 1 billionth of a meter); light in this range is referred to as "visible light." The overall electromagnetic spectrum runs from approximately 10^{-3} nm (gamma rays) to 10^{12} nm (radio waves). Visible light represents only a very, very small portion of the overall electromagnetic spectrum, less than one-percent. Light outside of the visible light range is not perceivable by us, yet such light represents the bulk of the electromagnetic spectrum, and that huge portion of "reality" is not part of our selective reality because it is not detectable by our visual sensory apparatus. It's not that that reality does not exist, but, rather, it is simply beyond our range of perception. When considering the small portion of the electromagnetic spectrum that we can perceive as compared with the electromagnetic spectrum in its entirety, it is not an exaggeration to state that humans are virtually blind in this energy domain.

Bees are capable of seeing a broader spectrum of light than humans can, and therefore their experience of "reality" is much different than ours. This fact is dramatically illustrated when we compare photos of flowers taken in natural light (what *we* can see) with photos taken in ultraviolet light (what *bees* can see): an

Evening Primrose flower to our eye appears as solid yellow, but to a bee it is pinkish-white with a bright red center. That red-appearing center has a practical purpose; namely, to draw the bee to the pollen and nectar. But that aspect of the reality of the flower is hidden from us and is thus not part of our experience. Likewise, as anyone who has ever owned a dog knows, dogs can smell scents and hear sounds beyond the sensory range of humans. Snakes can detect infrared radiation, bats use ultrasound, dolphins use sonar. The point is that there is a huge chunk of reality "out there" that is denied to us simply because of the limitations of our sensory organs.

13.2 Processing: The Brain

Our perception of reality can be further restricted or distorted by factors other than the limitations of our sensory organs. Recall, from our discussion of how we perceive reality, that stimulus energy is taken in by our sense organs and decoded into electrical signals that are passed to the brain where they are then processed into our perception of reality. In the case of the sense of sight, those electrical signals are edited and changed by the temporal portion of our brain lobe (the part of the brain that, among other things, interprets visual stimuli) before being sent to our visual cortex (the part of the cerebral cortex, located in the back of the brain, responsible for processing visual information).[125] Research indicates that our brain uses "context-sensitive predictions" in an attempt to interpret what an image might represent, then assigns a "best guess interpretation" of what the viewed object is – and then the person *sees that object.*[126] Indeed, there is evidence to suggest that about half of what we "see" is, in truth, the result of this prediction/best-guess process of the brain piecing together our perception of reality.[127]

The extent to which our brain is responsible for what we "see" is dramatically revealed by experiments performed by neuroscientist Paul Bach-y-Rita in neuroplasticity and sensory substitution and his efforts to treat patients with neurological-related disabilities. Sensory substitution involves processes intended to transform the characteristics of one sensory modality into stimuli of another sensory modality in the hope that such sensory substitution can help handicapped people to utilize sensory information from a functioning sensory modality in lieu of that lost due to their defective sensory faculty.

One such experiment suggested that signals sent to the brain from the skin were being processed in the visual cortex, thus allowing blind subjects to "see" via touch stimuli. In the experiment, people who had been blind from birth sat in a specially designed chair containing a bank of four hundred vibrating plates resting against the blind user's back. The plates were connected to a video camera via a computer which converted the camera-captured video into vibrations in the plates, thus creating a pixelated representation of the video image in the form of skin-sensed vibration patterns. What is interesting is that, after some usage, the blind subjects were able to recognize objects, via the felt stimulation patterns, with surprising detail, even to the extent of experiencing their perceptual episode as occurring in a 3D space in front of them, rather than on the surface of their skin. The results of this experiment led Bach-y-Rita to declare, "We see with our brains, not our eyes." In a similar experiment employing stimulation of the tongue, which is rich with tactile nerve endings, a blindfolded subject was able to reach out and catch a rolling ball simply using the rerouted sensory-substituted stimuli from her tongue.[128] While these findings offer much promise for people with cognitive disabilities, they also strikingly illustrate the extent to which our brain and sensory apparatus system interpret and modify the sensory data by which we perceive our environment.

A striking example of how our sensory organs and brain can restrict or distort our perception of reality is the phenomenon known as perceptual blindness (also called inattentional blindness). Perceptual blindness refers to a situation wherein a person fails to notice an unexpected stimulus, even though it is in his or her field of vision, because their attention is focused on other activities. The extent to which one can totally miss something that is glaringly obvious is mind-boggling, and a bit frightening. A fascinating illustration of this can be found in a video clip widely available on the internet known as the "Selective Attention Test" – it can be viewed at YouTube (just Google "Selective Attention Test").

As much as I'd like to discuss the details of this test, I don't want to give anything away and ruin it for people who want to take the test fairly. Suffice it to say that the first time I took the test, I completely missed the "unexpected stimulus," and when I viewed the clip later, knowing what to look for, I simply couldn't believe that I had missed it. In most groups of test subjects, 50% of the subjects did not notice the unexpected stimulus. As I said, it's a bit frightening. But it says a lot about how inaccurate our perception of reality can be.

An experiment exploring how our brain adjusts to visual distortion of reality that has gained wide public exposure in recent years, and has been much repeated, is the inversion goggles experiment. In the experiment a subject wears a specially designed pair of goggles that causes the wearer to see everything upside-down. Needless to say, the sense of disorientation caused by such goggles is extreme enough to make navigation and the performance of simple, routine acts virtually impossible (videos of people wearing such goggles are available on the internet, and they are both humorous and fascinating). Similar studies have been done using goggles that transpose right with left. What is interesting is the discovery that, after wearing such goggles for a matter of weeks, the subjects find that their brains have somehow adapted to the unnatural situation so that everything appears normal – so much so that subjects are even able to perform complex tasks such as riding a bicycle while wearing the goggles. Thus the brain has taken the distorted visual stimulus, as input by the eyes, and altered it to such a degree that the human subject is now responding to that altered version of reality.[129]

Distortions in our perception of reality are not limited to our sense of sight. It turns out that our sense of hearing can also be subject to imprecise interpretations of external stimuli (auditory stimuli, in this case). In an article in *The New Yorker* (Jan. 28, 2013) entitled "Music To Your Ears" which discusses the technological pursuit of 3D sound production, author Adam Gopnik relates a story told to him by scientist Edgar Choueiri about an experiment conducted at Carnegie Hall during World War I in which people listened to an operatic soprano and a tinny-sounding Victrola recording, both hidden from the audience's view; surprisingly, the listeners were unable to distinguish the recording from the live performance. Mr. Gopnik's summary of the experiment is quite revealing: "The audience's will to hear perfect sound mattered as much as the perfection of the sound heard. And it's alarmingly easy to mistake the apprehended sound for the actual signal."[130] What is pertinent to our discussion is Mr. Gopnik's observation that our *will* to hear will effect what we *perceive* we hear, so much so that it can change our perception of the actual sound to match our expectation or intention. Again, as with the visual examples discussed previously, this calls into question the accuracy and reliability of what we hear, or, in truth, what we *think we hear*.

Further along in the same article, Mr. Gopnik relates a conversation he had with Daniel Levitin, a producer and sound engineer in the music industry who went on to study psychology and neuroscience and who heads up a lab studying music at McGill University in Montreal. During their conversation, Mr. Levitin explained that the soundboard on most pianos isn't long enough to produce the lowest notes (i.e., the bottom octave), so those notes are "actually inferred rather than heard" by the brain's neurons firing at the correct frequency of the missing notes via association with the notes' overtones, which the piano can produce.[131] A similar situation exists with regard to male voices and most telephones, wherein the brain fills in missing information due to an inability of telephone speakers to accurately reproduce the fundamental frequency of a male voice, which is too low.[132] Thus we have situations in which the brain *infers* sounds that are not actually heard, and *fills in* missing auditory information.

Another interesting (and amusing) example of a misperception of reality is when our perceptions are fooled. I recall seeing a 3D movie at an Imax theater wherein one scene took place in the hold of a ship where wet chains were hanging down; the scene was incredibly realistic, and with the 3D technology it appeared as if the chains were hanging right in front of me. In fact, the impression was so realistic that I could see people in the theater reaching out with their hands as if to touch the chains. I was even doing it myself, without realizing it! I was laughing aloud at the fact that so many of us had been fooled into thinking that the chains were really there, even though we *knew* that they weren't. Another Imax 3D experience I had involved a movie scene filmed from the perspective of a biplane that was flying over New York City among the skyscrapers. I'm a bit leery of heights, and the 3D effect was so vivid and lifelike that my heart began racing and I instinctively grabbed my seat. Then I thought to myself, "This is ridiculous; I'm sitting in a movie theater ... not flying over Manhattan." Nevertheless, in spite of me *knowing for a fact* that what I was seeing was not real, my anxiety and racing heart continued until the scene ended. One final but very humorous example occurred during my military service. At this particular point in my service I was a commissioned officer in the U.S. Army stationed in West Germany. A travelling fair was making a stop in a nearby city and, since my duty assignment was a missile base in a rural area with few forms of available entertainment, most of the soldiers in my unit were eager to attend. One of the attractions at the fair was housed in a huge tent with folding chairs set up in the center and a great many movie screens placed in a wide circle around the walls of the tent. Apparently each movie clip shown had been specially filmed so that each of the screens showed the perspective from the center looking out in that particular direction. The overall effect was astonishing – it actually felt like you were inside of and experiencing the activity appearing on the screens. In one clip the perspective was from inside a boat moving along a body of water. At one point a water skier zooms by and, turning, splashes water in the viewer's direction. Well, *everyone* in the theater simultaneously screamed and threw up their hands in an effort to block the water! But best of all was another clip that portrayed a ride on a roller coaster. When the rollercoaster went through a complete 360° loop, one of the men in my unit was so caught up in the experience that he and his folding chair flipped over backwards! Everyone was laughing hysterically, not only at his slapstick tumble but also because they could fully sympathize with how and why it had happened.

At the time, I was merely amused by the situations above, but now I see a more serious side to them; namely, the fact that, *in spite of possessing certain knowledge to the contrary, our minds can be fooled into believing that an artificially created illusion is actual reality*. Once we realize that this is possible, we have to ask ourselves: *"What else is our mind misinterpreting as 'reality'?"* And furthermore: *"Is the everyday 'reality' we experience actually an interpretation, by our senses and brains, of something utterly different from how it appears?"* These are uncomfortable questions to consider, but they are vitally important if we are to understand the reason for, and purpose of, our existence. For, if human beings *do* have a purpose, then the reality in which we exist must play a key role in that purpose – after all, it is the setting and stage for the human drama that is being played out.

13.3 Output: A Perceived Reality

In titling the sections contained within this chapter I've used the terms that broadly represent how a computer does its work, namely: Input, Process, and Output. Data (information) are received by a computer through one or more of its input devices (mouse, keyboard, etc.), the data are processed by the computer's CPU (central processing unit), and the results of that processing are displayed as output through one or more output devices (monitor, printer, etc). As we've seen, our body perceives reality in much the same manner. Our sensory organs acts as input devices effecting input of data (stimulus energies), our brain processes those data, and the output is our perception of reality. And that is the critical point that can be easily overlooked: our "reality" is a *perceived* reality – the result of an intermediate processing phase performed by our brain – it is not a direct experience of reality. The disquieting truth is that *the reality we experience takes place in our mind*, not in our external environment. There is no guarantee that the external, objective reality and our perception of that reality are one and the same. As we've seen in the previous sections, the way in which we perceive reality is subject to limitations of the sensory organs, and also to distortions or misapprehensions caused by the brain due to a variety of factors. Thus the picture of reality that we are getting may be neither complete nor accurate. And once we become aware of *some* situations in which our sensory-perceptual system presents us with an imperfect or imprecise picture of reality, it is inevitable that we begin to wonder how much *else* of our perceived reality is untrustworthy and unreliable. To what degree are our senses and brain modifying whatever-it-is that is "out there"? Is it possible that the true external reality is vastly different from the "reality' we perceive? And if it is, then exactly *what is* that external reality? And why are we designed to modify it into an experience that is perceptually different from its true nature? These are huge questions, and they are unsettling questions. Nevertheless, they are questions to which I intend to provide definitive answers.

To return to the computer analogy for a moment, consider what is happening when you use your computer to access the internet and visit a web page. The web page appears on your monitor screen and you read the text and view the pictures presented therein. But let's just take a few seconds to really think about that web page: What is it, exactly? And for that matter, *where* is it? That web page does not exist – in the physical sense – *anywhere*. There is no actual physical representation of that page *out there*. The web page is a visual construct created out of binary digits – 1's and 0's – which themselves are merely translations of electrical signals. The entire web page is a phantasm – it exists in perception only, yet it contains meaningful information that you can comprehend and it contains visual images that you can see. Nonetheless, in truth, that web page has no physical existence; it is the result of the computer inputting electrical signals, processing them, and artificially creating output which is the web page: input – process – output. Sound familiar?

It turns out that there is a model of reality which suggests that what we *perceive* as "reality" may be no more substantial than a web page, that our "reality" might very well be nothing more than an energy-information construct which is processed by our brain and converted into what we experience as "physical reality." This model has many adherents in the scientific community, and it boasts some very convincing scientific evidence to support it. We will explore that model in great detail in Chapter 17. Before we do, however, let's first take a look at some fascinating situations from mathematics and science that strongly suggest that the scientific edifice upon which our "concrete" reality stands may contain some serious cracks.

Chapter 14

Cracks in the Foundation
of Our Understanding of Reality

The laws of Nature are but the mathematical thoughts of God.

- Euclid, mathematician

As far as the laws of mathematics refer to reality, they are not certain; as far as they are certain, they do not refer to reality.

- Albert Einstein, physicist

"Contrariwise," continued Tweedledee, "if it was so, it might be, and if it were so, it would be; but as it isn't, it ain't. That's logic!"

- Lewis Carroll, "Through the Looking Glass"

[T]here are known knowns; there are things we know we know. We also know there are known unknowns; that is to say, we know there are some things we do not know. But there are also unknown unknowns – the ones we don't know we don't know.

- Donald Rumsfeld, U.S. Secretary of Defense (2002)

The conjuring rod of reason turns out to be fairly weak magic, after all.

- Terence McKenna, author

This chapter deals with several thought-provoking topics that I find absolutely fascinating and riveting, and about which, in some cases, I feel very passionate.

We are going to delve into select areas of science and mathematics, and the purpose of this seeming digression is two-fold. First, we will look at some scientific and mathematical concepts that support the thesis that our reality may be much different than we perceive it to be. We will see that, as science and mathematics probe deeper into an understanding of "reality", their findings become ever more bizarre and unreal, and the notion of a concrete, deterministic reality becomes ever more fanciful. The second aim of this chapter is to examine select areas of science and math that suggest inherent limitations, weaknesses, or inaccuracies in these fields. This last point, I feel, requires further elaboration, lest my intentions be misconstrued. I think it is important to note that my intention here is *not* to bash science and/or mathematics. Far from it – I harbor a deep love of mathematics and a deep respect and awe for the discoveries made by science. However, I believe it is important to realize three things about math and science: (1) These two fields of knowledge are not perfect – they are incomplete and still evolving, and they may have flaws; (2) They are not the exclusive arbiters of "truth" (as they often claim to be); and (3) As knowledge in these fields increases and fuels attempts to understand the nature of reality, the findings become ever more unconventional and outlandish and, interestingly, they also become more in sync with millennia-old concepts of ancient wisdom traditions and with ideas expressed by near-death experiencers and life-between-lives hypnosis subjects.

The overall premise being presented here is that the old and long-held scientific notion of a concrete, physical, deterministic, clockwork reality is being proved untenable by science itself, and the old process of scientific reductionism is inadequate and unsatisfactory as a method for studying a reality that is clearly holistic and interconnected. My contention here is not that science and mathematics are "wrong" but, rather, that they are incomplete, and that they are hampered by a false belief that they *are* complete. An honest search for knowledge and understanding involves a healthy combination of open-mindedness and skepticism. But we must remember that open-mindedness does not mean naive gullibility, and skepticism does not mean dogmatic denial. Indeed, the etymology of the word "skepticism" involves the notions of inquiry and contemplation as well as uncertainty; the moment we think that we have all the answers is the moment when our pursuit of knowledge stagnates and the truth becomes lost in the unreachable realms residing beyond the periphery of our tunnel vision.

With that philosophy in mind, let's have a look at some of the amazing, stimulating, and mind-boggling concepts that have emerged from the fields of science and mathematics.

For whatever reason, the structure and processes of our reality are capable of being expressed and understood through the mental activity known as mathematics. Pythagoras, the Greek philosopher of circa 500 BC, famously stated, "All is number," and Isaac Newton, considered by many to be the most brilliant human being of all time, believed that "God is a mathematician." These statements derive from a fact with which all of us are familiar, namely, that everything in the physical universe appears to be capable of being described in the language of mathematics: motion, weather, finance, gambling, electricity, genetics, music ... seemingly every aspect of our material experience is expressible and describable by mathematical formulae. Indeed, the relationship between mathematics and reality is so obviously ubiquitous that we take that relationship as being axiomatic. But it is precisely because that relationship is accepted as a "given" that a hugely important question often goes unconsidered: *Why* does mathematics so accurately describe the world in which we live? And a related question: Why are our minds so constructed that we are *able to comprehend* mathematical concepts? As Albert Einstein wisely observed: "The most incomprehensible thing about the world is that it is comprehensible." We often take the comprehensibility of the world for granted. And we also take for granted the fact that mathematics is the agency through which such comprehensibility is possible.

Reality seems to be made up of things that are "sensible" (i.e., things that can be perceived by the five senses) and things that are intelligible (i.e., things that can be perceived only via mind). The intelligible things are incorporeal, but can be perceived indirectly by how they manifest in the physical world. Mathematics is an example of an intelligible thing ("time" may be another). The thesis developed throughout the previous chapter is that our human consciousness creates our reality. We know that mathematics is the language by which that reality can be described. And we also know that mathematics is a mental phenomenon, a conceptualized system of abstract ideas and formulations. Thus it is perhaps not so amazing that *mathematics* is the language of *reality* – they are both, after all, products of mind. Reality and the language that describes reality share the same source – human consciousness.

Isaac Newton's discovery of the laws of motion and universal gravitation in the 17th century set the stage for the belief in a "clockwork universe" – the mechanistic notion that the universe is akin to a huge machine running with the gear-driven precision and predictability of a mechanical timepiece. Newton's findings also strongly suggested that mathematics was the language that best described how that clockwork universe ran. Later scientific findings, such as James Clerk Maxwell's equations describing electricity, magnetism, and optics, only served to further confirm the seeming truth of the clockwork universe doctrine. For some reason, there appeared to be a direct relationship between abstract mathematics and the way things in the physical world worked.

Mathematics has long been known as "The Queen of Science" because it is the basis for all the other sciences. Mathematics is also known as the "exact science" because it is built upon a foundation of logic and proof. But how "exact" a science *is* mathematics? And how solid is the foundation upon which it is built? Mathematician and philosopher Bertrand Russell described mathematics as, "The subject in which we never know what we are talking about, nor whether what we are saying is true."[133] While I'm sure that Dr. Russell intended a degree of facetiousness in this statement, there is nevertheless an element of truth lurking behind the humor, for there is serious evidence suggesting that mathematics – the language describing how the clockwork operates – may be less than "exact", and that subatomic particles – the components making up the clockwork – are not completely predictable.

14.1 Caveat

Before we dive into this chapter's content, I'd like to take a moment to make some observations concerning how most authors typically introduce similar material and how I intend to differ from such practices.

It has been my experience, on occasions too numerous to mention, that whenever an author is about to discuss a topic that involves mathematics they inevitably preface that discussion using some combination of the following:

- They make some lame joke about how "difficult" math is and how most people "loathe" and "fear" it.
- They apologize for including material involving math in their book.
- They offer the reader the option of skipping past the math section if he/she should find it too intimidating or difficult.

This chapter is devoted in its entirety to a discussion of topics from the fields of mathematics and science, and I intend to employ none of the above excusatory dodges. Indeed, I emphatically propose an attitude that is completely in opposition to those unfortunate and ridiculous notions. Here is *my* preamble to this material:

- The concepts covered in this chapter are fascinating in the extreme, and I am certain you will find them exciting, engrossing and thought-provoking; rather than fearing them, you should embrace them with a vigor and hunger for personal edification and for the acquisition of exhilarating new ideas.
- The concepts are not difficult, and I am confident that your mental acuity is more than adequate to understand them; I think most readers will find the material *new* and *non-ordinary*, and as such might require some contemplation and/or a second read-through, but it is by no means above anyone's head; therefore, any inordinate difficulty you may encounter reflects an inadequacy on *my* part, not on yours.
- I make absolutely no apologies for including mathematics and science in my book; these fields represent a very important aspect of the methods we employ in our attempt to understand and conceptualize our reality; math and science are essential elements in any discussion of the nature of reality.

- Finally, I implore you *not* to skip over this chapter: not only are these topics vitally essential to the discussion at hand, but they are also mind-expanding, intriguing, and stimulating; the intellectual rewards offered by such material more than compensates for any challenges faced while endeavoring to comprehend it. Whether or not you consider yourself to be "good at" math (whatever that means), I feel certain that you will find the topics discussed in this chapter to be fascinating and provocative.

Constant references to the presumed notion that most people find mathematics impossibly complex and morbidly dreadful is insulting to our intelligence and serves to promote that false belief ever deeper. I refuse to participate in such intellectually elitist bullshit. Don't let anyone convince you that you might not be smart enough to understand something, and that, therefore, it is permissible, or even advisable, for you to avoid it. Jump in with both feet and give it a go. Am I saying that we will all understand everything we read? No, of course not. If anything, I've found that the more I learn, the more I become aware of how much I *don't* understand. But that doesn't deter me from *trying* to learn more and to understand more. If I read something and, after I've finished, I find that I've understood only 20% of it, then that's 20% more knowledge I've acquired; and perhaps the next thing I read – or the next time I read that same thing – I'll understand a little bit more. Don't sell yourself short, and, most definitely, *don't let anyone else sell you short*.

Okay, that's my view on this. So now, let's dive in and see what mathematics and science have to contribute to our discussion.

14.2 Not Exactly Exact – Hairline Cracks in the Foundation

I've noted previously in this book that I have long held a love and a fascination for mathematics, precisely for the reasons that it is considered an "exact science" – I greatly admire the structure, formality, logic, and exactitude inherent in mathematics, and I derive a sense of comfort and security from math's stable concreteness and mechanistic precision. It was thus that, as a mathematics major in college, I was shocked and disheartened when I began to discover subtle mathematical facts that not only defied common sense but also appeared to violate some basic concepts of mathematics itself. It was then that I first began to suspect that mathematics – the "exact science" – was not exactly exact.

$$1^{\infty}$$

My personal descent into mathematical demoralization began while taking a course in Advanced Calculus as an undergraduate math major. I had noticed in the course's textbook a statement to the effect that one raised to the infinity power (i.e., 1^{∞}) is *undefined*, which in the mathematical sense means that the expression has no meaning and thus can have no value assigned to it. This baffled me since, to my understanding, the number 1 raised to any power should be equal to 1. Recall from your own math studies that exponents, or "powers", refers to how many times a number should be multiplied by itself: so, for example, $3^2 = 3 \times 3 = 9$ (i.e., 3 multiplied by itself two times), while $2^5 = 2 \times 2 \times 2 \times 2 \times 2 = 32$. The number 1 has the unique property that 1 multiplied by itself is 1, regardless of how many factors (multipliers) of 1 are considered; thus:

$1^2 = 1 \times 1 = 1$, and $1^7 = 1 \times 1 \times 1 \times 1 \times 1 \times 1 \times 1 = 1$.

In fact, even $1^{1,000,000} = 1$, that is, "one to the one-millionth power equals one." This derives from the fact that the number 1 is the "multiplicative identity" which is a fancy way of saying that multiplying any number by 1 leaves that number's value unchanged. So, naturally, when I read in my advanced calculus textbook that one raised to the infinity power (i.e., 1^∞) is undefined, I was aghast! Common sense, logic, the mathematical concept of exponents, and the mathematical definition of the multiplicative identity all suggested – to my way of thinking – that 1^∞ should be equal to 1. After all, *no matter how many times you multiply one by itself, the result you get must equal to one.*

One day after class I approached my professor and explained my befuddlement over this "one-to-the-infinity-power" enigma. I opened the book to the page containing the ghastly assertion and, pointing, said, "The book states that one to the infinity power is undefined, but I think it should be one."

"No," he said calmly, "It's undefined."

"But isn't one raised to any power equal to one?" I asked, confused.

"Yes," he agreed.

"Then I would think that one to the infinity power should equal to one," I reiterated.

"No," he said, shaking his head, "it's undefined."

"But *why*?" I persisted, seeking a meaningful explanation for this conundrum.

"Because it's defined that way," he replied.

That was the answer my advanced calculus professor gave me: One to the infinity power is undefined because it's defined that way; in other words, his explanation was: it's *defined as being undefined.* To say that I felt the earth lurch and wobble beneath my feet would be an understatement. *This is not mathematics*, I thought; at least not mathematics as *I* considered it to be – namely rational, structured, and precise. My professor's "explanation" struck me as being some sort of demented circular logic and carnival sleight-of-hand. It most certainly did not seem like mathematics. Either that, or there was an even more disturbing possibility: *mathematics was not what I thought it to be.*

I've since learned that mathematics, and physics, (which is, in large part, applied mathematics) possess yet more unsettling qualities of inexactitude that call into question the lofty pedestal-position they have been granted as the undisputed expositors of truth and reality. Let's take a look at some of these fascinating scientific and mathematical anomalies.

Gödel's Incompleteness Theorems

In 1931 mathematician Kurt Gödel published a paper in mathematical logic that contained the proofs for two theorems that have become known as Gödel's Incompleteness Theorems. Those theorems established, in essence, that any axiomatic system which is capable of arithmetic is either incomplete (meaning there are true statements that cannot be proved or disproved from axioms within the system) or it is inconsistent (meaning that the system could lead to a contradiction; i.e., it is possible to have a statement that can be proved both true and false simultaneously).[134]

While many erroneous conclusions have been drawn from Gödel's Theorems (such as the ridiculous suggestion that mathematics and science have been rendered fallacious), the more sober truth is that Gödel's findings have brought to a halt the dreams of Hilbert, Whitehead, and others of establishing a rigidly formal axiomatic basis for mathematics. Moreover, Gödel's Theorems also appear to end any hope of finding the holy grail of physics – a Theory of Everything (ToE) that would fully explain and link together all known physical phenomena. The idea of a ToE derives from Hilbert's sixth problem, presented in 1900, where he tasked physicists to develop an axiomatic basis to all of physics. However, as a direct result of Gödel's Incompleteness Theorems, many prominent physicists – including Freeman Dyson and Stephen Hawking – now believe that finding such a Theory of Everything is impossible.[135]

All of a sudden, with the discovery of Gödel's Incompleteness Theorems, the satisfying precision of the clockwork universe begins to seem a bit rusty: mathematics – the "exact science" that is built upon pillars of immutable logic and indisputable proof – is either incomplete or inconsistent; and esteemed physicists now consider the long-sought goal of physics – a Theory of Everything – to be unattainable. Since mathematics describes and likely determines our physical reality, Gödel's Incompleteness Theorems hint at some rather alarming possibilities regarding the nature and structure of reality itself.

A fascinating take on Gödel's Incompleteness Theorems comes from esteemed philosopher Alan Watts. According to Mr. Watts, Gödel's Theorems suggest that the axioms that serve as the foundation for any logical system must come from a *higher system* – that is, they cannot be formulated from within the system they support. This interpretation is particularly interesting in light of our discussion of Plato's Cave from Chapter 15: perhaps the *higher system* to which Mr. Watts alludes is, in fact, a *higher reality*, of which our reality is merely a shadow. That could explain why these axioms are not provable or disprovable within their given system, and also why such axioms are considered in mathematics to be "self-evident truths." You may recall from your own study of high school geometry that Euclid constructed the entire system of plane geometry from five basic axioms, each of which was unprovable and considered self-evident (although "self-evident" is a bit of a stretch in the case of the so-called parallel postulate – but that's another story). It is quite possible that the fundamental assumptions upon which any body of knowledge is built – or, for that matter, *the cornerstones of any facet of our reality* – must originate in a higher reality; i.e., they are the higher-order objects which serve as the sources for the shadow-objects that make up our lower-order reality. This thesis might also explain the mysterious behavior and ethereal nature of subatomic particles as set forth in the two doctrines from quantum physics known as Heisenberg's Uncertainty Principle and the Copenhagen Interpretation.

Heisenberg's Uncertainty Principle and the Copenhagen Interpretation

In 1927 physicist Werner Heisenberg published a fact about subatomic particles (such as electrons) that flies in the face of our everyday worldly experience. Heisenberg's Uncertainty Principle (also known as the principle of indeterminacy) states that the more precisely the position of a subatomic particle is determined, the less precisely its momentum is known in that instant, and vice versa. In other words, any attempt to measure the velocity of a subatomic particle will cause it to move in an unpredictable manner, thus making a simultaneous measurement of its position impossible.[136] Thus, at the subatomic level, "[t]he very concepts of exact position and exact velocity together, in fact, have no meaning in nature."[137] The implication of this principle is that subatomic particles – the building blocks of our "solid" and "stable" reality – are never completely at rest but are, instead, in constant motion. Further muddying the waters of determinism is another quantum principle known as the Copenhagen interpretation, formulated by Heisenberg and Niels Bohr, which holds that subatomic "particles" exist *not* as precise entities but rather as states of potential whose location or motion is derived from a set of probabilities.[138]

In classical (i.e., pre-quantum) physics, particle behavior is described by Newton's equations of motion, while wave behavior is described by Maxwell's wave equations. These behaviors, being deterministic in nature, lie at the very heart of the notion of causality (the belief that the future motion of a particle can be precisely predicted if one knows its present position and momentum and all of the forces acting upon it). This is *determinism*, the bedrock philosophy underlying the concept of a clockwork universe.

Under quantum physics, however, matter behavior is calculated using Schrodinger's wave equations, the results of which are *probabilities* – that is, solving the wave equation will give a *statistical likelihood* of where the particle will *most likely* be found.[139] Hence, at the subatomic level, determinacy is not possible; if one cannot precisely assess the simultaneous position and momentum of a particle, then one cannot presume to calculate the particle's future position. In the quantum world, determinism and causality are no longer tenable concepts. The clockwork collapses.

The very idea of using words such as "incompleteness" and "uncertainty" to describe principles of mathematics and physics is unsettling, to say the least. But the sheer irony of using these words in this context dramatically drives home the point that our view of reality, even from the perspective of science, is changing in ways both striking and heretofore unimaginable.

One final point of interest: the nullification of the notions of determinism and the clockwork universe necessarily also calls into question the idea of the inevitability of fate. The probabilistic nature of quantum mechanics, coupled with the uncertainty principle, have led some to speculate that these quantum concepts might serve as the explanation for the existence of *free will*. Thus we have a potential scientific basis for yet another claim made by Life Between Lives hypnosis subjects and near-death experiencers. Albert Einstein firmly believed that, "God does not play dice with the universe." While God Itself might not play dice with the universe, it appears that humans have been granted precisely that prerogative through their ability to exercise free will.

Chaos Theory

If the uncertainties inherent in quantum theory did not completely put the notion of deterministic predictability to rest, then Chaos theory should finish the job.[140] In everyday usage the word "chaos" generally refers to randomness and disorder, but under the branch of science known as "Chaos Theory" the concept of chaos takes on a much subtler meaning. Chaos theory is also known as "dynamical system theory" because it studies the natural processes we experience in everyday life, and these processes are often erratic, fluctuating and discontinuous – altogether different from the conveniently "clean" textbook examples studied and suggested by the deterministic notions of classical physics. It is important to reiterate the fact that the dynamical systems studied by Chaos theory are *not* random; they are deterministic systems that are extremely sensitive to initial conditions, but that very hypersensitivity to initial conditions makes them unpredictable.[141] Weather patterns, the stock market, brain and heart activity – these systems, and most of real world experience, do not behave in a linear, predictable manner. The world is, in truth, largely non-linear in its behavior; yet science and mathematics, in the pre-chaos era, were hampered by a bias favoring activities that are regular, orderly and solvable. Thus the nonlinear systems exhibiting true chaos were "rarely taught and rarely learned."[142] The folly of this attitude was succinctly and emphatically expressed by physicist Enrico Fermi when he stated, "It does not say in the Bible that all laws of nature are expressible linearly!"[143] and by physicist Richard Feynman's observation that, "Nature isn't classical dammit..."[144]

The seeds of what would become Chaos theory were planted back in 1900 when mathematician Henri Poincare' noticed that classical Newtonian physics could not accurately describe planetary movement in our solar system (the "Three Body

Problem").[145] But it wasn't until the early 1960s when M.I.T. research meteorologist Edward Lorenz, while attempting to model weather turbulence using a computer, noticed that making small changes in initial conditions led to dramatically different and unpredictable outcomes. In a 1963 paper, Lorenz illustrated this phenomenon using the image of the flapping of a butterfly's wings in one part of the world dramatically affecting weather conditions thousands of miles away (e.g., a butterfly flapping its wings in the United States might cause a hurricane to occur in China). Thus this "sensitivity to initial conditions" – a hallmark of Chaos theory – became known as the "Butterfly Effect."[146] Other scientists made discoveries similar to Lorenz's and it soon became apparent that such aperiodic systems – not quite random, yet also not deterministically predictable – were ubiquitous throughout nature.[147] Indeed, with the acceptance and popularity of Chaos theory in the sciences "there has been literally a flood of papers demonstrating that chaos is more like the rule in nature, while order (= predictability) is more like the exception."[148]

The Butterfly Effect represents a death-blow to scientific determinism because it clearly implies that since it is impossible to know the exact state of all of the initial conditions in a complex system, there is no way to precisely predict the end state of the system. One very important lesson taught by the Butterfly Effect is that scientists could no longer ignore so-called "negligible effects" in their experiments and studies. But probably the most profound realization to emerge from Chaos theory was the discovery that "chaotic" behavior can arise out of surprisingly simple deterministic models, yet such behavior – seemingly random and unpredictable – actually contains a degree of underlying order and pattern. If the idea of a chaotic system possessing a substrate of order sounds like a contradiction, then consider the real-world example of weather: from day to day the weather appears to be utterly chaotic and unpredictable, so much so that meteorologists armed with computers and satellites can barely come up with a forecast that is accurate beyond 24 hours; yet this same system of unpredictable day-to-day weather encompasses the seasons of winter, spring, summer, and fall, which reoccur in cycles with an astonishingly reliable and predictable precision. Thus we see that order and chaos can, and actually *do*, coexist within the same system. A look at any of the amazing fractal animations available on the internet will illustrate this fact in a spectacular and striking manner (for example, try doing a web search on "Mandelbrot set animation").

The term *fractal* refers to a mathematical set of curves that often appear irregular or fractured but which exhibit patterns which are "self-similar," meaning that at different scales the fractal pattern is found to repeat either exactly or almost exactly.[149] Fractals display some unique properties that are as disorienting and counterintuitive as any of the unusual concepts from math and physics discussed earlier, and as such they serve as further evidence that our physical reality is far stranger than we've heretofore imagined.

One rather unusual property of fractals is that they can have *fractional dimension*. In other words, a fractal shape can have a dimension that is not a whole number – a "seeming impossibility."[150] To fully appreciate the utter outlandishness of this concept it will be useful to once again recall your math studies from high school. In your high school geometry class the teacher likely began the course by introducing the concept of a theoretical non-dimensional object called a point, mystically defined as "position without dimension." You were then introduced to the concept of one-dimensional objects called lines and line segments which possessed a single dimension usually referred to as "length." Most of your geometry course, however, was devoted to an in-depth study of two-dimensional objects: squares, rectangles, triangles, etc. These were flat objects having two dimensions, length and width. You then learned that by adding an additional dimension – depth – you could form objects that were more accurate representations of reality, such as cubes and spheres (instead of squares and circles). These objects are three-dimensional objects and are usually covered in a different course typically entitled "solid geometry." At some point in your geometry course it was inevitably noted that the reality in which we all exist is a three-dimensional reality, a *solid* reality. But the point being made here is that dimensionality, as typically understood, is represented by positive whole numbers – 1, 2, 3 – as illustrated below:

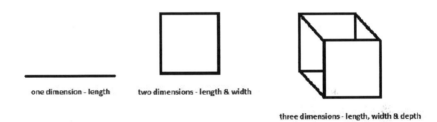

one dimension - length   two dimensions - length & width

three dimensions - length, width & depth

But a fractal shape can have a dimension that is not 1, 2, or 3 – its dimension can be a number that is *not a whole number*. As an example let's consider a famous fractal known as the Koch curve. A Koch curve is formed as follows: take an equilateral triangle (i.e., a triangle whose 3 sides are of equal length) and then on the middle third of each side form a triangle similar to the original triangle but one-third its size; then continue on indefinitely in this manner, as shown below:

Evolution of Koch snowflake from Koch curve

Using this process one can form an object commonly referred to as a Koch snowflake:

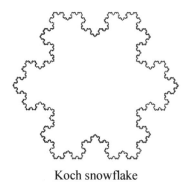

Koch snowflake

The Koch curve has the amazing property that its dimension is (approximately) 1.26 ... not 1, not 2, not 3 ... but 1.26. This is so foreign to our basic understanding of dimensionality that it seems like the ravings of a science fiction writer on a bad LSD trip. Oh, but it gets better: The Koch curve has an *infinite perimeter* but a *finite area*. In other words, if you circumscribed a circle around the original triangle and then proceeded to form the Koch curve from the triangle, that Koch curve would never extend beyond the confines of the circle (thus its area is bounded, or finite), yet the length of the Koch curve (i.e., the perimeter of the "snowflake") would increase infinitely. Think about that for a moment: by comparison, if you increase the perimeter of a square (i.e., if you increase the lengths of its sides), then its area will naturally and obviously increase as well; same with a triangle, a rectangle, a cube, and so on. But in the case of a Koch curve the situation is completely at odds with both common sense and our fundamental sense of measurement and geometry: with a Koch curve you can increase the perimeter indefinitely – to *infinity* – but the area will never extend beyond the area of the circle in which the Koch curve is contained.

We can now get a better sense of the property of fractal curves, alluded to earlier, called *self-similarity*. To say a fractal curve is self-similar means that the shape of the whole curve is identical, or very similar, to the shape of its parts. The Koch snowflake discussed above illustrates this property nicely.[151] It is basically a pattern that repeats over and over again, *ad infinitum*, as the fractal evolves, with the only difference being one of scale. This disquieting idea of "a part being equal to the whole" will be of considerable importance as the theses of this book are developed further.

One last comment regarding Chaos theory: it is interesting to note that Chaos theory describes a hidden level of order underlying apparently chaotic processes, while Heisenberg's Uncertainty Principle and the Copenhagen Interpretation describe a hidden level of probabilistic incertitude underlying apparently solid matter. *What is going on with our reality?* (A theory offering a possible explanation for this bizarre interplay of chaos and order will be presented in Chapter 21).

The Big Bang Theory

So far we've been discussing reality primarily on two levels: (1) the experiential level – what reality "looks" like and how we perceive it; and (2) the subatomic level – the substructure underlying our reality. But a much larger question, and most definitely a pertinent one, is: *Where did it all come from?* That enquiry falls under the purview of cosmology – the branch of astrophysics that studies the origin, evolution and structure of the universe. Cosmology's answer to the question *Where did it all come from?* is known as The Big Bang Theory. The Big Bang Theory posits that, approximately 13.8 billion years ago, our universe – all of it: matter, energy ... the works – sprang into existence in an instant out of what is called a "singularity," which is conceptualized as an infinitely small, infinitely dense, and infinitely hot state of existence. In spite of the use of the phrase "big bang" the birth of our universe out of this singularity is not considered to have been an explosion but rather a rapid expansion of the singularity. Continued expansion and cooling has led to our universe in the state in which it presently exists (with it yet continuing to expand and cool further). Esteemed physicists such as Stephen Hawking and Roger Penrose believe that *nothing* existed prior to the singularity – i.e., matter, energy, space, time – none of these existed prior to the singularity; the singularity's origin, purpose, and medium of existence are all unknown.[152]

Now think about this Big Bang theory for a moment: basically, it is saying that *everything* sprang from *nothing*, in an *instant*, for *no reason*. This is about as unscientific an explanation as I've ever heard. The religious concept of "God" as an omnipotent being – which science ridicules – is no less fanciful than this theory. Terence McKenna's comments on the Big Bang Theory are priceless: "[It] is the limit test for credulity... I mean, hell, if you can believe *that*, you can believe anything ... try and think of something more improbable than that contention." And this: "It's just the limit case for unlikelihood that the universe would spring from nothing, in a single instant, for no reason! What the philosophers of science are saying is 'Give us one free miracle.'"

"One free miracle" – that's the fundamental point here: no matter how arrogantly science beats its chest and congratulates itself on its adherence to strict standards of empirical and measurable evidence, sober principles of reasoning, and dispassionate objectivity, the fact is that science still seems to need *that one free miracle* to kick things off. Another area in which science requires the intervention of the miraculous is the theory that human beings are solely the product of Darwinian evolution.

Darwin's Theory of Evolution

As part of our basic education we are all taught that the human race, and, indeed, all life on this planet, evolved slowly over eons of time from a common ancestor in accordance with a process that is known as "Darwin's Theory of Evolution." The theory is named for English naturalist and geologist Charles Darwin, who first published his theory of evolution in his 1859 book entitled *On the Origin of Species*.[153] Darwin's theory of evolution posits that complex life forms evolve from their less sophisticated ancestors naturally over long periods of time via a process that is contingent upon the combined effects of random mutations and what Darwin termed "natural selection." The theory suggests that as an organism undergoes random genetic mutations, the beneficial mutations – those that enhance the organism's chances of survival – are preserved by the organisms that are fortunate enough to posses them and are then passed on to their offspring. So, for example, if an organism experienced a genetic mutation that resulted in it possessing greater speed, then that greater speed would obviously enhance that organism's survivability over other like organisms that did not possess the mutation (greater speed would, for example, result in superior hunting skills and improved evasion of predators); the organisms with the "speed mutation" would outlive their non-mutated cousins and would soon become the predominant organism. That is, the natural processes of survival would "select" in favor of organisms possessing this particular beneficial mutation – thus "natural selection." According to the theory, the accumulation of multiple beneficial mutations over long periods of time would ultimately result in a vastly different organism, [154] thus species *evolve* over great stretches of time (as in the evolution of modern humans from primitive primates). In short, Darwin's theory of evolution can be succinctly described as natural selection acting on variations.

This theory's appeal is quite obvious – it is easy to understand and it sounds eminently logical. It is also a beautifully elegant theory. But, as any mathematician will tell you, while elegance is a *necessary* quality of a good theory, it is not a *sufficient* one. I, personally, accept that much of biological evolution proceeds in precisely the manner that Darwin proposed. But problems arise with trying to use Darwin's theory to explain cases of extreme biological complexity, and with using it to explain the *origin* of life. First, Darwin was a naturalist, not a biologist – a naturalist is someone who studies plants and/or animals in their natural environment using an approach that is more observational than experimental; in other words, a naturalist is not truly a scientist. Second, the state of scientific knowledge and biological knowledge at the time when Darwin formulated his theory – before 1860 – were quite limited when compared to what we know today: technology – the primary tool of scientific study and exploration – was elementary and limited, and important fields of biology such as genetics and cell theory – fields highly relevant to understanding life processes and, hence, the evolution of life – were in their earliest crude stages. Third, genetic mutations, one of the two pillars upon which Darwin's theory rests (i.e., *variations* and natural selection) are mostly non-advantageous to the survivability of living organisms: "Most non-neutral mutations are deleterious."[155] This is why cells posses a remarkable ability, and go to great lengths, to repair DNA mutations when they occur. Mutations, like all random events, are mostly entropic – they represent *disorder*. Fourth, the fact that Darwin's theory depends heavily on the *random* nature of genetic mutations, coupled with the fact that most of these random mutations are harmful to life, means that this is a theory whose very foundation is grounded in *improbability*. This is an astonishing state of affairs for a scientific principle: the process of Darwinian evolution depends upon and requires *the improbable* in order to function as described. Science typically rejects such notions out of hand.

Many books have been written, and videos produced, that point out a multitude of specific weaknesses in Darwin's theory, and I have no intention of reiterating them all here. However, to provide an idea of some of the criticisms, I will briefly discuss two specific situations which dramatically illustrate the problematic nature of the Darwinian model: they are the Cambrian explosion and the concept of irreducible complexity.

Paleontologist Stephen Jay Gould stated, "The fossil record had caused Darwin more grief than joy. Nothing distressed him more than the Cambrian explosion, the coincident appearance of almost all complex organic designs." [156] The reason why the Cambrian explosion so distressed Darwin goes to the very heart of his theory.

Darwin's theory necessitates a multitude of transitional forms as a species slowly evolves in accordance with natural selection acting upon genetic mutations. That is, each time natural selection selects in favor of a beneficial mutation the organism undergoes a transformation; while a single such transformation might be relatively minor, the progression of a sequence of multiple transformations will, over time, collectively result in noticeable and dramatic changes in the organism, and, thus, it evolves. Think again of the supposed evolution of modern humans from primitive primates: we've all seen the chart showing the successive phases of an early simian gradually morphing through various hominid forms – it's arms shortening and it's posture becoming more upright – as it evolves into *Homo sapiens*. Well, the problem for Darwin is that during the Cambrian explosion, which began approximately 542 million years ago, the first fossils of most major animals appeared suddenly, geologically speaking, and without any precursors in the geological record;[157] the transitional forms required by Darwin's theory have not been found. Rather than the gradual, step-by-step development required by Darwinian evolution, there was an explosive burst of complex biological structures appearing suddenly and without any geological record of their predecessors. To truly appreciate the "explosive" nature of this occurrence, consider the following: for about the first 87% of the history of life on this planet there were only single-celled organisms; then, during a very short period of time amounting to only .2% (that's $\frac{2}{10}$ of 1 percent) of the history of life on earth, we see fully developed, complex organisms appear. *For almost 90% of the history of life on earth we have only simple one-celled organisms, then, in less than 1% of that timeframe, complex biological organisms possessing complex structures suddenly pop onto the scene with no geological record of an evolutionary transition from the simple to the intricate.* Darwin was well aware of the serious problem this posed for his theory, and he addressed it in *On the Origin of Species.* He believed that the "explosion" was merely due to an incomplete fossil record, and he hoped that in time further discoveries would fill in the record and corroborate his theory. Thus far, 155 years after the publication of his theory, such evidence has not been forthcoming.

The other bane of Darwin's theory to be discussed here has come to be known as *Irreducible Complexity*, an expression originated by biochemistry professor Michael Behe. As defined by Dr. Behe, an *irreducibly complex* system is "a single system composed of several well-matched, interacting parts that contribute to the basic function, wherein the removal of any one of the parts causes the system to effectively cease functioning."[158] The reason why the existence of an irreducibly complex biological system would cause problems with Darwin's theory of evolution was clearly expressed by Darwin himself:

> If it could be demonstrated that any complex organ existed which could not possibly have been formed by numerous, successive, slight modifications, my theory would absolutely break down.[159]

An irreducibly complex system cannot come about as the result of "successive, slight modifications" of a precursor system because, as the term implies, the system is *irreducible* – it is incapable of being made simpler: any simpler, less evolved, precursor system that is lacking a part would be unable to perform the system's intended function.

Modern technology has given scientists the ability to study life processes at the cellular level, capabilities that were not even remotely possible in Darwin's day. Many systems of incredible complexity and structure have been revealed via this technology, and some of them appear to possess the requisite characteristics of irreducible complexity. Of particular interest in this vein are systems falling under the category of "molecular machines" – protein complexes that perform a variety of cellular functions. An article in the journal Accounts of Chemical Research describes a molecular machine as "an assemblage of parts that transmit forces, motion, or energy from one to another in a predetermined manner" (as cited in Casey Luskin, 2010).[160] Among other functions, molecular machines enable cells to ingest food, swim, and copy themselves. Molecular machines also capture and store energy, turn cellular switches on and off, and even build other molecular machines.[161]

One of these molecular machines – the bacterial flagellum – is particularly amazing in regard to its complexity, structure and function. The bacterial flagellum is a biological mechanism that propels bacteria by means of a rotary motor which functions in much the same way that a propeller does on an outboard motor. In fact, diagrams and animations illustrating the structure and function of the bacterial flagellum look uncannily like an actual outboard motor.[162] Such animations can be found via an internet search, and also on a DVD entitled *Unlocking the Mystery of Life*. The bacterial motor is powered by an acid-regulated proton flow, and can generate a rotor spin rate of up to 100,000 times per second.[163] According to a statement by Scott A. Minnich, associate professor of microbiology, removal of "one of the components of the type three secretion system of the flagellum" results in the cell being unable to move.[164] This is precisely the criteria for irreducible complexity – cessation of function due to removal of a part of the system.

Critics of irreducible complexity argue that a system like the bacterial flagellum could have borrowed the necessary parts for its construction from parts already existing in other systems. This argument is known as co-option. However, only 10 of the 40 parts constituting the flagellar motor are known to exist in other systems; the other 30 parts are unique to the flagellum. Also, critics fail to address how the *assembly* of the flagellar motor can be explained or accomplished.[165]

But, all scientific semantics aside, I think you will find that, on a strictly intuitive level, if you view an animation of a bacterial flagellum you will be awe-struck: this thing *looks like* a machine and it *functions like* a machine – to a degree that is truly astounding. It is difficult to view this biological molecular machine and imagine it as having come about as the result of a series of genetic accidents, regardless of how much time is allowed. In fact, I find the claim that such a structure could have resulted from successive selection of favorable mutations to be preposterous in the extreme, and a clear violation of Occam's razor (a scientific principle which holds that, for competing theories attempting to explain the same phenomenon, the simpler theory is usually the better one). Many other molecular machines display similar degrees of structural and functional complexity.[166]

While the Cambrian explosion and the apparent irreducible complexity of certain molecular machines cast a credible shadow of doubt over Darwin's theory of evolution, I personally think that the most compelling evidence against Darwin is mathematical: probability calculations of the likelihood of the chance formation of a *single protein* – let alone a human being – are so high as to be impossible.[167] Philosopher David Berlinski has stated, "I know dozens of mathematicians who scratch their head and say, 'You guys think that this is the way life originated? It's absolutely a preposterous theory.'" He also claimed that the great mathematician John von Neumann laughed at Darwinian theory.[168] English astronomer Fred Hoyle likened the possibility of higher life forms resulting from Darwinian evolution to that of a tornado blowing through a junkyard containing all the parts of a Boeing 747 and *by chance* assembling them into a fully functional aircraft.[169]

So, the Cambrian explosion, irreducible complexity, and statistical improbability: Am I suggesting Darwin's theory of evolution is a bunch of nonsense? No, absolutely not. On the macro level of biology I think Darwin's theory is a totally plausible model of how species evolve. It seems completely logical to me that finches with longer beaks will prevail genetically because of the functional advantage such beaks offer with regard to gaining access to seeds. On the macro level, Darwinian evolution makes perfect sense. However, to then extrapolate from the finch's beak to the *entire finch* – or to a human being – is a leap of faith I am reluctant to take and a presumption I am reluctant to make. I believe that natural selection is a process that takes over *after* the initial formation of a complex organism: I see natural selection as a macro-phenomenon, *a maintenance system of environmentally induced self-regulation that fine-tunes an organism for maximum survival potential*. I do not believe that natural selection can account for the initial formation of complex systems, or for the assemblage of cellular-level or molecular-level complex systems into higher-order complex organisms. Those cases are, I believe, misapplications of Darwin's theory.

As an analogy, consider the free market concept of capitalism wherein the production, distribution, and prices of goods and services are dictated by supply and demand. The free market is self-regulating: if a product or service is shoddy, or if there is little demand for it, then the company offering that product or service will fail; companies that offer high-demand products of superior quality, however, will prevail and thrive. The market will also drive, to a certain extent, the decisions a company makes with regard to the products it offers. *But* ... did the market *create* the company? Certainly, a company might *be created* precisely because of market factors, but the market cannot be credited with the *actual creation* of the company. *Something else* created that company. That "something else" may have been inspired to create the company because of market factors, and, once created, that company will be subject to – and respond to – market influences, but the market itself did not create the company. The market is merely an environmental system in which the company exists, and that system will impact upon the company by communicating to it the need to make occasional advantageous changes if the company intends to survive in the market. But the market – i.e., the *environmental system* – does not *create* the company.

It's very tempting to latch onto an attractive idea and run with it. It's in our nature to solve puzzles and figure out mysteries, and we experience a heady and intoxicating feeling of satisfaction when we do so. But we must take care not to let our zeal overtake rational thought and objectivity. Just because theory T explains phenomenon P, it does not necessarily follow that it will also explain related phenomena Q, R, and S; it *might* explain them, and it would be grand if it did, but we must objectively *test* whether or not it does; and if it doesn't, then we must be mature enough and honest enough to accept that. In physics, Newtonian mechanics explains *a lot* about the physical world, but it doesn't explain *everything*. At one time it was *hoped* that it would and it was thought that it did, but advances in knowledge and technology proved otherwise. And physics, to its credit, adapted accordingly. In geology, when the theory of continental drift was first proposed it was ridiculed as fanciful nonsense; now it is accepted as indisputable fact. Early astronomers thought that the sun revolved around the earth – it certainly looks that way – but now, contrary to appearances and wishful thinking, we know otherwise.

It is one of the great ironies that, of all the sciences, biology is the one that refuses to adapt to changes in its environment. It doggedly resists and defies the influences of natural selection, even as it desperately clings to that very concept. And we all know what happens to species that fail to adapt.

In our present society and culture it is impossible to discuss the subject of Darwinian evolution without also addressing the idea of intelligent design. Intelligent design is a theory that proposes an intelligent cause, rather than an undirected process, as being the best explanation for certain features of life and of the universe. Intelligent design is not creationism, and it is not a religious doctrine. Because of an unfortunate Hatfield-and-McCoys contentiousness between science and religion that goes back many centuries, and because of the erroneous association of intelligent design *with* religion, many scientists dismiss intelligent design out of hand. But the truth is that intelligent design is a *scientific theory* that is accepted by some scientists and rejected by others.

I find it astoundingly ironic that, while many scientists scoff at the idea of intelligent design, science itself – by its very methods and conduct – *presumes* rational design in nature. If it didn't, then there would be no hope of understanding the structure, processes and functioning *of* nature. The very act of *doing* science requires and expects nature to be rationally designed. Our understanding of what constitutes intelligent, meaningful design is completely in sync with the way nature is structured. The most plausible explanation for why we *can* study and understand the world is because we are intelligent beings studying a world that is intelligently designed.

For a long time science saw the universe as being comprised of only two things: matter and energy. Now science has added a third ingredient to the mix: *information*. Information, in the scientific sense, has been defined as a "reduction of uncertainty",[170] and as the "negative of entropy"[171] – in other words, it is something that is not random, not disordered. To me, this implies design and intention.

So, where does this leave us? I, personally, accept that the evidence presented above is sufficient to cast serious doubt upon the ability of Darwin's theory to explain all biological systems. Does that lead me to believe it necessarily follows that *God* created biological systems? No. Not at all. I am totally open to the possibility that some new theory might arise that can explain complex biological systems by means of some natural process or processes. I *don't* believe, however, that Darwin's theory is it. I am also open to the possibility that intelligent design may be totally explainable without resorting to religion or God. In fact, I strongly suspect that there are a great many aspects of the universe that our science has yet to discover and explain, and I also suspect that they will be found to be explainable without any needed recourse to an hypothesis involving God. Scientists and religious fundamentalists both seem to be under the mistaken delusion that explaining the existence of life on Earth comes down to a choice between God or Darwin. That is a ridiculous, small-minded supposition, and both groups should be ashamed of themselves for even entertaining such a limited perspective on an issue of such staggering complexity and scope.

DNA

DNA (deoxyribonucleic acid) is a biological system for encoding and storing an organism's hereditary information. The *information* that DNA stores involves genetic instructions for assembling proteins from amino acids (proteins are large, functional molecules that do most of the work in cells and are necessary for the structure, function, and regulation of the body's tissues and organs). The *encoding* of that information is accomplished by means of four chemical bases: adenine (A), guanine (G), cytosine (C), and thymine (T); the order in which these bases are linked determines the information stored in the DNA. Each base attaches to a sugar molecule and a phosphate molecule to form a nucleotide. A single DNA molecule is simply a chain or strand of nucleotide units; when two long strands of nucleotides join together with the bases pairing off – A with T, C with G – they form the familiar twisted ladder shape of DNA known as the *double helix*, with the base pairs forming the ladder's rungs and the sugar and phosphate molecules forming the ladder's side rails. The set of instructions for the construction if a particular protein is thus a subsection of a DNA molecule, i.e., a linear sequence of base pairs; and it is precisely such a sequence of nucleic acid base pairs that constitutes what is known as a *gene*.[172]

DNA is of particular interest and relevance to our discussion here for three important reasons: (1) the mind-boggling complexity of organization and function through which proteins are formed utilizing DNA-encoded instructions; (2) the linguistic features possessed by so-called "junk DNA"; and (3) the misconception, under which biology operated for over 50 years, that DNA was a self-activating, unalterable blueprint of hard-wired genetic programming. Let's explore each of these points in more detail; first, the process by which genes direct the production of proteins.

If the intricate structure and deliberate functioning of the bacterial flagellum gives one pause when considering complex biological systems, then the process by which proteins are produced under the direction of DNA-encoded genetic instructions will absolutely knock your socks off. I will attempt to describe the process here, but again, as with the bacterial flagellum, an animation is worth 10,000 words, so I strongly advise the reader to seek out a video animation of the process on the internet or on a DVD (the DVD mentioned previously –*Unlocking the Mystery of Life* – does an excellent job).

The construction of a protein from genetic instructions involves two processes known as *transcription* and *translation*. In the nucleus of a cell, the instructions for constructing proteins are stored in genes which, as noted above, are stretches of a DNA molecule (i.e., sequences of base-pairs). During the process of *transcription*, the genetic information needed to construct a particular protein is copied from the DNA and transferred to a DNA-like molecule called messenger RNA (mRNA); this transcription occurs in the cell nucleus. The actual transcription is accomplished via an actual splitting of the DNA double helix, performed by a molecular machine, into two single strands. One of these strands then acts as a template, if you will, for the information to be copied. The mRNA carries the copied information out of the nucleus and into the cytoplasm (the cell substance between the cell membrane and the nucleus, i.e., everything in the cell that is outside of the nucleus but enclosed within the cell membrane). The next step in the process of protein construction, known as *translation*, occurs in the cytoplasm. Once there, another molecular machine called a ribosome "reads" the sequence of bases in the mRNA, three at a time, and uses this code to build the protein. Each sequence of three bases (called a *codon*) represents the instructions for one particular amino acid. An assemblage of hundreds or thousands of amino acids into a unique three-dimensional geometric structure determines the specific function of each individual protein. This assembling of amino acids into a 3D protein structure is performed by yet another molecular machine called transfer RNA (tRNA). The combined processes of transcription and translation are known as *gene expression*. The information flow from DNA to RNA to protein is a fundamental principle of molecular biology known as the "central dogma."[173]

Let's take a deep breath for a moment and really think about what is happening here (as I said earlier, a visualization of this process via an animation is priceless both in understanding what is happening and in appreciating how truly amazing it is): We have instructions for how to build a protein in the form of information that is encoded into a molecule called DNA. These instructions are meaningful and purposeful – they describe, after all, how to build something (i.e., a protein) that performs a practical biological function – and they are encoded by means of entities called bases (which function like letters of the alphabet) grouped into codons (which are like words) that are in turn grouped into genes (which are like sentences). That alone is mind-boggling. But then we have molecular machines that: (a) copy the information and transport it, (b) read it, and (c) interpret and execute it to build a protein. I find this absolutely, positively *astounding*. And then there are the more subtle, unstated aspects of this process that are often glossed over, such as: What is directing this entire process? How does the body know which protein is needed at any given time and where it is needed? How did *the first* mRNA and tRNA get made, before there *was* mRNA and tRNA to perform the transcription and translation that I presume was necessary for *their* construction? ... I could go on, but I think you get the idea. All of this activity is happening in a living organism at the cellular and sub-cellular levels; it is complex, it is purposeful, and it is information-rich and information-dependent. How can all of this possibly *not* be intelligently directed? If astronomers were to receive a meaningful sequence of bits they would interpret it as a potential sign of intelligent life. But biologists have this incredible, elegantly marvelous transcription-translation process of gene expression – a process whose very function and essence specifically entails the storage, transfer, and encoding/decoding of purposive information – and they see it as the result of random processes and natural selection. I'm not saying that genetic expression *proves* intelligent design, what I'm saying is that to not at least *suspect* intelligent design in such a process reeks of non-objectivity, close-mindedness, and a conclusion formed without argument or consideration. That is not science. Ironically, it is more akin to *religion*.

The second area of interest for us with regard to DNA has to do with so-called "junk DNA." As we learned earlier, DNA is a system for encoding the instructions for constructing proteins. But it turns out that not all DNA serves this purpose. Indeed, in humans it is estimated that less than 2% of our DNA is involved in encoding for protein production. The remaining 98% of DNA is commonly referred to as "junk DNA" (a term first coined by geneticist and evolutionary biologist Susumu Ohno), because much of it has no discernible biological function. The adjective "junk" notwithstanding, subsequent discoveries have indicated that some junk DNA does indeed serve a biological purpose, and it is thought that other junk DNA may have an as yet unidentified purpose, or may have served a purpose that is now obsolete. For these reasons the term "junk DNA" is now thought to be a misleading and (unintentionally) unflattering identifier, and has been replaced by the more appropriate and meaningful label "noncoding DNA"; another term used in lieu of "junk DNA" is *intron* (an intron is a segment of a DNA or RNA molecule that does not code for proteins, while exons are stretches of DNA that do code for proteins). Nevertheless, *as much as 50% of human DNA is thought to be of the noncoding type with unknown function.*[174]

This last fact is a bit startling, particularly in light of Darwinian evolution. Given the complexity of design and intricacy of function inherent in DNA it seems quite unlikely that nature would devote so much effort to creating and maintaining such an elaborate system if it had no practical purpose. Natural selection, by definition, favors efficiency and discourages inefficiency; having upwards of 50% of a system as complex as DNA be without purpose is grossly inefficient.

For our present discussion, the aspect of noncoding DNA that is especially intriguing involves the discovery that this so-called junk DNA appears to possess a linguistic structure. Due to the coding function of DNA both the scientific community and the general public have often employed DNA-as-language metaphors (e.g., references to DNA being the "book of life" or the "language of life"), but analyses of noncoding DNA suggest that the relationship between linguistics and DNA might be more than just a figure of speech. One such finding is that noncoding DNA possesses linguistic properties consistent with Zipf's Law, a statistical feature of human languages involving word frequencies.[175] There is even the possibility that noncoding DNA exhibits characteristics of grammar.[176] These findings are highly suggestive that noncoding DNA is not "junk" and, hence, has some purpose. Adding to this possibility is the intriguing fact that noncoding DNA is more common in complex organisms such as humans while being less common in simple unicellular organisms such as yeast and bacteria. In other words, it appears that the more complex an organism is, the more noncoding DNA it will contain.[177] This implies the possibility of a direct relationship between the two (i.e., between complexity and noncoding DNA). When one considers the function and capabilities of DNA, rumination as to the possible roles played by noncoding DNA can be quite intriguing, and, indeed, a variety of theories have been proposed suggesting that noncoding DNA does, in fact, have an as yet unidentified purpose. A particularly tantalizing hypothesis in this vein posits that noncoding DNA is a dormant instruction set which, when activated by certain environmental stimuli, will initiate an evolutionary upgrade of the human race. That theory will be discussed as part of a broader context in Chapter 20: The Dimension Shift.

Our third and final reason for discussing DNA has to do with the long-held belief that DNA is a self-activating, unalterable blueprint of hard-wired genetic programming. The Central Dogma of molecular biology discussed previously (DNA-RNA-   protein) has long been considered the process controlling biological life, with DNA credited as being the program, or instruction set, guiding the process. Initially it was only our physical characteristics that were attributed to this DNA-guided mechanism, but fascination with the theory, coupled with zealous extended application, led to a belief that our behavior was also subject to, and determined by, this genetic programming mechanism.[178] However, while it is true that genes contain the instructions for building proteins, and that there are particular genes associated with various biological behaviors and characteristics, the fact is that genes cannot turn themselves on or off. New research has shown that *signals from our environment* are responsible for activating DNA expression.[179] Furthermore, environmental factors can cause genetic modifications – which are not the result of alterations of the linear nucleotide sequence in the DNA molecule – and those modifications are inheritable by later generations. The study of such heritable yet blueprint-preserving changes in gene activity is known as epigenetics.[180]

It turns out that, before the instructions in DNA can be read, regulatory proteins that behave like a sleeve covering the DNA must first be removed, and such sleeve removal is effected by environmental signals. Thus the process of biological control no longer begins with our DNA, but with signals from our environment. These environmental stimuli cause the regulatory protein to unbind from the DNA, exposing it and permitting the process of transcription that we discussed earlier.[181] This realization results in a dramatic change in our perception of ourselves, our biology, and the degree of control we can have over our lives: we are no longer the hapless victims of hard-wired, inflexible hereditary programming, born pre-disposed to set-in-stone characteristics, traits, diseases, and so on. By taking control of our environment, we can affect gene activation.

So, for example, you might have a gene for a specific cancer, and that gene can be expressed *as a result of a signal from your environment*. That signal might be stress-related, or maybe it's diet-related; by taking steps to alter the relevant environmental conditions you could possibly prevent the expression of that gene. That is, you are not *fated* to fall victim to that cancer. You can exert control and thereby you can influence the way events will unfold. This is a degree of personal power and self-mastery the likes of which we have heretofore been denied.

But let's take this a step further. In Chapter 13 we saw that the environmental stimuli affecting us are subject to the limitations of our sensory organs and *the decoding of those stimuli signals by our brain*. Thus, ultimately, *our perception of our reality* is the starting point for the activation of our genes. And, as we also saw, our perception of reality is strongly influenced by our *beliefs* about "reality." Can you change what you believe? You bet you can. And therefore you can change how certain environmental stimuli are perceived, decoded and interpreted – and the regulatory proteins that permit or deny gene expression, then, should react accordingly.

So the process that fifty years ago was thought to begin in our DNA can now be traced back to our beliefs. Well, where exactly do our beliefs come from? They are instilled in us from an early age, when we are most impressionable, by parents, schools, religion, media, ideologies, culture – and so on. In other words, our "programming" is external, not internal. But we can change that programming, and the degree to which this is possible is nothing short of astounding. This topic will be explored further in Chapter 18, entitled "Hacking Reality."

I'd like to conclude this chapter with a return to my favorite area of the sciences, namely, mathematics. Specifically we will look at three mathematical concepts which keenly illustrate the two objectives that inspired my writing this chapter and which were explained at its outset: (1) that our reality may be much different than we perceive it to be; and, (2) that select discoveries in science and math suggest inherent limitations, weaknesses, or inaccuracies in those fields. Also, the sequential discussion of these three topics will build nicely to set the conceptual groundwork for the final point to be made in this chapter, a revelation which – when I first became exposed to it, and still to this very day – I find monumental in its implications and significance.

The final three topics of this chapter are: imaginary numbers, Cantor's theory of infinite sets, and transcendental numbers.

Imaginary Numbers

Numbers represent the absolute bedrock of mathematics. It is easy to forget that the complex and abstract discipline of modern mathematics sprang from something as basic and obvious as simple numbers. Whether it was the need of an ancient shepherd to tally the sheep in his herd, or the earliest desire to measure time or distance, the field of mathematics – this exotic, alien world of symbols and formulae and ultra-logic – can be traced back to the humble roots of number. Before I can get to the point of this section – imaginary numbers – I must first provide some background on how numbers are categorized.

Numbers evolved over time, beginning inevitably with the simple and practical – the counting numbers: 1, 2, 3, etc. – and expanding into ever more conceptual representations – fractions, decimals, and so on. These different ways of representing numerical quantities, or different classifications of numbers, are today expressed in the language of sets. Set theory was first conceived by mathematician Georg Cantor. In mathematical parlance a set is defined as a "well-defined collection of distinct objects" where the objects can be anything – numbers, things, ... even other sets.[182] For our purposes here we will limit our consideration to sets of numbers. (note: sets are typically denoted by squiggly brackets {}, and the objects making up a set are referred to as the *elements* of the set).

While you may never have had cause to think of numbers within the framework of set theory, the truth is that you will find the underlying notions and definitions familiar and comprehendible from your everyday use and understanding of commonplace numbers. Number sets, as with numbers themselves, begin at the most basic level and then gradually grow into ever more elaborate representations. The most fundamental set of numbers is known as the **Natural numbers** (also known, for an immediately obvious reason, as the Counting numbers): {1,2,3,...}. This set is clearly a set containing an infinite number of elements, and such will be the case for each number set we will discuss. If we add the element zero to the set of Natural numbers we create a new number set called the set of **Whole numbers**: {0,1,2,3,...}. So far, so good; nothing weird or esoteric here, just our everyday numbers being grouped together in different ways. As you get the hang of this, you are probably thinking ahead and anticipating the inclusion of fractions to create yet another number set – and you are correct; but before we can open that can of worms we must first consider one more set of "whole" (in the sense of non-fractional) numbers. Probably around the eighth grade or so, you were introduced to a mathematical concept which, at that point in your life, may have seemed a bit bizarre and unreal: the idea of "negative numbers." You learned that each number with which you were familiar (excepting zero) had a negative counterpart: 2 and -2, 7 and -7, etc. (If your experience was anything like my own, you inevitably referred to such numbers verbally by saying "*minus* 2" or "*minus* 7" and you were immediately rebuked by your math teacher who insisted that you use the word "negative" in lieu of "minus.") When we adjoin the negative counterparts to the set of Whole numbers we have yet another number set known as the set of **Integers**: {... -3,-2,-1,0,1,2,3,...}.

Needless to say, as humanity became comfortable with the idea of using numbers to represent quantity and measurement, at some point the need arose to represent portions or parts of whole quantities, and this need gave rise to the idea of fractions. If we add fractions to the set of integers we form the new number set known as the set of **Rational numbers**. Two important points need be noted here:

first, we are using the term *fraction* here in the strict sense of the ratio of two integers, numerator over denominator (where the denominator cannot be zero); and second, it is difficult to represent the set of Rational numbers using the convenient symbolic set notation we have heretofore been using (i.e., the {} brackets), the reasons being that there are *so many* fractions possible and it is exceedingly difficult to attempt to present a select sample in strict numerical sequence. In other words, for integers and whole numbers we know that 2 follows directly after 1 and 3 follows directly after 2, and so on; but what follows *directly after*, say, ½ ? Choose any fraction that comes after ½ and you can still think of another fraction that comes between that fraction and ½. There *is* a way to represent the Rational numbers using set notation, but it's a bit complicated and not germane to this discussion so I won't go into it. Suffice it to say that it does not employ the "representative sample" technique used to typify the Natural numbers, Whole numbers, and Integers. For the sake of convenience, mathematicians also use capitol letters to represent the various number sets, so, for example, **N** represents the set of Natural numbers, **Z** the integers, and **Q** the Rational numbers.

Continuing on with our development of number sets: as you know, there is a way to represent parts of whole quantities other than via fractions – namely, decimal numbers. While it is true that every fraction can be represented in decimal notation (e.g., ½ = .5), the converse is not true: there are many decimal numbers that cannot be represented as fractions; such numbers – decimal numbers that cannot be expressed as the ratio of two integers – are called *irrational numbers* (as distinct from *rational numbers* which, as we recently saw, are numbers that *can be* represented as the ratio of two integers). Examples of irrational numbers would be pi (π) – which is often *approximated* as 3.14 – and the square root of 2 ($\sqrt{2}$). When we group the irrational numbers together with the set of Rational numbers, we form a new set known as the set of **Real numbers (R)**, often referred to informally as "the Reals." For the purposes of everyday life, the set of Real numbers constitutes the extent of our experience with numbers – the Real numbers are all the numbers most of us will ever need or see. But that doesn't mean the Real numbers are the end of the story, and this is where things, number-wise, start to get weird.

It turns out that mathematicians have conceived of another species of number that lies outside the realm of the Real numbers. This point alone is worth reflecting on: If the Real numbers constitute all of the numbers we use and consider in everyday life – namely, the Integers (positive and negative whole numbers and zero), the rational numbers (fractions), and the irrational numbers (decimal numbers that cannot be represented as fractions) – then what else is there? The set of Real numbers seems to account for every possible number one can imagine – try to think of a number that is *not* a positive or negative whole number, *not* zero, *not* a fraction, and *not* a decimal. There aren't any, at least not within the conceptual framework of the notion of "number" as we understand it. That's why the set of Real numbers is called "Real" – they are the numbers that we need and use to function in our *real*ity, to measure and quantify our reality.

So, what other kind of number could there possibly be? Well, if it's not a Real number, then it must be ... *unreal*. And, by God, it is! This new species of number is called an *imaginary number*, and to create it requires breaking some rules.

Before we can understand what an imaginary number is, we must first review the mathematical notion of square root. The square root of a number *k* is a number which when multiplied by itself gives *k* as the result. So, for example, the square root of 4 is 2, since 2 x 2 = 4; likewise, the square root of 25 is 5, since 5 x 5 = 25. Simple enough. Except... we mustn't forget to consider the negative numbers. Recall from your school days that, when you first began working with integers (sometimes referred to as "signed numbers"), you learned some important rules for multiplying these signed numbers, namely:

- a positive times a positive yields a positive result: 2 x 2 = 4
- a negative times a negative yields a positive result: (-2) x (-2) = 4
- a positive times a negative yields a negative result: 2 x (-2) = -4
- a negative times a positive yields a negative result: (-2) x 2 = -4

In mathematics parlance, we refer to the result of a multiplication operation as a *product*. Thus we can restate the above rules more succinctly as follows:

- the product of two numbers with the same sign is positive.
- the product of two numbers with opposite signs is negative.

We now see that the number 4 actually has two square roots, namely 2 and -2. More generally, every positive number has two square roots, one being positive and the other being negative (so, for example, the square roots of 25 are 5 and -5). Zero – which is considered to be neither positive nor negative – has only one square root, namely itself (zero). But what about square roots of negative numbers? This is where things get interesting.

The rules for multiplying signed numbers, considered together with the concept of square root, lead to an important realization: Since the product of two numbers with the same sign must always be positive, and since the square root of a number is the product of a *number times itself*, we must conclude that *a negative number cannot have a square root*. Think about it: a "number times itself" will always be a case of a positive times a positive or a negative times a negative, and will thus always yield a positive result. In other words, there is no possible way we can have a situation wherein a number times itself will give a negative result. Let's look at an example: Suppose we are asked to calculate the square root of -4 ($\sqrt{-4}$); this is asking us to find a number which when multiplied by itself will yield -4 as the result. Not possible! *There is no number which, when multiplied by itself, will give us -4 as the result*: 2 x 2 = 4 (since a positive times a positive gives a positive result), and (-2) x (-2) = 4 (since a negative times a negative gives a positive result). In other words, a number times itself – regardless of whether that number is positive or negative – will always yield a *positive result*. Thus a negative number cannot have a square root.

Unless...

Remember my earlier observation that mathematics is the "exact science" that is not exactly exact? If you're willing to break the rules, then anything is possible. We can resolve this annoying inconvenience by *defining a new number into existence*. "Wait a minute, that's cheating!" you say? Remember my math professor "explaining" to me that 1^∞ is undefined because it is *defined* that way? Apparently the act of "defining" things in mathematics allows for the circumventing of fundamental principles. But such "thinking outside the box" often leads to fascinating results.

Mathematicians resolved the dilemma of the impossibility of square roots of negative numbers by expanding the concept of number to include a new type of number, aptly named (as previously noted) the *imaginary number*. The imaginary number (or imaginary unit) is denoted by the letter *i* and is defined as follows:

$$i = \sqrt{-1}$$

And from this simple sleight-of-hand we have now allowed for the possibility, and very existence, of square roots of negative numbers, since:

$$\text{if } i = \sqrt{-1} \quad \text{then it follows that} \quad i^2 = -1$$

Then we can say that, for example:

$$\sqrt{-4} = 2i \text{ (since } 2i \times 2i = 4i^2 = 4 \times (-1) = -4)$$

If that last part is confusing to you, don't sweat it. The important point here is that mathematicians have defined into existence a new species of number, the imaginary number *i*, which they've defined as being equal to $\sqrt{-1}$.

I have to admit that when I first learned about imaginary numbers I found the notion troubling because it appeared to me that fundamental concepts of mathematics were being violated with casual recklessness. As I noted above, mathematics provides a clear definition of what it means to calculate a square root, and it also provides very clear rules for multiplying signed numbers: together, these concepts preclude the possibility of a square root of a negative number. Mathematics is a very strict and rigorous enterprise; to circumvent its principles and doctrines by defining forbidden entities into existence struck me as, at the very least, sloppy, and, at worst, a degrading violation of the foundational framework upon which the entire edifice of mathematics is constructed. Now, in hindsight, I suspect my attitude was naïve and narrow-minded, but I have to go on record as stating that, even to this day, I get a little twinge of uneasiness whenever I think about the concept of imaginary numbers. My mathematical neuroses aside, it turns out that imaginary numbers are an instrument of convenience enabling complex computations that would otherwise be incredibly difficult or impossible.

The truth is that imaginary numbers play important roles in mathematics and science, and they are by no means considered "imaginary" by mathematicians. Imaginary numbers serve as a useful mathematical tool in enabling the discovery of new theorems as well as in expanding the reach of existing theorems. Indeed, it was this utility of imaginary numbers that persuaded mathematicians, some of whom (such as Descartes) initially rejected the concept, that there must be a logic to this strange beast and it should be taken seriously.[183] Furthermore, imaginary numbers have proven to be an invaluable aid to physicists and engineers in making complex calculations related to signal processing, fluid dynamics, electric current, relativity theory, quantum mechanics, and even in biology for analyzing neuronal activity in the brain. [184] Also, imaginary numbers actually have a geometric interpretation (though it is not linear [185] and involves rotations in a coordinate plane [186]). Thus, as a handy tool that facilitates difficult mathematical calculations and computations, imaginary numbers can be viewed as "an upgrade to our number system, just like zero, decimals and negatives were."[187]

The truly amazing thing about imaginary numbers is that *they work*. And this, then, raises a critically important question – one that is highly relevant to our discussion of the nature of reality: How is it that this artificial – arguably illegitimate – mathematical construct turns out to be helpful in solving equations related to actual natural processes? Perhaps imaginary numbers actually do have a "true existence" on some level of reality outside the scope of our everyday experience. This possibility is not as far-fetched as it sounds, and is, in fact, strongly hinted at by the most elegant, beautiful and sublime equation in all of mathematics: Euler's Identity. Let's take a look at this most fascinating mathematical statement.

Euler's Identity

$$e^{i\pi} + 1 = 0$$

This equation combines five of the most important mathematical constants into one deceptively simple formula. We have:

e: Euler's number, the base of the natural logarithms.
π: pi, the ratio of the circumference of a circle to its diameter.
i: the imaginary unit.
1: the multiplicative identity.

0: the additive identity.

(also note that 0 and 1 are the two digits of the binary number system, the simplest number system possible and the mathematical basis of computer logic).

To have these five important constants (and *only* these constants) appear together in one simple, elegant equation is nothing short of astounding. The implications of this formula with regards to the interrelationship of these five values can scarcely be imagined: *What*, exactly, is this formula telling us? And how is it that the *imaginary* number *i* gets equal billing with the other four critically important *real number* constants? I, personally, cannot help but read into this equation the suggestion that *i* is more than an artificial construct created for the convenience of mathematicians; to me, it says that *i* has real meaning in the real world, on par with *e*, **π, 1** and **0**.

Also, note that by subtracting 1 from both sides of the equation, we arrive at the result:

$$e^{i\pi} = -1$$

Really? How does an expression as complicated as $e^{i\pi}$, a numerical expression that involves two non-terminating decimal numbers and an imaginary number, simplify down to plain old -1 ? Seriously, think about what this expression entails numerically:

e (Euler's number) is a non-terminating decimal equal to: 2.7182818284...

π (pi) is a non-terminating decimal equal to: 3.1415926535...

i (the imaginary unit) is equal to $\sqrt{-1}$

Thus $e^{i\pi}$ actually means $(2.7182818284...)^{(\sqrt{-1})(3.1415926535...)}$

And that ridiculously inexact and convoluted expression calculates to a nice, simple number like -1 ? Come on! But it does; that's the inexplicable truth of it.

At the risk of sounding over-dramatic, I honestly sense that there is an important and profound piece of information hidden in Euler's equation, something that goes well beyond mathematics into realms philosophical, alchemical, and eerily magical.

Another mathematical expression that I find to be as eye-poppingly astounding as Euler's Identity is the following:

$$i^i = \frac{1}{\sqrt{e^\pi}}$$

Let's take a moment to fully comprehend what this amazing equation is saying. On the left-side we have the imaginary number i raised to the ith power – in other words, we have an imaginary number raised to an imaginary exponent (I can't even *begin* to guess what that means, or how to interpret it) hence the left-side involves only imaginary quantities. On the right-side of the equation we have an expression involving 1, e, and π; these are all numerical quantities that are Real numbers. So what we have here is *a mathematical equation that expresses an equivalence between an expression that is strictly imaginary and another expression that is strictly Real*. How is that possible? Real numbers and imaginary numbers are completely distinct from one another, they represent two entirely different and *mutually exclusive* number sets. Also, recall that the very concept of the imaginary number is artificial – it's a *man-made notion* devised to facilitate solving equations. Yet here we have an expression solely involving imaginary numbers (i.e., the left-side) *that is equivalent to* an expression solely involving Real values (the right-side). How can an imaginary quantity be equal to a Real quantity? Again, by their very definitions they are supposed to be mutually exclusive. The very existence of such an equation would seem like a mathematical impossibility. And to add intrigue to incredulity, we have the additional mind-blower that the real side of the equation involves those two extremely important constants π and e. How is it that, of all the infinitude of real numbers out there, *those two* real numbers are the ones that come into play here? (As we will shortly see, there is another property of the numbers π and e that leads to an even more astonishing fact, a fact that I suspect may be the most important mathematical concept of all).

It's all too easy to look upon something like this equation and simply shrug one's shoulders, scratch one's head, and say, "Huh! That's odd." But the fact is that something this strange and impossible is usually a beacon pointing the way to a deeper insight of profound import. There is a very good reason why author Isaac Asimov said, "The most exciting phrase to hear in science, the one that heralds new discoveries, is not 'Eureka!' (I found it!) but 'Gee, that's funny ...' " It is often those *"Gee, that's funny ..."* situations that point the way to gold. As such, they demand to be explored.

Well... How's that for taking stuffy old math and breathing a little excitement and mystery into it? Now that we've talked about imaginary numbers, and, in the process, laid the groundwork regarding sets of numbers, let's move on to another topic of mathematics that is just as strange and implausible and intriguing as imaginary numbers.

Cantor's Theory of Infinite Sets

As noted in the previous section, Set theory, as applied to mathematics and logic, was the brainchild of mathematician Georg Cantor. A set, in the mathematical sense, is described simply as a collection or aggregate of objects which possess similar properties; these objects, referred to as the *elements* of the set, can be numbers, things, points on a line, ... even other sets. Starting from this concept, Cantor went on to develop an algebra of sets which specifies rules for performing operations on sets that are analogous to the operations of arithmetic. As simple as this concept may sound, the importance and brilliance of Cantor's insight cannot be overstressed. Set theory now stands as the logical basis, as well as the purest form, of all mathematics and is widely considered to be one of the most significant modern contributions to this field.[188] Cantor formulated these concepts as part of his work with infinite sets and his theory of transfinite numbers, and it is with these areas that we are concerned.

Cantor's ingenious and controversial mathematical insight involved the realization that there are different orders, or magnitudes, of infinity. Prior to Cantor, the consensus of thought regarding infinity was that all infinities were the same[189]; in other words, two separate collections containing an infinite number of things were seen to be of the same magnitude, if you will, because the very notion of *infinite* presupposed the unique qualities of innumerable scope and limitless unboundedness. And I think you would agree that, from a common sense perspective, this is a perfectly logical and rational understanding of what "infinite" means. Certainly, that had always been my take on what "infinite" implied. At least, that was the case until I learned about Cantor's ideas.

When I was first exposed to Cantor's theory of infinite sets I simply couldn't believe it – it went completely against my own common sense notions of what the term "infinite" meant. And, apparently, I wasn't alone, for it turns out that Cantor's ideas in this regard were considered highly controversial when he first proposed them, and were initially met with scornful criticism and hostility from many of his contemporaries (and, sadly, contributed to his bouts of depression, nervous breakdowns, and institutionalizations).[190] Nevertheless, as noted above, Cantor was ultimately vindicated; his theories of sets and transfinite numbers have become cornerstones of the field of mathematics. Indeed, the brilliant German mathematician David Hilbert referred to Cantor's work as "the finest product of mathematical genius and one of the supreme achievements of purely intellectual human activity."[191]

Cantor's radical proposal was that there are different orders of infinity; that is, it is possible to have one infinite set that is, in a sense, "bigger" than another infinite set ("bigger" meaning that, although both sets contain an infinite number of elements, one set may contain infinitely *more* elements than the other set). This way of thinking is utterly foreign to our gut-level sense of the meaning of "infinite" – after all, endless is endless: how can anyone even conceive of one bottomless pit running deeper than another bottomless pit? They're both *bottomless* – right? Well, no. Once again, in the realms of deeper mathematics, our common sense fails us. However, it is critically important to realize that, unlike some other scientific theories or questionable "definitions", Cantor's ideas regarding infinite sets are *proven facts*. And I mean "proven" in the mathematical sense of the word; namely, proven to be *absolutely true beyond any doubt*. These ideas are not conjectures and they are not theoretical musings – they are mathematical certainties that have been established as such via rigorous mathematical proofs.

In essence, Cantor made a distinction between what are called countable (or denumerable) sets, and non-countable (or non-denumerable) sets. That distinction can be explained as follows: A **countable set** is one in which the elements of the set can be placed into a one-to-one correspondence with the elements of the set of Natural numbers[192] (recall that the set of Natural numbers is denoted by {1,2,3,...}, and is also called the set of *Counting numbers*). In other words, if the elements of some set can be placed into a one-to-one correspondence with the elements of the set of Natural numbers, then what we are saying is that each element of the original set can be individually accounted for by pairing it up – or labeling it – with an element from the set of Natural numbers. That is, although the set is infinite in size (i.e., has an unlimited number of elements) each particular element can nevertheless be individually distinguished, identified, and associated with one of the counting numbers {1,2,3,...}. Some interesting and counterintuitive results follow from this.

For example, let's consider the set of positive even integers {2, 4, 6, 8, ...}. This set is clearly an infinite set since it has an unlimited number of elements – there is no end to the even integers – yet it is a countably infinite set because we can set up a one-to-one correspondence with the set of Natural numbers by pairing up each number in the Natural numbers with its double:

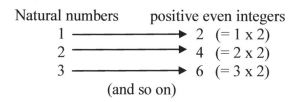

Natural numbers   positive even integers
    1 ───────────► 2 (= 1 x 2)
    2 ───────────► 4 (= 2 x 2)
    3 ───────────► 6 (= 3 x 2)
           (and so on)

Do you see what's happening here? We're simply labeling each element of the set in question (in this case, the even integers) with the Counting numbers 1, 2, 3, etc. If you can do this with a given set, then that set is considered to be a *countable set*. Countable sets are the "smallest" class of infinite sets (something Cantor designated by the transfinite number *aleph-zero*), and all countably infinite sets are considered to be of equal "size".

Now here's the first counterintuitive result to derive from this: We might naturally think of the set of positive even integers, {2, 4, 6, ...}, as being "half" the size of the set of Natural numbers, since the Natural numbers includes all the even integers (except zero) *plus all the odd integers*. It seems reasonable to think that the set that contains {1, 2, 3, 4, 5, 6, ...} is in some sense twice as big as the set that contains only {2, 4, 6, ...}. But that is, in fact, not the case. According to

Cantor's findings, the set of positive even integers is *the same size* as the set of Natural numbers. The set of even integers is only *a part of* the set of all integers – in fact, the exact terminology is that the set of even integers is *a subset of* the set of all integers, as indicated in the diagram below:

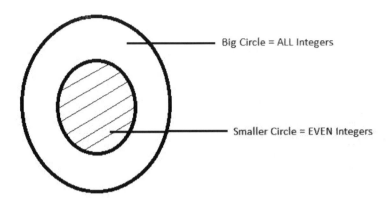

Big Circle = ALL Integers

Smaller Circle = EVEN Integers

The set of Even integers is a SUBSET of the set of All integers, yet, in accordance with Cantor's discoveries, the two sets are the same "size"

– thus what we have here is the paradoxical situation where *the part is equal to the whole*! This is as utterly illogical and counterintuitive a situation as one can imagine; yet it is a proven mathematical fact. Incredibly, such a situation also turns out to be a fundamental property of holograms, and this point will be of critical interest in Chapter 17: The Holographic Model of Reality.

Even more shocking is the fact that the set of Rational numbers (integers and fractions) is also a countable set. I say this is shocking because, when one considers all of the possible fractions that can be formed, it would seem impossible to be able pair up all the fractions with the Natural numbers; yet it *is* possible, and Cantor did it with an amazing stroke of ingenuity – Cantor *proved* that the set of Rational numbers is actually a countable set.

The irrational numbers, however, are another matter. Irrational numbers (i.e., decimal numbers that cannot be expressed as fractions) constitute what is called a **non-countable set**. And since the set of Real numbers includes the irrational numbers, it too is a non-countable set (which Cantor denoted with the transfinite number *aleph-one*). Non-countably infinite sets represent a "larger", or higher order, infinity than countably infinite sets.[193] The fact that the Real numbers are non-countable should not seem strange or unreasonable and, thankfully, mathematics is in agreement with our intuition on this matter.

But there is another conclusion that results from Cantor's work with infinite sets that is absolutely mind-blowing, and I, personally, consider it to be the single most amazing mathematical fact I have ever encountered. Furthermore, I consider this finding to be staggering in its metaphysical implications and in its relevance to the nature of reality.

Transcendental Numbers

In our discussion thus far we've seen several different sets of numbers: Natural numbers, Integers, Real numbers, etc. And we've seen that, besides these standard number sets, it is also possible to consider other number sets where the elements all possess the same properties or adhere to the same rule. A recent example we discussed is the set of even integers, which can be defined as the set containing integers that are divisible by 2. We could then conceive of the set of (all) Integers as being composed of two subsets: the set of even integers and the set of odd integers (in case you're wondering, zero is considered to be even). As you might surmise, there are many different ways to define number sets, and to split up existing sets, depending upon what criteria you choose to govern inclusion in your sets. Of interest to us in this discussion is a particular way that mathematicians have split up the set of Real numbers.

For most people whose experience of mathematics is limited to typical, real-world applications, the set of Real numbers qualifies as being the set of "all" numbers (the imaginary numbers notwithstanding) – the set of Real numbers encompasses the integers, the fractions, and the decimal numbers, which, for most of us, pretty much covers everything, number-wise. One way we can view the set of Real numbers is as a compilation of the set of Rational numbers and the set of irrational numbers. The Real numbers can also be broken down into a completely different pair of component subsets: the set of *algebraic numbers* and the set of *transcendental numbers*. Looking at the Reals in this way led Georg Cantor to an incredible discovery. Bear with me as I lay the necessary groundwork.

Let's start by defining what is meant by an *algebraic number* and a *transcendental number*. An *algebraic number* is a number that can be the solution to an algebraic equation having integer coefficients[194]. For example, consider the algebraic equation $2x - 6 = 0$: the = sign identifies it as being an equation, the variable x makes it an algebraic equation, and the coefficients, 2 and -6, are integers; thus the expression $2x - 6 = 0$ qualifies as an algebraic equation having integer coefficients. Any number that is a solution to this equation (i.e., any number which when put in place of x would cause the left side to evaluate to 0) would thus be considered an algebraic number; in this example that number is 3 (since $2(3) - 6 = 6 - 6 = 0$). As you might guess, algebraic numbers include the types of numbers the average person is thoroughly familiar with – again, the kinds of numbers we all use on a routine basis: whole numbers, integers, fractions. Well, if that's true (and it *is*), then what about the other set – the set of *transcendental numbers*? What are they?

Well, a *transcendental number* is defined, simply, as being a number that is not algebraic.[195] Okay, that's all well and good: any number that does not qualify as an algebraic number is considered to be a transcendental number – except, if the algebraic numbers include the whole numbers, integers, and fractions, then what else is left that is *not* algebraic? Good question: it turns out that the transcendental numbers are, *from the perspective of our everyday experience*, quite rare. But you do actually know of at least one transcendental number: π . That's right, the extremely important mathematical constant π is an example of a transcendental number. Another transcendental number of which you might be aware (and which we mentioned earlier) is the very important mathematical constant: *e* (Euler's number).[196] But, for the most part, those are the only two transcendental numbers most people are aware of. There definitely are other transcendental numbers out there, but they're not commonplace and they don't come up in your normal, everyday mathematical situations.

Now here's the perplexing enigma, and it is the one mathematical fact that I find most astounding: The set of algebraic numbers – the numbers we are most familiar with and most aware of – is a *countably infinite* set, whereas the set of transcendental numbers – the numbers, like π and *e*, that are uncommon in our experience and unfamiliar to us – is a *non-countably infinite* set. Let's make sure the full import and meaning of this is understood: ***The set of transcendental numbers is infinitely larger than the set of algebraic numbers***.[197] And let me be clear that this state of affairs is a mathematical fact – it has been proven true beyond any doubt. Here's how one of my math professors explained it to my class:

> Imagine all the Real numbers put into a huge hat: if you were to repeatedly reach into the hat and arbitrarily pull out a number, that number would ***almost always be a transcendental number***; rarely would you get an algebraic number.

But the conundrum here is that our real-world experience of numbers is exactly the opposite! Virtually every number we know and use is algebraic. Few of us know of any transcendental number other than π, and perhaps *e*. How can it be that the numbers that are commonplace and plentiful in our experience (i.e., the algebraic numbers) are, in truth, the rare numbers, whereas the numbers that are uncommon and scarce in our experience (i.e., the transcendental numbers) constitute, in actuality, the vast majority of numbers? How can that possibly be? Furthermore, why is it the case that two of the most important numbers in mathematics – namely, π and *e* – are transcendental numbers? And, lastly, where the hell *are* all those transcendental numbers? The implication appears to be that the transcendental numbers are mysteriously hidden away from us ... yet they are extremely important!

I will have more to say about transcendental numbers in Part IV of this book.

14.3 Sir James Lighthill's Apology

In this chapter we've looked at several topics from mathematics and science that starkly illustrate the often overlooked fact that these fields are not the rock-solid arbiters of truth which they often present themselves to be. We've seen that they are subject to inherent limitations and flaws, make assumptions that are sometimes questionable, and present theories that are occasionally rooted in the improbable. We've also seen that, as the fields of science and mathematics mature and advance, their cutting-edge discoveries are often perplexedly bizarre and disturbingly counterintuitive. Yet many of these same discoveries are also practically useful, esthetically beautiful, and proven to be factually true. And therein lie the two key premises of this chapter: (1) As knowledge in these fields expands, the findings become ever more unconventional and outlandish, and, interestingly, they also begin to concur with millennia-old concepts of ancient wisdom traditions and with ideas expressed by near-death experiencers and life-between-lives hypnosis subjects; and (2) The old and long-held scientific notion of a concrete physical deterministic clockwork reality is being proven untenable by science itself, and the old process of scientific reductionism is found to be inadequate and unsatisfactory as a method for studying a reality that is clearly holistic and interconnected.

Terence McKenna has noted that, in every era of the modern age, science has claimed that it has figured out 95% of everything there is to know, and that the remaining 5% will be understood shortly. The fallaciousness of this claim is evidenced by the fact that it has been made repeatedly for the past three hundred years. As I stated at the outset of this chapter, my contention here is not that science and mathematics are "wrong" but, rather, that they are incomplete, and that they are hampered by the false belief that they *are* complete. In this light I'd like to end this chapter by presenting the text of a statement that has come to be known as "Sir James Lighthill's Apology."

Sir James Lighthill was a British mathematician who, among many other laudable achievements, was Lucasian Professor of Mathematics at Trinity College, Cambridge, from 1969 until 1979 (he was succeeded in that position by Stephen Hawking).[198] In a paper entitled "The Recently Recognized Failure of Predictability in Newtonian Dynamics" (which appeared in the *Proceedings of the Royal Society of London* in 1986) he made the following statement, which, I think, speaks for itself (note that Sir James' use of the word "mechanics" is referring to the branch of physics that deals with the action of forces on bodies and with motion, often called "classical mechanics" or "Newtonian mechanics"):

> Here I have to pause, and to speak once again on behalf of the broad global fraternity of practitioners of mechanics. We are all deeply conscious today that the enthusiasm of our forebears for the marvelous achievements of Newtonian mechanics led them to make generalizations in this area of predictability which, indeed, we may have generally tended to believe before 1960, but which we now recognize were false. We collectively wish to apologize for having misled the general educated

public by spreading ideas about the determinism of systems satisfying Newton's laws of motion that, after 1960, were to be proved incorrect.[199]

This statement, widely referred to as "Sir James Lighthill's Apology," is remarkable for its candidness, particularly from such an eminent scientist. While Sir James' remarks were in reference to Chaos theory, we can nevertheless extend his sentiment to a deeper level of meaning; namely, that science and mathematics are never *complete.* These fields of knowledge are ever-growing, and as they grow they become more refined, more precise, and, hopefully, more representative of reality. In this manner science gradually approaches the Aristotelian concept of entelechy, a state of full realization, of actuality as opposed to potentiality. Then, and only then, will science be able to provide us with its long-promised insight into the true nature of reality.

As an intriguing footnote to all of this, recall from the previous section on Chaos Theory that scientists have discovered that chaotic systems, found to be ubiquitous throughout nature, appear to be the rule rather than the exception; now consider the degree to which we humans appear to be chaotic systems: normal heart rhythm and normal brainwave activity are now seen to be chaotic in nature, and human physiology (e.g., lungs, intestines, vascular system) displays many of the characteristics of fractal geometry. And, amazingly, medical science is finding that human pathologies are indicated by *non-chaotic* behavior; during an epileptic seizure, for example, the degree of chaos in the epileptic's brain activity actually *decreases.* In other words, a chaotic state is often a healthy state, whereas an ordered state can be pathological. As Crystal Ives so elegantly notes: "From seizures to leukemia, disease is finally being recognized for what it is: an acute attack of order".[200]

An interesting contradiction to contemplate is the fact that, while chaos seems to be "the rule in nature" most people find the seeming disorderly nature of chaotic systems to be repugnant or unnatural. I say this is a contradiction because one would think that our inherent esthetic proclivity would be consistent with how nature is structured, rather than in opposition to it. This anomalous state of affairs is due, I think, to science (and societal systems) having instilled in us an artificial affinity for order and predictability, deriving from the Newtonian-Euclidean-Darwinian notion of a mechanistic clockwork reality. In other words, we have all been, in a sense, brainwashed into believing in a reality – mechanistic, reductionist, and deterministic – that is by and large incompatible with the true nature of reality, a reality which modern science itself is revealing to be chaotic, interconnected and holistic. This, I think, is the essence of Sir James Lighthill's apology, and it is also the central point I've attempted to make in this chapter. Reality is much more complex than we have heretofore been led to believe, and mathematics and science, to their credit, are now doggedly unraveling that frustratingly tangled Gordian knot.

Chapter 15

Waves, Frequencies and Multiple Dimensions

Although we may think we are physical beings moving through a physical world, this is an illusion; we are really "receivers" floating through a kaleidoscopic sea of frequency.

- Michael Talbot, Author

I want you to know that there are no colors in the real world, there are no fragrances in the real world, that there's no beauty and there's no ugliness. Out there beyond the limits of our perceptual apparatus is the erratically ambiguous and ceaselessly flowing quantum soup.

- Sir John Eccles, Nobel laureate, Physiology or Medicine

If we are not fully informed as to the nature of reality, we should correct that oversight.

- Terence McKenna, author

If you want to find the secrets of the universe, think in terms of energy, frequency and vibration.

- Nikola Tesla, Engineer and inventor

15.1 Matter and Energy

Albert Einstein is most famous – at least among the general public – for his equation $E=mc^2$, where E represents energy, m is mass, and c is a constant representing the speed of light. This equation is known as "the principle of mass-energy equivalence" because, in essence, it implies that mass and energy are interchangeable, that they are "different aspects of the same thing."[201] This is of great significance with regard to a discussion of the nature of reality because it suggests that reality is *not* comprised of two fundamental constituents – matter and energy – but only one.[202] More recent work by Bernard Haisch, Alfonso Rueda, Hal Puthoff, and others, suggests an even more fundamental and profound realization, namely, that mass *is* energy, i.e., "there is no such thing as mass – only electric charge and energy, which together create the illusion of mass."[203]

The objects which comprise our physical reality are composed of matter, in the form of atoms, and "matter" is most commonly defined as any substance that has mass and occupies space.[204] But according to the findings mentioned in the previous paragraph, there is no such thing as "mass" – mass is, in essence, energy. Thus our physical reality is, ultimately, nothing more than an energy construct.

15.2 Waves and Frequencies

Energy exists in many different forms: heat, light, kinetic, electrical, and others. *Waves*, in the scientific sense, are traveling energy. *Frequency* refers to how many waves move past a given point during a set amount of time, typically one second. The more energy in a wave, the higher its frequency, and vice versa. A *Field* is, in the sense of classical physics, a substance that pervades space and in which every point has a "measureable state"; fields allow us to visualize, for example, light as the propagation of waves across space.[205]

As we saw in Chapter 13, our perception of reality begins with our biological sensory apparatus (eyes, ears, etc.) taking in stimulus energies from the external environment. These energies correspond to different frequencies and wave-lengths, and they travel in waves by means of fields. We also saw that our sensory organs are not always capable of accessing the full range of stimulus energies (recall the examples of light and sound, also from Chapter 13). Putting the information from Chapters 13 and 14 together, we discover that physical reality (matter) is related to mass, mass is energy, and our sensory organs are not capable of detecting the full ranges of various forms of energy. Thus we are "receiving", if you will, only a portion of physical reality. As an analogy, consider a radio tuner.

When you turn on a radio tuner and turn the channel selector in an attempt to pick up a particular station, you are tuning the receiver to a particular frequency. The channel selector knob lets you scan through the various frequencies; to tune into a desired radio channel, you set the tuner knob at the frequency over which that channel is broadcasting. Let's say your radio is set to receive a jazz music channel: the radio is tuned to the frequency of that channel and thus receives the signal being transmitted at that frequency, and you hear the jazz music being broadcast by that channel. While you are enjoying the jazz music, the fact is that the space all around you is awash with signals being broadcast at other frequencies – classical music channels, hard rock channels, all-news channels, etc. – but since your tuner is not set at those other frequencies, you are not aware of the information they contain. They're *there*, but you are simply not set to receive them. In a like manner, it is entirely possible that there are other realities coexisting with our own reality but involving frequencies that are outside of our perceptible range; those realities are *there*, but we are not receiving them because our biological tuning equipment is not designed to tune into those frequencies.

15.3 Other Dimensions

Some people think those other realities might be other dimensions, or other realms. In particular, it is thought that the Spirit Realm may simply be another reality coexisting with our own reality but functioning at a higher frequency. According to this theory, matter is merely a low frequency (and thus low energy), high density state of being. Conversely, the Spirit Realm exists at a much higher frequency (higher energy) and a much lower density. This concept is actually very consistent with what we know of the afterlife from the Newton Model, namely that the Spirit Realm and its inhabitants (souls) are by all accounts ethereal in nature – non-solid and composed of light (which is a form of energy). Furthermore, recall that many NDErs and LBL hypnosis subjects insist that there is no time, as we know it, in the Spirit Realm; we experience time as a linear one-way transit from past to future, but in the Spirit Realm time is experienced as an "eternal now." Time, in our sense of it, is an artifact of three-dimensional space. The three spatial dimensions of 3D reality – length, width, and height – are measured using the concept of distance, and time is intimately related to distance – think back on the simple formula from your school days: *Rate x Time = Distance*. If there is no time in the Spirit Realm, then there is no "distance" there, i.e., there is no 3D/solid reality there – the Spirit Realm reality must be something entirely different. Also, according to Albert Einstein, time slows down the faster you travel: as one's speed approaches the speed of light, time approaches zero. *At the speed of light, time becomes zero*, i.e., at the speed of light time ceases to exist. Now, consider the claim that souls are light-beings and the Spirit Realm is a realm of light, and the fact that both NDErs and LBL subjects tell us that *there is no time* in the Spirit Realm! That is exactly as we would expect according to the dictates of physics: The Spirit Realm and the souls inhabiting it are composed of light, thus that reality exists at the speed of light, and therefore, according to Einstein, there is no time there. The claims made by NDErs and LBL subjects regarding time are borne out by the laws of physics.

On a more personal and practical level, we can refer to our own everyday experiences as a means of discerning the logicality of these ideas. Think of situations where you have become completely absorbed in some activity – reading a good book, listening to beautiful music, writing, researching, daydreaming, etc. In such situations, there is a feeling of lightness-of-being that is not experienced in our usual everyday activities. The more we remove ourselves from material/physical experience, the lighter – or less dense – we feel. Furthermore, when we finally extract ourselves from such absorbing experiences we are often amazed to discover how much time has elapsed since we first began the activity. Our sense of time is altered to the extent that, for a while, *we did not experience the passage of time.* This effect is particularly pronounced during meditation and hypnosis. When I had my hypnosis session with Mira Kelley the hypnosis portion alone lasted about five hours. When Mira took me out of the hypnotic state and told me the time, I simply couldn't believe it! From my perspective, it felt as though perhaps only two hours had elapsed. I've also found that, contrary to my expectations, right after meditating or undergoing hypnosis I feel invigorated and energized. I honestly believe that by partially removing ourselves from physical experience we raise our frequency and energy levels, and thus we become in a very real sense lighter, i.e., less dense. For those of you who have tried meditation and/or hypnosis, think about how you are advised to prepare yourself: you are told to find a quiet place where there are no distracting sounds, close curtains and blinds to block out light, get into a comfortable position, close your eyes ... in other words, *you are told to cut yourself off as much as possible from the sensory stimuli of physical reality.* As we move further and further from material reality, we experience a higher frequency and energy state, we feel less dense, and we lose touch with our experience of the passage of time. And, once again, this "subjective" experience is borne out by science: What happens when an object moves further and further away from a planetary body (i.e., a dense material mass)? Gravity decreases! The object becomes *lighter.*

All of the above observations are consistent with the widely held notion that our physical, three-dimensional reality is a high-density, low-energy reality where objects appear solid and where time is experienced as a linear, one-way affair; the Spirit Realm, however, is a light-based, low-density, high-energy reality that is ethereal rather than physical, and where time is experienced as an "eternal now." In this regard, it is theorized that the Spirit Realm may exist in another dimension, one that possibly coexists with our own reality in much the same way that different radio channel frequencies coexist simultaneously in the same space. However, our "receiving hardware" – i.e., our sensory organs and brains – are designed to receive signals only at the frequency of 3D reality and *not* at the frequency of the Spirit Realm (at least, not while we're alive). In other words, we are like radio tuners that can only receive one channel – the 3D reality channel – and therefore other realities or dimensions which might coexist with our reality are not accessible by us and thus are not part of our experience. Interestingly, the various flavors of String Theory all require additional dimensions beyond our three spatial dimensions and one temporal dimension: Bosonic String theory (the original version of String Theory) requires 26 dimensions, Superstring theory requires 10 dimensions, and M-theory requires 11 dimensions.[206]

Chapter 16

Is Reality "Real"?

Reality is an illusion, albeit a very persistent one.

- Albert Einstein, physicist

There is no out there, out there.

- John Wheeler, physicist

What we observe is not nature itself, but nature exposed to our method of questioning.

- Werner Heisenberg, physicist

We are basically bogged down in the superstition of materialism, which says that sensory experience is the crucial test of reality.

- Deepak Chopra, M.D., author

Our brains mathematically construct 'hard reality' by relying on input from a frequency domain.

- Karl Pribram, neurophysiologist

The question posed by the title of this chapter – Is Reality "Real"? – is asking, in effect, if the way we *perceive* reality is an accurate representation of the way reality actually *is*. Or, to put it another way: Is the true nature of the objective, undistorted external reality consistent with our perception of that reality? We can even carry the question a step further by contemplating whether there is any kind of external reality at all; we can reasonably ask: Does reality have an existence independent of its perception by human beings? We saw in Chapter 13 that our reality is a perceived reality subject to processing and modification by our brain and sensory apparatus. In this chapter we will develop that premise further in an attempt to ascertain the true nature of the external reality, and to understand how our sensory organs and brain actually transform that raw reality into the processed reality that we experience.

In his short video "What is consciousness?" Deepak Chopra, M.D., states: "We experience the world from our subjective point of view. We see objects and beings as existing in their own right, separate from us. This is an illusion."[207] The idea that our physical reality is an illusory reality is actually a belief that goes back thousands of years. Hinduism, Buddhism, and Sikhism all speak of the concept of *Maya*, or life as illusion.[208] Likewise, the Kabbalah, a Judaic set of ancient esoteric teachings and wisdom, endorses the belief that there is no objective, perceptible, external reality; instead, Kabalistic philosophy posits that, "The entire world is within us, and we feel that we are influenced from the outside because we are created this way."[209] Rabbi and author David A. Cooper states that Kabbalah is, in fact, "a way of perceiving the nature of reality."[210] One must ask oneself why Albert Einstein, Deepak Chopra, and other great minds, as well as ancient belief systems thousands of years old, all suggest that the reality we experience as being "out there" is actually an illusion. This is a bold and controversial claim, and one that is surely not made lightly and without good reason.

Part of the reason, it turns out, goes back to our earlier discussion of the fact that our reality is a perceived reality, and that our perceptions are dictated by the biological apparatus of sensory impression with which we are equipped. Our brain is, in effect, *constructing* a "reality" out of sensory data inputted via our sensory organs. Clearly, something "out there" is transmitting the energetic stimuli which are picked up by our sensory organs and decoded by our brains, and the product of those decrypted stimuli is our perception of reality. The question is: What is the *source* of those energy stimuli? What it all boils down to, basically, is this: When I see a chair in front of me, is it really a chair – as I'm perceiving it – or is it something else that is being decoded into the image of a chair by my brain? Amazingly, the scientific evidence suggests that it is *something else*.

16.1 Atoms and Subatomic Particles

For about two thousand years – from the time of the ancient Greeks until the formulation of quantum theory – the scientific model of reality was, understandably, a materialist model that painted a picture of a concrete, physical reality constructed of solid particles. At first atoms were thought to be the fundamental constituents of physical reality, and they were imagined as being akin to miniscule billiard balls. As scientific understanding and technology improved, it was discovered that atoms themselves are composed of more elementary particles – sub-atomic particles; specifically, the atom was then envisioned as being comprised of a central nucleus, containing protons and neutrons, which was orbited by electrons. This is the model of reality I was taught in high school, and those sub-atomic particles – the protons, neutrons, and electrons – were themselves described to me as being solid particles. So reality was still being presented – in the early part of my life – as being, fundamentally, something solid, albeit by means of a refined theory that was uncovering ever smaller particles to serve as the basis of the concrete reality.

While this notion – that microscopic solid particles are the building blocks of our perceived solid macro-reality – might make sense on an intuitive level, the fact of the matter is something quite different: when one considers the relative magnitudes of the sub-atomic particles that make up an atom, one discovers that what we consider to be solid matter is, in truth, mostly empty space (99.9999999% empty space).[211] By way of an analogy, if the nucleus of a hydrogen atom was the size of a basketball, then the electron circling that nucleus would be 20 miles away – everything in between is empty.[212] Thus the apparent, or perceived, solidity of the matter that makes up reality is, in truth, anything but solid; it is mostly empty space.

Furthermore, not only are the sub-atomic particles that make up atoms infinitesimally small in relation to the size of the atom, but those sub-atomic particles themselves turn out to be very un-particle-like. With the advent of quantum theory it has been discovered that the so-called sub-atomic "particles" do not possess attributes typically associated with matter. An electron is now described as being a "point particle" that has "no spatial extent."[213] That is, an electron does not possess dimension.[214] Meinard Kuhlmann, in his Scientific American article *What is Real?*, noted that what physicists think of as "particles" are nothing like the popular conception of "tiny billiard balls" and that, while physicists often use the term "particles" to refer to the components of nature, the truth is that "there are no such things."[215]

So, although the world around us appears to be made up of solid objects which themselves are composed of microscopically small particles called atoms, we find that the sub-atomic constituents of atoms are so widely spaced apart, and are so exceedingly small themselves, that the atoms which they comprise are in actuality mostly empty space. Furthermore, those tiny sub-atomic "particles" that occupy that vast space are, in fact, not particles at all. So much for reality being physical and concrete. But if reality isn't made up of solid objects, then what exactly *is* it made of?

16.2 Wave-Particle Duality

In Chapter 15 we saw that the objects which comprise our "physical" reality are composed of matter (in the form of atoms) and that "matter" is most commonly defined as any substance that has mass and occupies space. We also learned that there is no such thing as "mass" – mass is, in essence, energy. (Recall also that *waves* are traveling energy, and that the concept of a *field* was introduced by scientists as a way to explain the mechanism by which waves propagate across space). Thus we have the conundrum of a seemingly solid, physical reality composed of sub-atomic "particles" that, upon inspection, are anything but particulate. The obvious question is: Which is it? Is our physical reality composed of particles or of waves? The surprising answer is: both ... or neither.

In the early nineteenth century Thomas Young performed a now-famous experiment to determine if light consists of particles or if it exhibits wave-like behavior. The results were completely contrary to what common sense would dictate.

Such an experiment involves a coherent light source, such as a laser, illuminating a plate containing two vertical slits. The light passes through the slits and strikes a screen on the other side of the plate, and a so-called *wave interference pattern* appears on the screen; this pattern results from the constructive and destructive interference of two waves, one going through each slit. This indicates the wave nature of light. The same result is obtained by firing a stream of electrons. If the stream of electrons is slowed to one electron per second, the electrons do behave as particles in the sense that they strike the screen individually; however, with time these individual strikes build up to form the wave interference pattern! *How?* At such a slow rate, each electron (or photon) is *not* interacting with other photons to produce the interference pattern – there are not two waves to create the interference pattern since each electron is passing through a single slit by itself. What is the electron reacting *with* to form the pattern? And, for that matter, how does the electron "know" that there are two slits present? But wait – it gets better. If a measuring device is placed at the slits to "see" what is happening (i.e., to determine which slit the electron or photon goes through), the electrons change from waves to particles and leave a particle pattern on the screen – the interference pattern is not produced! In other words, if the human observer looks for a particle (using particle detectors), then a particle is found, but if he/she looks for a wave (using a wave detector), then a wave pattern is found. This is the concept known as *wave-particle duality*: a quantum entity has a dual *potential* nature. This experiment illustrates what is known as "The Measurement Problem" in quantum physics: reality at the quantum level cannot be perceived directly, and so it must be measured through the use of instruments; but this very act of attempted measurement disturbs the energy and position of the subatomic particles.[216]

While the double-slit experiment demonstrates the wave-particle duality of light, French physicist Louis de Broglie later established that matter (i.e., sub-atomic particles) also possesses wave-particle duality.[217]

16.3 Beginning to Put the Pieces Together: Perception and Reality

The double-slit experiment, Louis de Broglie, and the resulting insight into the wave-particle duality of quantum entities suggests the following conjecture: When we look at or attempt to measure an electron, the electron collapses from being a wave into a particle; that is, sub-atomic particles – the fundamental particles of "reality" – only behave like *particles* when someone is looking at them, otherwise they behave like waves (i.e., not solid). This "collapsing of the wave function" caused by observation/measurement is how our perception creates the "reality" we perceive: Our five senses, in conjunction with our brain, cause the energy construct in which we exist to collapse into what we perceive as "physical reality". When we're *not* looking, reality is a wave phenomenon, but when we *do* look, the wave function collapses into a particle state and we perceive reality as solid.

The above hypothesis is one of the most important concepts presented in this book, and as such it bears restating: The true nature of the reality in which we exist is not physical but, rather, energetic; our experience of reality as seemingly physical is the result of our biological perceptual apparatus (i.e., our sensory organs) and our brains decoding an energy construct into the appearance of physical reality by collapsing the wave function to a particulate state.

We translate the energetic reality into an illusion of physical reality. This is possible because the energetic reality is not a random, chaotic amalgamation of energy but, instead, is a structured energy rich with information. And we are biologically equipped to decode that information and translate it into a perceived physical experience. How that might be accomplished will be developed further as we proceed through this part of the book.

16.4 Fields

In Chapter 15 we defined some basic scientific terms that are fundamental to our understanding of reality. Of particular importance is the concept of a *Field*. The notion of a field is a conceptualized generalization introduced by scientists as an attempt to explain the mechanism by which waves propagate across space and influence distant objects.[218] That is, a field can be thought of as a medium of energy propagation in the form of waves. A familiar example is a magnetic field, whereby a magnet exerts an invisible influence on iron by attracting it. Although there is nothing "material" connecting the magnet and the iron, the influence of the magnet on the iron is perceptible and measurable – and that influence is measurable at every point within the field. That explanation is, at least, the way classical physics viewed things. Under quantum physics, however, the concept of a field has changed: the measured quantities present at every point in the "classical field" are now seen –in the "quantum field" – as being replaced by a "spectrum of possible quantities."[219] Quantum fields are envisioned as resulting not from forces, but rather from an exchange of energy between our old friends the "particles," which are themselves not actual particles but bundles of energy.[220] These energy packets arise out of (and reintegrate with) the underlying field like droplets of water out of a churning ocean. From the perspective of quantum theory, then, we see that the old classical notion of a "particle" is nothing more than a manifestation of energy temporarily arising out of the underlying field, then remerging with it. In other words, *the essential, primary reality is the underlying field itself.*

What most people consider to be the "empty" space surrounding us – the space in which everything exists – has been demonstrated by science to be anything but empty; that supposed vacuum or nothingness is, in actuality, a "giant reservoir of energy" known as the Zero Point Field.[221] At the sub-atomic level, elementary particles interact with one another via an exchange of energy that is accomplished through "virtual particles" – quantum particles that emerge from, and remerge with, the Zero Point Field in the briefest fraction of a second. As noted in the paragraph above, quantum fields result from this virtual particle-mediated energy exchange. These field-spawned particles, and the resulting energy fluctuations and fields, all exist within the *Zero Point Field* – what author Lynne McTaggart refers to as "a field of fields."[222] Recall again that a field is nothing more than a medium for wave propagation, and a wave is nothing more than traveling energy, and mass (matter) *is* energy: thus the Zero Point Field – the "field of fields" womb out of which quantum particles and energy are born – can be seen as the primary and fundamental sub-structure of our perceived reality.

16.5 Fourier Transforms

In the early nineteenth century, the French mathematician Jean Baptiste Joseph Fourier made a discovery of such monumental importance as to qualify for the short list of the most significant mathematical advances of all time, putting his discovery in the company of such portentous breakthroughs as Isaac Newton's invention of the calculus.[223] Joseph Fourier discovered that every differentiable function, no matter how strange its graph, can be represented by an infinite series of sine and cosine functions.[224] If you think back to your high school classes in trigonometry, you will remember that the sine and cosine functions are wave functions; thus Fourier's discovery amounts to the realization that mathematical functions can be built up from, and broken down into, waves (it should be noted that scientific formulas are a type of mathematical function, and such formulas are used to describe and model our reality). The mathematical tool by which this is accomplished is called a Fourier Transform, [225] and the branch of mathematics dedicated to expressing periodic functions as the sums of sines is called "harmonic analysis"; as Alfred North Whitehead has noted, both the abstract theory of periodic functions and their applications to physical science are "dominated" by Fourier's Theorem.[226]

Fourier transforms play a key role in signal processing and as such have applications in a vast variety of technological disciplines, including image processing, television and radio transmissions, and computer graphics. [227] (As a young boy watching television I always wondered how it was possible for the video of a TV show to be sent through the airwaves, picked up by my TV's antenna, and then reconstructed into the video I was seeing on my TV screen; it seemed like magic to me – now I know that the "magic" was due to Fourier transforms). Of particular significance to our discussion is the fact that Fourier transforms can be used to translate patterns into waves and vice versa; in other words, Fourier transforms provide the means by which optical images can be translated into mathematical wave functions, and by which those wave functions can be translated back into optical images. In fact, engineer Dennis Gabor utilized Fourier transforms in his discovery of holography, for which he was awarded the Nobel prize in physics.[228] (As we will later see, holography is the cornerstone of the model of reality toward which we are headed).

16.6 More Pieces of the Puzzle: Perception and Reality

In what has become known as the de Broglie hypothesis, the de Broglie postulate, or wave-particle duality, French physicist and Nobel Laureate Louis de Broglie "postulated the wave nature of electrons and suggested that *all matter has wave properties*."[229] [italics mine]. Notice what is happening here: We have a set of mathematical tools – i.e., the Fourier transforms – that gives us the means of translating waves – energy – to and from optical images – in essence, geometry. In other words, *Fourier transforms provide a mathematical bridge between the sub-atomic energy domain level of reality (waves) and the visually perceived macro-level of spatial-geometric reality (patterns, forms)*. That bridge could be the key to understanding how our perception of reality operates; to wit: Is it possible that we humans are somehow biologically equipped to utilize Fourier transforms to translate an external energy-information construct into what we perceive, via our senses, to be "physical" reality? Amazingly, there exists some very convincing scientific evidence suggesting that this is precisely what is happening.

Discoveries from research conducted in the 1960s demonstrated that brain cell activity in the visual cortex is pattern-dependent – different brain cells fire depending on the nature of the pattern perceived; for example, looking at a horizontal line will stimulate certain brain cells, while looking at a vertical line will stimulate different brain cells. Using these findings while researching perception of spatial information and how it is analyzed and encoded in the brain, husband and wife neurophysiologists Russell and Karen DeValois made a profound discovery: neurons in the visual cortex responded to the *wave forms*, derived via Fourier mathematics, of plaid and checkerboard patterns.[230] This finding suggests that our brain may be using Fourier transforms to translate wave forms into visual images. Additional research has suggested that our other senses – hearing, smell, touch and taste – also function as "frequency analyzers"[231] culminating in what might be thought of as a "Fourier Approach to sensory perception." [232]

As an analogy, consider the following scenario: You walk into a café that offers wireless access to the internet; the internet in that café exists as an invisible energy-information field – you can't see it, you can't feel it – but if you have a laptop or tablet computer that has the WiFi capability needed to access that field, and if it also has the software capability to decode that field, then all of a sudden that energy-information field becomes a perceivable "reality" – the reality of the Web pages on the internet. With the proper equipment you can transform that invisible energy field into a perceivable and meaningful reality. That is precisely what is happening with us: our sensory organs access the energy field, and our brains decode the energy into our perceived reality.

Our sensory organs and brains are creating our reality, a seemingly physical reality derived from the true (or truer) primary energetic reality of The Field. Our eyes are converting light waves into images, our ears are converting waves of disturbance in the air into sound. But "sound" is merely a relationship between the vibrations in the air and a sensory organ (our ears). If there were no ears, then there would be no sound – there *would be* vibrations in the air, but there would be no "sound." Likewise, our eyes are converting electro-magnetic waves into the images we perceive visually. In a world without eyes there would be no "things" – as we perceive them to be – but simply their unconverted vibrations or energies. Our sensory organs and brains decode an environment of energetic information into "reality" – in other words, *the totality of our perceived reality is nothing more than a subjective experience that is reconstructed from sensory data; we have no idea to what extent, if any, our perceived reality corresponds to the objective, external reality.*

This realization has elevated the role of human consciousness from being a mere *observer of reality* to that of a *participant in the creation of reality*. St. Francis of Assisi said, "What you're looking for is what is looking." Now science has provided the incredible explanation for that mysterious statement: Our consciousness creates our reality.

The brilliant philosopher Alan Watts made the point very eloquently by noting that in order to have a rainbow there must be: moisture in the atmosphere, sunlight striking that moisture at a particular angle, and an observer to perceive the rainbow. The observer is a necessary ingredient for the existence of the rainbow; without the observer there is *no rainbow* – there is merely sunlight striking moisture in the atmosphere at a particular angle.

16.7 The Puzzle Complete: Perception and Reality

There is a concept from Taoism called *hun-tun* that refers to a state of chaos: not "chaos" in the western sense of confusion and disorder, but rather a cosmic egg kind of chaos – a primal state of infinite possibility and potential out of which all creation occurs. [233] In my opinion, *hun-tun* and the Zero Point Field are one and the same. When physicists speak of electrons or other quantum particles existing as a wave, they mean a wave of possible locations where the electron could manifest as a particle when it is observed – i.e., a wave of possibilities ... a probability wave. This "wave of possibilities" in which the quantum world exists has been called by many names:

- The Quantum Wave Function
- The Implicate Order (Bohm)
- The Zero Point Field
- The Unified Field
- The Field of Infinite Potentiality
- The Matrix
- The Energetic/Informational Construct
- The Ocean of Existence
- The Field of Intelligence

... or simply, "The Field" – a field of unlimited possibilities out of which everything is created. Everything in existence – matter, energy, forces – are merely ripples in this field, waves of vibration in the field. There is no objective, independent "physical" reality – at least, not in the way we've been led to believe. The true reality is a domain of waves and frequencies. It is our brain's decoding of those waves and frequencies, via Fourier transforms, that creates the illusion of the seemingly "concrete" reality that we perceive. When we interact with The Field using our senses and our brain we cause the wave functions to collapse to their particulate state, and we then comprehend the resulting "reality" as being solid, physical, and composed of discrete and distinct constituent parts. This is what near-death experiencers and life-between-lives hypnosis subjects are referring to when they say that life on earth is an "illusion" and that "everything is one": The Field is "everything-as-one," and the transformation of The Field by our sensory-brain system into "physical reality" is the illusion. Everything that we perceive of existence is actually the result of one single process that diversifies: that one single process is the Field, and the diversifications are the collapsed wave functions. Everything in existence truly is *one*, in the sense that everything arises out of that single Zero Point Field; The Field is the source of all creation. In its pure, underived form The Zero Point Field is the true reality. Our perceived reality, on the other hand, is an illusion; it is an artificial experience that is derived and decoded from the primary reality which is The Field.

So, then – Is the Zero Point Field, as the womb of creation, *God*? In my humble opinion: No, not quite. Recall that the true external reality is an energy-*information* construct. The chaos of Chaos Theory has been found to possess an underlying *order*. *Order* (i.e., structure) implies *information*. We are still missing the informational component of the reality construct. As the old saying says, "It takes two to tango." The womb cannot conceive and give birth on its own – the egg must first be fertilized before creation can occur. Recall that the Field is considered – by both physicists and metaphysicists – to be an ocean of *potentiality*, a field of *probability waves*, some of which occasionally collapse into a particle state to form our perceived reality. The Zero Point Field is thus the *egg of creation*, the raw material out of which the fruits of creation are born. The *seed* – the thing that fertilizes that cosmic egg – is what I call the Organizing Principle (OP). The Organizing Principle is the information source that gives structure and coherence to the raw disordered stuff of the Field; i.e., it is the intelligence that organizes the chaos of the Field into form (I will discuss the Organizing Principle in depth in Chapter 21). The Creative Source of All, then, is more accurately seen (in my opinion) as the concresence of The Zero Point Field with the Organizing Principle, the merging of a chaotic collection of symbols with a set of grammatical rules specifying syntax and usage. Interestingly, this is consistent with the concepts from Chinese philosophy known as *yin* and *yang*, two "complementary (rather than opposing) forces that interact to form a dynamic system..."[234]

The ancient religious belief systems – the so-called pagan religions – possessed an important feminine component that has been all but excised from the patriarchal monotheistic religions of modernity. Under pagan doctrine, male and female were assigned equally important roles to play in the divine plan. I propose that this ancient yin-yang cosmology of interdependence is closer to the truth in its description of the nature of reality than are present-day religions, including the religion of scientism. The Zero Point Field represents the female aspect of the creation of reality, providing the egg component of the creation equation in the form of the raw material of the ocean of potentiality. The male aspect is the Organizing Principle, providing the information that organizes the disordered chaos of the Field into the structured forms of "reality." That Organizing Principle utilizes – or *is* – mathematics. The idea that reality and mathematics are synonymous is not as far-fetched as it sounds: Physicist Max Tegmark of the Massachusetts Institute of Technology in Cambridge believes that math not only governs our universe, but that reality itself is a mathematical structure. This theory is known as the Mathematical Universe Hypothesis (MUH).[235]

Well, then, what of we humans? What role, if any, do *we* play in this cosmic dance between energy and mathematics? Considering all we've learned thus far, it would seem quite possible that we are the agents of the Organizing Principle: we collapse the wave functions, we transform the energy-information construct into a perception of form, we ... *create*. Perhaps this is the meaning behind the enigmatic statement ascribed to Jesus in John 10:34 and Psalm 82:6 that, "Ye are gods."

16.8 Plato's Allegory of the Cave

In his work *The Republic*, the Greek philosopher Plato presents a dialogue between Plato's brother Glaucon and Plato's mentor Socrates that has become known as *The Allegory of the Cave* or *Plato's Cave*. In this parable Socrates describes a group of people who have lived their entire lives chained in a cave and facing a blank wall, with a fire burning behind them. As people and things pass between the prisoners' backs and the fire, shadows are cast upon the wall the prisoners are facing. The prisoners' entire experience of reality is limited to their viewing of these shadows, and they have absolutely no idea or comprehension of the true nature of the people and objects that are the sources of those shadows. To the prisoners, the shadows *are* reality.

I think we humans are in a situation very similar to the prisoners in Plato's cave: the "physical" reality we perceive is merely a series of shadows cast by a higher reality – namely, The Field – but we are falsely interpreting those shadows as being the true reality. If we are to break the chains of scientific materialism and reductionism, then we must think deeper and harder about what might be the source of the shadows we are perceiving, and we must take care not to accept the superficial forms of our perception as being the true nature of reality.

Chapter 17

The Holographic Model
of Reality

Surprising new clues are emerging that you and I and even space itself may actually be a kind of hologram. That is, everything we see and experience – everything we call our three-dimensional reality – may be a projection of information stored on a thin, distant, two-dimensional surface...

- Brian Greene, Theoretical physicist, string theorist

Is the three-dimensional world an illusion, in the same sense that a hologram is an illusion? Perhaps. I think that I'm inclined to think "Yes," that the three-dimensional world is a kind of illusion, and that the ultimate precise reality is the two-dimensional reality at the surface of the universe.

- Leonard Susskind, Theoretical physicist

The tangible reality of our everyday lives is really a kind of illusion, like a holographic image... Underlying it is a deeper order of existence, a vast and more primary level of reality that gives birth to all the objects and appearances of our physical world in much the same way that a piece of holographic film gives birth to a hologram.

- David Bohm, physicist

In the preceding chapters of Part III we've seen evidence that our reality is not the physical, deterministic reality traditionally described by science; rather, it appears to be more along the lines of an energy-information construct possessing a fractal structure and probabilistic nature that are typical of chaotic systems. By many accounts, both ancient and modern, our "physical" reality is considered an illusion, a shadow-world of a greater and deeper reality.

We also learned that our experience of reality is selective and subjective, due to: (1) the limitations of our sensory organs, acting as our reality input devices; and (2) the decoding and editing of environmental signals performed by our brain, acting as our reality processing unit.

Finally, the tantalizing relationship existing between reality and mathematics, considered in conjunction with the purposeful and complex structure of DNA and other biological molecules, strongly suggest the likelihood of intentional design underlying the foundation and formation of reality.

Any meaningful model of reality must address all of these features. And, lest we forget where our journey started, such a model should also be somehow consistent with our model of the Afterlife, since, after all, our reality is the stage upon which reincarnation and the resolution of karma are carried out. It turns out that, going as far back as at least the 1980s, such a model has existed, and, in the intervening years, a growing body of evidence has emerged confirming the validity of this model. This controversial yet intellectually reasonable and robust model is known as the Holographic Model of Reality.

17.1 Michael Talbot: The Holographic Universe

By far my favorite pastime is reading, and, while it is true that I derive much enjoyment from works of fiction, my greatest passion lies in reading non-fiction. I find the acquisition of new knowledge to be the most exciting, rewarding and satisfying pursuit of all. As such, if I were asked to recommend what I believe to be the most important and worthwhile nonfiction books one should read, my choices for numbers one and two on the list would be Michael Newton's *Journey of Souls* and *Destiny of Souls*. Following very close on the heels of those two books you'd find my choice for the number three position – the late Michael Talbot's extraordinary book *The Holographic Universe*. Just as Dr. Newton's two books represent the "go-to" books regarding the Afterlife model, Mr. Talbot's book is surely the "go-to" book when it comes to the Holographic Model of Reality, as it brings together much of the information pertinent to the holographic theory available at that time (the book was originally published in 1991). In the years since, a great deal more evidence has surfaced in support of the holographic theory, and it is not uncommon nowadays to learn of many mainstream scientists who openly subscribe to this model or, at least, seriously entertain it (as the epigraphs introducing this chapter clearly illustrate).

Talbot reasonably traces the modern origin of the Holographic Model of Reality to physicist David Bohm and neurophysiologist Karl Pribram, each of whom developed their theses independently of one another, and from the unique perspectives of their respective disciplines.[236] Modern views notwithstanding, one could make an arguable case that the concept is far older, as there are interesting parallels between the holographic model and the belief, held by many ancient wisdom traditions, that our reality is illusory. And, as you now know, this is also the understanding reported by near-death experiencers and life-between-lives hypnosis subjects. But before we can explore the development and features of the Holographic model we must first be clear on what a hologram is.

17.2 Holograms

The discovery of the hologram was a consequence of work performed by physicist Dennis Gabor in the 1940s to improve electron microscope technology (Dr. Gabor was awarded the Nobel Prize in Physics in 1971 for his discovery and development of holography).[237] Perhaps the most famous example of a hologram is the holographic message recorded by Princess Leia and stored in the robot R2D2, as depicted in the original *Star Wars* movie (a Google search of "Princess Leia hologram" should provide multiple links to related video clips).

A hologram itself is a kind of three-dimensional "photograph" of an object created by recording the interference pattern formed by two intersecting light waves. As such, a hologram is somewhat analogous to a sound recording, but, whereas the sound recording involves sound waves, a hologram derives from interfering light waves. And just as an audio recording can be played to reproduce the original sound, so too can a hologram be "played" (i.e., reconstructed) to reproduce a virtual image of the original source object. Specifically, holography works as follows: A beam of light from a laser is split into two beams by a beam splitter such that one beam (the "object beam") is reflected off of the object to be "holographed", then through a diffusing lens which spreads the beam, and onto a holographic plate or film; the other beam (the "reference beam") is reflected off a mirror, also spread via a diffusing lens, and directed in such a way that it intersects with the first beam at the holographic plate. When the two beams converge their waves cause an interference pattern that is recorded on the holographic plate/film. This recorded interference pattern is the hologram.[238] See the illustration below:

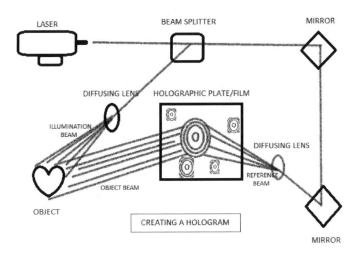

CREATING A HOLOGRAM

Unlike with a photograph, you will not see an image of the holographed object when you look at the holographic plate; rather you would see what appear to be rough concentric circles and swirls of various sizes (it almost looks like the cratered surface of the moon). To again use the analogy with recorded music, just as holding a music CD to your ear would not result in you hearing any music, so looking at a holographic plate would not reveal an image of the object that was holographed. However, when an appropriate laser is shined through the holographic film its beam is diffracted in such a way that it recreates the original object beam as it was before it intersected with the reference beam; your brain interprets the light from this diffracted beam as a virtual three-dimensional image seemingly projected out in front of you. In truth there is no image floating about; in spite of how realistic some holograms may appear, if you attempt to touch the hologram, your hand will pass right through it. Furthermore, any attempt to measure any unusual energy presence at the hologram's apparent location will prove futile;[239] the holographic image you perceive is a *virtual* image – it is an illusion: the laser passing through the holographic plate is recreating the *original object beam* (the beam that was reflected off the object when the hologram was created), which, when your eyes detect it, is then interpreted by your brain as if it were a beam of light being reflected off of an actual object.[240] Thus there is no image where you think you see one – the hologram resides solely on the holographic plate, and your brain is fooling you into perceiving an image where, in fact, nothing exists (recall our discussion from Chapter 13 regarding ways in which our brain deceives us into perceiving a false or distorted reality).

Another amazing property of holograms – and one particularly relevant to a theme being developed throughout this book – is the fact that if a holographic film is cut up into pieces, and if you were to then shine the appropriate laser through any one of the pieces of that holographic film, you would see *the complete image* of the object that was holographed rather than merely a part of the image; in other words, *each piece of a holographic film contains all the information necessary to reconstruct the entire holographic image*. We've already seen several variations on this theme elsewhere in this book: (1) in living organisms, each cell contains the full set of DNA code necessary to recreate the entire organism; (2) in fractal mathematics, fractal curves (such as the Koch snowflake discussed in Chapter 14) possess the property of *self-similarity*, meaning that the whole curve has the same shape as that of its parts; (3) mathematician Georg Cantor proved that for certain infinite sets it is possible for a portion of a set (i.e., a subset) to be equal in size to the set itself. As you might imagine, this idea of *the part being equal to the whole* has important ramifications with regard to the claims made by NDErs and LBL subjects – and even some physicists – that everything in existence is, in actuality, One.

Having seen what a hologram is, we can now begin to formulate an impression of what is being suggested by the notion that reality itself is a hologram. Specifically, the Holographic Model of Reality is proposing that our so-called "reality" is an ethereal medium which presents us with the illusion of form and substance. Just as with a hologram, our reality may look solid and appear to be three-dimensional, but in truth it is an insubstantial phantasm of the mind and sensory organs. As disorienting as this idea may feel, it turns out that there is actually an impressive amount of "real world" evidence to support the Holographic Model of Reality, and that brings us back to Michael Talbot and his book *The Holographic Universe*.

As noted at the beginning of this chapter, Mr. Talbot's book highlight's the work of physicist David Bohm and neurophysiologist Karl Pribram as laying the original groundwork for the Holographic Model of Reality. Working from the unique perspectives of their respective disciplines, and initially unaware of one another's work, these two scientists independently arrived at the startling conclusion that the universe may be a giant hologram, the formation of which may be due, at least in part, to the human brain. How and why these scientists were led to this thesis is not only a fascinating story, but also serves to provide some of the evidence in support of this theory.

17.3 Karl Pribram: The Brain as Hologram

In Pribram's case, the seed for the holographic model idea was planted when he was working with neuropsychologist Karl Lashley at the Yerkes Laboratory of Primate Biology in the 1940's. Lashley was trying to locate the area of the brain responsible for memory storage, and his approach involved training rats to run a maze and then methodically removing portions of their brains; his plan was to retest the rats' ability to run the maze after each surgery until that ability was lost, thus pinpointing the area of the brain responsible for memory. However, contrary to his expectations, Lashley found that the rats' memory of how to navigate the maze persisted regardless of what portion, or how much, of their brain was surgically removed. Indeed, even when the volume of brain tissue removed was massive, the rats were still able to run the maze successfully (interestingly, the rats were successful even when the brain removal was so extensive that it impaired their motor skills to the extent that physical movement was difficult).

As a result of these experiments, Pribram surmised that memory in the brain was not confined to a specific location but, rather, that *memory is distributed throughout the brain.* At the time, however, there was no known model to explain how this might be possible. But in the 1960's, Pribram read an article discussing laser holograms in *Scientific American* and he then formulated the hypothesis that memory in the brain was functioning like a hologram;[241] that is, memory appeared to be disbursed throughout the entire brain in much the same way that the information to completely reconstruct a holographic image was present in every piece of a holographic plate. When other experiments revealed a similar state of affairs involving the visual cortex of the brain, they served to confirm Pribram's suspicion that the brain functioned in a holographic manner.[242] Further confirmation came by way of the ironic when biologist Paul Pietsch, endeavoring to prove Pribram wrong by conducting extensive experiments involving alterations of the brains of salamanders, discovered (much to his surprise) that the feeding behavior of his salamander test subjects remained intact in spite of the extreme surgical modifications to which he subjected their brains. Pietsch's dramatic findings converted him from a skeptic to a believer.[243]

Pribram's conclusion, then, was that memories in the brain are not encoded in the neurons, but, rather, they are represented by patterns of reticulated nerve impulses pervading the entire brain like a web, very much like the interference patterns imprinted on a holographic plate containing a holographic image.[244] Thus, to Pribram's way of thinking, our brains function like a hologram. When you consider this idea in conjunction with the critically important role our brain plays in determining our perception of reality (as discussed in chapters 13 and 16), the implications are staggering.

17.4 David Bohm: The Implicate and Explicate Orders

While Pribram's insight was inspired by biological phenomena, physicist David Bohm's revelation regarding the holographic nature of reality resulted from his fascination with quantum interconnectedness and his work with plasma systems.

One of the strangest results to come out of quantum physics pertains to particular pairs of subatomic particles whose interaction is such that the quantum state of each particle cannot be described independently; in such cases measurements of certain physical properties are mutually interdependent. Thus, for example, two particles making up such a pair might be related in that they each have opposite spin, or they may have identical angles of polarization. This interdependency is known as *quantum interconnectedness*, or *quantum entanglement*. If you recall our discussion from Chapter 16 regarding the double-slit experiment and wave-particle duality, it was noted that subatomic particles actually become "particles" only when observed; because of this, physicist Niels Bohr maintained that the properties of such particles (e.g., spin or polarization) cannot be determined until they are observed or measured. The strangeness aspect of quantum entanglement arises from the fact that the measured results of the shared property of two such particles will be found to be appropriately correlated *regardless of how far apart they are*; that is, if, for example, the polarizations of two complimentary particles were simultaneously measured while the particles were a significant distance apart, their polarizations would be found to be equal, thus suggesting that the two particles were somehow instantaneously communicating with one another to insure the required consistency (since the property being measured was indeterminate until the measurement was made). This apparent instantaneous communication is known as *nonlocality*. The problem here is that such instantaneous communication violates the provision of Einstein's Special Theory of Relativity which states that nothing can travel faster than the speed of light. Due to this conundrum Einstein considered quantum mechanics to be incomplete, and he referred to the nonlocality attributed to quantum entanglement as "spooky action at a distance." [245]

Bohm was intrigued by the concept of quantum interconnectedness, and this fascination was later magnified during his work with plasmas at the Berkeley Radiation Laboratory. It was there that he discovered that when a gas became a plasma the electrons ceased behaving like individual entities and, instead, began to behave like a coordinated and unified whole, via a process of apparent self-organization. Bohm grew increasingly dissatisfied with quantum theory and, after discussing his doubts and concerns with a like-minded Albert Einstein (while they were both at Princeton University), he decided to pursue an alternative view to quantum theory's description of reality. [246]

In particular, Bohm noted that the mechanistic notion of classical physics (i.e. the "clockwork universe" concept discussed in Chapter 14 and elsewhere), and its attendant reductionist approach of viewing and studying reality as though it were composed of separate independent parts (which Bohm referred to as "the fragmentary approach to reality"), were inconsistent with the models of reality described by relativity and quantum physics, and were also breeding a "confusion of the mind" that was at odds with nature and was causing problems not only in science but in the individual and collective human psyches as well. Bohm came to view the reductionist approach as an illusion, and he made a convincing case for it being a causative factor underlying many destructive human tendencies and behaviors. [247] Einstein's theory of relativity had moved physics away from the mechanistic/reductionist mentality by supplanting the primacy of particles with a theory involving fields. Quantum theory, with its features of discontinuity, wave-particle duality, and non-causality, further and even more dramatically diminished mechanistic reductionism. [248]

In preparing to develop his alternative theory of reality Bohm began with those two existing dominant theories, namely Einstein's theory of relativity and quantum theory. However, he noted that these theories stand in opposition to one another in three key areas: relativity theory rests upon the assumptions of continuity, causality, and locality, while quantum theory requires the exact opposites: non-continuity, non-causality, and non-locality. Thus Bohm logically decided that the best place to begin the formulation of *his* theory would be in an area in which relativity and quantum theory were in agreement, a shared conceptual element he called "undivided wholeness" – an idea diametrically opposed to the old reductionist approach.[249] As you might guess from the meanings of those words, Bohm's notion of "undivided wholeness" is consistent with the claim made by NDErs and LBL hypnosis subjects that "all is One."

Bohm's thinking was guided by an assumption very much akin to the idea illustrated by Plato's Allegory of the Cave (which was discussed in Chapter 16). Bohm began by assuming that there must be a deeper level of reality underlying the quantum level espoused by modern physics. [250] Bohm referred to this deeper level of reality as the *implicate order*, and he envisioned it as a totality in which "everything is enfolded into everything."[251] Bohm saw the implicate order as a fundamental level of reality which lies beyond our human threshold of perceptibility, but which contains, enfolded within itself, the totality of forms needed to manifest our perceived reality. When these forms are "unfolded" out of the implicate order they appear, on a different level of reality, as the matter and forces constituting our worldly experience. This other level of reality – *our* level of existential experience – Bohm called the *explicate order*.

Thus the implicate order is a primary level of reality which contains, enfolded within itself, the basis for all forms in a state of unified and undifferentiated wholeness, while the explicate order is a different level of reality derived from the implicate order via the unfolding of these forms into things (e.g., particles and fields) manifesting each in its own region of space and time. By way of analogy, Bohm relates the way a television broadcast is carried by a radio wave and how, when that wave is intercepted by a television receiver, the information of the wave is translated into a visual image. Bohm likens the radio wave transmission to the implicate order, and the "unfolding" of that wave into an image by a TV set as the explicate counterpart.[252] As a further analogy, Bohm makes reference to holograms. And, at this point in our discussion, I think that you can piece together the analogy yourself: The holographic film corresponds to the implicate order, with the interference patterns of the recorded image being "enfolded" throughout the entire holographic plate; when a laser illuminates the plate and causes the holographic image to be projected we now have the explicate order, essentially the "unfolding" of the holographic image into a visually perceptible form.[253]

Bohm found that his theory of the implicate order provided plausible explanations for some of the more unconventional concepts emerging out of quantum theory. For example, the notion of quantum entanglement – where two subatomic particles appear to engage in instantaneous communication (as discussed above) – is revealed, via the theory of the implicate order, as resulting from the fact that *there are not two particles*, and hence no actual communication, because what we perceive as two separate entities are, in truth, nothing more than expressions of the continuous, undifferentiated wholeness of the implicate order. In other words, there is only the singular oneness of the implicate order which we falsely (because of our perceptual limitations) subdivide into the illusion of separate forms. We see specificity where there is, in fact, only unity. Indeed, according to Bohm's view of reality, not only are material objects an illusion of the explicate order, but space and time are as well. In the "truer" reality of the implicate order, space and time are included in the enfoldment of everything into itself: there are no separate things, no three dimensions of space, and no past-present-and-future. Everything – matter, energy, space, time – the totality of all-that-is exists as a singular, concurrent, indistinguishable unity of being. The mystifying statement which God made to Moses – "I am that I am" – can now be understood in this context, for how else can one describe the all-encompassing singularity that is the implicate order? (Interestingly, God made this statement in Exodus 3:14; note that the transcendental number π = 3.14...). Also, recall from our discussions of near-death experiences and Newton's Model of the Afterlife (chapters 2 and 7) that it is repeatedly reported that time *as we know it* does not exist in the afterlife, but that past-present-and-future coexist in an "eternal now."

17.5 Form arising out of non-form

As far back as the 4th century B.C., the Greek philosopher and mathematician Plato formulated what has become known as "Plato's Theory of Forms" or "Plato's Theory of Ideas." The essence of this theory is that there exists a realm of abstract, non-material, archetypal forms which represents a level of reality that is more fundamental than our own "physical" reality (the choice of the word "forms" was, I think, unfortunate because nowadays we think of *form* as meaning "physical" or "structured" whereas in Plato's usage the meaning is entirely different: to Plato the word "form" represented a nonmaterial essence that served as a generic template from which material objects were designed and created). This realm of forms was, to Plato, the "essential basis of reality", and the forms themselves were considered to exist outside of space and time.

Furthermore, Plato believed that the objects constituting *our* physical reality are merely representations or shadows of those fundamental forms [254] (recall again Plato's Allegory of the Cave discussed in Chapter 16); as such, these forms serve as the "causes" of the objects making up our material reality. One final but important feature of Plato's theory is that these forms are "systematically interconnected."[255] The correspondence between Bohm's ideas and Plato's Theory of Forms is obvious: Bohm's implicate order can be seen as the analog of Plato's realm of forms. In each theory, the things constituting our material world arise out of the deeper reality of that more primal realm; also, according to each theory, that primal realm is the "true" (or, at least, "truer") reality, while our material reality is but an illusory phantasm.

Interestingly, many ancient wisdom traditions assert long-standing cosmologies that are remarkably similar to Bohm's concept of the implicate and explicate orders: Buddhists, Hindus, Native Americans, Hawaiian kahunas, as well as Kabalistic, shamanistic, and Hermetic traditions, all affirm beliefs that the material reality is a "second generation" and illusory reality and that, on a fundamental level, all of nature is interconnected.[256]

We've been seeing this theme – of form arising out of non-form – recurring repeatedly throughout our discussions: Chaos theory, DNA, quantum physics, holograms, and now in Bohm's theory. Our reality – the "physical" world – is a world of form, and as we look at the evidence it becomes quite apparent that the idea of form arising out of non-form is not as contradictory as it first seems.

17.6 The Holographic Model of Reality

And thus we've arrived at the crux of the matter: *Our physical reality is the result of a system whereby wave-elicited forms arise out of an undivided wholeness of non-form*. But this is just another way of describing a hologram. What we find is that the holographic model is amazingly consistent with the picture of reality that is emerging from modern science – a picture we explored at length earlier in this book, and which I will briefly review now.

In chapters 15 and 16 we learned that: (1) mass is, in essence, energy; (2) energy travels in waves; and (3) a field is a medium of energy propagation in the form of waves. After a discussion of several contemporary scientific principles and theories we were led to the realization that there is no objective, independent "physical" reality – at least, not in the way we've been led to believe. The true reality is a domain of waves and frequencies (i.e., a Field). It is our brain's decoding of those waves and frequencies, via Fourier transforms, that creates the illusion of the seemingly "concrete" reality which we perceive. When we interact with The Field, using our senses and our brain, we cause the wave functions to collapse to their particulate state, and we then comprehend the resulting "reality" as being solid, physical, and composed of discrete and distinct constituent parts. The Field is "everything-as-one," and the transformation of The Field by our sensory-brain system into "physical reality" is the illusion. Everything that we perceive of existence is actually the result of one single process that diversifies: that one single process is the Field, and the diversifications are the collapsed wave functions.

As you can see, the description of reality given above is depicting a state of affairs that is remarkably similar to holography. The Field is analogous to a holographic plate, the waves in the Field are analogous to the interference patterns recorded on the holographic plate, and our brain is akin to the laser that is shined on the holographic plate to produce the holographic image – our sensory-brain system collapses the wave functions in the Field into the illusion of physical reality in much the same way as the laser illuminating the holographic plate produces the illusory holographic image. Thus our reality is nothing more than a huge, complex, elaborate hologram. Our perceived reality is no more "real" than is a hologram of an apple. The diagram below illustrates how the Holographic Model of Reality explains the creation of our perceived reality by means of a process very similar to holography:

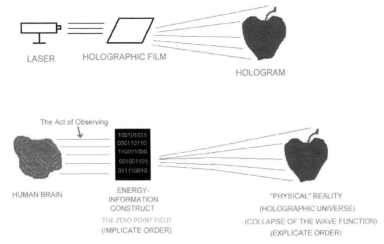

(Note: I will be refining the above diagram slightly in Chapter 21, after the introduction of some new information).

This, then, is the culmination of all the material covered in Part III of this book. Putting all of it together leads to a model remarkably similar to David Bohm's concepts of the implicate and explicate orders. And it also corresponds nicely with details of the Afterlife reported by NDErs and LBL subjects. The Holographic Model of Reality seems to provide the best and most accurate explanation of where and how our "physical" reality originates. The Holographic Model is elegant, and it is consistent with both science and experience. But, as the old saying goes, "talk is cheap." One could reasonably ask: "All speculation aside, is there any actual *evidence* that the Holographic Model of Reality might seriously be a true representation of the way things really are?" Incredibly, there is.

17.7 String Theory: Wave-induced Form

According to the cutting-edge field of physics known as String Theory, the ultimate fundamental units of reality are thought to be *vibrating strings*, and the classic fundamental "particles" of reality – e.g., photons, electrons, quarks – are simply different manifestations of that one primary object (the string) vibrating in different ways.[257] A vibrating string is a wave phenomenon, so String Theory, at its core, is postulating a situation where the fundamental "particles" of physical reality – i.e., the basis of form – are born out of wave phenomena. This is much like holography, where the holographic image and its holographic projection are the result of light waves. (Going back to the Spirit Realm, recall that upon arriving in the Afterlife one of the first things that many LBL subjects report is a sense of *sound* – music or a humming/vibration).

17.8 Cymatics: Form from Non-form

Cymatics is a process of visualizing sound by vibrating a medium of liquid or particles. This is accomplished by placing a thin layer of, for example, sand on a metal plate whose surface is then made to vibrate. What results are remarkably complex and symmetrical geometrical patterns in the excited medium. I urge you to go to YouTube and run a search on "cymatics" – seeing this in action is truly amazing. Not only are the physical forms that arise amazing in and of themselves, but even more astonishing is that many of these cymatic forms resemble patterns and forms found in nature. Also, *the complexity of the created patterns increases as the frequency of the sound increases* [258] (recall that the Spirit Realm is thought to be another dimension existing at a *higher frequency* than that of our level of reality). If we generalize this idea, we have a wave phenomenon (sound) somehow causing form to emerge into existence. This is precisely what is happening in the case of a hologram, except that the wave phenomenon is electromagnetic – light – instead of sound.

Well, this idea of form arising out of non-form as the result of wave phenomena is something we saw in Chapter 16 in our discussion of the Zero Point Field. To refresh your memory, the Zero Point Field was considered to be the "field of fields", the womb out of which quantum particles and energy are born – i.e., the Zero Point Field can be seen as the primary and fundamental sub-structure of our perceived reality. Clearly, the Zero Point Field sounds just like Bohm's implicate order, even to the extent of how our physical reality (the explicate order) grows out of it. Also, both the Zero Point Field and the implicate order posses the quality of being an undivided wholeness – a totality or plenum in which everything is folded into itself. This, once again, is in complete agreement with the belief, held by many ancient wisdom traditions and often expressed by LBL subjects, that "all is one".

17.9 Bell's Theorem: All is one

Recall our earlier discussion of quantum entanglement, or quantum interconnectedness, which postulates that if two subatomic particles shared a mutual association then they will maintain their interconnectedness across time and space. This led to the implication that instantaneous (i.e., faster than light) communication between such interconnected pairs (i.e., non-locality) must be the case. Since this contradicted Einstein's finding that nothing can travel faster than light, Einstein concluded that quantum mechanics was necessarily incomplete. In 1964 physicist John Stewart Bell published a paper in which he demonstrated mathematically that the frequency with which correlated properties of entangled particles would occur under normal probabilistic conditions was violated by quantum physics experiments. This contradiction suggested that one of Bell's original assumptions had to be false: either the assumption of locality (the opposite of non-locality, as displayed by quantum entanglement) was wrong, or the assumption of physical reality was wrong [259] (this method of "proof by contradiction" is known as *reductio ad absurdum*). Since experiments have confirmed Bell's findings, scientists are put in the position of rejecting either locality or realism; most have chosen to reject locality, which means they accept the validity of quantum entanglement.[260] Bohm's theory and the Holographic Theory of Reality, however, suggest that perhaps they should have rejected the assumption of physical reality instead. Nevertheless, the interesting thing is that, even if we accept their approach and agree to play in their park, so to speak, the results are the same – as follows:

Let's begin by assuming that quantum entanglement and non-locality are valid: then two entangled particles will remain interconnected, with their properties correlated, across all time and space. However, according to the Big Bang Theory, *everything* currently in existence was concentrated in the solitary singularity that existed prior to the Big Bang. According to quantum entanglement, then, that original pre-Big Bang interconnectedness must be preserved: thus *everything presently in existence is fundamentally interconnected* – that is, *All is One*. This is an astonishing realization: Two scientific principles –The Big Bang Theory and Quantum Entanglement – considered together demonstrate the indisputable truth that All is One. This is precisely David Bohm's contention that the implicate order is one of undifferentiated wholeness, and it is consistent with the property of holograms wherein any piece of a holographic plate is capable of producing the entire holographic image. And, lest we forget, *All is One* is also a claim repeatedly made by NDErs and LBL hypnosis subjects.

17.10 The Holographic Universe

In the years since the publication of Michael Talbot's book the idea that our physical reality might actually be a hologram has gained growing acceptance among scientists, and has led to the radical yet seriously-taken theory that the *entire universe* is a holographic projection. The evolution of this theory and the underlying scientific thinking that led up to it make for a fascinating peek into the birthing process of a new paradigm.

As part of his groundbreaking discoveries regarding black holes, Stephen Hawking postulated that once a black hole evaporates, all of the information contained within it is destroyed along with the black hole. While the mathematics employed by Hawking were sound, some physicists objected to his theory on the grounds that it violated a fundamental axiom of quantum mechanics which holds that information cannot be destroyed. Since Hawking used quantum mechanics in the formulation of his theory, its violation of what we might call the "preservation of information" axiom led to an obvious contradiction. The physicists who disagreed with Hawking were thus challenged with the task of trying to discover how the information contained in a black hole might be preserved after the black hole's demise. Rising to that challenge, they discovered that the information in a black hole is equal to the black hole's surface area; in other words, they discovered that all the information contained in a 3-dimensional region can be accurately mapped onto a 2-dimensional surface. This is, in essence, the situation that exists with a hologram, thus the black hole's surface can be likened to a hologram of the immediate surrounding space-time. It was soon discovered that this situation with black holes had broader significance; namely, that there is in fact a universal relation between information and areas of surfaces. Thus the idea emerged that the relationship existing between a black hole's information and its surface area could be extended to the universe as a whole: that is, *it is possible that all the information contained within the entire universe can be mapped onto a two-dimensional surface surrounding the universe*, and, therefore, that our 3D reality is merely a holographic projection of the data on that surrounding 2D surface. In other words, there exists a sound scientific basis for the possibility that the universe – our "real world reality" – is but a holographic illusion.[261] Compelling mathematical evidence for the holographic universe theory has recently emerged in the form of two scientific papers published by a team of Japanese physicists. As reported in an article entitled "Simulations back up theory that Universe is a hologram" appearing in the scientific journal *Nature*, the Japanese physicists' findings have "provided some of the clearest evidence yet that our Universe could be just one big projection."[262]

In the holographic universe model one can see an obvious correspondence between the 2D information-containing surface surrounding the universe and David Bohm's concept of the implicate order. That 2D surface is also intriguingly consistent with Plato's notion of the realm of archetypal forms. The perceived *stuff* of so-called physical reality is thus revealed to be nothing more than an illusory holographic projection from an information-rich 2D surface surrounding the universe. The implications of this theory, and the fact that mainstream scientists discuss it seriously, are nothing short of astonishing.

17.11 Light: The Fundamental Component of Reality?

Throughout chapters 15 and 16 I presented scientific evidence that makes a strong case for the thesis that our perceived reality is *not* an objective, independent "physical" reality but is, in fact, a domain of waves and frequencies – an *energy* domain – that is decoded by our brain, using Fourier transforms, into the illusion of the seemingly "concrete" reality of our experience. Our reality, the evidence suggests, is an energy-information construct. In the current chapter we've seen further scientific evidence that has refined the energy-information construct hypothesis into the theory that our reality is a holographic projection of a higher-dimensional, information-rich domain. In a true hologram, the *information* is contained on the holographic plate, and the *energy* that converts that information into the illusory holographic projection is *light*.

In terms of physics, *light* refers to electromagnetic radiation. In our everyday experience we typically think of light as being the stimulus energy our eyes detect when we "see" – that is, the portion of the electromagnetic spectrum perceptible by the human eye. This type of light is referred to as "visible light" or "the visible light spectrum." But, as we learned in Chapter 13, visible light represents only a very, very small portion (less than one-percent) of the overall electromagnetic spectrum. So bear in mind that the word "light" – in its broadest and most accurate sense – refers to electromagnetic radiation across the *full* electromagnetic spectrum, to include, but by no means limited to, visible light.

Light is conceptualized as being comprised of discrete bundles of electromagnetic energy called *photons*. Photons are the result of a release of energy by an atom when an agitated electron moves from an unstable higher energy state to its normal, lower energy level (commensurate with the atom's ground state).[263] Historically, our conception of light has been a schizophrenic oscillation between particle and wave theories. Isaac Newton, in his formulation of the science of optics, considered light to be composed of discrete particles. By the 1800s, the discovery of the wave properties of electromagnetic radiation caused a shift away from the notion of light as particulate to that of it being a wave phenomenon. In the early 1900s, Einstein's concept of light as quantized energy revived the Newtonian notion of the particle nature of light. Now we know, as discussed in Chapter 16, that, as demonstrated by the double-slit experiment, light has a *dual nature*, commonly referred to as the "wave-particle duality of light."[264]

Well, since light is the energy source responsible for holographic creations, and since some scientists believe our universe/reality is a holographic projection, then we should expect that light is of fundamental importance to our reality – in fact, it might well be the case that light is *the* fundamental component of reality. If light truly does play this singularly significant role in reality, then we can reasonably expect light to possess some very interesting and unique properties. And so it does.

The first fascinating and anomalous property of light we will note is mentioned above and was discussed at length in Chapter 16; namely, the "wave-particle duality of light." This is an idea that has received a lot of press over the years and has thus lost much of its exoticness due to overexposure, but let's just step back for a moment and give this notion some serious thought. Light sometimes behaves as a particle – i.e., a material "thing", a localized object with physical properties – and other times light behaves as a wave – i.e., travelling energy. This in itself is quite bizarre; yes, we've already seen that mass and energy are *fundamentally* identical, but on the whole the components of our reality maintain their preferred mode of existence – energy behaves like energy, and things behave like things; energy exhibits energetic properties and things exhibit physical properties. But light insists on having it both ways. Besides being peculiar, this property is especially interesting because of the fact that matter is, fundamentally, energy. The operative word here is "fundamentally" – *Light naturally exhibits the wave-particle duality that is fundamental to everything that makes up our reality*. To make things even more interesting, light behaves like a wave when unobserved, but it collapses to its particle state when being observed. In other words, *light appears to be the bridge between the energy level of reality and the solid-seeming illusion of our perceived reality*: unobserved, light behaves like energy, but, when observed, light assumes its physical persona and behaves like a particle – it is energy when we're not looking, but matter when we are looking.

While light displays a duality with regard to its wave and particle manifestations, there is another area where its very *lack* of a dual nature is suspicious: *Light has no antiparticle*. Most kinds of particles studied by physicists possess an associated antiparticle, which has the same mass but opposite charge of the original particle. Thus, for example, the antiparticle of an electron is a positively charged electron called a positron. A rare few particles, however, do not have an antiparticle, or, said another way, such particles are their own antiparticles. A photon is such a particle. What's more, the other particles that have no antiparticles – gravitons and weakly interacting massive particles – are *hypothetical* particles[265]: their existence is surmised, but unproven. Thus photons may uniquely possess this property. What is fascinating about this particular property is that, by not possessing an antiparticle, the photon has in effect dropped out of the dualistic nature of material reality. Up and down, black and white, hot and cold, north magnetic pole and south magnetic pole, positive electric charge and negative electric charge, past and future, good and evil – everything in our world appears to have an opposite, and, furthermore, each thing is defined precisely via comparison with its opposite. By all accounts we seem to live within a dualistic reality. Ancient wisdom traditions, however, talk of a higher, more perfect domain of existence which exists outside of duality. This philosophical view is known as *monism* and posits that everything derives from One single source, and that perceived distinctions are merely manifestations of One single ultimate reality. Photons are the unique component of our reality that possess this property *in this reality*. Now recall that one of the most important revelations experienced by NDErs and LBL hypnosis subjects is that *All is One*: the differences we perceive are illusions, everything is interconnected and interrelated in a single whole; dualism – the notion of opposites – is a false perception. Well, photons actually live this truth, if you will; a photon has no opposite, even within a world awash with, and predicated upon, opposites. This is a very Zen-like attribute, the overcoming of dualism as exemplified in the Zen phrase "not two."

A truly unique property of light, and perhaps its most important property, is the speed at which light travels. Denoted by *c* (as in Einstein's famous equation: $E=mc^2$), the speed of light in a vacuum is approximately 186,000 miles per second. What is of particular interest regarding this speed – besides the obvious fact that it is incredibly *fast* – is that it is a universal physical constant of great importance in many areas of physics.

First of all, according to the equations of Einstein's theory of Special Relativity, *the speed of light is the maximum speed at which all matter and information in the universe can travel*.[266] Think about that: The speed of light is the *limiting velocity* for matter and information. That is a decidedly key role to play in our physical reality.

In the late 1600's, Danish astronomer Ole Rømer made the first quantitative measurements of the speed of light and, although he did not calculate a specific value for it, he determined that the speed of light was finite. In 1865, James Clerk Maxwell proposed that light was an electromagnetic wave and thus concluded, in accordance with his theory of electromagnetism, that light travelled at the speed c. In 1905, Albert Einstein made the bold and counterintuitive assertion that *the speed of light is independent of the speed of the light source*. This is yet another of light's bizarre properties and, as such, it merits clarification. If I am sitting in a moving train and holding a ball in my hand, then from my perspective the ball is not moving; but to an observer standing outside the train on a station platform, that ball is moving at the speed of the train. This situation we can all readily accept as being consistent with our experience. Now let's say that, while sitting on the moving train, I throw the ball to the far end of the car in the direction that the train is moving: to the observer on the station platform the speed of the ball is now the *sum* of the train's speed and the speed which I imparted to the ball by throwing it – it stands to reason that, to the platform observer, the ball is moving at the *combined speeds* of the train and the throw. But with light such is not the case: if I were to shine a light on the opposite wall of the train car, towards the train's front, the speed of the light's photons would be the same, whether the train was moving or at rest. This is contrary to what common sense would suggest and appears to contradict the laws of physics. Nevertheless, the truth of the matter is that the speed of light is a physical constant of nature – the speed of light is invariant.[267]

Yet another intriguing property of the photon is that *it has no mass*. This troubled me for a long time (and still does to some degree), for I kept coming back to the question: "If something *exists*, then how can it not have mass?" Since I'm not a scientist, that is probably a naive question. But from the perspective of a layperson, I find the conundrum troublesome and vexing. The answer, it seems, has to do with yet three more astonishing facts associated with the speed of light. According to Einstein's Special Theory of Relativity, as speed increases, mass increases while time and length decrease; at the speed of light, mass becomes infinite while both time and length become zero. Since photons are the fundamental constituents of light, they, by definition, travel at the speed of light; if a photon had mass, then its mass at speed c would be infinite, which is impossible.[268]

One final characteristic of light that I find provocative is the role it plays in the electromagnetic force. Physics recognizes three fundamental forces of nature: Gravity, the Electroweak Force, and the Color Force. The Electroweak Force represents the electromagnetic force and the weak nuclear force, which are two different aspects of the same force. The electromagnetic force refers to the forces between charges (opposite charges attract, like charges repel) and the magnetic force. Although we are all familiar with this force from science courses taken in school and from our experiences with magnets, most of us don't fully understand exactly how the force operates; that is, what exactly is happening that causes, for example, a proton (positive charge) to be attracted to an electron (negative charge)? According to physicists, the electromagnetic force that causes a proton and an electron to be attracted to one another results from the electron emitting a *virtual photon* which the proton absorbs, then the proton emits a virtual photon which the electron absorbs, and on and on, back and forth. In this context, the virtual photon is referred to as a "force carrier."[269] Thus light plays a fundamental role in the forces of nature.

Let's recap these fascinating and unusual facts associated with light, and let's consider them in conjunction with the Holographic Model of Reality. Here's a bullet list of the amazing "facts of light":

- Light has a dual nature: particle when observed, wave when unobserved
- Photons have no mass
- Photons have no antiparticle
- The speed of light is the limiting velocity for matter
- The speed of light is independent of the speed of the light source
- At the speed of light mass becomes infinite while time and length become zero
- The electromagnetic force results from the exchange of a virtual photon

Each one of the above facts is nothing short of incredible, and I'm using the word "incredible" here in its most literal meaning of "beyond belief or understanding." At the very least they are highly counterintuitive, and most of them seem impossible. Indeed, the first four properties strongly suggest that light exists outside of material reality. And the last property implies that light is responsible for holding a good part of our reality together. I firmly believe that, collectively, these light properties make a powerful case for the claim that light is singularly significant in our reality and – when considered in conjunction with the Holographic Model – that *light might very well be the fundamental component of our reality*.

One very intriguing theory posits that matter is nothing more than "frozen light' – i.e., light that has been "slowed down" and is thus of higher density. [270] This concept becomes clearer if we make an analogy between light and water: water in its liquid state is formless, but when frozen water adopts highly structured crystalline forms (think of snowflakes); likewise, light in its normal state is also formless, but when "frozen" – slowed down – it assumes structure and become matter. Like the process of cymatics discussed earlier, this is another example of form arising out of non-form, and, quite interestingly, both are dependent upon vibration.

The possibility that matter can actually be created from light is taken quite seriously by mainstream scientists. Quantum electrodynamics predicts that the mutual annihilation of two high-energy photons colliding under the right conditions will produce pairs of electrons and positrons – i.e., matter. Scientists have proposed a design for a photon-photon collider using gamma ray beams to test this prediction. [271]

If it can be conclusively demonstrated that matter can be created from light, either via colliding photons or the "frozen light" hypothesis, then we are a giant step closer to confirming the premise that light is truly and literally the fundamental component of matter, and thus, of reality.

This belief that matter can be created from light has a particularly interesting ramification that is worth noting. While writing this book I had mentioned to my son that I was going to include a section that discusses the premise that light is the fundamental component of reality, and I told him about the unique properties of light that I was planning to address. When I mentioned the fact that light has no mass, he remarked that perhaps light was the substance constituting the singularity that preceded the Big Bang (recall from our discussion in Chapter 14 that the Big Bang Theory posits that, approximately 13.8 billion years ago, our universe – all of it: matter, energy ... the works – sprang into existence in an instant out of what is called a "singularity," which is conceptualized as an infinitely small, infinitely dense, and infinitely hot state of existence). I was intrigued by his suggestion and, after giving it some very serious thought, I imagined the following: Suppose that the singularity that preceded the Big Bang was simply a mass of super-compressed photons. Since photons are mass-less this would account for the singularity being a virtually non-existent point – an accumulation of mass-less "particles" would still be mass-less. Now suppose that the singularity ruptured and released all those compressed photons in the event that we call the Big Bang. As these photons expanded outwards at the speed of light, some of them collided with one another. As we learned above, quantum electrodynamics postulates that some of these collisions could result in the annihilation of the photons and the subsequent release of pairs of electrons and positrons – i.e., *matter and antimatter*. In other words, it would be entirely possible for the matter (and antimatter) of the universe to have been born out of a singularity that was composed of nothing but photons. The Big Bang may have been an event as simple as a bursting forth of light. This is eerily consistent with the Bible's version of creation (in Genesis 1:3): "And God said, 'Let there be light.'"

(For yet another possible explanation of the Big Bang Theory, see Chapter 21).

17.12 The Missing Stuff

Transcendental Numbers

In Chapter 14 I discussed the perplexing enigma of transcendental numbers; namely, the fact that the set of transcendental numbers (the numbers, like π and e, that are uncommon in our everyday experience and thus unfamiliar to us) is a *non-countably infinite* set, whereas the set of algebraic numbers (the numbers we are most familiar with and most aware of) is a *countably infinite* set. This fact means, in essence, that **the set of transcendental numbers is infinitely larger than the set of algebraic numbers.** To make the import of this fact crystal clear I had quoted one of my college math professors as follows:

> Imagine all the Real numbers put into a huge hat: if you were to repeatedly reach into the hat and arbitrarily pull out a number, that number would **almost always be a transcendental number**; rarely would you get an algebraic number.

I ended that discussion in Chapter 14 by asking three questions:

1. How can it be that the numbers that are commonplace and plentiful in our experience (i.e., the algebraic numbers) are, in truth, the rare numbers, whereas the numbers that are uncommon and scarce in our experience (i.e., the transcendental numbers) constitute, in actuality, the vast majority of numbers?
2. Why is it the case that two of the most important numbers in mathematics – namely, π and e – are transcendental numbers?
3. Where the hell *are* all those transcendental numbers?

It is the last question that is of interest to us here. My professor's statement above is a mathematical fact, yet it is completely in opposition to our everyday experience. The world of our experience is a world of algebraic numbers: if we were to scour books, newspapers, magazines, and web sites (even those devoted to mathematics, science, and engineering) and note each and every number we encountered the truth is that the vast, vast majority of those numbers will be *algebraic numbers* – i.e., the numbers that mathematics can *prove* are *so rare as to be almost impossible to turn up*. Why, when it comes to numbers, does our reality so blatantly violate the laws of mathematical probability? It is akin to someone continually picking the winning lottery numbers week after week! So, again, the big question is: If the transcendental numbers represent the vast majority of numbers and yet we seem to hardly ever encounter them in our everyday interaction with our reality, then *where the hell are all those transcendental numbers?*

Well, the shocking truth appears to be that most of them are missing – missing from *our reality*, that is. We know for a fact that they're out there, and we know for a fact that they far, far outnumber the algebraic numbers. But, in our experience of our reality, the transcendental numbers appear to be inexplicably missing.

Dark Matter and Dark Energy

It turns out that the transcendental numbers are not the only things missing from our experience of reality. Interestingly, cosmologists have determined that there is a large quantity of matter and energy that is also mysteriously unaccounted for, and they refer to these missing entities as *dark matter* and *dark energy*.

In the 1990's astronomers and physicists studying the expansion of the universe were particularly interested in the question of whether the universe would decelerate but expand indefinitely, or whether it would at some point cease expanding and ultimately collapse in upon itself (a kind of reverse Big Bang sometimes called the "Big Crunch"). In 1998 observations from the Hubble Space Telescope led scientists to conclude that the expansion of the universe is accelerating – something not expected. In seeking an explanation for this surprising discovery, scientists have determined the causal agencies to be dark matter and dark energy; "dark" because they are not directly observable by normal means but nevertheless can be inferred and measured through gravitational effects on the material universe analyzed via mathematical modeling. What is particularly intriguing is that the scientist's calculations reveal the startling fact that normal matter – atoms – accounts for *less than 5% of the universe*! Dark matter and dark energy – those invisible, unobservable aspects of our universe – account for 95.4 %.[272] In other words, most of the matter and energy making up our universe ... *is missing*. Once again, as with the transcendental numbers, scientists know it's out there, they just can't find it.

Let's stop for a moment and really consider the ramifications of what we've been discussing here: The vast bulk of the real numbers – namely, the transcendental numbers – are inexplicably rare in our experience of reality; likewise, the vast bulk of matter and energy (more than 95% of it) – the so-called dark matter and dark energy – is also inexplicably undetectable by us. What science is telling us is that *most of the numbers, most of the matter, and most of the energy that constitute our reality are invisible to us*! In other words, from our perspective: *most of reality is missing*. This is phenomenal and staggering in its implications. Why are the most important and fundamental components of our reality – almost in their entirety – unperceivable by us? And where, exactly, *is* all this missing stuff?

DNA

One other point – previously covered in Chapter 14 – might also be relevant here: the concept of "junk DNA." Recall from that earlier discussion that biologists have determined that less than 2% of our DNA is involved in encoding for protein production. The remaining 98% of DNA is commonly referred to as "junk DNA" because much of it has no discernible biological function. While this junk DNA itself is not "missing," its function and purpose most definitely are.

However, it turns out that, junk DNA aside, there actually is a large portion of our DNA that *is* missing. This particular enigma only came to light as a result of the Human Genome Project (HGP), an "international, collaborative research program whose goal was the complete mapping and understanding of all the genes of human beings."[273]

Guided by a "one-gene, one-protein" doctrine and the fact that human physiology involves over 100,000 proteins and about 20,000 regulatory genes, geneticists logically expected that the human genome would require more than 120,000 genes.[274] The actual finding, however, was much, much less than geneticists expected: with the full sequencing completed in 2003, the HGP determined the existence of approximately 20,500 genes constituting the human genome.[275] This startling finding left scientists with roughly 100,000 expected human genes unaccounted for.

So, then, this is our conundrum: The vast bulk of matter, energy and numbers is missing – we know for a fact that they're out there, but we can't locate them. Similarly, a complete mapping of the human genome reveals that upwards of 80% of the expected genes aren't there; furthermore, when we study DNA – the molecules that make up our genes – we can't find the purpose for most of it. This is a perplexing state of affairs, and it begs for an explanation. Here's one possibility:

Suppose our reality is truly, as presented throughout this chapter, a holographic projection of a higher reality. Then our reality would be expected to possess *some* of the properties and features of its source reality but, being a mere shadow of that higher reality, it certainly would not possess every property and feature. Our reality, being a semblance of the higher reality, possesses only a subset of the qualities of that higher reality, much as a holographic image possesses only some of the qualities of the source object. This, I believe, may explain the elusiveness of dark matter, dark energy, and transcendental numbers: we can detect them indirectly because they are necessary for the creation and existence of our reality, but they are not part of our reality – except at the rare points where the two realities inevitably overlap; then we have a bleed-through that results in extraordinary things like π and e. As for junk DNA and our missing genes, perhaps they play a role as part of the interface mechanism between our reality and the higher reality of which we are a projection. This is all, admittedly, only speculation. But quandaries such as dark matter, dark energy, transcendental numbers, missing genes, and junk DNA are huge red flags that should not be swept under the rug because they are uncomfortable or vexing. It is precisely these types of anomalous bugaboos that lead to the most startling and important scientific discoveries. Remember Isaac Asimov's wonderful quote, mentioned previously: "The most exciting phrase to hear in science, the one that heralds new discoveries, is not 'Eureka!' (I found it!) but 'Gee, that's funny ...' "

17.13 The Great Chain of Being

This idea of coexistent and hierarchical levels of reality actually boasts a long-standing tradition traceable as far back as Plato and Aristotle – and continuing on through Descartes, Spinoza and Leibniz – called "The Great Chain of Being" or the *scala naturae*. It involves the notion that all of reality is divided into stratified levels of existence (or "heavens") analogous to a set of concentric spheres, with God occupying the outermost sphere. That uppermost level – the God level – represents perfection and independence; the lower levels devolve into increasingly less perfect states that are dependent on, and reflections of, the more perfect levels above them. [276] Significantly for our discussion, it was believed that the relative proportions of "spirit" and "matter" determined positioning within the hierarchy, with higher spirit concentrations implying existence at a higher level of the system.[277] The number of levels, or "heavens", varies but is generally cited as being nine, ten, or eleven.[278] What I find particularly interesting and relevant about this ancient cosmology is: first, that it is eerily like the holographic universe theory's notion of a higher-level, information-containing surface existing as a shell around our lower-level reality; second, that the notion of nine, ten, or eleven concentric levels of reality corresponds to string theory's postulation of the existence of 11 or more dimensions; and, third, that each subsequent level in the hierarchy (moving down from the top level) is a less spiritual/more material reflection of the levels above it. The degree to which millennia-old beliefs correspond with cutting-edge scientific theories is absolutely astonishing. More and more it appears that we are now rediscovering truths about the nature of reality that were, remarkably, known to the ancients.

17.14 How True is the Holographic Model?

In this chapter, which represents the culmination of Part III of this book, I have assembled a vast collection of information from many diverse sources in the presentation of an alternative theory of reality that is drastically different from the long-standing materialist view of a concrete, physical reality functioning with clock-like mechanical precision. The new theory – the Holographic Theory of Reality – posits a reality that is a light-based holographic projection of some higher reality, and whose design appears to be structured in accordance with the fractal property of self-similarity. Furthermore, I have suggested that our holographic reality has been purposely created to serve as a school in which souls from the Spirit Realm are given opportunities to evolve spiritually via a process based upon karma and reincarnation. I think the evidence presented here, both scientific and spiritual, makes a compelling case for the plausibility of the Holographic Model. Nevertheless, I freely acknowledge that the Holographic Theory is, even in light of the evidence presented, a tough pill to swallow: one need only wrap one's knuckles on a table surface to initiate a rebuttal of the theory. So the big question, as is always the case with theories and models, is the degree to which it reflects the actual state of affairs; in other words: Is it *true*?

A story is told about the mathematician and philosopher Ludwig Wittgenstein that, while addressing a group of students regarding some philosophical concept, one of the students interrupted him and said, "Professor, this is all very interesting – but is it *true*?" To which Wittgenstein is purported to have replied, "It's *true enough*."

I think the same applies to any question about the validity of the Holographic Model of Reality: it might not be a precisely accurate representation of the way things are, but, given our current level of knowledge and understanding, and considering the extent to which it is supported by scientifically sound evidence, we can surely make the claim that "It's *true enough*."

17.15 A Rethinking of the Afterlife Model

If we are willing to at least consider the possibility that our earthly reality is, in fact, a holographic illusion rather than a physical/material reality, then we open the door to a fascinating reinterpretation of the Afterlife Model and its interconnectedness with the earth plane.

One day, while pondering some of the enigmas associated with the Afterlife Model (see Chapter 10: The Elephants in the Room), I was struck with the realization that a revision of the Afterlife Model, in light of the Holographic Model, could resolve many of those enigmas. Consider the following:

What if each one of us is the *only real soul* in our particular, unique life incarnation experience? Suppose that everyone and everything else is an artificially created holographic illusion designed solely to present *that single soul* with possibilities, circumstances and settings through which it can have experiences that will both test it and offer it opportunities for spiritual growth. That soul's choices, responses and actions are then later (in the Spirit Realm) evaluated (by that soul, its Council of Elders, etc.) to determine its overall level of spiritual growth, and to identify those areas in which it is lacking and requires further attention. This theory – that only the subject soul is real and that everything else in each earth life-experience is an illusion – provides very satisfying explanations for the following:

- How details of *future lifetimes* can be presented to us in the Place of Life Selection.
- Why "reality" appears to be a hologram.
- How other supposed souls can do bad things to assist in our spiritual growth yet not be tainted by those evil deeds.
- Why both NDErs and LBL hypnosis subjects claim that, after they are given total understanding and knowledge, everything in the world – *including all the suffering and misery* – makes sense and is acceptable and understandable.

- How particular lifetimes can be *tailor-made* for each soul's karmic needs for spiritual growth.
- Why we are so easily "forgiven" in the Spirit Realm for the bad things we do during a lifetime.
- How such an incomprehensibly complex tapestry of interconnecting and interacting lives – supposedly assisting one another in mutual spiritual growth – is possible.
- Why both NDErs and LBL hypnosis subjects claim that the entire earth experience is an illusion.
- Why we often feel (during our earthly lives) that far-reaching phenomena occur specifically to have an impact on us, individually, or as a result of a particular action on our part (e.g., the "It-rains-whenever-I-wash-my-car" syndrome).

I find the theory offered above very appealing because so many of the problematic aspects of both the Afterlife Model and the Holographic Model are explained by it. This new spin on the Afterlife Model presents a situation analogous to an airline pilot training on a flight simulator: everything feels real and reacts to the pilot's actions realistically, but, being a simulation, if the pilot crashes or errs in some catastrophic way, *no harm is done*. What better way to train souls than in a virtual reality environment? Our earthly lives can be preprogrammed to precisely suit our spiritual growth needs. And we're free to do as we please because, no matter how badly we screw up, no one is actually harmed. I'm not saying that I'm certain that this is the way things are, but I must admit that I am seriously considering this to be the most likely explanation.

This idea is actually not particularly original, as it is in some ways an extension of a philosophical notion which goes as far back as the ancient Greeks; known as *solipsism*, it posits that "the self is the only existent thing." [279] Under the solipsistic view, the perceiving self is all that exists and everything else – the external world, other people, etc. – has no independent existence. While originally little more than a fanciful exercise in mental musing, nowadays solipsism becomes a more plausible possibility when one considers modern virtual reality (VR) technology and scenarios like that portrayed in the movie "The Matrix." Once we realize that the human mind can be made to experience artificial settings and experiences as though they were real, then we can't help but wonder where "reality" ends and *virtual* reality begins. How do we know – how *could* we know – if our experience of everyday reality is not simply a VR program being fed directly to our minds? To the ancients the solipsistic view was little more than an intellectual curiosity to be idly contemplated in the abstract, but to us living in the 21st century the notion is entirely rational and well within the realm of possibility.

Chapter 18

Hacking Reality

Therefore I tell you, whatever you ask for in prayer, believe that you have received it, and it will be yours.

- Mark 11:24 (Holy Bible, New International Version)

If you believe you can or if you believe you can't ... you're right.

- Henry Ford, engineer and industrialist

The power of the imagination is a great factor in medicine. It may produce diseases in man and it may cure them.

- Paracelsus, alchemist and physician

Science believes the world is truly there – it is naive in its empiricism. *Magic* knows that the world is ... a construct of forceful imagination.

- Terence McKenna, author

The stuff of the world is mind-stuff.

- Sir Arthur Eddington, astrophysicist

Before I begin the content of this chapter, please allow me to issue a very important warning. Some of the topics discussed in this chapter relate to matters of health and, in particular, to unconventional approaches in treating health-related problems. Please understand that by discussing these approaches I am not endorsing them, nor am I endorsing *any* specific modes of care or treatment for medical matters. I am not a doctor. I have no medical training or expertise. Even with my own personal battle with cancer I sought the advice of mainstream medical doctors, received external beam radiation treatments, and I am still under the care of a medical doctor. I personally choose to supplement the mainstream medical care I receive with some of the unconventional modalities mentioned in this chapter; I do not use these modalities in lieu of mainstream medical care – that was my own personal decision which I made for myself. In line with this philosophy, let me repeat the disclaimer that is printed in the early pages of this book:

Disclaimer

It is not the intention of the author to advise on health care. The information in this book is provided as an information resource only, and is not to be used or relied on for any diagnostic or treatment purposes. This information is not intended to be patient education and should not be used as a substitute for professional diagnosis and treatment. Please see a medical professional about any health concerns you have.

Now, on to *Hacking Reality*…

18.1 Lynn Grabhorn: Deliberate Creation

Many years ago I was watching a video of a talk given by Deepak Chopra during which he made a statement, as an aside to his main topic of discussion, that literally brought me to the edge of my seat. I no longer can recall the title of his talk nor the particular topic he had been discussing, but I vividly remember him pausing and somewhat parenthetically remarking that it is possible for humans to affect external reality through the power of their minds. Back then this was a novel idea – certainly one that I had never heard before – and I remember thinking to myself: *Is such a thing actually possible?* It seemed like magic to me, and if such a claim had been made by anyone other than Deepak Chopra I would have dismissed it as ludicrous. But I had read several of Dr. Chopra's books and had viewed many of his video lectures – I had even attended one of his talks in person in Manhattan – and as a result I had come to consider him an intelligent and level-headed person of integrity. Thus I took his claim, incredible as it was, quite seriously, and I slid my butt to the edge of my couch and leaned towards the TV in excited anticipation of hearing how one might accomplish this feat. Much to my dismay, Dr. Chopra did not elaborate on his claim but simply returned to his main topic of discussion. His assertion – that people can influence material reality via thought – haunted me for quite a while but, as is often the case, over time it was gradually forgotten.

Several years later I read a very short blurb in a magazine about a book by Lynn Grabhorn entitled *Excuse Me, Your Life Is Waiting*. The blurb was so brief that it wasn't particularly clear what the book was about, but it noted that people were getting together and "doing the book" in groups. That comment caught my attention – I had never heard of people coming together to "do a book" and I wondered what exactly that meant – so, intrigued, I took a chance and purchased a copy of the book. In retrospect, it was one of the best gambles I've ever made.

As I began to read Ms. Grabhorn's book it quickly became clear that the subject matter was precisely related to Deepak Chopra's disturbingly provocative claim that we can affect reality through our will – a capability Ms. Grabhorn calls "deliberate creation." After having my appetite so teasingly whetted by Dr. Chopra, I greedily devoured Ms. Grabhorn's book, and I was both surprised and grateful to find that she explained the process by which this "deliberate creation" can be accomplished very early on in the book (unlike many other authors who save the Big Revelation for the very last paragraph while devoting the rest of the book to the cultivation of maddening curiosity and frustration on the part of the reader). Throughout the period of time that I was reading the book I would discuss its amazing content with my wife, who, to say the least, is highly skeptical of any and all new age, "airy fairy" concepts. She predictably shrugged off the entire notion and found humor in my exuberance over it.

One day during that period I had seen an ad in a newspaper indicating that one of the premium cable channels was going to air a production of one of my favorite plays – Sam Shepard's "True West" – starring actor Bruce Willis. Being a big fan of both "True West" and Bruce Willis, I was deeply upset over the fact that, not being a subscriber to any premium channels, I would not get to see the play. I had seen the PBS American Playhouse production of "True West" (starring John Malkovich and Gary Sinise) several times, and I had also attended a live performance of the play (with Daniel Stern) off-Broadway at the Cherry Lane Theater. This is a play that I truly love, and I was extremely distraught at the thought that I would not get to see this new production. I drove my wife crazy that week, bitching and moaning about how badly I wanted to see the play and about how unfair it was that I would not be able to.

That weekend I awoke in the middle of the night, unable to sleep. I got up and did sometime I virtually never do: I sat on the couch and started to channel-surf. Round and round I went, cycling through the channels and finding nothing worth watching – until... On one of the channels there was an announcement that coming up next would be "True West" starring Bruce Willis! *What?* I thought, *I don't get that channel.* I checked the channel my TV set was tuned to and then I checked the TV Guide – sure enough, my TV was set to the premium channel that was scheduled to air "True West." At first I was mystified, but then I remembered that my cable provider occasionally ran promotions where they would broadcast a premium channel for several hours for free as a come-on to entice subscribers to add that channel to their account. I presumed that this was the case, thanked my lucky stars, and settled in for a wonderfully unexpected viewing of Sam Shepard's great play. When the play ended I grabbed my TV Guide to check what else this premium channel would be showing, my plan being to tape it for viewing with my wife the following night. As I flipped open the TV Guide the transmission abruptly ended and my TV screen went to snowy static. I sighed, turned off the TV, and went to bed.

The next morning I said to my wife, "You won't believe what happened last night," and I proceeded to relate the entire story to her. I brought my story to a close by saying, "Isn't that unbelievable?"

My wife simply laughed. "It's that book you're reading," she said matter-of-factly.

"Huh?" I replied.

"That book," she reiterated. "All week you did exactly all the stuff that you've been telling me about from that book."

And by God, my skeptical, non-believing wife had realized what I – the new-age believer in spirituality and mysticism – had been too blind to see: I had precisely applied – unknowingly – Lynn Grabhorn's method of "deliberate creation" to manipulate reality. Inexplicably, the extreme unlikelihood of the amazing coincidence and incredible luck required for me to wake up and stumble upon that broadcast precisely at its beginning, and then the bizarre fact of the transmission ending immediately after the play ended, had never occurred to me. It was only after my wife opened my eyes that I realized the almost statistically impossible confluence of events that was necessary to bring about my opportunity to watch that play. It was at that moment that I began to take Ms. Grabhorn's premise of "deliberate creation" very seriously.

18.2 The Law of Attraction/Intention

As I'm sure most of you know, the idea that one can affect material reality via an effort of thought and will is now a commonly held notion – going by names such as "the law of attraction" and "intention" – and has been covered in a multitude of books by many famous authors, including the likes of Gregg Braden, Wayne Dyer, Lynne McTaggart, and Deepak Chopra, among many, many others. Probably the single greatest factor in popularizing the law of attraction has been Rhonda Byrne's book (and DVD) *The Secret*.

The idea behind the law of attraction is surprisingly simple. The principle is based upon the premise that thoughts are composed of energy and that "like energy attracts like energy."[280] Often coupled with this notion is the belief that we exist in a field of infinite potentiality (akin to the Zero Point Field) and that the thoughts and emotional energies we transmit to that field will result in the manifestation of whatever desires are underlying those thoughts and emotions. An important point often made about the law of attraction is that it is non-judgmental and morally neutral: positive thoughts will result in positive experiences and manifestations, while negative thoughts will bring about negative results – one possible interpretation of the Bible's, "As ye sow, so shall ye reap."

The process by which one employs the law of attraction generally involves: (1) picturing in your mind precisely what it is that you wish to manifest; (2) fueling or empowering those thought-forms with strong emotions; (3) firmly believing that you can, and will, manifest that which you desire; and (4) vividly picturing yourself as already having or experiencing the object of your desire.

There are many subtle variations in technique and method, depending upon which proponent's book you read, but the core process typically involves at least the four points indicated above.

In retrospect, I realized that during the week leading up to the airing of Bruce Willis in "True West" I had unwittingly, yet vigorously and repeatedly, performed steps (1), (2), and (4) of the law-of-attraction process: I continually imagined how the play would be with Bruce Willis in the role of Lee, and because I knew much of the play by heart, my imaginings were very detailed and specific. Also, my imaginings were always accompanied by very powerful emotions – anger, sadness, longing. Without realizing it I had assembled the ingredients necessary for an application of the law of attraction, and I then proceeded to mix them with gusto. The result was, needless to say, astounding.

18.3 A Personal Experiment

I have to admit that, before this unplanned test of the theory, I had my doubts about Ms. Grabhorn's claims regarding the law of attraction. But after my "True West" experience I began to take the idea much more seriously. To see if this law-of-attraction thing was truly legit, I decided to do an experiment: I would *intentionally* apply the process to attempt to bring about a desired result. After days of thinking, I decided to try it on an upcoming and recurring source of misery for me: seasonal hay fever.

At that time in my life I had suffered year after year, without exception, awful hay fever symptoms which would begin with amazing precision the last week of August and continue on to the first week of October. Each year, during this approximately seven-week period, my nose would get so runny and my eyes would tear so profusely that I would have to place boxes of tissue as well as bags for the used tissue at various strategic locations about my house. It was an awful, awful time of the year for me which I faced with utmost dread as the month of August would come to a close.

So my plan was to try to avert my hay fever misery by applying the law of attraction/intention to the problem. Specifically, I would take a few moments several times each day and picture myself getting through the upcoming months with clear, dry eyes and a dry and free-breathing nasal passage. I would mentally *see* myself in my mind's eye going about the routine business of life with absolutely no hay fever symptoms whatsoever. I used the powerful emotions of my extreme dread of that seasonal torture to empower my mental imagery. And I used my amazing experience with "True West" to reinforce my belief in the reality and effectiveness of the process. The result? That year, during my usual hay fever period, I barely had a sniffle. Honestly, I sneezed a couple of times and had to blow my nose once or twice, but other than that – *nothing*. As I went around my house in early October collecting up the tissue boxes and plastic bags I marveled over the fact that they were all unused. I remember thinking: *This Grabhorn thing really works!*

18.4 Hacking Reality

The model of reality developed throughout Part III of this book maintains that our so-called "physical" reality is merely *perceived* by us as being a material reality but is, in actuality, an energy-information construct designed in accordance with mathematical principles and possessing many attributes typical of holograms and holographic projections.

It is no accident, then, that I have sometimes used the computer as an analog for our reality. Computers are, after all, also energy-information constructs – they use electricity as their energy and they rely on intelligently-designed instructions, in the form of firmware and software, to direct their processing of data. Furthermore, mathematics and logic serve as the basis for computer circuitry design, and, significantly, computers create real-seeming experiences (web sites, applications, games, etc.) that are, in truth, merely light-based illusions with no actual material existence (again, akin to holographic projections). So the analogy between our holographic reality and the computer experience is quite strong and defensible.

But the analogy can be carried even further. A "binary system" is a system that can exist in either of two possible states; in mathematics, the simplest number system is the binary number system, composed only of the two digits 0 and 1 (known as "binary digits", or "bits"): this is a complete number system in which all numerical quantities can be represented and all arithmetic operations can be performed. Computers, at their most fundamental level, operate in a binary environment: data is represented in a computer by means of electricity – a circuit either *has* electricity passing through it (ON = 1) or it *does not have* electricity passing through it (OFF = 0); decisions are made in computers by means of logic gates that evaluate conditions as being TRUE or FALSE. The entire basis of computer function and design is predicated upon the binary system. Now consider our physical reality: magnetism involves a NORTH POLE and a SOUTH POLE; electricity involves a POSITIVE CHARGE and a NEGATIVE CHARGE; in biology there is MALE and FEMALE. Our reality is dependent upon polarities; at its core, our reality is a binary reality – a *digital reality*. Author and computer systems designer Greg Braden has extended this analogy between computers and reality to encompass wave-particle duality, as follows: when subatomic particles exist in wave form they are in their OFF state, when they exist as physical entities (matter) they are ON. He then quotes physicist John Wheeler: "Every *it* – every particle, every field of force, even the space-time continuum itself – derives its function, its meaning, its very existence entirely from binary choices, *bits*. What we call reality arises … from the posing of yes/no questions." [281]

Well, if the design and function of our reality is so strikingly similar to that of a computer, then it's quite logical to suspect that, as with computers, *our reality is capable of being hacked*. That, I believe, is precisely what is happening with the law of attraction/intention and also with other heretofore unexplained phenomena such as ESP, precognition, remote viewing, and the like. Just as with computers, if someone is well-versed enough in understanding how the system functions, then he/she should be able to "break into" that system, gain control over it, and manipulate it in ways that are inconsistent with the expected functioning of the system. There are countless examples, across many diverse areas, of people intentionally and successfully hacking our reality. Let's take a look at several of these extraordinary cases.

18.5 Hacking Reality: Examples

The Placebo Effect

If there is any truth to the claim that we possess an ability to alter reality through the power of our minds, then it stands to reason that we would enjoy the greatest possible success when applying the process to our own bodies, for if mind can truly affect matter, then the best chance for doing so should be with matter that is most directly connected *to* mind. True to expectations, the most numerous examples of mind-over-matter hacking of reality are to be found in situations related to human health and healing.

The expression "placebo effect" is a phrase used by the medical field to describe situations where an illness is cured or an injury healed as a result of so-called "fake" treatment as opposed to "real medicine"; in other words, a placebo effect is a healing that results from an intervention that does not involve an active chemical substance or a medical or surgical procedure recognized and validated by mainstream medical science. Placebos are typically used as controls in drug trials and medical research: patients are given a pharmacologically inert pill ("sugar pill"), an injection of saline solution, or sham surgery so as to provide a frame of reference to evaluate the effectiveness of the actual therapy being studied.[282] Interestingly, placebos used in trials involving disorders that are amenable to psychological factors often demonstrate an effectiveness equal to or almost equal to that of the therapy under scrutiny. [283] While the medical establishment has been aware of the placebo effect for many decades, its view of the phenomenon was largely narrow-minded: first seen as little more than a bothersome artifact of clinical trials, it is now gradually being recognized as a treatment modality worthy of study in its own right. Indeed, the study of how a patient's attitudes, beliefs, and expectations impact their health and their ability to heal is now the subject of a special field called *psychoneuroimmunology*.[284]

The placebo effect is a perfect example of how reality can be hacked. What is happening here is that the patient's physical body is literally being changed (in this case, healed) simply because the patient has been led to believe that something has been done to that body – chemically or surgically – that will cause it to heal; the *reality* of the situation is that no chemical has been introduced and no surgery has been performed, but the *perceived reality*, on the patient's part, is that some medically valid intervention has occurred, and that *perception of a false reality* is enough to effect the healing. Thus reality has been hacked: the patient's physical body has been healed solely by convincing the mind that it is so. This is analogous to hacking a computer program or web page by going directly into the source code or HTML script and rewriting it.

While the medical profession may have shrugged off the placebo effect as a "mere" mind-over-matter phenomenon, the implications of the effect are potentially huge – it has all the markings of one of those Asimovian "Gee, that's funny..." situations, and as such demands formal and honest study. If aspects of our mental state and attitude can affect our physical health, then the likely rewards are enormous: placebo pills and sham surgeries are not only much cheaper than prescription drugs and fully invasive surgeries, they are also much safer and involve little or no side effects. To ignore the possibility of such an avenue to healing is unconscionable.

Fortunately, western medicine's heretofore narrow-minded attitude towards the therapeutic potential of placebos is changing. Headquartered at Beth Israel Deaconess Medical Center, the Program in Placebo Studies and the Therapeutic Encounter (PiPS) is "the only multidisciplinary institute dedicated solely to placebo study." One of its founders, Ted Kaptchuk, an acupuncturist and associate professor of medicine at Harvard Medical School, champions the need for an in-depth study of the mechanisms underlying the placebo effect: he believes that dismissing the evidence that placebo treatments appear to affect certain ailments "is like ignoring a huge chunk of healthcare." "[W]e should be using every tool in the box,"[285] he wisely notes.

A study by Mr. Kaptchuk dramatically illustrates the power of the placebo effect. In Mr. Kaptchuk's trial the subjects were seeking relief for severe arm pain; half of the subjects were given pain-reducing pills, while the other half received acupuncture treatments. The subjects were warned of possible side effects involving sluggishness, swelling, and pain. About one-third of the subjects, coming from both groups, experienced the side effects. Most of the other subjects reported genuine relief from their arm pain, with the acupuncture group claiming the more effective results. What was most telling about these results, however, was the fact that *both treatments had been shams*: the pain-relief pills were simple corn starch, and the supposed acupuncture needles were retractable needles that never pierced the skin.[286] In spite of the completely bogus nature of the "treatments," subjects nevertheless experienced effects, both positive and negative, that they were led to expect. It should be noted that sham treatments that cause negative effects are known as "nocebos," while the term "placebo effect" refers to positive effects resulting from such treatments[287]. Another nocebo example involved a chemotherapy study in which 30 percent of the *control group* – i.e., the folks receiving the placebo – lost their hair.[288]

In meta-analyses of clinical trial data (both published and unpublished) for antidepressant drugs, Irving Kirsch, Associate Director of the Program in Placebo Studies and a lecturer in medicine at the Harvard Medical School and Beth Israel Deaconess Medical Center, showed that the effectiveness of certain antidepressant drugs over placebos was "not clinically significant."[289] Kirsch attributes such results to what he calls "response expectancy theory" which posits that people experience results, at least in part, from what they expect to experience.[290]

In eleven separate trials involving colitis patients, fifty-two percent of the patients treated with placebo reported feeling better, and assessment via sigmoidoscopy indicated that fifty percent of the inflamed intestines actually looked better. [291] The sigmoidoscopy results highlight the important point that positive results from placebo treatment are not limited to subjective patient reports of improvement but often include actual physiological changes – such as shrunken tumors, elimination of warts, dilation of airways, and increased blood flow – confirmed by medical tests. Placebos appear to be effecting *genuine healing*.

A scientific explanation for this expectation-experience connection is suggested by the work of neuroscientist Fabrizio Benedetti at the University of Turin, who has studied the effects of placebos on brain chemistry. "What we 'placebo neuroscientists'…have learned [is] that therapeutic rituals move a lot of molecules in the patients' brain *[sic]*, and these molecules are the very same as those activated by the drugs we give in routine clinical practice," Benedetti has noted. "In other words, rituals and drugs use the very same biochemical pathways to influence the patient's brain."[292]

Dr. Benedetti's findings raise an important point: as a method for hacking reality, I am not suggesting that the placebo effect (or, for that matter, any of the other "hacks" to be discussed) is some kind of spooky, supernatural mojo working through an unfathomable agency; on the contrary, I firmly believe that these methods for hacking reality employ natural processes that are very much a part of this reality. However, I think that the mechanisms through which they function address reality at a much more fundamental level than that which we routinely experience, and the processes they employ are of a deeply subtle nature. There is no magic happening here; rather, it is a manipulation of our reality that is being accomplished through avenues and methods presently unknown to us, and occurring at a level of reality presently hidden from us. At some point in the process, the placebo effect then integrates into material reality and utilizes normal biological mechanisms and avenues to actuate the healing.

In his wonderful book *Fighting Cancer from Within*, medical doctor Martin L. Rossman notes that, "The human brain is the world's greatest pharmacy" citing its ability to make chemicals that control a multitude of bodily functions as well as relieve pain and stimulate the immune system. [293] If we do indeed possess our own internal pharmacy, then perhaps the placebo effect is an indication of how we can take steps to access that pharmacy and exploit its resources. It would seem that our bodies already possess the ability to heal themselves – what *we* must learn is the process by which that self-healing can be activated.

The literature and internet are rife with similar examples of the placebo effect, and as such there is no reason to belabor the point here. Suffice it to say that there is more than enough evidence available in this area to justify a formal and rigorous study of how and why the placebo effect works, and for seriously considering its utilization as a therapeutic intervention in its own right. Before I move on to other areas, there is one more case I'd like to highlight because it strikingly illustrates just how powerful the placebo effect can be.

An absolutely amazing case involving the placebo effect was reported in an article entitled "Psychological Variables in Human Cancer", from the Journal of Projective Techniques, Vol.21, No.4, (December 1957), concerning a cancer patient referred to as Mr. Wright. The patient was suffering from advanced malignancy involving the lymph nodes (lymphosarcoma). Among other problems, Mr. Wright had tumor masses "the size of oranges" in the neck, armpit, groin, chest and abdomen. He was diagnosed as untreatable and terminal, and his doctors assessed a life expectancy of, optimistically, two weeks. But Mr. Wright had read about a new drug called Krebiozen and became convinced that it would be his salvation; he begged his doctors to administer it and, although he did not qualify under the trial criteria, his doctor relented and gave him his first injection on a Friday. When the doctor next saw Mr. Wright, on that following Monday, he was astounded to see his patient in excellent spirits, no longer bedridden but walking about and cheerfully chatting with people. The tumor masses were reported to have "melted like snowballs on a hot stove" and in those few days had shrunk to half their original size. Within ten days Mr. Wright was discharged with "practically all signs of his disease having vanished." Barely able to breathe only two weeks earlier, Wright was now able to take out his plane and fly it at 12,000 feet with no discomfort. Wright remained in almost perfect health for two months until he began reading reports that Krebiozen had proved ineffective. As a result, Mr. Wright lost faith in the drug and quickly relapsed to his original state. Wright's doctor, now realizing why his patient had previously recovered so miraculously, decided to lie in order to see if Mr. Wright's original mind-induced recovery could be repeated. The doctor told Wright that Krebiozen was indeed effective, but that it had "deteriorated on standing"; he then claimed he expected to receive a more refined, more powerful product. After a couple days the Doctor announced he had received the product and gave Mr. Wright an injection (of what was, in reality, merely "fresh water"). As a result of this placebo injection, Wright's second recovery was even more dramatic than his first – tumor masses once again melted, chest fluid vanished, and he was back on his feet and even resumed flying. The water injections were continued and Mr. Wright remained symptom-free for more than two months. However, upon reading an American Medical Association press release stating that Krebiozen was worthless in the treatment of cancer, Mr. Wright again lost hope, was readmitted to the hospital near death, and died two days later.[294]

By virtue of Mr. Wright's (unwarranted) faith in the healing potential of Krebiozen, and his (false) belief that he had received injections of it, his mind was able to effect a recovery from terminal cancer that was nothing short of miraculous. This happened in direct defiance of the reality of Mr. Wright's situation – Krebiozen was, in fact, determined to be ineffective against cancer, and Mr. Wright had, in fact, not been injected with it in any case. Yet Wright's mind was able to somehow utilize some unknown healing potential, presumably inherent in his body, and vaporize huge tumors. Physical reality was altered – hacked – with no discernible physical cause apparent.

The doctrine of scientific materialism holds not only that *matter* is the fundamental substance in nature, but also that *all phenomena are the result of material interactions*. What we are seeing in the placebo effect, however, are material results springing from non-material causes: instead of the physical excisions of surgery or the chemical effects of drugs, we have, in the placebo effect, physiological changes resulting solely from mental processes. And *that* is the unique feature that distinguishes the hacking of reality from the normal process of reality: *when one hacks reality one is bringing about changes in physical reality exclusively through the use of one's mind*. And notice the interesting correspondence between the placebo effect and the steps involved in the law of attraction: in these placebo cases the participants are given a clear picture of the results they should expect, they are given reason to believe that they will get those results, and (presumably) there are powerful emotions implicit in their desperate desire to be healed. That is virtually a step-by-step application of the law of attraction/intention.

While the placebo effect is most often associated with drugs – the placebo as "sugar pill" – it turns out that there is also a placebo counterpart associated with surgery. So-called "sham surgeries" are fake surgeries in which routine aspects typical of surgery – e.g., anesthesia, incision, pre- and post-op care – are performed on a patient, while the step that is thought to be therapeutically necessary (i.e., the actual repair or removal) is omitted. As is the case with placebo pills, sham surgeries have frequently been found to result in the healing of the condition for which treatment was sought. Again we have a situation where the health problem itself is not being addressed via any physical intervention, but where *deceiving the mind* into believing it was so addressed is sufficient to effect healing. Examples of healings due to sham surgery are often even more dramatic than those of the sugar pill variety.

A study was conducted by the Baylor School of Medicine to evaluate the relative effectiveness of two types of surgical procedures used to treat osteoarthritis of the knee. One of the surgical procedures, arthroscopic lavage, involves a washing or flushing out of the knee joint, while the other surgery, arthroscopic débridement, involves shaving and removal of damaged cartilage. The study began with 180 patients randomly divided into three groups: one group received arthroscopic lavage, a second group received arthroscopic débridement, and the third group was a control group which received placebo surgery consisting of incision and "a simulated débridement without insertion of the arthroscope." The results were not what the doctors expected: "At no point did either of the intervention groups report less pain or better function than the placebo group." The study's conclusion says it all: "In this controlled trial involving patients with osteoarthritis of the knee, the outcomes after arthroscopic lavage or arthroscopic débridement were no better than those after a placebo procedure."[295] Dr. Mosley, first author of the study, was refreshingly blunt in his assessment of the results: he discounted any benefits due to actual surgery and gave full credit for the "entire benefit" to the placebo effect. [296]

Other examples of placebo surgeries proving equally effective as true surgeries include: cases of angina pectoris (chest and arm pain due to decreased blood flow to the heart), where tests indicated actual improvement of blood flow in addition to patients' reports of pain relief [297]; vertebroplasty, a surgical procedure for "fixing broken backs by injecting them with a special kind of medical cement" [298]; brain surgery for Parkinson's disease [299]; and laser surgery to improve cardiac blood flow. [300] Again, as with placebo medications, reports of the effectiveness of placebo surgeries are voluminous. But the core point is the same: If the mind can be fooled, then it can override reality. When one considers the dangers inherent in invasive surgery as well as the phenomenal monetary costs and the limited availability of qualified surgeons, sophisticated medical technology, and hospital facilities, then one must wonder *why* considerable effort is not being expended to understand and harness the process underlying the incredible effectiveness of the placebo effect.

What is especially interesting with regard to placebo surgery is the fact that some medical professionals are acknowledging its extraordinary effectiveness as a counterargument to those who complain that use of sham surgeries in medical trials is unethical. This ironic situation has come about because critics have objected to the use of sham surgeries as experimental controls on the grounds that trail participants who receive the sham surgery "have no prospect of benefit from the trial, yet they are exposed to all the risks of the sham intervention"; these critics therefore claim that using sham surgery in clinical trials is unethical. After all, participants in the control groups are not getting the potential rewards of the "real" surgery, yet they are being exposed to all the potential dangers associated with other aspects of the surgery – infection, anesthesia risks, etc. Proponents *for* the use of sham surgery as experimental controls, however, counter the critics' claims by noting that the proven effectiveness of placebo surgeries suggests that they *do*, in fact, offer potential benefits to the subjects. A direct quote from the abstract of a relevant professional paper says it all: "[T]he placebo effect associated with sham procedures can often be substantial and has been well documented in the scientific literature. We argue that, in light of the scientific evidence supporting the benefits of sham interventions for pain and Parkinson's disease that stem from the placebo effect, these sham-controlled trials should be considered as offering potential direct benefit to participants."[301] Thus the medical profession is acknowledging that the healing potential of sham surgery is "substantial," which is precisely what the evidence shows.

The placebo effect, as we have seen, is dependent upon fooling the subject into believing in the reality of something that has, in fact, not occurred. What if we could knowingly and successfully employ the mechanism behind the placebo effect and us it intentionally to heal? Would that not be a desirable application of this miraculous ability? After all, the placebo effect is telling us that the ability to heal ourselves via our minds actually exists. It seems logical that our next step should be to learn to exploit this ability and use it in a more direct manner. Fortunately, people have been doing exactly that for a number of years.

Guided Imagery

Sometime during the 1980s I saw a TV show about a man who travelled around the U.S. visiting children's cancer wards at various hospitals. He would sit with the young patients and coach them in the use of a technique known as "guided imagery" wherein the patient creates mental imagery designed to coax the immune system to vigorously battle the disease. In this particular case, the man trained the children to use imagery that they could relate to consistent with their young age; for example, he might advise them to picture their immune system's T-cells as knights wearing armor and carrying swords, doing battle with and destroying the cancer cells, which were imagined as dragons. Clearly, this is imagery that a child can easily understand, and for which he/she can generate vivid mental imagery and intense enthusiasm. Other scenarios could be sci-fi-based, involving ray guns and aliens. The show reported that the man was having remarkable success in achieving remission of the cancer in many of the children, including some with severe cases.

Guided imagery appears to utilize the same, or similar, mechanism that is induced by the placebo effect. But whereas the placebo effect results from deceiving the subject into believing a false situation exists, guided imagery is a knowing and intentional technique designed to effect physiological healing strictly by use of mental processes. This is clearly a more direct and efficient means of activating mind-induced healing.

Imagery (also referred to as "visualization") is a mental activity wherein a person generates thoughts that possess sensory attributes – i.e., thoughts that can be seen, smelled, heard, or felt in one's mind. Vivid dreams or memories are examples of imagery that we routinely experience. Detailed and realistic mental planning also qualifies as imagery. *Guided* imagery, as the phrase implies, is imagery that results from purposely directed thoughts that are generated and coordinated with a specific goal in mind.[302] In other words, in its broadest sense, guided imagery is a skillful and deliberate application of the imagination that is intended to create vivid mental representations for the purpose of effecting an outcome in the material world.

Guided imagery, as applied to self-healing, is predicated upon the belief that the mind and body are connected, and that the body responds to mental imagery as though it were real.[303] Those very premises – that the mind and body are connected, and that the body responds to mental imagery as though it were real – are convincingly demonstrated, I believe, by the massive volume of documented instances of the placebo effect.

The theory behind guided imagery, at a deeper level, posits that the mind and body exist in a dynamic interrelationship as part of a shared energy field; a change in consciousness effects a corresponding change in the energy field, which then manifests as a change in the physical body.[304] A more mainstream, but arguably similar, explanation for the mechanism by which guided imagery operates suggests that, due to the connection between the visual cortex in the brain and the involuntary nervous system, activation of the visual cortex via mental imagery as opposed to direct visual stimuli can influence physical and emotional states and thereby evoke physiological changes in the body.[305] Imagery would thus appear to serve as the bridge connecting the material body to the mind's mental energy: as noted earlier, form and energy appear to be the two basic features of reality; in guided imagery, the mental image provides the form and the mind provides mental or psychic energy. In my opinion, all methods of hacking reality go back to this basic premise: the need for form and energy.

Guided imagery is used as a healing modality for a variety of purposes: to promote relaxation, to lower blood pressure, to relieve pain, to stimulate blood flow, and to stimulate and direct the immune system, just to name a few.[306] Many studies have indicated that guided imagery has demonstrated significant effectiveness in treating a variety of medical conditions.[307] In the example I used to kick off this section – the man helping children fight cancer – it is easy to imagine how his imagery scenarios involving knights as immune cells and dragons as cancer cells could create a situation in the body where such imagery would stimulate T-cells into action against cancer cells.

Dr. Carl Simonton, a radiologist who specialized in the treatment of cancer, began using visualization with his patients in the 1960s. His method of imagery utilization is very much like that referenced earlier in the treatment of children with cancer (and I suspect it is possible that the gentleman conducting those treatments was inspired by Dr. Simonton's work): patients are taught how to get into a relaxed, meditative state; they are then asked to visualize a scenario in which their cancer cells are destroyed (say, for example, by their white blood cells or by the energy of radiation therapy) and then flushed out of their system; the patient concludes their visualization by picturing themselves healthy and well. The case of one of his patients is instructive: Bob Gilley, age 40, came to see Dr. Simonton with a diagnosis of cancer and a survival prognosis of 30%. Adapting Dr. Simonton's visualization techniques to create a "game of it" Mr. Gilley would visualize his cancer as a "vicious animal" such as a snake, and his white blood cells as "white husky dogs by the millions." The dogs would tear the snakes apart, then lick up the remains leaving his bodily interior clean. Gilley did three 10 to 15 minute visualizations per day; after six weeks his tumor had shrunk by 75%, and after two months a cancer scan showed no trace of the disease remaining. [308] In a study involving 159 of Dr. Simonton's cancer patients who were deemed incurable and with a projected national norm survival time of twelve months, 63 of those patients were still alive four years later; the group's overall average survival time (24.4 months) was more than twice the expected twelve months. [309] It is important to note that Dr. Simonton's methods are intended to be used in conjunction with standard medical treatments for cancer (e.g., radiation therapy, chemotherapy). [310] Although I was not aware of Dr. Simonton's work in the early years of my battle with cancer, I nevertheless employed imagery techniques very similar to his in order to augment and enhance the external beam radiation treatments I received for prostate cancer, and I still use imagery today in an effort to boost my immune system and hopefully keep the cancer in remission.

My Utilization of Imagery

In my fight against prostate cancer I used several different forms of imagery which I devised myself so as to be compatible with my personality. As an Army veteran, I found it natural to envision my T-cells and the cancer cells as soldiers in battle, and I would, of course, "see" my T-cells as exhibiting superior numbers and superior fighting skills as compared with the cancer cells. At other times I would take a more spiritual approach and imagine a bright, healing light enter through the top of my head and permeate my entire body, cleansing it not only of cancer cells but of anything harmful to my health; although I would imagine my entire body being saturated with the white light, I would specifically focus pointedly on my prostate. Additionally, I purchased and used a CD by Belleruth Naparstek which contained anti-cancer imagery and health-promoting affirmations. And, as you already know, I underwent hypnosis sessions conducted by two different hypnotists. I also decided to get a bit creative and try an original approach: To assist my mind in forming the mental imagery, I downloaded an actual photo, taken with an electron microscope, of T-cells destroying a cancer cell. I used graphics software to create a before-and-after set of pictures where the cancer cell was present in one picture (this was the original photo) and then another picture (the doctored photo) in which the cancer cell was missing, suggesting that it had been eradicated by the T-cells. I would (and still do) stare at these two pictures and imagine the T-cells attacking the cancer cell, spraying or injecting it with toxins, and then the cancer cell ultimately dissolving into nothingness. I found that using these pictures helped me to focus, and more clearly define, my mental imagery. Whether any of this actually helped me is, of course, impossible to determine as I had also employed several other treatment modalities, to include external beam radiation treatments, diet and exercise changes, and dietary supplements. I think it important that I reiterate the point expressed in the Disclaimer from the beginning pages of this book: I am NOT offering any medical advice here or elsewhere in this book. I have no medical training or expertise and it is not my intention to advise on health care. Please see a medical professional about any health concerns you have.

While I'm on the topic of my own personal use of guided imagery, allow me to take a moment to mention an exciting idea that occurred to me while I was engaging in this practice.

Whenever I would use my self-created before-and-after photos of the T-cells killing the cancer cell I would experience a very subtle but powerful feeling that the imagery was working, i.e., that it was highly effectual in fighting the cancer. I cannot say why I felt this, nor can I describe exactly what I was feeling, but the impression was (and still is) extremely compelling. On one level it was most definitely an emotional feeling, but there was also what felt like a vaguely perceptible physiological sensation. Perhaps it was because the photos were very dramatic and vivid, and they made forming a mental picture of the process extremely easy and accessible. In any event, I became very impressed and intrigued by the effect these photos had on me, and I devoted much thought to it. Then, one day, I came up with an idea of how the method I had employed could be greatly enhanced: it occurred to me that viewing an *animation* of T-cells killing cancer cells would be much more graphic and, presumably, more effective. From that notion I formulated an idea for a controlled scientific study of my supposition. I contacted a scientist who had published a paper along somewhat similar lines and I emailed her with my idea. While she said she thought the idea had merit, the primary concern, she noted, would be the acquisition of funding. So, for the sake of anyone reading this book who might have the means or the connections to make this study happen, allow me to present a brief description of how I envision this study being designed and carried out.

Guided Imagery Experiment Proposal:

The experiment would first involve creating a computer animation that vividly and realistically depicts T-cells destroying cancer cells. The experimental subjects would be people who all have the same type of cancer, at the same stage, and who are receiving, or have received, the same type of treatment. Since I'm personally familiar with prostate cancer I'll use that to illustrate the specifics. So, for example, the subjects might consist of men with prostate cancer with the same T-scores and Gleason scores, and who all have received the same form of treatment (surgery, radiation, what have you); other variables (e.g. age, alcohol use, smokers vs. non-smokers, etc.) would be controlled for as deemed necessary. A preliminary assessment would be made using standard diagnostic tools such as PSA, tumor size, or what have you. The subjects would then be divided into three groups: one group would be educated as to how the body fights cancer as well as the methodology of guided imagery, and they would then be required to view the T-cell computer animation two or three times per day for a specified length of time as an aid to their utilization of guided imagery; the second group would also be educated as to how the body fights cancer and the methodology of guided imagery, but they would only be asked to conduct their own personal mental guided imagery without the benefit of the computer simulation; the third group is the control group and would not receive any instruction whatsoever regarding the immune system or guided imagery and would not have access to the computer animation. At the end of the testing period the diagnostic tools would be re-administered and the resulting PSAs, tumor sizes, etc., of each group would be compared to see if either form of guided imagery indicated a statistically significant advantage.

If the experimental results of this study were to indicate that guided imagery – especially the computer-assisted approach – represented a synergistic enhancement of the immune system's ability to eliminate cancer, then it would suggest a safe, inexpensive, and natural means for combating cancer. It would also offer cancer patients a satisfying and uplifting sense of personal empowerment in that they could now play an active role in their own treatment, rather than the passive, helpless role commonly experienced.

The Witch Doctor's Curse

I vividly recall a highly dramatic illustration of the nocebo effect from a video I saw of Deepak Chopra addressing a group of medical doctors at a hospital where his physician brother worked (I cannot remember what video it was, and I was unable to find any reference to it on the internet, so, unfortunately, I cannot provide a citation). To the best of my recollection, the following paragraph summarizes the content of Dr. Chopra's talk.

Dr. Chopra told the story of some anthropologists who were studying a primitive tribe. A member of the tribe would occasionally hire a witch doctor/medicine man to place a curse on another member with whom he was in conflict. The medicine man, who wore distinctive and identifying clothing, necklaces, etc., would approach his target, make a hand gesture, and speak the magic word of the curse. To the anthropologists' amazement, the cursed individual would gradually become progressively ill and would eventually die. The scientists wondered, "Is there really magic occurring here?" Baffled, they recruited some medical doctors to study the situation and soon learned that no magic was transpiring; the MDs determined that the tribal people believed so strongly in the medicine man's powers that, when cursed by him, they would grow extremely fearful and depressed, they would stop eating and drinking, their immune system function would shut down, and they would slowly but inevitably succumb to dehydration and physical deterioration. The doctors being addressed by Chopra nodded knowingly at the outcome to the story – science had prevailed in explaining away a silly superstition. Then Chopra hit them with the punch: he noted that whenever one of *them*, in their role as doctor, wearing their distinctive and identifying white lab coat and stethoscope, told a patient that he or she had cancer, that doctor was *doing the exact same thing* and *having the exact same effect* as the medicine man issuing his death curse. The effect on the gathered group of physicians was dramatic – the doctors' jaws dropped and the looks of cocky pride fell away from their faces. But Deepak Chopra had made his point: the nocebo effect – a negative mind-over-matter effect – unwittingly practiced in modern medicine, can be just as deadly as the tribal medicine man's curse. When a medical doctor points at a patient and says "cancer" that doctor has just issued the equivalent of a modern-day curse: the aura of lethality which our society associates with cancer, and the authority with which medical doctors are invested, combine to create a situation in which a diagnosis of cancer is often interpreted by the patient as the equivalent of a death sentence.

Another example of the nocebo effect, albeit less dramatic than the witch doctor's curse, is related by biologist Rupert Sheldrake in his fascinating book, *Science Set Free*. While a student at Cambridge, Dr. Sheldrake witnessed one of his physiology instructors hypnotize a student whom he told would be touched on the arm with a lighted cigarette as part of an experiment regarding skin response to heat. In truth, the instructor touched the student's arm with the cool, flat end of a pencil; nevertheless, the skin at the location of contact with the pencil reddened and blistered. [311]

If you believe strongly enough in a curse, then it will have power over you. The nocebo effect is likely the explanation behind claims that voodoo spells and hexes actually work. But let's not fall into the trap of accepting the placebo and nocebo effects as mundane rationalizations for otherwise mysterious phenomena – the fact is that the placebo effect *itself* is a mysterious phenomenon; it is a means for hacking reality, for causing physical effects in reality that have no discernible cause under a materialist paradigm. The placebo effect is not an answer to a mystery – it is the mystery itself.

Yogi Mind-Induced Body Control

There are many cases of Indian Yogis and Tibetan monks exerting control over physiological processes to a degree heretofore thought impossible, with studies conducted under laboratory conditions having confirmed what had long been claimed anecdotally. Employing various deep meditation techniques, these adepts have demonstrated the ability to: significantly raise and lower their heartbeat; produce brain wave patterns, while awake, typical of a deep sleep state; sit naked in cold environments covered by cold, wet sheets, and generate body heat sufficient not only to prevent hypothermia but also to melt snow and dry the wet sheets. [312] Many documented cases exist of people who demonstrate imperviousness to fire and heat – so-called "fire immunity" – by walking across hot coals or hot lava, or by handling red-hot metal, without evidencing any pain or injury. [313] And, while not demonstrated under laboratory conditions (at least, not to my knowledge), there are many reports of people levitating their bodies before large numbers of witnesses. [314]

It would seem that all humans possess an innate *potential* ability to hack reality, but that tapping into that ability requires the development and application of a certain technique and state of mind that somehow enables or activates the ability. Calming the mind, visualization, and belief appear to play keys roles in the process. Clearly, it is an *internal* process, and I believe that our societal preoccupation with the external material world hampers the ability and causes it to atrophy.

Visualization and Training

Several experiments have established a relationship existing between visualization imagery and athletic performance. Athletes who have spent most or all of their preparation time by practicing in their mind using visualization imagery have performed as good as or better than athletes who spent their full prep time in actual physical training. This method of practice, sometimes referred to as "mental rehearsal" or "implicit practice," involves the athlete visualizing the experience in a multisensory mode from a first-person perspective; in addition to rehearsing the activity, the athlete also envisions his/her bodily sensations, the setting, the crowd, and as many other details of the experience as possible. They also imagine themselves achieving victory. [315] Once again, the methodological similarities to the law of attraction/intention are obvious. This is a great practical application of hacking reality: the idea of preparing for an athletic event while sitting in an armchair with your eyes closed is an amazingly convenient option – it can be done at any time of day or night and under any weather conditions, it presents no risk of injury to the athlete, and it can even be performed *by* an injured person.

What is also of tremendous practical value is the possibility that such "mental rehearsal" need not be limited to athletic events. The brilliant French pianist Hélène Grimaud appears to utilize such mental rehearsal herself, having the ability to prepare for a concert "without actually playing"; when once asked if she had practiced for an upcoming concert, Ms. Grimaud replied, "I played the piece two times in my head." [316] If this ability exists in each of us, then the possibility of being able to develop and improve technical skills via mental visualization has enormous implications on both the personal and the societal levels.

With regard to mental practice of athletic events, there is solid evidence that the benefits of such visualization are not limited merely to perfection of skill and technique. *People who visualize athletic activity display neurological and physiological responses consistent with the actual physical performance of such activity.* Studies have shown that the brain transmits the same signals to the body whether the subject was thinking about engaging in a particular physical activity or actually doing it. Likewise, "implicit practice" studies involving weight training showed that the groups that engaged only in mental weight training nevertheless increased both strength and muscle size by almost half as much as the groups that physically exercised. [317] Think about this for a moment: you can get the actual, physical results obtained from weight training (i.e., increased strength and muscle size) simply by imagining yourself lifting weights! Here's a scenario to consider: You come home from work too exhausted to exercise and, besides, it's raining out and you don't feel like traveling to the gym – no problem; just plop down in your recliner chair and visualize yourself lifting weights, and you can conceivably get as much as half the benefit you would have gotten by actually going to the gym and physically lifting the weights. And it's safer too. If this isn't hacking reality, then I don't know what is.

Age Regression

In 1981 psychologist Ellen Langer conducted a study involving men in their seventies and eighties in which she was able to reverse the biological age of her subjects solely by employing a psychological strategy. The method utilized by Dr. Langer is as striking in its simplicity as it is in its effectiveness. The elderly gentlemen were divided into two groups that each participated in a one-week retreat at an old monastery in New Hampshire. Both before and after the retreat the men were subjected to a multitude of physical and cognitive tests intended to measure age-related characteristics. During the week-long retreat, the men in one group were told to behave as though they were back in the 1950's: they were to talk in the present tense of that time period, wear IDs with personal photos from that era, and even discuss their jobs as though they were still working rather than being retired. The environment in which they lived was similarly rigged to promote the illusion that they were back in the 1950s: magazines, TV, music, and movies all were from that era. Discussions were restricted to topics current in the 50s as well: e.g., Khrushchev, Eisenhower, Mickey Mantle. The experiment was structured so that every detail of life for that week pertained to the time period of the late 1950s. The second group of men – the control group – was merely told to reminisce about that era, but their actual environment was left unaltered and thus reflected the true and then-current time period. The results of the study, determined via comparison of the biological age profiles from the before-and-after mental and physical test data, were stunning: the men in both groups showed signs of age reversal, but the results were significantly more prominent in the group that lived in the simulated 1950s environment. Amazingly, those subjects demonstrated measureable, *physiological* signs of age-reversal: hearing, vision, posture, muscle strength, manual dexterity, memory and IQ test performance all showed dramatic improvement – by all accounts their bodies appeared to have actually and literally become younger. [318]

Note the similarities between this age-regression experiment and the methods employed in placebo healing, imagery healing, the law of attraction/intention, and so on: in each situation we are fooling the mind into believing something other than that which is actually true. Except, let's exchange the phrase "fooling the mind" for a more appropriate phrase: "redirecting awareness." In truth, genuine deception is really only happening in the placebo cases; in all the other situations – imagery, yogi body control, visualization training, the law of attraction, and this age-reversal study – the mind's awareness is intentionally and knowingly being redirected for the purpose of achieving a desired and preconceived goal. This is a technology, if you will, for altering reality; but it is strictly a *mental* technology, for – be it by deceit or design – all of these techniques share one common denominator: they function and operate *via mind*. All of these phenomena are variations on a single, incredible theme: it is possible to hack reality solely through the power of one's mind.

Multiple Personality Disorder and Physiological Illness

An absolutely astounding situation in which reality is altered in ways that are inexplicable within the limits of our current scientific knowledge has to do with physiological conditions and illnesses experienced by people afflicted with Multiple Personality Disorder.

Multiple Personality Disorder (MPD), also referred to as Dissociative Identity Disorder (DID), is a condition in which a person's identity fragments into two or more distinct personalities that coexist within one individual. The degree to which such multiple personalities can differ is striking, with the distinct personalities often possessing different: names, ages, genders, IQ, language fluency, posture, mannerisms, tones of voice, and memories (among other traits). [319] One might look at this list of differing traits and explain it away as a bizarre mental or psychological phenomenon, but it turns out that, fascinating though those differences might be, they are only the tip of a very explanation-defying iceberg.

For, it is also common for an MPD patient's various personalities to possess differing biological and medical conditions.[320] These distinctions are based in human physiology and are thus dependent upon the structure and function of the living body. But, in the case of an MPD patient, *there is only one physical body.* The disturbing question then arises: How can different physiologically-dependent medical conditions coexist in a single physical body? The documented examples of such cases are mind-blowing.

It is not uncommon in MPD cases for a medical condition afflicting one personality to inexplicably disappear when another personality takes control. There are cases where all sub-personalities but one are allergic to orange juice and exhibit the associated swelling and rash, while the sole non-allergic personality experiences no reaction whatsoever; this occurs even to the extent that, should an allergic personality in the throes of allergic reaction suddenly switch to a non-allergic personality, the rash will instantly begin to fade. [321] Other biological changes exhibited among coexisting MPD personalities relate to: allergic reaction to wasp stings, instant transition from drunkenness to sobriety, differing responses to prescription drugs or anesthesia, visual acuity (with some patients needing to carry several pairs of eyeglasses), colorblindness, and women having several menstrual periods per month due to the differing cycles of their sub-personalities. There is even a case cited wherein a woman admitted to a hospital for diabetes exhibited no diabetic symptoms when one of her non-diabetic personalities came to the fore. The different personalities of an MPD patient also exhibit differing brain wave patterns. [322] Scars and wounds can appear and disappear from one personality to another, as well as left- and right-handedness, seizures, and eating disorders. Even blood pressure readings can vary dramatically. A study in which MPD patients were subjected to a battery of ophthalmological tests showed not only differences in visual acuity among the different personalities, but also significant changes with regard to curvature of the eye and refraction; Dr. Scott Miller, the psychologist who conducted the study, described the case of one patient who "had had his left eye injured in a fight, so that it turned out. But the condition only appeared in one of his personalities. It disappeared in the others, nor was there any evidence of muscle imbalance." [323]

Well, you get the point: In all of these cases we have the rather paradoxical situation of a single physical body exhibiting wildly varying, and often conflicting, physiological conditions and symptoms. How can a drunk person turn instantly sober? How does a diabetic suddenly become non-diabetic? How do physical features of one's eye change with no discernible physical cause? If nothing else, these cases prove that it is possible for the human body to drastically alter a wide variety of biological conditions and attributes *without the need for any external causative agent*. If we could understand the mechanism by which this is happening, and then harness that mechanism, we could conceivably devise techniques to enable people to self-generate cures and healing for a variety of common medical afflictions. How far we might then extend that mechanism is anyone's guess. Are there cases in which one sub-personality of an MPD patient has cancer but another personality does not? I couldn't find any such cases, but as a person with prostate cancer I can tell you that I damn well would like to know. The point is that these MPD patients are *hacking reality*, albeit unknowingly and unintentionally. And they are doing it by some method that is outside the scope of our understanding of how reality operates. The simple fact that they are doing it is proof that it can be done.

18.6 Hacking External Reality

The majority of examples of reality hacking presented in this chapter have been limited to changes affecting internal human physiology. This should not be a surprise since the human mind and body are physically, directly, and intimately connected; one would expect that any mental altering of physical reality would be most easily accomplished in that context, i.e., by the mind altering the physical body to which it is biologically connected. In many ways, the utilization of mental imagery for personal healing – though miraculous and wonderful in its own right – may represent the most elementary and obvious application of this extraordinary phenomenon. My own example regarding my experience with the televising of the play "True West" is a glaring exception, as it involved an application of the law of attraction that appeared to manipulate events in the external world. This extended application of reality hacking represents a broader utilization of this amazing ability – namely, to reach beyond our bodies and somehow use our minds to affect *external reality* – yet it is nevertheless completely consistent with the scientific basis to be discussed below. And, indeed, this situation is not uncommon: Rhonda Byrne's book and DVD of *The Secret* are filled with such examples (as are other books and DVDs) – from things as mundane as finding a parking space to more serious matters like getting the house of one's dreams, selling thousands of copies of one's book, or meeting one's "perfect partner." [324] In this vein there are also myriad examples of groups of people using their combined prayers or directed intention to heal a sick person miles away [325], or to reduce incidents of violence in a specific geographic area. [326] In his book *The Divine Matrix*, author Gregg Braden discusses a video (which is widely available on the internet) of the healing of a woman's malignant bladder tumor, in a hospital in Beijing, China, that was accomplished by three "practitioners" utilizing only "focused emotion and energy" and the repeated utterance of the phrase "already done, already done"; no anesthesia or sedatives were administered and no surgery performed, and the entire process, including sonogram images of the fading tumor mass, was presented in real time. [327] But perhaps the most dramatic example of the hacking of external reality was given by author Michael Talbot.

18.7 The Invisible Daughter

In his wonderful book *The Holographic Universe* author Michael Talbot relates an amazing story of an event that he personally witnessed in the mid 1970s. Talbot had been invited to a get-together of friends hosted by his father to which a hypnotist had been hired to entertain the guests. The hypnotist selected a friend of Talbot's father as a good candidate for hypnosis and then put the man into a deep trance. After putting the subject through some typical, amusing hypnotically-induced antics (such has having him believe that a potato he was eating was an apple) the hypnotist then told the subject that his teenage daughter, who was present in the room, would be invisible to him. He had the daughter stand directly in front of her father and then took him out of his trance state. Asked if he could see his daughter, the father visually scanned the room and, apparently looking right through his daughter, said , "No." When the hypnotist asked if he was certain, the subject again, despite his daughter's giggling, responded in the negative. The hypnotist then went behind the girl, took something out of his pocket, and placed it against the small of the girl's back, out of view of everyone present. When asked to identify the object the subject leaned forward and, seemingly oblivious of his daughter's presence, correctly stated that it was a watch; when asked if he could read the inscription, the man, with obvious effort, correctly relayed the name and message inscribed on the watch. The hypnotist passed the watch around so that all the guests could confirm that the inscription was exactly as stated by the hypnosis subject. When Talbot later spoke with the man, he affirmed that he had indeed not seen his daughter but had only seen the watch cupped in the hypnotist's hand. In considering an alternative explanation, Talbot notes that it was possible that the subject was somehow receiving information about the watch telepathically from the hypnotist. [328]

While telepathy might explain the subject's ability to identify the watch and its inscription, it does not explain the man's inability to see his daughter standing directly in front of him. This is a case where tinkering with a man's mind resulted in a significant change in his perception of reality; and, as we've already learned, our *perception* of reality is our *experience* of reality. Somehow, the hypnotist's suggestion affected this man's mind in such a way that his brain was programmed to not register his daughter's presence even when she was directly in front of him – his visual sensory input was selectively hacked to omit registering one specific, particular object. This is nothing short of astounding. If a simple hypnotic suggestion can make a person oblivious to the presence of physical matter – particularly of a living being with whom he is closely connected – then the possibilities for hacking reality would seem to be almost endless. Reality *can be* hacked. The question is: *How?*

18.8 Hacking Reality: A Scientific Basis

When you consider all the examples discussed above – of the different means by which people are successfully hacking reality – the one common denominator is the human brain: if there is only one certain conclusion that can be drawn from an analysis of these cases, it is that the human brain seems unable to distinguish between "actual" reality and what it "thinks" is reality. And that is the key to the methodology and basis for hacking reality.

In a piece entitled "Your Brain on Fiction" published in the *New York Times*, author Annie Murphy Paul discusses several scientific studies which indicate that written words activate not only the language-processing area of the brain but also the relevant sensory-processing areas. Utilizing brain scans, such studies have revealed that reading words that possess a strong olfactory association, such as "perfume" or "coffee", causes the brain's primary olfactory cortex – the part activated by actual smelling – to light up, while words having no sense-of-smell association, like "chair" and "key", do not. Similar findings were noted regarding the relationship between written metaphors involving texture and the portion of the brain involved with perceiving texture through touch. Likewise, when subjects read sentences describing motion, the part of their brains responsible for the control and execution of movement was activated, even to the point of accurately corresponding to the pertinent body part (e.g., arm movement or leg movement). As Ms. Paul states, "The brain, it seems, does not make much of a distinction between reading about an experience and encountering it in real life; in each case, the same neurological regions are stimulated." [329] The findings from these studies, considered in conjunction with our other examples of reality-altering, would appear to provide a scientific basis for explaining the mechanism by which the hacking of reality is accomplished.

In the placebo and imagery examples discussed earlier we learned that, if the brain is led to believe that an effective drug has been ingested or that the body's T-cells are attacking cancer cells, then the body physiologically responds accordingly; on the flip side, if people are convinced they have been cursed with death, either by a disease diagnosis or a voodoo witch doctor, they become ill and die; in the age regression study, when the brain is led to believe that chronological time has been reversed by twenty years, then the body undergoes a corresponding age-reversal; when athletes mentally practice sports events, or when Hélène Grimaud plays a piano piece in her head, the effect upon their bodies is as if they had actually, physically performed those activities. All of these situations, in conjunction with the studies cited by Ms. Paul in the *Times*, strongly suggest that *our mind-body complex is incapable of distinguishing an imagined event from a real event.*

If one were to get down to the very essence of what constitutes our reality, the unavoidable conclusion would have to be: Energy and Form. Until fairly recently science had deemed matter and energy to be the most fundamental constituents of reality. But as we've seen in previous chapters, that paradigm has been further simplified with the realization that matter is, in truth, merely an aspect of energy. Thus we appear to be left with only energy as the basis of reality ... except, in our experience of reality it is clear that energy is *structured* in very particular and precise ways. Our ability to experience reality in a world involving three spatial dimensions necessitates that energy be spatially arranged into recognizable and meaningful patterns. Energy unregulated would be mere chaos, but when form is imposed upon energy the result is an ordered, coherent and comprehensible experience. Thus *form and energy* constitute the most basic and fundamental components of our reality.

Now, think about the four steps involved in the law-of-attraction process for hacking reality: You must *picture* in your mind precisely what it is that you want to manifest, and you must then *picture* yourself as already having it – in other words, you are mentally giving *form* to the thing you are trying to manifest; the other steps in the process entail fueling your thought-forms with powerful emotions and belief – this constitutes the *energy* aspect of the process. Thus, hacking reality involves evoking a process that attempts to manipulate reality *by going to the very heart of what constitutes reality itself – form and energy*. This is an utterly logical and reasonable explanation for *why* the hacking of reality is possible. But the other half of the question is: *How* is it possible?

There are actually two answers to that question, and we have already covered the groundwork material in earlier sections of this book. First, recall from our discussions in Chapter 13 that our reality is a *perceived reality*: our sensory organs act as input devices that receive external environmental stimuli in the form of energy signals; those organs *filter* those signals, and then send the filtered signals to our brain for *processing*. The filtering and processing result in editing and interpretation of those stimuli data, a redacting and decoding of the signals into a mental representation of the signal sources. That mental representation constitutes our experience of reality. By the time the filtering and processing are complete, we have no idea to what extent our internal mental perception of reality corresponds to the actual external reality.

Well, if our experience of reality is so heavily, if not entirely, dependent upon our perception of that reality, then it stands to reason that we should be able to manipulate our *experience* of reality by manipulating our *perception* of reality. In other words, if we could affect the way our brain processes stimulus signals, or if we could affect the signals themselves, then we could manipulate our experience of reality – i.e., we would be able to hack reality. The evidence from the hacking reality examples discussed above seems to imply that, at the brain-level of reality processing, "*all* experiences, whether real or imagined, are reduced to the same common language of holographically organized wave forms." [330] Thus imagined experiences are interpreted, by our brain, as being no different than real experiences.

Ironically, it is mainstream science itself that provides the second answer to the question of how it may be possible to hack reality. Referring once again to material covered earlier in this book, in Chapters 15 and 16 the thesis was developed that everything in existence – matter, energy, forces – are merely ripples in the Zero-Point Field, i.e. waves of vibration in the field. There is no objective, independent "physical" reality – at least, not in the way we've been led to believe. The true reality is a domain of waves and frequencies. It is our brain's decoding of those waves and frequencies, via Fourier transforms, that creates the illusion of the seemingly "concrete" reality that we perceive. When we interact with The Field using our senses and our brain we cause the wave functions (e.g., electron probability clouds or orbitals) to collapse to their particulate state, and we then comprehend the resulting "reality" as being solid, physical, and composed of discrete and distinct constituent parts. When we combine the Copenhagen Interpretation formulated by Heisenberg and Bohr (which holds that subatomic "particles" exist not as precise entities but rather as states of potential whose location or motion is derived from a set of probabilities) with the finding of Louis de Broglie (that electrons and other sub-atomic particles possesses wave-particle duality) and the double-slit experiment (that human observation causes subatomic particles to collapse from their probabilistic wave state to a particulate state), we have a very clear scientific model for how humans can hack reality; to wit: If we, through our act of observation, are the causative factor in transforming wave phenomena into "physical" (or, more accurately, holographic) reality, then we should be able to exert intentional control over that process and thus manage and direct the unfolding of reality.

To a surprising extent, this is already being accomplished: all the examples offered above serve collectively as a testament to the fact that *human beings can hack physical reality through the application of nothing more than mental energy*. The incredible truth is that the ability of human beings to hack reality, using their minds, is supported by a large body of documented evidence and is completely consistent with cutting-edge scientific theories regarding quantum physics and the nature of reality.

.

Part IV

Summation and Synthesis

God, therefore, is not Mind, but Cause that the Mind is; God is not Spirit, but Cause that Spirit is; God is not Light, but Cause that the Light is.

– Hermes Trismegistus, author of the Hermetic Corpus

Isn't it odd that anything exists? It's most peculiar, really, because it requires effort, it requires energy, and it would be so much easier for there to have been nothing at all.

– Alan Watts, philosopher

There's no question that we need a greater consciousness of who we are.

– Terence McKenna, author

Sell your cleverness and buy bewilderment.

– Rumi, Sufi mystic

Chapter 19

The Answers to the Great Questions of Existence

I have said, "Gods ye are, And sons of the Most High -- all of you"

- Psalm 82:6 (Holy Bible, Young's Literal Translation)

Jesus replied, "Truly I tell you, if you have faith and do not doubt ... you can say to this mountain, 'Go, throw yourself into the sea,' and it will be done.

- Matthew 21:21 (Holy Bible, New International Version)

Very truly I tell you, whoever believes in me will do the works I have been doing, and they will do even greater things than these...

- John 14:12 (Holy Bible, New International Version)

Science has steered us deeply into the notion that nature is soulless and spiritless, and the practice of this idea has led us to the brink of catastrophe – global and species and ecological catastrophe.

– Terence McKenna, author

As a young boy I was taught by my religion that humans are vile sinners, and I was taught by my secular schooling that humans are a biological accident – neither notion offering much hope for a self-image of dignity or meaningful purpose. But then, as I grew older and began reading and researching for myself, I discovered that quite the opposite appeared to be true: from a biological perspective, I learned that human beings are nothing short of miraculous – human anatomy, neurology, DNA ... the entirety of human physiology is phenomenally complex and awe-inspiring; and when I read the Bible I noted several references claiming that people are gods, fully capable of performing miracles on their own. I found this disparity – between what I was "taught" about humanity versus what the source material indicated – astounding; it was not simply a subtle difference of degree but, rather, a glaring contradiction: people cannot be both gods and sinners, biological miracles and biological accidents … Or can we?

After many years of studying spirituality and science I've come to believe that we are gods who sin, and that we are biological miracles embedded in a probabilistic reality. We are flawed diamonds of remarkable beauty that, with the right cutting and polishing, can aspire to perfection. Furthermore, I believe that our experiences in the Spirit Realm coupled with our many earthly incarnations constitute the process by which this pursuit of perfection is accomplished. All of the previous chapters of this book were written in an attempt to develop and articulate the details of that process.

In this book's Introduction I deconstructed its title in an effort to present a broad overview of its theses, describing how I intended to explore, in depth, a model of the Afterlife, a model of reality, and a theory of how the two might be interrelated. As we now begin the last section of this book we have finally come full circle – the details of the models have been presented and discussed, and we are now ready to take all of that material, condense it, and synthesize it into a single cohesive model that will explain exactly what this crazy and complicated human life experience is all about.

For the sake of review, let me begin by summarizing the Afterlife Model and the Model of Reality, and then I'll consolidate the two models into a Unified Model of Reality. From that vantage point we'll have the information needed to formulate some rather precise answers to the Great Questions of Existence.

19.1 The Newton Model of the Afterlife: Synopsis

Drawing heavily on the Life-Between-Lives findings of Michael Newton, with additional supplemental and confirmatory research by Delores Cannon, C.V. Tramont, Joe H. Slate, and Robert Schwartz, and the further supporting evidence of near-death experiences as documented by Raymond Moody and Jeffrey Long, plus the past-life recall work of Ian Stevenson, as well as my own explorations via regressive hypnosis – not to mention the work and research of many others – we have the information necessary to formulate an impressively detailed model of what happens to us after we die. It is important to reiterate a point that was made earlier in this book: because most of our information about the afterlife is provided by souls who are still in the reincarnation cycle, that information is necessarily limited to the portion of a soul's spiritual existence that occurs during the reincarnation phase; what happens to souls after they have graduated and moved beyond the reincarnation phase is occasionally hinted at but is, by and large, unknown. Thus our Afterlife model is confined almost exclusively to the experiences of souls that are still engaged in the reincarnation cycle.

In a concise format, the Afterlife model tells us the following:

The true nature of each human being is an eternal soul, comprised of energy (possibly light). The true home of human souls is an ethereal realm, also comprised of energy (again, most likely light), known as the Spirit Realm or the Afterlife; it is the place from which we come before we are born and it is the place to which we go after we die. The two foundational concepts upon which the Afterlife model depends are reincarnation and karma, both of which go hand-in-hand. Reincarnation refers to the transmigration of the soul – the notion that the soul, after death, passes from one body to another body. In between incarnations, the soul returns to the Spirit Realm for: (1) assessment of its conduct in its most recent life; (2) planning the details for its next life; and, (3) some well-deserved rest and relaxation.

The soul's circumstances and experiences in its upcoming incarnation are in large part dependent upon the quality of its conduct in its previous life. This "quality of conduct" is the essence of the notion of *karma*, which is a universal law of cause-and-effect whereby our acts and deeds in any given lifetime become determining factors of conditions and events experienced by us in future lives; the purpose of karma appears to be two-fold: spiritual evolution and balance. Thus the karma-reincarnation process dictates that a person's fortune or misfortune in subsequent lives is the result of the qualitative assessment of the deeds they performed in previous lives. Areas in which a soul is found wanting become the focus of attention in future earthly lives, and, indeed, those lives are precisely chosen so as to offer opportunities to address those areas of deficiency.

In a sense, one can view the Spirit Realm as the place where the theoretical work of spiritual advancement is done, while the incarnations experienced as physical earth lives offer the opportunity for practical application of that theory. During the portion of our existence in the Spirit Realm to which we are privy, much of a soul's experiences revolve around reviewing and analyzing its conduct and decisions from previous earthly incarnations, and then making preparations and decisions for its next earthly incarnation. Souls attend classes, do research at libraries, engage in private contemplation, and consult with Spirit Guides, soul group members, and a Council of Elders for advice and guidance. Once it is determined that a soul is ready for its next incarnation, it visits the Place of Life Selection to decide upon one of several alternative life situations. This decision involves consideration of very specific details of our next life, to include: who we will be; who our parents will be; and the time, place, setting, and circumstances of our new life. Once this decision is made, the soul is ready to embark upon another life adventure in the physical earth plane.

19.2 The Holographic Model of Reality: Synopsis

As the environment in which the hands-on portion of spiritual evolution is played out, the Earth plane plays a crucial role in the karma-reincarnation process. As such, an understanding of the nature of earthly reality is critical to resolving the mystery of who we are and why we're here. I'm of the opinion that our "physical" reality on earth was intentionally designed and created to facilitate our spiritual progress. For millennia humans have taken the nature of reality for granted with benign acceptance, if not resignation. But in more recent times people of diverse ilk, from the science-minded pragmatist to the spiritual-minded mystic, have begun to question and explore the reality paradigm; surprisingly, their findings, though originating from points of extreme intellectual polarity, have led to a singular conclusion: contrary to long-held belief and everyday experience, our reality is not the physical, material reality we thought it to be. The new model of reality that is emerging is so contrary to normal perception and discernment, and so diametrically dissimilar from the old model, as to be almost unthinkable. And yet the body of evidence in support of this new model grows ever more voluminous and convincing. This new model of reality is a true concresence of science and mysticism, a fusing of the intellect and the imagination into a refreshingly original and liberating existential outlook.

The new model of reality posits that our reality exists within, and springs from, a field of pure energy known as the Zero-Point Field, or, simply, The Field. Everything in existence – matter, energy, forces – are merely ripples (waves of vibration) in the Field. The true reality is a domain of waves and frequencies, a field of unlimited possibilities out of which everything is created. The human brain is designed to decode those waves and frequencies, using the mathematics of Fourier transforms, into the illusion of the seemingly "concrete" reality that we perceive. When we interact with The Field using our senses and our brain we cause the wave functions to collapse to their particulate state, and we then comprehend the resulting "reality" as being solid, physical, and composed of discrete and distinct constituent parts. Everything that we perceive of existence is actually the result of one single process that diversifies: that one single process is the Field, and the diversifications are the collapsed wave functions. Scientific discoveries actually suggest the mechanism by which this might occur.

The Copenhagen Interpretation of Heisenberg and Bohr postulated that subatomic "particles" exist not as precise entities but rather as states of potential whose location or motion is derived from a set of probabilities; Louis de Broglie noted that *all matter* has wave properties; the double-slit experiment demonstrated that human observation causes subatomic particles to collapse from their probabilistic wave state to a particulate state; and mathematician Jean Baptiste Joseph Fourier discovered a set of mathematical tools – the Fourier transforms – that enable the translating of waves (i.e., energy) to and from optical images (in essence, geometry) – in other words, Fourier transforms provide a mathematical bridge between the sub-atomic energy domain of reality (waves) and the sensorially perceived macro-level of spatial-geometric reality ("physical" reality). We humans appear to be biologically equipped to utilize Fourier transforms to translate an external energy-information construct into what we perceive, via our senses, to be "physical" reality.

This view of reality turns out to be remarkably similar to holography: The Field is analogous to a holographic plate, the waves in the Field are analogous to the interference patterns recorded on the holographic plate, and our brain is akin to the laser that is shined on the holographic plate to produce the holographic image. That is, our sensory-brain system collapses the wave functions in the Field into the illusion of physical reality in much the same way as the laser illuminating the holographic plate transforms the recorded interference patterns into an illusory holographic image. Our reality, therefore, is nothing more than a huge, complex, elaborate hologram. The Holographic Model of Reality intimates that our so-called "reality" is an ethereal, light-based medium which presents us with the illusion of form and substance; just as with a hologram, our reality may look solid and appear to be three-dimensional, but in truth it is an insubstantial phantasm of the mind and sensory organs.

19.3 Synthesis: A Unified Model of Reality

As I noted in the Introduction to this book, combining the phrases "The Afterlife" and "The True Nature of Reality" together in the book's title suggests that the two topics are somehow interrelated. I've made no secret of the fact that I do consider these concepts to be very closely connected, and on several occasions I've more than hinted at what I believe that connection to be. Now, having covered the Afterlife and Reality models in great detail throughout Parts I, II, and III of this book, and then having summarized those models above, we can finally introduce a unified model that addresses precisely how and why the afterlife and our reality are interconnected and, in so doing, we can derive some surprisingly direct answers to the great questions of existence.

It is quite clear from a study of the Afterlife Model that human souls require a locale and setting in which they can experience circumstances and address situations that are designed to afford them the opportunity to learn spiritual lessons, resolve karmic issues, develop an attitude of love and a sense of the unity of all things, and, in general, evolve towards a desired state of spiritual perfection. As noted earlier, while the Spirit Realm serves as the environs in which we get the *theoretical "classroom"* portion of our spiritual education, it is our earthly "physical" reality that serves as the *practicum* counterpart of our educational process: our reality is where we get to employ and experience, by way of practical application, the abstract spiritual concepts we contemplate in the Spirit Realm. Our physical reality is the hands-on laboratory, the setting in which this learning takes place. Pertinently, the Judaic tradition of Kabbalah speaks of the interconnectedness of all realms of reality and, in particular, of the *symbiotic interconnectedness* of heaven (the spirit realm) and earth (the material world). [331] This is the important connection between our physical lives on earth and our spiritual existence in the afterlife, and it is the reason why it is vitally important that we understand the true nature of our reality.

The earth reality is an important part of the process by which we strive to attain spiritual perfection. Through multiple lifetimes lived in a variety of circumstances we gain wisdom and understanding by way of direct, personal experience of joy and suffering; we learn via repeated and varying lessons and opportunities which are designed to cleanse us of negative traits and tendencies while encouraging the development of a spirit of empathy, compassion, and love. Thus our physical reality is the setting in which this learning-by-doing phase takes place: the experiences we have, the people with whom we interact, the places we go, our life circumstances, ... all of it can be seen as a stage play, or virtual reality, that was designed expressly for the purpose of giving us exactly what we need to in order to learn and advance, and in which we are the central character with the ability to rewrite the script and redirect the action in real time. Such a design has to be structured, yet flexible; it must be an environment of form, yet malleable enough to respond to our actions, thoughts, and feelings, and adjust accordingly. The old Newtonian notion of a concrete physical reality functioning with mechanical, clockwork predictability is not such a reality. But a holographic reality is a much more likely candidate: after all, if you change the energy flow, adjust the waves, and alter the fields, then you've changed the interference patterns, which changes the holographic plate, which then changes the holographic projection. An illusory holographic, light-based reality is easily altered, via energy; we humans perceive that reality by interpreting that energy, and we also affect that reality by projecting our energy into it. Our perception of the reality changes in accordance with the fluctuations in its energies; but we can also affect those energies ourselves, thus having a degree of personal control over the process (hacking reality), and we typically refer to this ability to personally affect reality as "free will". Thus the Holographic Model appears to be a perfect fit for the type of reality that is required to provide us with a scenario for the resolution of karmic issues and the attainment of spiritual awareness, while also permitting us a level of participatory influence via the process of creative free will.

A cornerstone of the Hermetic tradition is the maxim "As above, so below," a principle suggesting that "whatever happens on any level of reality ... also happens on every other level." Personally, I believe that "As above, so below," is evincing (among other ideas) the fact that everything in existence is structured in accordance with fractal geometry. Even a cursory look at nature strongly suggests that this is the case: solar systems are structured like atoms, and galaxies like solar systems; our bodily system of human organs has its counterpart, at the cellular level, in cellular organelles; the pattern of twigs on a tree branch matches the pattern of the branches coming off the tree's trunk; branching in the human lungs, blood vessels and nervous system is patterned likewise; reflexology (and, to some extent, acupuncture) relies on a belief that the entire human body – every part, gland and organ – can be mapped onto corresponding zones on the hands, feet, and ears; Coulomb's Law for the measure of the electrostatic force of interaction between two point charges $F = k_e \dfrac{q_1 q_2}{r^2}$ is strikingly similar to Newton's law of universal gravitation $F = G \dfrac{m_1 m_2}{r^2}$, ... I could go on and on. The point is that nature appears to be designed in accordance with the self-similarity property of fractal geometry. One would expect, then, that our reality and the Spirit Realm would also be in self-similar correspondence. Indeed, the *Zohar* (the foundational work in the Jewish tradition of Kabbalah) suggests precisely such a doctrine: "The Holy One has disposed all things in such a way that everything in this world should be a replica of something in the world above" [332] which is virtually identical to the Hermetic principle "As above, so below." According to the reports of NDErs and LBL hypnosis subjects, the Spirit Realm does indeed appear to possess many holographic properties, suggesting that perhaps our earth-based holographic reality is but a self-similar, lower-order representation of the higher order reality of the Spirit Realm. Recall that many NDErs and LBL hypnosis subjects insist that time as we know it does not exist in the Spirit Realm: contrary to our experience of time as a linear progression of past-present-future, the Afterlife is reported as existing in an "eternal Now." If we relate to that notion the fact that, according to Einsteinian physics, at the speed of light time becomes zero, then we can surmise that there is no time in the Spirit Realm precisely because it is a holographic light-realm *existing at the speed of light*. The Spirit Realm is also reported as being ethereal in nature, a completely non-material reality; this is very much a holographic quality. Also, non-material implies non-spatial, and this is, again, consistent with Einstein's finding that at the speed of light length, like time, becomes zero. The obvious common denominator of the Spirit Realm is Light: the entire Spirit Realm itself is described as being composed of light; during the process of passing, upon death, from our reality to the afterlife NDErs and LBL subjects describe a journey through a tunnel towards a bright light; and they are often met by what they describe as "beings of light." The Afterlife is often associated with higher frequencies and vibrations, and it is sensed as being "less dense" than the earth realm. Interestingly, many NDErs and LBL subjects describe the things "seen" in the afterlife as being sharper, brighter, richer, and clearer than their counterparts in the earth realm – so much so that the claim is frequently made that the Spirit Realm is the true reality while the earthly existence is an illusory reality.

Recall from Chapter 17 that mainstream science is now seriously considering the possibility that all the information contained within our universe can be mapped onto a two-dimensional surface surrounding the universe, and, therefore, that our 3D reality is merely a holographic projection of the data on that surrounding 2D surface. When one takes into account the details about the Afterlife model – in conjunction with: the scientific theories of a holographic universe, Bohm's implicate and explicate order, and fractal self-similarity – one cannot help but speculate as to the possibility that *the Spirit Realm might well be the 2D information-containing surface surrounding our universe*; that is, the Spirit Realm may very well be David Bohm's implicate order and Plato's realm of archetypal forms – a source realm from which our physical reality derives in the form of a holographic projection. *Our reality can thus be seen as a lower-level self-similar fractal iteration of the higher domain of the Spirit Realm, with both levels of reality being light-based and holographic.* That, then, is the Unified Model of Reality that emerges when we combine Newton's Afterlife Model with the Holographic Model of Reality.

The Spirit Realm is our true and eternal home, but it also serves, in conjunction with our physical reality, as the school in which we strive for spiritual perfection. The two realms – the Afterlife dimension and our holographic "physical" dimension – are intertwined in the coordinated, interdependent purpose of fostering the spiritual evolution of human souls.

19.4 The Great Questions Answered

Having synthesized the Afterlife and Reality models into a Unified Model of Reality we find, contained therein, the answers to the great questions of existence:

Where do we go after we die? and *Where do we come from before we are born?*

- The Spirit Realm is our destination after we die, and it is our point of departure before we are born. But it is much more: it is the eternal home of our true nature, of our immortal soul; and it serves as the source domain, or informational template, of which our earthly reality is but a holographic projection.

Why are we here?

- We are here to develop and perfect our soul, to hone, within our nature, the qualities of love, compassion, and empathy.

What is the true nature of reality?

- The setting in which we work that honing is the "physical" earth plane, which, in actuality, is a holographic, light-based, illusory reality. The true nature of our earth-based reality is an energy-information construct that is custom-designed to facilitate the pursuit of spiritual perfection within the context of a spiritual process grounded in reincarnation and karma.

What role do we play in the formation and process of reality?

- Contrary to what is commonly believed, we are not the hapless victims of blind fate, an aloof god, or a random and heartless natural order. We regularly and routinely impact upon the unfolding of reality in our exercising of free will, where we continually rewrite the scripts of our lives, making frequent course corrections – both constructive and destructive – as a result of the decisions we make and the actions we take. But we are beginning to learn that the exercise of free will might well be only one aspect of the role we play in the reality process. It now appears that, with an understanding of the true nature of reality and the sustained phenomena by which it manifests, we can learn to hack that reality, to alter it and control it in ways once thought miraculous.

For me, learning the answers to the great questions of existence has been a personal, life-long quest, and one that, quite frankly, I never imagined I would see resolved. So I am not exaggerating when I say that writing the section above was an extremely moving and profound experience for me. Yet now, having discovered those answers, I find there is yet one more great question that is begging for an answer: *Where are we going?*

Chapter 20

The Dimensional Shift

Just look at us. Everything is backwards, everything is upside down. Doctors destroy health, lawyers destroy justice, psychiatrists destroy minds, scientists destroy truth, major media destroys information, religions destroy spirituality and governments destroy freedom.

— Michael Ellner, hypnotist

The most radical and least likely future of all, it seems to me, is a future in which we continue just to stumble forward as we have been since the industrial revolution. That's no longer an option.

— Terence McKenna, author

In the next few years we will either transcend or self-destruct, because nature does not sustain disharmony.

— Nassim Haramein, founder, The Resonance Project Foundation

The real question is "Is Man good?" you know, because we're going to find out.

— Terence McKenna, author

And I saw a new heaven and a new earth: for the first heaven and the first earth were passed away.

- Revelation 21:1 (Holy Bible, King James version)

In tune with the sentiments quoted above, Terence McKenna was also fond of saying, "'Business as usual' is no longer an option." And, truly, when one looks around oneself at the state of the world today, it is immediately and indisputably apparent that our world is broken. The notion that human civilization is on the brink of collapse – a notion that was once the exclusive purview of "the end is nigh" millenarians, conspiracy theorists, and believers in religious apocalyptic eschatology – is today acutely sensed across an amazingly diverse cross-section of the population. Average people with no interest in, or knowledge of, biblical end-times prophecies or ancient end-times calendars nevertheless harbor a strong suspicion that we've reached the end. And this feeling of impending doom is not without merit or justification. Exposure to any form of mainstream media results in a bombardment of stories about: economic collapse, war in the Middle East, war with Russia, more terrorist acts, worldwide spread of Ebola (or any number of other pandemic outbreaks of deadly diseases), ecological collapse, global warming, depleting oil reserves, water shortages, … on and on and on. And if all that is not enough to darken one's spirit, we have the irony that much of our "entertainment" is just more of the same: violent TV shows and movies, violent video games, and morbid reality TV (drug abusers, infidelity, child abuse, spousal abuse); if the subject matter of these productions doesn't entail violence, then it usually deals with disease, criminal behavior, or some other dark aspect of the world. When we look to those who lead us to provide a way out of this nightmare, we discover to our horror that we are lead by the least among us: politicians, bankers, Wall Street honchos, CEOs – all are perceived as corrupt liars and thieves; priests are feared as pedophiles; big pharma as purveyors of poison; doctors and hospitals as cold, heartless and uncaring … again, the list goes on. Even to a confirmed optimist, this world appears to be irreparably, hopelessly broken.

In addition to the inevitable anxiety and fear it induces, the current state of affairs begs the question: *Where are we going?* As McKenna notes, wherever we *are* going, it had better not be in the same direction we've been going, because that way clearly lies madness and destruction. Apocalypse? To some, that fate seems inevitable; the serious hype over the Mayan calendar end-date of 12/21/12 (not to mention Tim LaHaye and Jerry B. Jenkins' popular *Left Behind* book series and the endless post-apocalyptic movies) is telling.

Well, the Mayan end-date has passed and we are all still here. Yet there is no collective sigh of relief, because the conditions in this world have, if anything, only gotten worse. Things are so bad that even the totally uneventful passing of a predicted and much hyped end-of-the-world date is not enough to dispel, or even dampen, our fears of an Armageddon.

Interestingly, among those who firmly believed that the world would "end" on the 2012 Mayan calendar end-date, as well as those who still believe the end is nigh, there are basically two schools of thought: one group believes the world is headed for total destruction, and humanity for total annihilation, from one or a combination of: nuclear war, an asteroid or comet strike, violent earth changes (e.g., the earth tilting on its axis), ecological collapse, or the like; the other group, taking a more optimistic tack, views the "end" not as a destruction scenario but as the dawning of a new age of peace and love – an uplifting of humanity to a higher state of being.

For myself, I was originally (i.e., pre-2012) in the "destruction" group – like McKenna, I couldn't see things going on the way they'd been going, but I also saw no hope that we could, or would, willingly take action to change course; so I just resigned myself to the inevitable death of the human race. I saw the other group – those who believed that the "end" was really a glorious new "beginning" – as being in denial, too frightened to face the horrible fact of a violent and tragic end to humanity, and thus having dreamed up a fantasy scenario that made the inevitable "end" a palatable thing (following the habit of virtually every speaker addressing a graduating class who, *ad nauseam*, proclaim: "This is not an ending, but a beginning.").

But then one day, as I was thinking about this topic, a thought occurred to me: Not everyone in this world is corrupt and evil – there are a lot of *good* people here – so it would be incredibly unfair and unjust if *everyone* were to perish in a world-wide catastrophe. I firmly believe that the Universe is, if nothing else, logical and just, so, upon deeper reflection, the destruction scenario no longer seemed plausible to me. But, on the other hand, I thought: The world is really in shambles, primarily due to a lot of vile and corrupt people. Considering that those vile people are the ones yielding the decision-making power, I didn't see any realistic possibility of human society making positive changes of its own volition. It was a dilemma: both scenarios seemed an inappropriate solution to the world problem, given that there are both very good and very evil people coexisting in this world and equally subject to whatever fate might befall it. I couldn't accept that the innocent would be horribly punished along with the guilty, and I found it equally unlikely that the guilty would (or *could*) uncharacteristically adopt a pure-hearted higher level of consciousness.

Then, one day, it hit me: Why can't *both* scenarios occur? Why can't there be a situation where the evil people face the fate they've created, while the innocent people move on to a higher state of peace and love? This idea appealed to me greatly – it seemed eminently fair, logical, and just. The only thing was, I didn't see *how* both scenarios could occur simultaneously.

Until I read Dolores Cannon's magnificent book *The Three Waves of Volunteers and the New Earth*.

20.1 Dolores Cannon: The New Earth

Dolores Cannon is a hypnotherapist and author who has been writing and researching since the 1970's. Her involvement with hypnosis began in 1968, and she has since developed her own unique hypnosis technique that affords her access to deep levels of human consciousness (and also, I believe, to a collective subconsciousness or over-mind); Ms. Cannon now teaches her unique method of hypnosis all over the world. She has also written many books – having read and greatly enjoyed many of them, I am a big fan. So it was without hesitation that, when Ms. Cannon's book *The Three Waves of Volunteers and the New Earth* hit the bookstores, I purchased a copy sight unseen. As I read the book I quickly realized that it contained a fascinating and satisfying solution to the dilemma of how the world could "end" without punishing the innocent or rewarding the wicked. This new scenario revolves around the concept of a "New Earth."

As Ms. Cannon explains in her book, the idea of the New Earth came about as a result of information that emerged gradually and piecemeal, over a five year period, from hypnosis sessions with her clients. She began to notice that her hypnosis subjects were all discussing a similar event, albeit using differing language, and in time the emergent pattern coalesced into a startling revelation about the future of humanity. [333]

In essence, the New Earth hypothesis claims that the planet Earth is undergoing its own evolutionary process and, as such, is experiencing an increase in its vibration and frequency that will result in a shift to a new and higher dimension. This New Earth will be born out of the currently existing earth, much as the mythological phoenix that bursts into flames and is reborn out of its own ashes. [334] What is particularly interesting – and relevant to the discussion at hand – is how humanity will be affected by the earth's shift into a higher dimension.

According to the New Earth theory, *in order for humans to make the shift along with the planet, their own frequencies and vibrations must be in alignment with that of the New Earth*. People who have succeeded in raising their personal frequencies to the required vibratory level will be brought along *with* the New Earth and will make the shift to a higher dimension; those unfortunate people who do not raise their frequency accordingly will be left behind on the old (current, low-frequency) earth.[335] The fates awaiting the two groups could not be more different.

The New higher dimensional Earth is described as a world of love, peace and beauty, devoid of all the negative attributes associated with the world in its current state: hatred, violence, greed, disease, ... even the karmic cycle will no longer exist on the New Earth; it is a dimension that appears to very closely approximate the Spirit Realm described earlier in this book. Indeed, although the humans who successfully make the shift to the higher dimension will initially retain physical bodies, it is claimed that the continued physical phase will be short-lived and that the evolved humans will ultimately be transformed into beings of light. [336]

Those people whose lower frequencies render them incapable of making the shift will find themselves remaining in the existing world, where, apparently, everything will devolve into the chaotic hellish nightmare that many currently see as the inevitable result if humanity remains on its present path of self-destructive behavior (McKenna's reference to "business as usual"). [337] One subject chillingly described the shift process as "cleansing the species of defective specimens." [338] Looked at in that light, what we have here is *an evolutionary leap of the human race*. In any evolutionary advancement what we always find is that the segment of the species that successfully adopts an advantageous survival adaptation is the one that survives and advances; the segment of the species that does not adapt is the line that dies out. In the case of the shift to the New Earth we are seeing an adaptation that is *energy-based* rather than matter-based, since it involves adopting a higher frequency and vibration: humans who have not progressed spiritually and thus whose frequencies remain low will be left behind, from an evolutionary point of view, while those people who *have* progressed spiritually and thus successfully raised their frequencies will make the evolutionary leap to the next level, i.e., the New Earth. This is evolution occurring on a level that is spiritual rather than biological (although there may very well be a biological component to it: e.g., some think that our so-called "junk DNA" might play a role in the process [339]). It is widely accepted that human evolution – on the biological level – "has either slowed down or stopped completely in most humans." [340] This suggests the possibility that the current and future evolution of humanity has either stagnated, or else is occurring on some other level. For example, Terence McKenna believed that technology was the new arena of human evolution. I personally find that notion interesting but, ultimately, neither persuasive nor attractive. The idea that human evolution might occur *in the spiritual domain*, however, is quite compelling, particularly when one considers that spiritual failings appear to be the fundamental causes behind the erosion and palpable collapse of human civilization (as is dramatically expressed in the quote from Michael Ellner at the beginning of this chapter). *If a degrading of spiritual qualities is bringing humanity to ruin and devastation, then the spiritual is precisely the aspect of our nature that needs to be improved, and thus positive spiritual qualities are the selective adaptations that need to be preserved and nurtured, evolutionarily, to insure the survival of our species.* This is, to me, a powerful argument in support of the New Earth shift theory.

I think it is therefore quite obvious why I would find the New Earth hypothesis to be a logical solution to the apocalypse dilemma: under the New Earth scenario, those people who have developed a nature of loving kindness and who have evolved spiritually will be exempted from any catastrophic future events which might occur on this planet, and will move on to a better life in a better world; on the other hand, people of a vile and cruel nature who have helped to create the hellish conditions currently existing here will be left behind to deal with the hell of their own creation.

I want to be clear here that I don't find this situation particularly appealing – I've long grown beyond a mindset of vengeance and punishment. This is not about reveling in seeing evil people "pay" for their sins – at least, to my mind it's not. I daily pray that *everyone* on this planet will experience a spiritual awakening in time to raise their personal frequency to a sufficient degree that we will *all* be able to make the shift to the New Earth. I pray that for *myself* every day as well; God knows that I have lived a far-from-perfect life in this incarnation and, while I think that I have improved greatly in my later years, my younger years were lived in a state far removed from anything spiritual. I know I carry much karmic baggage, and I have no idea where the "cut-off point" will be for determining who will ascend and who will stay behind. All I can do – all any of us can do – is work very hard to amend our ways and make a sincere effort to change for the better (more on how this can be accomplished in Chapter 22).

To me, Dolores Cannon's New Earth hypothesis seemed a logical and just resolution to the quandary of humanity's fate, and I found myself, after finishing her book, hoping that it was true. But I'm wise enough to know that wishful thinking doesn't make something so. Thus I decided to keep my eyes and ears open for any additional evidence that might tend to confirm the truth of Ms. Cannon's New Earth conjecture. I didn't have high expectations, but the information that presented itself, over the following years, was extraordinary.

(In one of those amazing "synchronicities" that seem to often occur at key moments in one's life, while writing this section about the Shift I received an email, as part of a subscriber mailing, from Inelia Benz – a self-proclaimed "messenger of personal and global ascension" – discussing a topic entitled "The Splitting of the Worlds" which spoke about the earth moving "into a higher vibration, occupying the same location, but a different space/time vibration" and (from her web site) "souls divided between light and dark, awakened and asleep, aware and blind." Needless to say, both the content and the timing of this email really blew me away; it's difficult to see such things as mere coincidence).

20.2 The Rapture

I first became aware of the theory of the "Rapture" when I read Hal Lindsey's fascinating book "The Late Great Planet Earth" way back in the 1970's. The book was an interpretation of then-current events through the lens of Bible prophecy, promoting the premise that world events indicate that we are living in the end times described in the Bible. I thought that Mr. Lindsey presented a strong argument in support of his premise, and I found his claims quite plausible. However, at that time, I found the business about a "Rapture" hard to swallow. While reading Dolores Cannon's New Earth book, some four decades later, it occurred to me that her clients' descriptions of the Dimensional Shift were in many ways reminiscent of details contained in the notion of the Rapture.

The term "rapture" is not found in the Bible per se, but the notion of a rapture was inspired by a variety of passages from Bible scripture. The term "Rapture" and the theory it represents first became popular in the United States in the late 1800's. A variety of books revived and perpetuated the theory throughout the next century, most notably Hal Lindsey's *The Late Great Planet Earth* and the popular *Left Behind* series, by Tim LaHaye and Jerry Jenkins.

The "Rapture" refers to the Christian belief that an event will occur during the end-times predicted by Bible prophecy wherein true believers in Christ will be miraculously taken from earth and into heaven by God, while all non-believers will be left behind for the tribulation period (a seven year period of worldwide destruction and desolation). [341]

This is clearly a scenario suggesting the salvation of the righteous (via the Rapture) and the punishment of the wicked (the unfortunate "un-raptured" who are left behind to suffer the horrors of the tribulation). The parallels to Ms. Cannon's New Earth theory are, I think, obvious: those whose advanced spiritual state and corresponding higher frequency vibration enable them to evolve to the higher plane of the New Earth represent the obvious analog to those who get raptured in the Christian scenario; likewise, the low-frequency people who do not make the transition to the New Earth and thus remain on the old Earth while it undergoes its apocalyptic throes clearly correspond to the non-believers who are left behind to face the horrors of the tribulation. I think the similarity between these two theories is tantalizing. While I consider myself to be a very spiritually-oriented person, I am not religious. I reject ideologies in general and, as I discussed at the outset of this book, I rejected Catholicism many, many years ago. But I don't necessarily reject every concept of every ideology, and I am, in fact, open to all ideas, theories, and knowledge. Given the Bible's advanced age and impressive survivability, I think its content deserves serious attention and consideration. The reason why I rejected the notion of a Rapture for many years was because of the claim that only Christians could be raptured; I find that particular aspect totally unacceptable and ridiculous. I've known many non-Christians who are wonderful people, and I don't believe that God – whoever or whatever God is – would base salvation on ideological affiliation rather than personal conduct and morality. But the *basic premise* underlying the Rapture hypothesis strikes me as being quite logical and reasonable, and the degree to which it agrees with the New Earth/Dimensional Shift reported by Ms. Cannon is remarkable.

20.3 Terence McKenna's "Funny Idea"

I've mentioned elsewhere in this book that I am a big admirer of Terence McKenna, and my prodigious use of quotations by him as lead-ins to the book's various chapters and parts should confirm that. Mr. McKenna was an amazing individual: he could speak very knowledgably on a wide variety of subjects, but his true brilliance was, to me, the way he interpreted knowledge and information and how he formulated new ideas from them. He was also an extremely eloquent and articulate speaker who would often express his ideas in memorable phrases of hilarious wit and sublime beauty. I've read a few of his books and I've watched countless hours of videos of his talks; I do not agree with all of his ideas, but I always find him interesting, thought-provoking, and entertaining. While his interests spanned many diverse subjects, he is most well-known as a promoter of the idea that plant-based hallucinogenic substances (especially psilocybin and

DMT) are boundary-dissolving and mind-expanding pabulums that were responsible for humanity's evolutionary leap from primitive primate to deep-thinking human, and he also believed that those same plant-based hallucinogenic substances offered the best opportunity for humanity to break out of the modern cultural morass of self-destructive habits and behaviors that threaten to send us hurtling toward our extinction. Mr. McKenna experimented widely with such hallucinogenic substances and often reported on the insights revealed to him during those experiences, frequently prefacing such reportage with phrases such as, "The mushroom told me…"

It was hearing one such mushroom-induced revelation related by Mr. McKenna that brought me to the edge of my couch because it bore an astounding correspondence to Dolores Cannon's New Earth/Dimensional Shift theory. I came across it in an audio file posted on the internet, apparently an audio recording someone made while attending one of Mr. McKenna's talks many years ago. The information it contained was so profound that I replayed the recording several times and attempted to write it down as accurately as possible. I've put the main points in the segment below, and while it may not entirely be a verbatim transcript of his words, much of it is, with the essence of the idea, I believe, accurately preserved (a citation is provided in the end notes: the audio file is widely available on the internet – just do a search on "Terence McKenna funny idea"). I want to note that I find *the entire idea* deeply profound and thought-provoking, not simply the portion that relates to the New Earth hypothesis. Here, then, is an abridgment of Terence McKenna's "Funny Idea":

> A few weeks ago I was meditating in my usual fashion, and I began to get this new idea … I was told a very funny thing which I will share with you. It's a funny idea. There's something in the universe called a "fractal soliton of improbability" – this means it's a unique event, it only happens once in the lifetime of a universe; you can think of it as a wavelength of one wave, that's why it's called a "soliton." And these things move not in ordinary three-dimensional space but in some kind of much higher spatial manifold.

> When [the soliton] collides with a planet, the time-stream of that planet is divided, and two copies of the entire planet spring into existence without either having any knowledge of it.

Mr. McKenna goes on to explain that this actually happened to the Earth in the past, causing a twin of the Earth to come into being in another dimension. The split occurred at or near the moment of Christ's birth. The Soliton of Improbability event has a quantum mechanical half-charge, so on one of the Earths Christ is born but on the other Earth he is not born. Thus the entire ideology that sprung out of Christ's existence did not occur on one of the Earths.

Consequently, as time passed, first decades and then centuries, the absence of this particular intellectual influence on that one world changed it radically, in the following way: Greek science did not suffer the suppression that occurred with the conversion of Constantine; the academies were not closed; the Hermetic knowledge was not repressed. Thus the empire was stronger and was able to repel the barbarian invasions of the 2nd to the 5th centuries. Mathematics, which halted in our world at Diophantus, proceeded through his disciple Hypatia to develop a calculus by AD 370, so that the millennium of Christian stasis that occurred in our world did not occur in that world... by around 850 they had ships that were able to cross the Atlantic Ocean and they encountered the Mayan civilization reaching its fullest flowering... This Greco-Roman imperial culture recognized the Mayan genius in math and astronomy, and Europe was transformed into an amalgamation – a Greco-Mayan civilization. One of the things the Mayans brought to Europe was their extremely sophisticated pharmacopeia and shamanism; this mated with neo-Platonism and Hermeticism so that, rather than science developing as it developed in our world, a kind of magical psychopharmacologic technology of thought and understanding developed [on the other Earth]...

In this alternate timeline/other Earth, McKenna relates, the Greco-Mayan civilization then contacted the Orient and merged with the Sung dynasty to create a global civilization. Eventually, they figured out what had happened with the split and they discovered our world. They then conceived of the notion of saving us – thus UFOs, astral travel, etc., are merely "a manifestation of this bizarre Greco-Mayan postmodern star-faring civilization trying to reach across the dimensions to save us from the momentum of our history by making us aware of their existence and also their technology, which is evolving toward a point where around 2012 ... the two time streams will be rejoined, and we will make peace with this civilization which is 1000 years more advanced than us, and with a totally different cultural history and completely different take on reality." [342]

According to McKenna's revelation, in the distant past the Earth splits into two earths, each occupying a different dimensional time-stream; one earth takes the higher ground, if you will, and evolves along a more spiritually and intellectually enlightened course, while the other earth – *our* earth – remains mired in an ever-stifling mindset of repressive and limiting ideologies and practices. At some future point in time (in the early 21st century) the two time streams rejoin.

In light of the above, Dolores Cannon's "New Earth" scenario can be reinterpreted as not an upcoming splitting of the Earth, but rather a rejoining of the (previously split) two time-streams as described by McKenna. We can extend this notion to speculate that when the two time streams rejoin, any people on our Earth who are vibrating at a higher rate of consciousness will be in resonance with the other Earth (which is likely at a higher planetary level of consciousness and thus also at a higher frequency) and will be absorbed into it, while people on this Earth who vibrate at a lower frequency will remain here. As with the theory of the Rapture, I find the correspondence between McKenna's "Funny Idea" and Ms. Cannon's New Earth to be astonishing. That these three concepts, coming from three utterly disparate sources, should dovetail so closely is impressive and, I think, highly significant. When considered alongside the prophecies of the Bible, Edgar Cayce, Nostradamus, the Mayans, etc., as well as the air of impending doom permeating our present-day culture and collective psyche, one can't help but wonder if there isn't some degree of factual basis underlying all these intimations of planetary and human transformation.

20.4 The Dimensional Shift as a Birthing Process

On another occasion Mr. McKenna asked the mushroom why our species was in such chaotic and dire straits, and he was told that humanity was in the throes of a birthing process: "The mushroom said to me once, it said 'This is what it's like when a species prepares to depart for the stars. You don't depart for the stars under calm and orderly conditions; it's a fire in a madhouse!' That's what we have – the fire in the madhouse at the end of time – this is what it's like when a species prepares to move on to the next dimension."

McKenna noted that just prior to the birth of a human baby, the mother and the fetus develop a kind of mutual antagonism – not a "hostility" but, rather, they have reached a point where the host/mother can no longer support the parasitic fetus; the fetus has been sapping nutrition and resources from its mother, and a stage is reached where the fetus becomes too much of a drain on the mother's resources, and it is then that nature (possibly via a hormonal exchange) kicks in and triggers the birth process. When one considers this view of mother and fetus with the current relationship between humanity and planet Earth, the correspondence is startling: humanity has become too much of a drain on Earth's resources, and perhaps nature must initiate a birth process on a planetary scale.

McKenna referred to the impending dimensional shift as a "transcendental phase transition." In his typically erudite and articulate manner he related the dimensional shift to the human birth process as follows:

> What is happening here at the end of the twentieth century is a kind of birth process. Think of the fetal life in the womb: you're endlessly adrift in the amniotic ocean, weightless, food and oxygen are being delivered – without even your awareness – through the umbilical cord. It is paradise, and if you were there and in control of your fate, you would choose to prolong it forever. But what happens instead is that you get squeezed into the birth canal; then the paradise turns into hell: strangulation, pressure – you are literally being squeezed to death ... So I believe that, culturally, we are in the birth canal and everything appears to be being destroyed: the oceans, the atmosphere, the very integrity of our own bodies because of all

these diseases, ideological contaminations, you name it. But we simply must push forward – it's a forward escape. [343]

Using the birth analogy on another occasion, McKenna suggested that we imagine how it would be if a person with absolutely no knowledge of the human birthing process walked into a hospital delivery room while a baby was being born: blood, crying, screams of agony – there is no way that an uninformed person would perceive this situation as the beautiful and miraculous event of the creation of new life; indeed, to someone who did not know any better, it would look like just the opposite – violent, bloody carnage. Perhaps this explains why our world is in such a horrible state – wars, terrorism, economic collapse, ecological collapse, disease, drought, starvation … *Perhaps we as a species are suffering the labor pains and hemorrhaging that must inevitably precede our birthing – our evolutionary leap – into a new species, the phoenix rising from the ashes.* This is species birth resembling individual human birth – the Hermetic "as above, so below" quality of fractal self-similarity. There is a logic and a symmetry to this that I find very compelling.

20.5 The Indigo Children

Many ancient cultures and wisdom traditions foresaw a future time of catastrophic earth changes preceding the emergence of a new golden age of humanity. [344] An integral part of, and catalyst in, this process of transformation is a new, superior species of human being, what Alberto Villoldo calls "Homo Luminous." [345] Many believe that we are now in the midst of the early stages of those predicted earth changes, and that "homo luminous" is already here.

This next evolutionary iteration of humanity goes by many names (children of the new millennium, crystal children, children of light), but the most common one is the "indigo children." In mystic and occult traditions, an indigo aura is the mark of a spiritually advanced soul (and recall from our discussion of soul auras in Chapter 7 that Michael Newton had determined that the more advanced souls possessed auras in the blue to purple range). This new, advanced segment of humanity became apparent beginning around the 1960s in the form of highly gifted and unusual children who dramatically stood out – intellectually, socially, and behaviorally – from their companions. Hence the name "indigo children." These so-called indigo children (or "indigos") share many common attributes that not only serve to identify them but also suggest why they are appearing en masse at this particular moment in human history.

Among the most common shared characteristics of indigo children are the following:

- high IQ
- heightened intuition

- creative
- wise beyond their years
- psychic/telepathic
- empathy and compassion for all life forms
- feel born to accomplish a special mission in life
- emotionally over-sensitive
- uncomfortable around noise and chaos
- feel out of place in this world (have trouble conforming)

What is particularly interesting about these children, and highly relevant to our discussion of a Dimensional Shift, a New Earth, and a human evolutionary leap, is that these children are often seen as "system busters" – it is believed that, when they reach adulthood, they will be responsible for fostering new paradigms across all the major cultural institutions: education, business, government, religion, etc. [346]

Well, to me, this "fostering of new paradigms" sounds a great deal like the creation of a "new earth" or, at the very least, a new human society; and when I look at their shared characteristics, these indigo kids certainly appear to be an evolutionary upgrade of the human race. As for the timing of their "arrival" – when I look at the horrid state of human society now, I'm not in the least surprised to find such a unique group of people appearing on the scene just at the moment when they are most needed. As I said earlier, there's a logic and a symmetry to this that simply cannot be ignored. But there's more.

Going back to Dolores Cannon's book about the "New Earth," recall that the title of that book is *The Three Waves of Volunteers and the New Earth*. In my earlier synopsis of Ms. Cannon's book I discussed the "New Earth" aspect of the theory, but I didn't address *The Three Waves of Volunteers* – well, now it's time to do precisely that.

The Three Waves of Volunteers refers to highly advanced souls who, although they do not need to, have volunteered to incarnate on Earth at this time to assist in this planet's vibratory leap into a higher dimension. These advanced souls, many of whom are described as "light beings," are of a higher vibratory state, and it is this high frequency energy, which they bring with them, that will: (1) help the earth to avoid catastrophe; and (2) facilitate the process of human ascendance to the higher dimension. Ms. Cannon makes it clear that the information she has received indicates that the Earth is going to make this dimensional shift with or without us; how many humans will accompany the earth is strictly up to us. These advanced souls have volunteered to help us in this process. [347] The *Three Waves* refers to three generations of these volunteers, the first wave having been born around the 1950s-1960s, the second wave born in the 1980s, and the third wave being the newest and youngest group, children and teenagers. According to the *Three Waves* theory, people on earth who will be making the shift to the new dimension are at present having their DNA altered to permit the necessary adjustment to the new frequencies and vibrations; but the Third Wave children are arriving with their DNA already altered and are fully prepared to comfortably make the transition. [348] To me, these Third Wave volunteers sound very much like the indigo children.

I have known a couple of children whom I consider to be indigo children (although I think their parents would find the notion silly and amusing). I am strongly of the opinion that, if indigo children truly exist, then these kids are the real deal. And I will tell you that they are not merely "bright kids" or even "gifted kids" – they are something entirely different; they are impossibly intelligent, incredibly quick studies, more morally mature than most adults, and possess a degree of conscientiousness that would be admirable in anyone, let alone a child. I'm talking about, for example, a young child choosing to become a vegetarian when neither parent is one. These kids are more than just young brainiacs; along with their extremely advanced level of intelligence they possess a highly evolved sense of ethics and morals, something that children of their young age simply have not had enough time to develop. Is it mere coincidence that nature has created a generation of humans being born with precisely the qualities that we as a species desperately need, and the very lack of which has led us to the precipice of disaster that we now face? I think not.

20.6 The CHANI Project

This section was one which, like the material in Chapter 11: Technology and the Afterlife, I hesitated to include in this book. The subject matter, as you will soon see, is on the more extreme end of occultism, and I had made up my mind when originally undertaking the writing of this book to avoid fringe content. For the record I want to state that I don't automatically dismiss such subjects and, in fact, I find them quite interesting; but I wanted this book to be more mainstream and moderate in both content and tone. Also, the CHANI Project information is almost impossible to vet for authenticity: it comes from a single, anonymous source who claims it bears a high level of security classification (if it's true, then it most surely would be highly classified). We are thus left in a position where, in order to accept this material as being true, we must accept one person's word for it, and that person is unknown and unidentified. I am generally very uncomfortable citing such information as evidence, for obvious reasons. But, upon much reflection and soul-searching, I ultimately decided that it would be better to include it in my book than not, with the above caveat regarding its unverifiable nature. I made the decision to include it for two reasons: (1) its relevance to, and conformity with, the Dimensional Shift we are discussing is extraordinary; and (2) the material it contains that deals with subjects other than the Dimensional Shift is quite profound and rings true from a spiritual as well as a current-events perspective.

Personally, I accept the possibility that the CHANI Project material *might* be true, but without additional supporting evidence the prudent decision must be that the jury is still out as to its credibility. Nonetheless, it is very powerful and intriguing material and, as I stated above, it bears an amazing congruity with both Dolores Cannon's Dimensional Shift and, particularly, with Terence McKenna's "Funny Idea."

The CHANI Project refers to a purported event that lasted from 1994 to 1999 in which a group of researchers with "access to an underground CERN-like collider facility in Africa" supposedly received communications from "an Entity who claimed to be from a parallel universe/dimension/timeline." The communications were apparently conducted via computer technology. Over the five-year period the researchers posed over 20,000 questions to the Entity and received answers to more than 95% of them. The Entity initiated contact because of an impending collision, or crossing/merging, of our solar system with the parallel reality of its parallel universe, and the desire to "prepare their civilization for our arrival/merge." The Entity had access to information about future events on our world, and thus its answers to the researchers questions appear as predictions about our near future. Its predictions are nothing short of staggering, particularly when considered in light of current world events, and the Entity's spiritual and philosophical observations are both moving and profound. But it is its mention of the impending merging of our reality with theirs that is relevant to our discussion at hand. In particular, the Entity noted that, "There are many of these circular timelines and sometimes they interchange or cross each other"; it also mentioned that, "When they intersect, some beings, or their developed awareness, they can jump from one to another..." while, "Others don't jump..."[349]

When I first read this article I had already read Dolores Cannon's book about the New Earth, so I immediately noticed a similarity of theme, but when I later heard Terence McKenna's talk about his "Funny Idea" I was astounded at how much it paralleled this story. The other version of earth that McKenna talks about would seem to correspond with the CHANI Entity's home world, and in each scenario – McKenna's and CHANI – our earth and the other world exist in parallel realities or dimensions, and they are approaching a point in time in the near future where the two timelines (CHANI term), or time streams (McKenna term), will cross paths and merge or rejoin. Finally, the Entity's world and McKenna's alternate earth are both aware of the impending merger of realities and are preparing for it. These two ideas are so amazingly similar that the suspicious side of me wonders whether the CHANI story was inspired by McKenna's "Funny Idea." If, however, the CHANI story is on the level, then we have a striking confirmation of McKenna's insight and, even more spectacular, the suggestion of an actual worldwide event (i.e., the merging of two different dimensional realities) that could serve as the factual basis for Dolores Cannon's New Earth theory, as well as for the Christian notion of the Rapture. And this brings us to one final point about the CHANI story, namely its claim that, "When they intersect some beings, or their developed awareness, they can jump from one to another..." while, "Others don't jump..."; this idea correlates highly to Ms. Cannon's claim that some people will make the Shift to the New Earth, while others won't, and to the claim of

Rapture believers that some people will be "raptured" and others not. That these three conjectures have so many specific points in common doesn't prove anything, but it is enticingly fascinating and provocative.

20.7 "Magnetic Reversals and Evolutionary Leaps"

A while back I was listening to an interview with a man named Robert Felix discussing his book *Magnetic Reversals and Evolutionary Leaps*. I found his theory extremely interesting, so much so that I purchased his book to learn more about it. After reading the book I found myself seriously considering the possibility that his theory was precisely what his book's subtitle claimed: "The True Origin of Species."

Mr. Felix's thesis, backed up by much documented evidence, is that repeated geomagnetic reversals throughout earth's history have played a key role in mass extinctions as well as in sudden evolutionary leaps among various species of plants and animals. [350] Since I had already been speculating that the portion of humanity that would be experiencing an increase in vibratory frequency, as part of the Dimensional Shift, might represent a "sudden evolutionary leap" of the human species, I realized that Mr. Felix's theory provided a plausible scientific basis for *how* that leap might occur.

The long-standing scientific belief in gradual evolutionary change has been replaced by a new theory, supported by the paleontological record, of "punctuated equilibrium" – the idea that most evolutionary change occurs suddenly; new species appear to arise abruptly, rather than via the slow and stepwise process of Darwinian evolution. [351] Many complex and unique animal types have appeared on the scene abruptly after mass extinctions, and "with no similarity to the animals they had replaced." [352] Such mass extinctions have occurred with surprising regularity throughout the history of life on this planet, they appear to be causally connected with planet-wide catastrophes, and they are typically abrupt. [353] In his book, Robert Felix demonstrates a significant correlation between the occurrences of magnetic reversals, ice ages, mass extinctions, and the emergence of new species. His explanation of the process by which magnetic reversals can cause extinctions and evolutionary leaps is scientifically sound and satisfyingly logical, and it can be summarized as follows:

When the earth's magnetic field undergoes a reversal (which is a flip-flopping of the planet's north and south magnetic poles) that magnetic field – the magnetosphere – is temporarily lost. Since the magnetosphere shields our planet from the sun's mutation-causing cosmic rays, our unshielded planet's surface is bombarded with cosmic rays during the reversal. These radiation bombardments, and their attendant ice ages, result in death and genetic mutations. However, while most genetic mutations are detrimental to life, a rare few cause changes that are advantageous; it is those rare positive mutations – "macromutations" – that result in the sudden appearance of new species. [354] According to mainstream science, evidence suggests that the next magnetic pole shift is imminent: earth's magnetic field is weakening at an ever increasing rate, the magnetic north pole is moving (toward Siberia), and the frequency of past reversals indicates that the next reversal is already long overdue. [355] Felix's evidence for his thesis, as laid out in his remarkable book, is voluminous and compelling.

Also worthy of note is the fact that Mr. Felix also establishes a correlation between magnetic reversals and precession of the equinoxes. [356] The phrase "precession of the equinoxes" refers to the phenomenon whereby the constellations appear to rotate around the earth, with each of the twelve zodiacal signs taking a turn at appearing to rise on the horizon. The entire precessional cycle – i.e., the time it takes for all twelve constellations to make a complete rotation – takes approximately 25,920 years, and each sign's period of apparent rise on the horizon lasts 2,160 years. This precession phenomenon, also known as "axial precession," is attributed to a wobbling of the earth's tilted axis of rotation, which traces a clockwise circular path around true north [357] (although there are other possible explanations: see, for example, Walter Cruttenden's fascinating book *Lost Star of Myth and Time*, which posits that the precessional effect is due to the gravitational influences that derive from our sun being part of a binary star system). I find Felix's correlation of magnetic reversals with the precessional cycle of particular interest because I believe it explains one of the great mysteries of human history. Many ancient cultures were fully aware of the precessional cycle; [358] this knowledge, inexplicable if one accepts that those cultures were primitive and scientifically unsophisticated, is often cited by, for example, proponents of theories involving Atlantis or ancient aliens as proof that some civilizations from earth's remote past were more scientifically advanced than has been officially acknowledged, their point being: How could a primitive civilization have been aware of an astronomical cycle that takes almost 26,000 years? But the question about ancient peoples' knowledge of precession that always intrigued me was not *how* they could have known about it, but *why did they care*? I always suspected that ancient man's otherwise inexplicable obsession with precession was because precession was somehow related to recurrent planet-wide cataclysms, and thus humanity monitored the cycle closely in order to predict the next impending catastrophe. Now Mr. Felix has, I believe, proved my long-held suspicion true: precession is indeed connected with world cataclysms, in the form of recurring geomagnetic reversals.

20.8 The Dimensional Shift

If we collectively consider the various theories and ideas discussed throughout this chapter – putting together Dolores Cannon's New Earth scenario with Terence McKenna's "Funny Idea," Christianity's notion of the "Rapture," the predictions of the CHANI Project, the so-called "indigo children," and Robert Felix's theory regarding magnetic reversals and evolution – we can formulate the following thesis:

- A portion of the human race will soon be, or is presently in the process of, experiencing an evolutionary leap of a spiritual or quasi-spiritual nature which involves an increase in vibration/frequency.

- A "New Earth" will be born out of the existing earth via a process whereby an increase in the planet's vibration/frequency results in its planetary double ascending to a higher dimension of existence.

- The planetary dimensional-shift and human evolutionary leap will be precipitated by a reversal of earth's magnetic field and its subsequent effect on the planet and on human DNA.

- The humans who experience this transformation will move to a higher dimensional plane of existence – along with the "New Earth" – where many of the negative factors currently affecting humanity will cease to exist.

- Those humans who do not experience the transformation will remain on this earth at its current level of dimensional frequency, where they may experience cataclysmic earth changes and societal collapse.

This, then, may be the answer to the final Great Question of where humanity, as a species, is headed: The human race may very well be on the verge of a major evolutionary upgrade, an ascension to a state of being closer to our true nature as ethereal souls, and to a new "world" that is more like our true home, the blissful place known as the Spirit Realm. Some of us may finally be about to leave the wheel of karma, and all its attendant negative baggage, forever behind.

20.9 A Grand Test

We live in a world where virtually every coercion and enticement is to do that which is wrong. Over and over we are presented with examples of people who have achieved "success" by violating basic principles of morals and ethics. In politics, finance, entertainment, business – you name it – we find that the people who succeed are often the most morally deficient. As if to encourage this materialistic mindset, the lure of materialistic pleasures is thrown in our faces incessantly by the media – the mansions, the sexy people, the techie "toys", the bling – the seduction of materialism is relentless. And we are led to believe that any price is worth paying – any compromise of our ideals, any abandonment of our ethics, any violation of our sense of right and wrong is justified by a Darwinian survival-of-the-fittest, end-justifies-the-means philosophy.

But I suspect that the world is that way by design. I suspect that we are all taking part in a grand test, a selection process designed to determine who among us will, through strength of character, resist those myriad seductions and follow a path of human decency and basic goodness. This is a culling of humanity into those who have achieved spiritual maturity and those who have not: Those who pass the test will graduate, and those who fail will be left behind.

Chapter 21

My Personal Insight Regarding the Nature of Reality

[1]In the beginning God created the heaven and the earth. [2]And the earth was without form, and void; and darkness was upon the face of the deep. And the Spirit of God moved upon the face of the waters. [3]And God said, Let there be light: and there was light. [4]And God saw the light, that it was good: and God divided the light from the darkness.

– Genesis 1:1 - 1:4, King James Bible

There are more things in heaven and earth, Horatio,
Than are dreamt of in your philosophy.

– Hamlet to Horatio, in William Shakespeare's "Hamlet"

[1] In the beginning was the Word, and the Word was with God, and the Word was God. [2] The same was in the beginning with God. [3] All things were made by him; and without him was not any thing made that was made. [4] In him was life; and the life was the light of men. [5] And the light shineth in darkness; and the darkness comprehended it not.

– John 1:1 - 1:5, King James Bible

21.1 An Awakening

One day a few years back I awoke from a deep sleep with a cascade of thoughts running through my mind. Initially, my comprehension of those thoughts was on a purely subconscious level, and my state of consciousness wavered between the sleep and waking states. As I gradually came to full wakefulness, the thoughts emerged into my conscious mind and quickly overwhelmed it. I lie in my bed, on my back and with my eyes still closed, mesmerized by the profundity of the concepts flitting through my head. *Wow*, I remember thinking, a part of my consciousness somehow detached from and observing the cascading thoughts, *Yes, that's fascinating! That's amazing!* As I opened my eyes, still perceiving those thoughts, I wondered who was relaying this captivating information to me. And then, finally, I realized with some degree of shock that the information was coming *from me*, arising out of *my* brain. I jumped out of bed, stumbling dizzily in search of pen and paper lest I forget these profound notions that were inexplicably bubbling up out of my subconsciousness. I then sat on the edge of my bed, in my underwear, furiously writing down those ideas, even as they began to dissolve into the fuzzy wisps of unremembered dreams.

The result of this crazy episode was several sloppily scrawled pages of notes that seemed to describe a theory of reality that was, to the best of my knowledge, original and unique. It also struck me as being surprisingly reasonable and plausible. The more I read over those notes, the more I felt that the theory they described had merit, and, moreover, I felt that these ideas could not have arisen out of my brain. As much as I wanted to take credit for this novel concept, I couldn't shake the feeling that it was somehow transmitted into my brain from elsewhere and that I was merely serving as a device to receive and broadcast it. I read the notes to a few people who expressed agreement with my sense that it was an original, credible, and profound idea. But, not having yet embarked upon the writing of this book, I merely shelved the notes as something interesting and unusual.

In October of 2011, more than a year after the incident related above, I had a long hypnosis session with hypnotist (and now also author) Mira Kelley. I had been watching videos of interviews with Dolores Cannon on YouTube, and in one of those interviews Ms. Cannon noted that the unique form of hypnosis she had devised for regression work was also demonstrating a remarkable ability to effect healing. My prostate cancer situation at the time was not looking hopeful due to fluctuating PSA levels, so I was desperate for a new intervention. Having read many of Ms. Cannon's books and thereby harboring great respect for her, I decided to give her style of hypnosis a try. I visited her web site, consulted a list of hypnotists certified in her unique hypnosis method, and after some research decided upon a woman named Mira Kelley. I contacted Ms. Kelley via email, explained my situation and what I hoped to accomplish, and we set up an appointment for the session. What resulted was a meeting that lasted about seven hours, approximately five or more of which involved me being under hypnosis. The session was mind-blowing in the extreme, and the things I learned and experienced were fascinating, awe-inspiring, and of inestimable value to my personal growth and spiritual awareness. Interestingly, in many ways the most remarkable aspect of the session was Mira herself. In addition to possessing remarkable skill as a hypnotist, Mira is also a person of extraordinary kindness and sensitivity. She made me feel very much at ease, and she guided me through the complex labyrinth of subconscious visions and perceptions with skillful expertise and inspired intuitiveness; her questions were intelligent and insightful, and they navigated me through the experience in such a way as to result in some truly awesome revelations which I believe would not have surfaced under the guidance of a hypnotist with less personal concern, skill, and interest. I feel extremely fortunate to have had Mira as my "tour guide" into the realms of my inner self. (Mira's web site: http://www.mirakelley.com/).

As for the hypnosis portion, I will simply say that the information imparted during my session with Mira explained a great deal about my current life, my personality, and the problems I've faced. It also revealed some wondrous and inspiring cosmological and spiritual principles which have enlightened and transformed me in ways I had never thought possible. And it is those cosmological principles, in particular, that are pertinent to the topic at hand.

As with my hypnosis sessions with hypnotist Amy Benesch, Mira began our meeting with a discussion about myself, my life experiences, and what I specifically hoped to address during the session. At no point during this discussion did I mention my experience, from a year or more earlier, of awakening to a deluge of insights about the nature of reality. Nevertheless, while under the deeper levels of hypnosis (attained via Ms. Cannon's special method), additional information was revealed that supplemented and expanded upon the theory that I originally jotted down on paper that day over a year previously. (I will provide selected verbatim portions of the transcript of my session with Mira later).

21.2 My Personal Insight into the Nature of Reality

Here, then, is a compiled summary of the interesting take on the nature of reality that was revealed to me in stages: first upon awaking in my bed at home, then during my hypnosis session with Mira Kelley, and, later, during a wakeful moment of clarity in which the new theory was reconciled with the holographic theory of reality.

The Organizing Principle

The Organizing Principle (OP) is a mathematical engine that takes primal, chaotic energy and transforms it into the encoded forms that serve as the basis for our reality. Our sensory apparatus – our sensory organs and brain (or, more accurately, sensory organs and nervous system) – are predesigned to decode those encoded energy forms into our experience of reality. The raw energy is transformed by the OP into the encoded forms of the underlying reality via mathematics, and our sensory apparatus then decode those forms into experienced "reality," also via mathematics. That is why nature/reality appears to obey mathematical laws and formulas, and also why we humans are able to comprehend mathematics.

Einstein's famous equation $e = mc^2$ equates matter and energy, but note something important: it does not say that matter equals energy directly but, rather, it says that matter must be *transformed* into energy, and that transformation, according to Einstein's formula, requires two things: light (c) and mathematics; specifically, the speed of light (c, a mathematical constant – i.e., a numerical value) must be squared (a mathematical operation), and then that value must be multiplied (another mathematical operation) by the mass. Thus both light and mathematics are needed to effect the transformation of mass into energy, and vice versa. What is energy (e)? Energy is wave phenomena. What is matter (m)? Matter is something that occupies space and has mass – i.e., substance having form. Wave phenomena can be converted into forms, and vice versa, using mathematics (Fourier transforms). Thus energy, mathematics, and encoded forms are the fundamental components of "physical" reality, the recipe by which matter is created out of energy. I think it is no coincidence that light, mathematics (particularly Fourier transforms), and encoded forms (interference patterns) are also the ingredients that make up a hologram.

The historical progression of physics can be succinctly condensed into a clear pattern leading up to this realization, as follows: Newtonian mechanics showed that reality can be described and understood using mathematics; Einsteinian relativity showed that matter and energy are equivalent, and that light plays a crucial role in that equivalence; Quantum theory demonstrates that light has a dual nature, particle and wave (i.e., matter and energy); String theory postulates that the ultimate basis of reality is energy (in the form of vibration). Thus the entire history of modern physics is, in essence, a series of stepping stones leading to the realization that *our material reality is merely energy converted into matter via light and mathematics* (with light serving as the bridge between matter and energy, and mathematics, via the OP, serving as the engine of construction). Everything else, as the saying goes, is just details.

Indeed, if we perform some simple algebraic manipulations on Einstein's formula and solve it for c, we get:

$$c = \sqrt{\frac{e}{m}}$$

That is, light is equivalent to both energy and matter (wave and particle). This is the wave-particle duality property of light (from the famous double-slit experiment) expressed mathematically.

The OP takes raw, chaotic energy and, using what we call mathematics, converts that energy into one of an infinite number of "form systems". There is nothing inherently special about this particular form system – it is, in truth, merely one of many possible assemblages of energy – except for the fact that we have been designed to decode that energy-form system into our experience of reality. Thus, *to us*, that particular energy-form system is special and unique: we call it an "ordered state". But it is not any more ordered than any other state – it is but one of an infinite number of combinations and permutations of energy. But it appears ordered to us because we are designed to decode it into something that has meaning to us, due to a consistency of structure and interpretation based upon mathematics.

Our reality is truly a "consensus reality" in much the same way that language is a consensus type of communication. The word "cat" conveys a meaning to someone who understands the English language, but there is nothing inherently special about the word "cat" or, for that matter, about the letters c, a, and t which form the word "cat". Those letters are only random squiggles – arbitrary shapes – to which we have decided to assign an agreed-upon meaning (to a Chinese or a Japanese, for example, "cat" has no meaning whatsoever and is utterly unrecognizable as serving any nomenclatural function). Likewise, if we form a sentence – "The cat chased a mouse" – we have created a richer and more complex meaning by manipulating those shapes (letters) and shape-groupings (words) in accordance with a set of syntactical and grammatical rules. I suggest that our reality works in much the same way as does language: The OP transforms random chaotic energy into encoded "shapes" via the rules of mathematics, and we have been designed in such a way that our sensory-neurological apparatus is able to use that same mathematics to decode those energy "shapes" into our consensus reality – we are all applying the same rules to those energy forms, so we all translate them into the same "meanings", giving us a shared and consistent experience of reality. But our reality is not something special: it is an arbitrary arrangement of energetic forms that simply has meaning to us because it follows a particular set of rules that we have been designed to understand.

This new view of our reality can be interpreted scientifically, as follows: The OP takes raw, chaotic energy and forms it into the fundamental building blocks of our reality – the quarks and electrons of quantum physics, or the strings of string theory – which are analogous to the letters of the alphabet of a language; these building blocks are then combined into more complex energetic structures – atoms, molecules, etc. (analogous to the words and sentences of a language) and ultimately into encoded energy forms using mathematics (with mathematics being analogous to the syntactical and grammatical rules of language) – and *we* then translate those energy forms into our experience of material reality by decoding them using that same mathematics. The collection of encoded energy forms corresponds to Bohm's implicate order, and to Plato's realm of archetypal forms, and to the Zero Point Field; the decoding of those forms, by us, into material reality is equivalent to Bohm's idea of the unfolding of the explicate order out of the implicate order – as in the double-slit experiment, where our observation of photons causes their probabilistic wave state (energy state) to collapse into their alternative particulate state (matter state): i.e., human consciousness causes energy to collapse into matter.

This insight about the nature of reality provides us with the opportunity to formulate an alternative interpretation of the concept of "entropy." Science defines entropy as a measure of disorder of a thermodynamic system, and the Second Law of Thermodynamics – arguably the most important law of science – says that isolated systems always evolve toward a state of maximum entropy; this is usually stated in more colloquial language as "the tendency of the energy in the universe to gradually move towards disorder, unless acted upon by an outside force." But I maintain that natural systems are not "tending toward" anything – all states are equally possible, and there are infinitely many possible states, none of which is "ordered." Designating a particular state as "ordered" is completely arbitrary. We might consider a particular state to be ordered because it happens to be consistent with our agreed-upon decoding scheme, but the truth is that our precious "ordered state" is just as arbitrary as every other possible state. Thus a new interpretation of entropy, and the Second Law, would go as follows: *Natural systems will arbitrarily assume any one of an infinite number of random states, unless acted upon by an outside force.* Systems that are not acted upon by an outside force don't "tend towards" disorder – they don't "tend towards" anything; they simply arbitrarily assume one of the zillions of other states that we call "disordered." The Second Law of Thermodynamics is not describing a "tendency toward disorder" but, rather, it is indicating the *mathematical likelihood* that a system not acted upon will assume, arbitrarily, one of the many possible *other* states available, all of which we have capriciously and anthropocentrically designated as "disordered."

In Chapter 17 I presented an illustration of the Holographic Model of Reality, and at that time I promised a slightly revised illustration after the introduction of some new information. Now, having described my theory of the Organizing Principle, I can present the revised diagram:

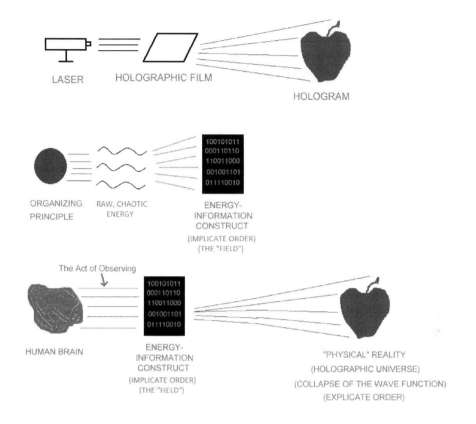

THE ORGANIZING PRINCIPLE AND THE CREATION OF REALITY

The Organizing Principle acts upon the raw energy of the Field and encodes it into an energy-information construct (one of many "form systems" as described earlier); we humans decode (via our brain and sensory apparatus) the encoded energy-information construct into our perception of "physical" reality. *The OP organizes chaotic energy to create the holographic plate, if you will, of the forms that make up our reality, and our human sensory-neurological apparatus decodes the interference patterns on that holographic plate into a holographic-like projection of what we perceive to be physical reality.*

The big question that arises out of this theory is: What, exactly, is the Organizing Principle? As I pondered that huge question, I decided to put aside, for a moment, the temptation to say that the Organizing Principle is "God" – I don't necessarily reject that notion, but I wanted a more explanatory and meaningful conceptual framework in which to come to an understanding of what the OP might actually be. I found that framework, I felt, in an idea proposed by Nassim Haramein.

Black Holes as the Organizing Principle

While viewing videos on YouTube I came across a video stating that someone named Nassim Haramein had posited that black holes might exist in the nuclei of atoms. [359] I had no idea who Mr. Haramein was, but I was intrigued by the notion of black holes existing in the cores of atoms because such an idea was consistent with my belief that fractal self-similarity is a fundamental property of natural processes and structures; after all, if black holes exist at the cores of galaxies (which science claims is so [360]), and since galaxies resemble atoms structurally, then it stands to reason that black holes might very well exist at the centers of atoms. Ruminating over this possibility leads to the following thesis:

Let's suppose that rotating mini black holes exist in the nuclei of atoms. These rotating black holes create a vortex which has a charge, positive or negative (depending on the direction of spin). In our reality, all black hole vortices are spinning in the same direction and thus are emitting the same charge – negative. On the subatomic level, a black hole vortex in a nucleus sucks in protons and electrons, and since the vortex is negative it attracts the protons to its center (since opposite charges attract one another) and it repels the electrons away from it (since like charges repel one another), even as the electrons are caught up in the vortex's rotation. Some of the protons are neutralized by the negative charge of the vortex, and these are transformed into neutrons; the remaining protons now exert an attracting force on the oppositely charged electrons, and this attracting force – together with the initial repulsion and the rotating orbital momentum – create a state of equilibrium in which the electrons now orbit the atom's nucleus (that nucleus being comprised of the neutrons and excess protons) thus creating an atom. Black holes of differing strengths would attract differing numbers of protons, resulting in the different atom/element configurations (as illustrated in the Periodic Table of the Elements). A similar situation exists in galaxies, hence the similarity of structure between galaxies and atoms; this would also explain the equivalent forms of the formulas for gravity and the electrostatic force between charged particles (see the section entitled "Synthesis: A Unified Model of Reality" in Chapter 19). Additionally, this might be the basis for duality, and why opposites are necessary in order to have form (Yin-Yang).

I suggest the possibility that *the black holes postulated to exist in atomic nuclei represent the mechanism, in 3D reality, of the Organizing Principle.*

21.3 My Hypnosis Session with Mira Kelley: Excerpts

As stated previously, the hypnosis portion of my session with Mira Kelley lasted in excess of five hours; as you might imagine, the topics and ideas that emerged were varied and far-reaching, ranging from the broadly general to the intimately personal. Of particular relevance to the subject matter of this book, however, was a surprising exposition on cosmological matters that provided further clarification of the idea of an Organizing Principle and, particularly, its relationship to reincarnation.

I thought it preferable to provide the verbatim transcript of this portion of my session, rather than to summarize it: I believe this information is best experienced in its original raw and unedited form, and I also believe that the emotions I experienced and the difficulties I had in attempting to grasp certain concepts provide for a dramatic and honest rendering of the overall gestalt of the experience. The transcript provided below is a small portion of the overall session. In order to provide some sense of context, let me briefly explain what I had experienced immediately prior to this part, and how that segment led into the cosmological one.

I had found myself floating out in space, surrounded by infinite blackness speckled with myriad pinpoints of light from distant stars. In this state I began to sense, firsthand, the Oneness of everything. Here's a sampling:

> **John:** I'm like in the darkness of space now, I see stars ... and the thing took me there ... it sent me there. it's ...unbelievable ...
>
> **Mira:** Tell me.
>
> **John:** I'm out in space; my ... like I'm standing on that platform; my arms are out, my legs are spread and I feel this tremendous energy.
>
> **Mira:** So it feels like your body is still there but your mind is out in space?
>
> **John:** I think so. I mean I can perceive my body in space, but I can't believe my body is there so I think it's just my mind, my perception ...
>
> **Mira:** Yeah ...
>
> **John:** And I'm feeling myself with my arms and legs spread out as though I'm drawing every ... I don't know if I'm drawing everything in or ... I'm feeling this connection, this awesome connection. Like I'm just out there in the middle of everything. And I'm connected to everything, and its ... amazing. This like vast, ... I don't know, it's ... it feels un ... inexplicably right to be there, I mean it feels crazy to be like a body out in space, just floating in the middle of nowhere but it's very comforting and very ... energizing. And it feels right. And it feels good. It's ... I feel like I'm connected all the stars that are in the distance ... and planets and...
>
> **Mira:** How does that feeling feel ... is it a feeling or is it a sensation in your body ... how does it feel, that connection?
>
> **John:** It's ... emotional ... it's like a powerful emotional feeling and also an impression ... it ... it almost feels logical at the same time that it feels emotional.

Mira: yeah ...

John: It's emotionally overwhelming in a positive way, and it's logically comforting because it feels right. It feels right logically and it feels wonderful emotionally. I either feel like I want to expand out into everything or I want to suck everything into me. I can't tell which ... or both. It's wonderful, it's ... it's like being an integral part of the universe, but not a thing in it; not like a planet but, ahhh, like it's, ahh, it's like the universe is a spider web and I am in the web, but it's not a bad thing ... it's ...

Mira: ... feels to you that the universe is also part of you...?

John: Yes. I almost feel like I could wiggle my fingers and I would see the stars jingle around.

Mira: yeah ...

John: It's like everything is totally connected ... and I'm, not in the center of it, I mean it almost feels like that but not that way. Ahhh ... Ahhh ... I can feel my individual self yet still feel completely totally utterly connected to everything at the same time. It's like a miraculous feeling. But I feel like I want to ... expand out into it more, if I ... I don't know if I could, like merge with it more.

Mira: See if you can do that.

John: I'm a little afraid. I don't want to lose my identity. And I feel like I would, maybe, if I expanded more. And I'm (laughs) ah ... I'm afraid if ... if I expand more into it I won't be able to experience it because I'm experiencing it now as myself, my individual self there, and I don't want to lose that feeling because it feels so good. But I feel this urge to, like expand or bloom or I don't know ...

Mira: Let's do that, because later you can shrink back if you want to experience it as an individual. But see what it feels like to expand even further into this.

John: Okay. (deep breath). Oh boy. There's a brightness that is almost blinding, it is white, bright, a milky white brightness. And it's just around me. It's bright and crisp and clean, and pure. Wow, it is so bright it's unbelievable. Oh my God ... Oh gee ... oh my God ... oh ... oh my God ... oh ... oh ... I'm a part of an energy that is unbelievable.

Mira: Describe it to me please.

John: It's like a milky white brightness, and it's vibrating in a very subtle way. It's very powerful ... I can't contain myself anymore, I'm intermixed with this but it's bigger than me ... and it's clean, it's so clean, it's so pure. There's like nothing else ... it's just this whiteness. I can almost perceive myself in it but not, not like before, like a vague, vague outline of that body but it's just barely there. I'm in this energy; it's almost, the vibration is almost too much to handle. It's not bad it's just ...

Mira: How does it feel?

John: It feels wonderful.

A bit later, after having fully merged with the bright light, I became slightly detached from it.

John: (long pause). I'm feeling slightly outside of it now. I'm still with it, but now I can feel a more distinctness of myself again. But it's still there and I'm partially in with it. Earlier I kept thinking it was God, but I ... thought that was my mind ... deducing that. Now I do feel like it's God and I'm before God in a way, that's why I've come out of it a little bit, to ... in order to perceive it as God I had to come out of it. I was in it before, and with it, and one with it. And I felt no distinction with anything. Now I'm a little bit out of it and I perceive it as this ..., in a way, partially ... and it's so much bigger than me. It feels totally benevolent, and loving. I still feel good, but nothing like I felt when I was in it. The contrast is unbelievable, and yet it's still a wonderful feeling but it's pitiful compared to what I felt before (laughs).

Mira: Right.

John: It's ... oh my God ... it's a confirmation of the oneness that I always ... not always, but that I do believe is everything. Or it was that. That's what that was, the other experience was a confirmation of that for me, a direct experience of pure oneness with everything. And now I'm ... feeling partly that connection and partly the usual sense of detachment that we have. But I think it was to let me know that, yes we are all one, it is all one, everything is all one ... that my suspicion of that is true. And I was having the experience to confirm that for me. So that there would be no doubts. Even though I believed it; now I know. Because I felt it. And I think ... it's telling me that that's what ... that feeling I had when I was with it, is what we're striving for, all the, uh, incarnations and the pursuit of, uh, spiritual perfection or whatever the hell it is we're pursuing ... but coming back and everything, that's it, that's the goal. And it is ... amazing and wonderful. It's what we strive for. And it feels so lonely to be out of that. So sad.

Mira : What is the reason ... there is a detachment out of it, because if it's so wonderful and pure to stay in it, why do we need to get out of it?

John: I don't know – that has plagued me and driven me crazy ... ever since I first became aware of this. Why do we have to go through all this crap? If we're perfect when we're there why do we need to learn anything? Why do I have to step down if I'm already there? I don't understand that. I don't ... (sigh) (long pause) just as I had to step out of it now ... to truly ... not appreciate it, because I appreciated it when I was in it, but I had to be, had to step out partially to *receive* it. When I was in it I wasn't aware of it, I mean I was aware of feeling good but ... it was, like I said, it was nothingness. It was *beautiful* nothingness, but it was nothingness. It was a one state of being, a beautiful state of being, but non-dimensional, non-... like, like a perfect blandness, and when I stepped out of it ... the lack of it impresses upon me the beauty of it. I had to know what it feels like and then know what it ... feels like not to have it in order to truly understand and appreciate what it is, because in and of itself from within ... it's nothing. But when you step out it, after having experienced it, you begin to comprehend the awesomeness of it, and the perfectness of it, and the goodness of it. I mean that's why I had to be stepped out now ... I don't know if that's telling me that ... if I'm supposed to carry that analogy further, and if that's supposed to be the explanation of why we have to come to earth, but it seems like it's analogous to that. Like taking it steps further now, because right now I still feel like I'm energy, and I feel like I'm almost partially connected to it, almost like a, uh ... if there was a sphere of energy and a little like a blob or pustule was pulling out of it, hadn't disconnected yet, but was pulling out. That's how I feel now, still one with it but not like I was before. I feel a limited detachment from it, enough that I can perceive it as something other than me ... and (laughs) ... oh God ... from out here it's not bland at all. From outside it's ... beautiful. It was beautiful inside but it was different. I couldn't perceive it from within, I could feel it and I could feel it was good, but I couldn't perceive it because it's all that was and it was nothing but white bright light and a vibration. Ahhh ... when I step out of it it's ... I want to be back in it. But I actually have a better sense of what it is when I'm outside of it than when I'm in it. Which I guess makes sense. I guess if you're in a building you can't see the building. It's not until you step outside the building – that's the image I'm getting now – I'm seeing myself in a building and I'm seeing the inside of the building, I have no idea what I'm in; now I walk out of the building, it's like a big skyscraper, and from the street I look up at the building and I'm like "Oh my God ... I was in *that thing*? I had no idea that I was in that huge building." And that's the image I'm getting now. When you're in the light you don't know it, you don't know what it is. You step out of it, and now you're awestruck. And then you want to go back. (long pause) I almost feel ... (laughs) a sense of guilt ... at wanting to be ... in there all the time. Because ... it's like doing nothing. But so what, I don't care. I don't care if I don't do nothing, I just want have that experience. But I feel like there's ... oh jeez ... oh no ... I can't, uh ... there's a purpose beyond that that I can't begin to fathom. There is a ... oh no ... it's almost crushing me. Ahhh ... there's more than that even, I have no idea what it is.

Mira: Tell me...

At this point I began to get tantalizing glimpses of something beyond the light that seemed to offer a deeper explanation of deeper truths, but the revelation proved elusive. Fortunately, Mira skillfully eased me past the blockage, and what was revealed were some of the most profound and astonishing concepts I had ever been exposed to.

John: But whatever it is ... ahhh ... apparently is the explanation ... of why ... we have to ... separate from it. It's ... it's not the end. There's more, but ... I can't even conceive of this and there's more, there's something else that's ... ahhh God, I don't even know, it's overwhelming … I almost want to cringe because it's so ... it's too much. It's too much. The infinitude is ... oh God it's ... ahhh ... I don't know, I don't know, I'm not getting any ... I'm getting a brief slight sense of something so big and so ... infinite that it's scaring the shit out of me. (long pause) It's just that there's more...

Mira: Is this more coming out of the light or is it more ...?

John: Beyond the light ...

Mira: Beyond the light ...

John: Beyond the light. There's something else beyond whatever that is, and that to me is the ultimate be-all and end-all, and I'm getting a sense that there's something beyond that, and that *other* something is waaaay beyond what I could ever even hope to begin to conceive a fraction of ... that I don't even, I can't even be exposed to it but ... the mere knowledge that it's there ... is somehow ... telling me that it's the reason why things have to be the way they are. It almost seems like a cop-out, like a priest telling you "Oh, you know, who knows the mysteries of God?" and that's the answer, which is a bunch of crap. But that's what it feels like, it feels like there's ... ahhh ... now, I don't know ... that's what, I don't know if it's my mind making that up but that's what I feel or that's what I'm sensing.

Mira: And you're saying that this feels like the explanation of why we need to be separate from the light?

John: Yeah. somehow, I don't ... I mean I get the feeling that the explanation was that – to perceive it. But then I'm getting also, uh, a sense that ... there's a deeper explanation, or a more profound explanation, or a clearer explanation ... maybe why we have to perceive it ...

Mira: Yeah...

John: And that I think is coming from something beyond ...

Mira: I want you to think about it and I want you to allow for the understanding to become part of you because you can, you can allow for this to become your understanding so you can explain it to me.

John: (long pause) I was briefly back in the white light, and now I'm in like ... or I'm seeing ... a kaleidoscope of colors ... in weird patterns, swirling almost like inks all swirling around. Black and red and blue and ... and it seems like it's beyond that bright light. It seems chaotic. Ahhh ... and it's more dark colors than light ... which is foreboding to me, I don't know if that's coming from within me or if it is foreboding, but ... it's a chaos of dark colors, swirling ... it's not giving me a good feeling. (long pause) It's a state of disorder and the white bright light is a state of order. The disorder is not good; my foreboding is correct. It's not a good thing. I don't sense an evil, nothing like that, just a not-rightness. It's the, the chaos of it and the darkness of it, and the ... the way the colors come together is not attractive, it's like an ugly ... ugly mixtures, ugly ... *ugly* [stated with a profound sense of disgust] patterns. It's not evil, it's ugly. And it's not right. So now I feel like my mind is working and again I don't know if it's me thinking ... or I'm told this. I'm think ... I'm feeling like I'm thinking ... that our reincarnating is part of a system, or a mechanism, that brings order out of the chaos. I don't know if I'm being told this or I'm coming up with this. But since that's what I was ... the question we were trying to get answered, I'm thinking it's the answer. I'm thinking they're showing me this chaos ... because it's the answer.

Mira: Yeah...

John: I don't know how much I'm inputting at this point, but I ... I'm assuming they're showing me this chaos, this ugliness, and it's distasteful. It's not evil, it's not like a Satan or anything, it's distasteful. It's like a mess. Just like a big mess. Like a messy room. So it's not evil, it's just ugly. It's unappealing, it's, uh ... it's just not pleasant to look at, not pleasant to [unintelligible]. And the white light is like perfect ... order. So perfect that it's ... like I said bland, like there's nothing. And maybe that's not ... good. The two extremes. Maybe ... now what I'm getting, I don't know if it's ...

ahhh ... the white light is one extreme, which is beautiful, and blissful, and perfect order. But ... *bland*. The other extreme is this ugly messy chaos. Ahhh ... I don't, I don't know if, if we are trying to create something in the middle of those two, because that would be a more ... balanced way of being? I don't know. In a way it seems to me we want to be in that bright perfection, but in a way it seems to me that that's too perfect. It's so perfect it's sterile. That it ... it's sterile. And while it's perfect and beautiful and blissful, it's sterile. And maybe sterility is not good either. I don't know. I'm almost sensing that ... we're trying to ... find or establish a happy medium between those two extremes. Is that what we're about? I don't know ... is that what we do when we incarnate, or is that part of a process to ... to do that? To bring together? Ah, to ... find something in the middle of those two extremes? Sterility is not a very appealing concept to me, now that I look at it that way. It's appealing because its ... it feels good ... but ... to what end? To what end? But why ... why does there need to be an end? Why does there need to be a goal? I don't know, I don't understand. I don't, uh, but I get that feeling that we need to be in the middle or something ...

Mira: Yeah...

John: (deep breath, long pause) I feel connected to the ... light; I don't feel connected to the chaos. And that seems odd to me. It seems to me like everything should be all ... one ... thing. But I don't feel a connection to that chaos, and I do feel a connection to the light. So I don't know if that chaos is a separate thing ... or if I'm just more ... down this end of the ... spectrum, if I'm so far removed from it that I don't feel ... like maybe there's a subtle connection to the chaos but it's, uh, I'm so far down the other end that I don't perceive it. I don't know ... I don't know if that's distinct from the light overall, or it's all one big thing. I feel one with the light, I feel we're all one with the light, I feel like everything is the light. Everything we know. And I can't resolve in my mind if the chaos is also part of that, or if it's a separate thing ... I'm getting the sense that it's separate, but that doesn't ... it ... feels like it shouldn't be, but nevertheless that's what I'm feeling. But I think that's my own ... I think the feeling that it shouldn't be is my own prejudice or whatever. My ... my own belief that everything should be one. But I ... and I think I was right about that ... I know I was right about that, but this ... this may be something else. This may be the thing outside the light. I'm thinking, I'm feeling that this is something else. There is the light, and we are all part of that, every ... thing we're aware of is all part of that light, and then there's this other thing, this chaos. I don't know if the light tames the chaos...

Mira: Could it be what you explained, that this chaos came from outside the light so that it knows the perfection and then can go back with it?

John: I don't… No, I don't feel that.

Mira: Okay.

John: I was thinking that, but when I came outside the light to experience the light, although I didn't separate from it, I didn't feel like I was part of the chaos. It's hard to describe but, I didn't feel like when you come out of the light forward to the chaos, it doesn't feel that way. It's one of two things: it's either that the chaos is totally separate from the light but I am part of the light, so even when I come out of the light I'm not really… I'm still separate from the chaos; or there's this long spectrum and the light is on one end of it, and the chaos is all the way on the other end, far away, and I'm… on the path between them but I'm so far over close to the light that the chaos seems separate from me. And I can't really tell if there is a connection with that chaos to the light and everything else, or not. It seems like it's not connected, but that conflicts with what I expect, I guess. But my sense is that it's not connected. It's another thing, that there's the light and there's the chaos. And that maybe that's it – that's everything: I mean to us everything is the light, we're part of that light, but that chaos exists out there somehow. And… I don't know if… If we're the balance between the light and the chaos, or we're supposed to tame the chaos … ah. Or maybe the light is supposed to merge with the chaos to create a new entity… And us reincarnating is part of that process. I don't know… But that chaos seems integral to the whole mystery, because it appeared when you asked me to see, and I didn't expect that.

Mira: yeah…

John: But it's funny because it's not that good and evil that we are all trained to believe in. I don't sense an evil from that. I sense that it's not… good, but… It's not good because it's a mess, not because there's an evil about it. It's just not the right… It's just … pandemonium, which is nothing constructive. But the light is bland. I mean, it was blissful while I was in it, but I didn't know what, you know, there was nothing there, it was kind of, you know, "okay, so what?" Like it's beautiful but… what? But when you're out in the muck here, it sure looks good. I mean, the blandness is not an issue because you want to get… if it's a choice being there or here, I want to be there without any doubt whatsoever. But on the other hand, ah … The thought of existing in that forever seems… pointless. As good as it feels, it seems pointless. And the chaos thing seems… worse than pointless. I don't know exactly how to say it but… It's like… a crazy person, it's like a sane person and a crazy person, and the chaos is the craziness – it's not necessarily bad, but it's craziness. There's nothing of any value there, it's just chaotic… noise, nonsense … And for that reason it's not good. But what it is in relation to us, what it is in relation to… God, I don't know. All I can say is it doesn't feel evil, but it's that side – if there is a counterpart to God, it's that. (long pause)…I don't know.

I then trailed off into a quiet state, apparently unable to go any further in this vein. Thus it was that Mira now gave me directions that would permit me to access my "higher self." I believe that this aspect of the hypnosis process might be the unique hypnosis methodology that Dolores Cannon developed. In any event, what seems to happen (in my view) is that the subject's consciousness is given access to higher levels of awareness, possibly even to a super-consciousness or over-mind, and thus has access to knowledge and information beyond his/her conscious knowledge or life experience. Interestingly, you will note that I often refer to myself while in this deeper state of hypnosis as "he" or "John" rather than "I" or "me," which would seem to indicate that someone/something else is providing the information. It was during this phase of the session that more information about the Organizing Principle was revealed.

Mira: I want to ask the higher self and level of understanding to explain to me what John saw outside of the light and that pure bliss and that pure nothingness. He felt there was this pressure, and then you showed him this chaos of colors and… Can you explain to me that? I want to understand it better.

John: He was given a vision not too long ago, and he's consciously aware of this, and the vision… What he was shown now was a clearer experience of that vision, and the vision that he was given is that… There is nothing – all of existence, everything – is nothing but information. And in its natural state that information tends towards disorder, just like the law of entropy from science, and this was the vision he was given. The information, left alone, seeks a disordered state, that's its natural state. And that was the chaos he was seeing. God is an ordering principle, a force of organization. And when that ordering principle acts upon the information, it orders it. It reassembles it into meaning, and that's the existence we perceive both on a physical level and on a spiritual level. It's nothing more than information – the only thing that exists – acted upon by the ordering principle, which is God. God is, in effect… When God acts on the information it's like a force that's resisting the natural tendency toward disorder, for that information. So the information naturally wants to go to this disordered, chaotic state. The force of God acts upon the information, pulls it away from the disordered state, and begins to order it or structure it. And out of that structure and ordering comes meaning, and out of that meaning comes existence. He got this vision upon awaking, it just was in his mind, and he was aware that it just was in his mind, unbidden. And he started to write it down. And he's fully aware of it. And it was such a powerful vision that … he couldn't help but believe that it was something important conveyed to him. But his self-doubts, which he has a lot of, make him wonder if it wasn't just a product of his mind, just some random bizarre thought, because he thinks about things like this and reads about things like this a lot. And what he saw now was a confirmation that the vision he had was a fairly accurate explanation of what's happening.

Mira: Where does this information come from…

John: It is. It is, it is… it is *All that is*. That is all that is, it's the only … thing that is. It exists.

Mira: So how does that connect to the light? That chaotic information.

John: The light acts upon the information, and somehow structures it, somehow organizes it into ordered... groupings, or something. It makes sense of it, in a way. It's like taking … uh … letters of the alphabet all jumbled together, like blocks … just a meaningless jumble in a pile, and forming words from them. The light acts on the information and creates meaning from it, by organizing it. It's an organizing principle.

Mira: What is the source of the light? Why is the light not, um, disorganized? Why is the light different?

John: The light is what we perceive of as God.

Mira: Okay.

John: It's an intelligence. It's an intelligence making sense … of … the information.

Mira: And why was the image of the information given to John as ugly, as messy?

John: In its chaotic form it's ugly, it's messy. There's nothing … it's meaningless in its chaotic form, and therefore has no value, no purpose. It's just…

Mira: How does this relate to incarnation, to the idea of people having lives and existing and striving towards spiritual development?

John:[long pause] It is… It is our individual pursuits of perfection that is the … that is the organizing principle. That, that … I mean, God is the organizing principle… Our pursuit of perfection is what is accomplishing the organization … for God, or *by God*. As we go through lifetimes and hopefully progress and improve and get closer and closer to spiritual perfection the more we are organizing the chaotic information. It's the mechanism by which God accomplishes the organization. And why that happens, I don't know... Or *how*. I mean, why that ... But we bring structure. Negativity is an outgrowth of the chaos, so there is no evil, per se. The chaos manifests as evil. It's the constant ... struggle. The ... uh ... The actual tendency to chaos pulls the information in that direction, and God, as an organizing principle, struggles to organize the information, so it's almost like two forces opposed to one another. But the natural tendency is for the information to be disorganized. And God is something else coming in, interfering with that natural tendency, imposing his organizing principle upon the information and in opposition to the natural tendency to be disorganized, forcing the information to structure, and somehow that's accomplished through us living and reincarnating. So I'm getting the sense that God, or the force that is God, is detached from the chaos and the information. That they are separate. But again it's not good and evil, its order and disorder ... and the information is the ... raw material that's acted upon.

Mira: So is the information also the source of both of them, or is there something else that's the source of both of them?

John: Both of what?

Mira: Of God and the disordered information.

John: No, I'm sensing either three separate entities or two separate entities. I'm sensing God is separate, and then possibly the information is separate and the disordering principle is separate, or, the disordering principle and the information are one. Because I keep sensing that ... the information's natural state is disorder, so I almost feel like they're not separate. And yet I do feel like the information is a raw material and the disorder is a force acting upon it just like the force of God is a force acting upon. Except I get the sense that God is external to this whole system, whereas the information and the disorder belong together naturally. It's the natural state of being for the disorder to act upon the information, or maybe for the information to be disordered. Maybe there is no disordering principle, maybe the information just exists and it exists in a natural state of disorder. But I do get the sense that God is separate from that, coming into the picture and then acting upon that information to order it. *That's* it! But the information's natural state is disorder, and it instinctively, or ... whatever ... naturally ... is made to maintain that state of disorder. So it's unnatural for it to be ordered, so in a sense it's resisting God's attempt to order it because that's not its normal state of existence. So God is almost making it go against its own nature by structuring it. That's clearer, I think, to what I'm seeing. And... And therein is the struggle, therein comes all the problems ... or there*from* ... because God is making this information do something that it naturally doesn't want to do. And in its natural resistance ... bad stuff comes out. But they're just outgrowths of the struggle. Again, there's no evil. There's not an evil force out there. So it's not bad versus good. It's disorder... a state of disorder and a force coming in and trying to structure and this thing naturally resisting that attempt at structure. And since it's going against its own grain, or against its natural state of existence, from that struggle or that friction, or whatever is occurring, in this attempt to order this stuff that does not want to be ordered, uh, we have all the things that we perceive as negative, or evil, or dark.

As you can see, this deeper state of hypnosis offered me access to a richer repository of information that significantly elucidated what the Organizing Principle is and how it operates; it also offered a tantalizing, but frustratingly incomplete, glimpse into the role that human incarnations play in the organizing process. Let's further explore some of the ideas that were raised here and consider them in conjunction with the theories discussed at length throughout this book.

A "Perfect Blandness"

My experience of merging with the bright light that I took to be God is eerily similar to that described by Dr. Eben Alexander, the neurosurgeon who had a profound NDE while in a coma for seven days (see Chapter 2). Dr. Alexander described his experience of God, or the Creator/Source, as an "inky darkness" that was nevertheless "full to brimming with light" and also as being "something akin to that of a fetus in a womb." [361] This, I think, conveys a sense similar to what I experienced of a bright light, extremely peaceful but boring – as I said, a "perfect blandness" and "a beautiful nothingness." Dr. Alexander also described a feeling of complete interconnectedness with the light and with everything, while simultaneously also maintaining some degree of self-awareness; [362] again, an experience very similar to my own.

Reincarnation as the Mechanism of the Organizing Process

The revelation from this portion of my session that I found most astonishing and original is the suggestion that human beings' pursuit of spiritual perfection via the process of reincarnation is "the mechanism by which God accomplishes the organization" performed by the OP; the notion that, somehow, "As we go through lifetimes and hopefully progress and improve and get closer and closer to spiritual perfection the more we are organizing the chaotic information." As I stated, I was not privy to *how* or *why* this happens – and therein lies the frustrating aspect of this – but I seemed certain that "... *we bring structure*." If this is indeed true – and, honestly, I don't know how much, if any, of this information *is* true – then it provides at least a partial answer to one of the conundrums discussed in Chapter 10: The Elephants in the Room, namely, *Why Are Physical Incarnations*

Necessary? When I first posed that question back in Chapter 10, I noted that, by all accounts, life in the Spirit Realm is pure bliss, and we souls appear to be pure and untainted while residing there. Why, then, do we bother to reincarnate into physical lifetimes on earth and experience all the attendant suffering and discomfort? The standard, and vague, answer is that we are "pursuing spiritual perfection," but the problem is that we already appear to be quite fine, spiritually, when we're in the Spirit Realm, so the need to come here and suffer appears to be unnecessary. Unless … unless *our incarnations serve some other purpose*.

I've noted elsewhere in this book that I strongly suspect that the information about the Afterlife, reincarnation, and our role in the grand scheme of things, that is revealed to us via LBL hypnosis sessions and NDEs is not complete. When one reads the transcripts of Michael Newton's sessions with his patients one is often haunted by the sense that we are not getting the whole story; there is a subtle impression that the hypnosis subject either doesn't know the answers to certain questions, or else is not allowed to provide certain information. I don't necessarily find it suspicious that selected information might be redacted by some overseeing authority; I can envision many reasons why it would not be in our best interests, or even possible, for us in our present human state to know the whole story. The truth is that I have a very strong sense that, for whatever reason(s), we are not privy to a large part of the mysteries of the Afterlife and our reality, and how the two interconnect. The fact that some knowledge is inaccessible to us was dramatically illustrated in the obvious frustration and overwhelming emotions I experienced in trying to describe what lies *beyond the light*:

> There's more, but ... I can't even conceive of this and there's more, there's something else that's ... ahhh God, I don't even know, it's overwhelming … I almost want to cringe because it's so ... it's too much. It's too much. The infinitude is ... oh God it's ... ahhh ... I don't know, I don't know, I'm not getting any ... I'm getting a brief slight sense of something so big and so ... infinite that it's scaring the shit out of me. (long pause) It's just that there's more...

> There's something else beyond whatever that is, and that to me is the ultimate be-all and end-all, and I'm getting a sense that there's something beyond that, and that other something is waaaay beyond what I could ever even hope to begin to conceive a fraction of ... that I don't even, I can't even be exposed to it...

There appears to be knowledge that we humans, at our present level of spiritual maturity, simply cannot fathom; something " … waaaay beyond what I could ever even hope to begin to conceive a fraction of …" – something so awesome that "… I can't even be exposed to it…" Such a possibility is, to me, as unnerving as it is intriguing.

A Possible Scientific Basis for the OP

Interestingly, there may actually be a scientific basis for accepting – or, at least, for seriously considering – this thesis of the Organizing Principle and the idea that we play a key role in its organizing process.

Recall that, according to quantum physics, the very core of reality is probabilistic (see the discussion of the Heisenberg Uncertainty Principle and the Copenhagen Interpretation in Chapter 14). This probabilistic basis of reality that is revealed by quantum theory might very well be the raw chaos that the OP structures into physical forms. In other words, it is possible that, either before or after being transformed by the OP, some vestige of that chaos remains at the core of material reality – that unprocessed chaos might be the source of quantum uncertainty and the probabilistic flux-state in which subatomic particles exist. Also recall that the human act of observation causes the probability function to collapse from its wave state to its particle state – in other words, according to physics, we humans actually *do* play a role in the formation of order out of chaos. These correspondences between the Organizing Principle theory and the findings of modern physics are intriguing and should not be cavalierly dismissed.

Aside from the fact that human observation appears to cause the collapse of the wave function, there is another way in which humans seem to play a direct role in the OP process. When a soul enters a body and takes on physical form, the situation is fractally self-similar to when a subatomic particle emerges out of the Zero Point Field: in each case, energy is transforming into matter, non-form is taking on form. When our eternal soul inhabits a human body we are effectuating the collapse of quantum probabilistic uncertainty into the explicit structure of material form: our soul energy manifests in a material body, tames the undisciplined resident host personality, and then uses that body as a vehicle for the creation of order in the physical plane – in other words, we, as souls, are the agents of the Organizing Principle at the macro level of reality.

Evil as a Byproduct of the Organizing Process

Another interesting notion that emerged from my hypnosis session pertains to the concept of "evil." My higher self repeatedly stated that there is no such thing as "evil" or "Satan" in the sense that we typically envision them, i.e., as a force and a being that exist independently and are inherently "bad." Indeed, I specifically stated – and I find this to be the other astonishing and original revelation to come out of this session – that what we consider to be "evil" is, in actuality, a byproduct, or a waste product, created by the process by which the OP organizes the chaos into ordered states (much like the carbon monoxide produced by an internal combustion engine when it converts fuel into energy). This is a fascinating idea, certainly a notion that never crossed my mind prior to my session with Mira. It is particularly relevant to the Afterlife Model because LBL hypnosis subjects repeatedly stress that *there is no such thing as evil or a devil*. Also, this problem of *Why is "evil" necessary?* was another of the conundrums I raised in the "Elephants in the Room" chapter (Chapter 10). That this OP theory might clear up yet another of those loose ends from the Afterlife Model is telling. To carry it all a step further, when we consider that "evil acts" are attributed to people, and that, according to the OP theory, people are the organizing mechanism of the OP and evil is a by-product of that process, we can see a very clear explanation for the causal connection between humanity and evil. Many people associate evil with materialism and its handmaiden, greed; it's not too much of a stretch to view materialism as being the OP unchecked, an out-of-control creation and acquisition of material goods. Perhaps there needs to be a balance between chaos and structure, and the problems we are presently experiencing in our world are the result of excessive over-structuring, i.e., the OP running amuck. When one considers the fact that cancer in the human body is out-of-control cell growth, the analogy of evil with an unbridled OP is as edifying as it is alarming. And just as cancer eats away at and destroys its host body, so too is our myopic obsession with materialism destroying our society and our world.

For a very long time I have harbored the opinion that the ideal level of human civilization is something at or near that of Native American societies. Living in small communities, utilizing limited "technology," and in a healthy balance with nature, the Native American culture strikes me as being the perfect stage at which to level-off and adopt a posture of maintenance rather than continued growth. Experience demonstrates that complexifying a system or process indefinitely is counterproductive; the normal path (no pun intended) is that of a bell curve where early efforts offer improvements but at some point an ideal level is reached – any progress beyond that point hinders more than it helps and results in a downward trajectory toward annihilation. Modern society long ago strayed off of the bell curve path and has pursued an ever-falling asymptotic line that leads to self-destruction.

What I find particularly fascinating about the OP theory is that, in addition to the conundrums from the Afterlife model that it answers, it also answers a disturbing conundrum from religion, namely, *Why would God create evil?* This is a question that every child exposed to religious doctrine asks at an early age, and the answers provided by members of the priesthood are generally less than satisfying – the usual "God works in mysterious ways" hokum. But from the perspective of the OP theory, a meaningful answer is possible: God unleashes – or *is* – the Organizing Principle, which creates reality out of chaos; that process of creation releases a byproduct, which is what we call "evil"; thus God does, in a sense, "create evil", but does so indirectly and unintentionally. Then we humans, in our pursuit of spiritual perfection and in our efforts to resist or overcome evil, are cleaning up the pollution caused by this unfortunate and unwanted waste product. Again, this is pure speculation, but it has an elegance and an air of credibility that is hard to ignore.

The Role of Language in the Formation of Reality

Yet another provocative concept expressed by my higher self was the analogy made between language and the Organizing Principle:

> The light acts upon the information, and somehow structures it, somehow organizes it into ordered... groupings, or something. It makes sense of it, in a way. It's like taking … uh … letters of the alphabet all jumbled together, like blocks … just a meaningless jumble in a pile, and forming words from them. The light acts on the information and creates meaning from it, by organizing it.

Terence McKenna often stated his belief that at the very core of reality we would find, not quarks and electrons, but *language*. If it is true that our thoughts create, or at least effect, reality (as discussed in Chapter 18), and that our experience of reality is a result of our brain's perception and processing of energy signals (as discussed in Chapter 13), then consider this: What would our experience of reality be if we didn't have language? Try to imagine what would be going on in your mind if it could not utilize language. While it is true that some of our thinking relates to pictures, most of our thoughts are language-dependent (even that last phrase – "most of our thoughts are language-dependent" – has meaning in the domain of language, but it cannot be represented mentally as a picture). I cannot even begin to imagine how I would experience reality without resorting to language; the experience would be so *different* that it is truly beyond imagining. So the analogy of the OP with language may hint at a fundamental connection between the two (in Section 21.2, in which I describe the OP in detail, I made liberal use of an analogy with language that I think conveys its relationship to the OP quite clearly). McKenna dramatically described the extent to which language can limit and dull our experience of reality in the following exposition:

> In the tradition of the West this has been viewed classically as "The Fall" – into "names" instead of "realities", into constructs of reality rather than reality itself. And this has been inculcated into every single one of us as the ability to be in, and reside in, language. For example, a child lying in a crib and a hummingbird comes into the room and the child is ecstatic; this iridescence of movement and sound and attention is just wonderful – it is an instantaneous miracle when played out against the dull background of the wallpaper in the nursery and so forth. But then mother, or father or nanny, comes in and says, "It's a bird, baby. Bird. *Bird*." And this takes this linguistic piece of Mosaic tile and places it over the miracle, and glues it down with the epoxy of syntactical momentum, and from now on the miracle is confined within the meaning of the word. And by the time a child is four or five or six no light shines through – they have tiled over every aspect of reality with a linguistic association that blunts it, limits it, and confines it within cultural expectation. [363]

Language is something that I think most of us take completely and utterly for granted, and we tend to presume that humans and language are fundamentally connected; I know I did for most of my life. On the timescale of human existence, however, language is a fairly recent phenomenon: spoken language is thought to be about 100,000 years old [364], while the earliest human ancestors are believed to go back at least two millions years. [365] What was going on in the minds of our pre-language human ancestors? How did *they* experience "reality"? When considering these questions in conjunction with Terence McKenna's moving observation quoted above, one has to wonder how different our experience of reality would be if it were not filtered through a brain whose thought processes are language-based.

Is the Organizing Principle *God*?

One huge point that needs to be addressed from my hypnosis session is the question: *Is the Organizing Principle God?* That possibility is strongly suggested throughout my discourse, and my higher self even states it directly at one point. But if God *is* the OP, then that means the chaos that I experienced is something other than God. That notion conflicts with the claim of many LBL subjects, NDErs, and ancient wisdom traditions – as well as what I myself believe – that God is *everything*. How can we resolve this dilemma?

In the passage from Genesis quoted at the beginning of this chapter, the claim that "the earth was without form, and void" can be interpreted as describing the chaos-state of the universe before being acted upon by the Organizing Principle; likewise, the point where God said, "Let there be light" can be interpreted as the unleashing of the OP (with the OP itself being that "light"). Note also that God saw the light as being "good" and He "divided the light from the darkness" (the darkness being the chaos). We can reinterpret this Biblical cosmology via the OP theory as follows: God created the Spirit Realm ("the heaven") and the universe ("the earth"), and the universe was in a state of chaos ("without form, and void"); God unleashed the Organizing Principle ("God said, Let there be light") which then transformed that formless void into our "physical" reality.

If this reinterpretation is accurate, then God appears to be something *other than* both the OP and the chaos; in fact, God appears to have *created* both the OP and the chaos, and then directed the OP to convert the chaos into form. So my tendency is to think that the OP is not God, per se. Recall that some of Michael Newton's more advanced LBL hypnosis subjects have suggested that the supreme intelligence or "Oversoul" often sensed by souls when meeting their Council (and construed by them to be God or the "Source") may actually be an aggregate of extremely advanced souls or else merely one member of a divine pantheon of Gods (see Chapter 8). This possibility could explain the relationship between God and the OP/Light: The OP/Light may be a force of creation created by the God of Genesis – i.e., a "lesser God" created by a "greater God" – and that force is interpreted by us humans to be a God in its own right – what we rightly call the "Source", the creative force. In that sense, the OP might be our *immediate God,* our *creator*, while *its* creator is another God existing in a hierarchy of Gods. This may not be as outlandish as it sounds: what we consider to be "everything" – the universe – might very well be only a small part of a vaster reality. Modern physics seriously entertains the prospect of multiple dimensions, and modern cosmology accepts the possibility of multiple universes (the so-called "multiverse").

My personal opinion – at least at this point in time, but subject to change pending further possible developments – is that the Organizing Principle is, in fact, what *we* think of as God. I think the OP fits the bill because: (1) the OP created everything that constitutes our experience of reality; (2) the OP is omnipresent in this reality, and is the force holding it all together (i.e., preventing it all from falling back into its natural state of chaos); (3) the OP is the quintessence of "intelligent design" – it *creates form and structure* out of chaos; and (4) the OP and the "Light" are described as being one and the same, just as God is so frequently equated with light in the Bible and elsewhere. I am fully open to the possibility that there are other Gods beyond, or above, the OP; but I think that what *we humans* have come to think of as God is, in actuality, the Organizing Principle.

The OP and the Big Bang

In Chapter 14 I discussed the cosmological concept called the Big Bang Theory, which is science's explanation for how our reality was created. To refresh your memory, allow me to repeat my summary of that theory. The Big Bang Theory posits that, approximately 13.8 billion years ago, our universe – all of it: matter, energy ... the works – sprang into existence in an instant out of what is called a "singularity," which is conceptualized as an infinitely small, infinitely dense, and infinitely hot state of existence. In spite of the use of the phrase "big bang" the birth of our universe out of this singularity is not considered to have been an explosion but rather a rapid expansion of the singularity. Continued expansion and cooling has led to our universe in the state in which it presently exists. Physicists believe that *nothing* existed prior to the singularity, and they offer no explanation to account for its origin.

I also noted, in Chapter 14, my opinion that this "theory" is about as preposterous an explanation as one can imagine. In essence, it claims that *everything* sprang from *nothing*, in an *instant*, for *no reason*. That's an awfully tough pill to swallow, even for the most gullible among us. The Big Bang Theory is, in point of fact, nothing more than a creation myth disguised as science. The OP theory, however, offers what I think is a more elegant understanding of the Big Bang event, as follows:

I believe that the Big Bang was not a bursting forth of "everything" out of a primary particle but, rather, *the expansion of the Organizing Principle wave through the field of chaos*. "Everything" was already there, in the form of unstructured chaotic energy. The OP was released into that mass of chaos and, as it spread through it, caused a continuous structuring of the chaos into interference patterns of energy that represent the forms that constitute our reality. This ongoing process of organization and complexification eventually led to the creation of living beings that possessed the necessary neurological and sensory apparatus to decode those interference patterns into an experience of "physical" reality.

21.4 "In the Beginning there was..." *Logos*

If The Big Bang Theory is science's version of the creation, then the Bible's version is expressed in John, Chapter 1:"In the beginning was the Word... and the Word was God" (John 1:1). In that sentence, the word "Word" is translated from the Greek word *Logos*, and "logos" does indeed mean "word." But *Logos* also has another meaning: The Greek philosopher Aristotle made a distinction in mathematics between *arithmos*, which referred to arithmetic calculations, and *logos*, which represented the foundation of logic and reason upon which mathematical argument is based. [366] To the Greek philosopher Heraclitus, *Logos* represented "a principle of order and knowledge" while the Stoic philosophers of ancient Greece identified *Logos* with "the divine animating principle pervading the Universe." [367] Seen in this light, the biblical phrase "In the beginning was the Word..." takes on a much different meaning, and one that is quite consistent with the OP theory. If we consider that the Organizing Principle is a force of organization that creates form and structure out of chaos, and that it was the primordial cosmological phenomenon responsible for the creation of the universe (à la the Big Bang), then an interpretation of *Logos* as meaning *the foundation of logic and reason upon which mathematics is based*, and "*the divine animating principle pervading the Universe*" makes much more sense than interpreting *Logos* as simply "word." For now we can render John 1:1 as follows: *In the beginning was a divine animating principle, using mathematical logic and reason, that pervaded the universe... and that divine animating principle was God.* This makes infinitely more sense as an explanation of creation than does the vague notion that a "word" was the causative agent.

While I don't subscribe to any particular system of organized religion, I do strongly suspect that there are profound truths contained in the Bible, many of which have been either intentionally or accidentally edited or redacted. In the case of *Logos*, I honestly believe that the original intent of that word was not its literal meaning of "word" but, rather, its deeper meaning of order, logic and reason.

As an explanation for the creation of reality, the theory of the Organizing Principle provides a degree of cogency, comprehensibility, and elegance that is sorely lacking in the vague and shadowy theories offered by science and religion.

21.5 Chaos and Mathematics

Chaos Theory Redux

One point worth contemplating is the notion of chaos as presented in the OP theory considered in light of mathematics. In Chapter 14 we saw that the relatively new branch of mathematics known as Chaos Theory studies processes that are erratic, fluctuating and discontinuous – deterministic systems that are extremely sensitive to initial conditions and are thus unpredictable (or, perhaps more accurately, prediction-resistant), such as weather patterns, the stock market, and brain and heart activity. These so-called "non-linear systems" represent most of the natural processes we encounter in our everyday experience of reality. But we also saw that there is a subtle level of order underlying these chaotic processes and that (as exhibited by, for example, weather patterns and fractals) order and chaos can, and actually do, coexist within the same system. This dichotomy of seemingly contradictory states, while baffling to our common sense and intuition, suddenly makes perfect sense when considered in light of the Organizing Principle theory. For if the OP is forcing order upon a resistant chaos, then we would expect to see evidence of this "struggle of opposites" manifesting in nature. And so we do, in the form of chaotic non-linear systems that demonstrate both erratic disorder simultaneous with predictable patterns. I suggest that what modern Chaos Theory has uncovered is the ongoing struggle between the OP and the chaos that it is attempting to tame. Indeed, *fractals might very well be a dynamic representation of the OP-chaos process in action.* And that may explain why so many natural phenomena display fractal features (such as: river networks, mountain ranges, lightning bolts, coastlines, trees, heart rates, earthquakes, snowflakes, crystals, blood vessels and pulmonary vessels, ocean waves, DNA, and various vegetables and fruit such as cauliflower, broccoli, pineapple). [368]

Transcendental Numbers Redux

In Chapter 14 I discussed mathematician Georg Cantor's work on infinite sets and higher orders of infinity, and in that chapter I promised that I would have more to say on the subject in Part IV of this book. Let me quickly review the material previously covered before I introduce some additional insights.

The set of Real numbers (the numbers with which we are most familiar – whole numbers, fractions, and decimals) can be divided into two subsets of numbers: algebraic numbers and transcendental numbers. In our human experience the algebraic numbers are by far the most commonplace numbers, whilst transcendental numbers are largely uncommon to our experience: π and e are likely the only transcendental numbers most people know of, while virtually any other number a person can think of would be an algebraic number. Yet Georg Cantor proved that the set of transcendental numbers is infinitely larger than the set of algebraic numbers. Recall the comment one of my math professors made in this regard:

Imagine all the Real numbers put into a huge hat: if you were to repeatedly reach into the hat and arbitrarily pull out a number, that number would almost always be a transcendental number; rarely would you get an algebraic number.

Back in Chapter 14, after having laid out the groundwork, I posed the following question: How can it be that the numbers that are commonplace and plentiful in our experience (i.e., the algebraic numbers) are, in truth, the rare numbers, whereas the numbers that are uncommon and scarce in our experience (i.e., the transcendental numbers) constitute, in actuality, the vast majority of numbers? This is an astonishing state of affairs! Why would our experience of numbers differ so dramatically from the actuality of numbers? The answer, I think, lies in the theory of the Organizing Principle. I suspect that the transcendental numbers are numbers that have not been acted upon by the Organizing Principle, that they are more "pure" – i.e., unstructured, chaotic, and unrefined – and thus represent the vast majority of numbers which exist in a realm outside of our reality (the realm of unstructured chaos), while integers and fractions are numbers that result from the effects of the OP – they are "cleaner" and more orderly and are thus naturally commonplace in our OP-created reality of form and structure (consider how much more pristine and precise a number like 3 or .5 is compared with π, which is a never-ending decimal equal to 3.1415926535...). Algebraic numbers are, by definition, simple and delimited (i.e., non-chaotic), whereas transcendental numbers are, clearly, imprecise and chaotic. It stands to reason that in a world of order, structure, and form (and that is populated by people whose neurological systems are designed to decode those forms), algebraic numbers, despite their rarity, would reign supreme.

Prime Numbers

Another intriguing area from mathematics where the OP theory might provide some insight is that of "prime numbers." A *prime number* is defined as any integer greater than 1 that is divisible only by itself and 1; so, for example, the number 17 is prime because its only divisors are 17 and 1. The first several primes are: 2, 3, 5, 7, 11, 13, 17, 19, 23, ... (the number 2 is the only even prime number, since every other even number is divisible by 2). Sometime around 300 B.C. the Greek mathematician Euclid (of geometry fame) proved that there are infinitely many primes.

While you might not be aware of it, prime numbers play a very practical and important role in our society: the security of financial transactions conducted over the internet (known as "RSA encryption") is dependent upon prime numbers. [369] The really interesting thing about prime numbers, however, is that *every integer greater than 1 either is prime itself or can be expressed as a product of primes* (this statement is known as the "Fundamental Theorem of Arithmetic"). Thus every integer greater than 1 can be created, or "built", out of the prime numbers.

This fact, taken together with the indivisible nature of prime numbers, has resulted in prime numbers being regarded as the "atoms of arithmetic." [370] What is particularly fascinating about the primes is that, although they can lay claim to the exalted role of being the building blocks of number – the very essence of the "exact science" of mathematics – the primes themselves occur in a pattern that is, to all appearances, random and chaotic. Despite attempts by the greatest minds of mathematics for more than two thousand years, no one has been able to come up with a formula to generate the nth prime number (meaning, a formula that will spit out, for example, the 8th prime number or the 63rd prime number). Just take a look at a listing of prime numbers and you will be struck by a pattern that appears random and disordered. Needless to say, the fact that the so-called "atoms of arithmetic" might be randomly dispersed does not sit well with mathematicians. [371] But, just as with the fractals and non-linear systems of Chaos Theory, it turns out that there seems to be a subtle order underlying the apparent chaos of the primes. Beginning with Johann Carl Friedrich Gauss in the late 1700s and on to Bernhard Riemann's Hypothesis of 1859, discoveries were made that demonstrated an unexpected and elusive regularity in the distribution of prime numbers. [372]

It is my belief that the bizarre chaotic-yet-ordered nature of prime numbers (together with their role as the building blocks of arithmetic) may be explained by the process of the Organizing Principle forcing order out of chaos. We've seen this inexplicable mix of order and chaos before with fractals and the non-linear systems of Chaos Theory, and also with chaos underlying order in the form of quantum probability lying at the heart of matter. I think that in each case – Chaos Theory, fractals, quantum probability, and prime numbers – what we are seeing is the struggle between the OP and the primordial chaos, and it is noteworthy that this contradictory chaos-order dichotomy seems to always occur at the *core* of the phenomenon in question.

I suspect that at the very essence of our reality there is a boiling tempest of conflict arising out of the ongoing struggle between the OP and the primordial chaos, and, further, that this struggle itself might be the source of the Zero Point Field and the quantum particles that emerge from, and remerge with, that Field. Our reality is literally being created out of the OP-chaos conflict: very close to the core of that conflict there is a mix of order and chaos as the process unfolds, while at the outer edge of that conflict – our macro-reality – all appears calm and orderly, the result of the process completed.

Chapter 22

Final Thoughts

> We can't solve problems by using the same kind of
> thinking we used when we created them.
>
> - Albert Einstein, Physicist

In one of his lectures, Deepak Chopra talks about the "Seven States of Consciousness," the first four states of which are as follows:

1. Deep sleep (the sleep state)

2. The Dream state

3. The Waking state

4. Transcendental Consciousness (glimpsing your own soul)

Dr. Chopra then directs you to recall a time in which you were having a vivid dream. The dream felt very real to you – you interacted with others, experienced sensations, felt emotions, and so on. While you were in the Dream state of consciousness, that dream seemed totally, unquestionably real. But when you awoke from the dream, your sense of the dream experience changed: although the dream *seemed* remarkably real, you now realize, from the perspective of the Waking state, that, in fact, it wasn't real – it was only a dream. The Waking state is now experienced as being the "real" state. But what happens, Dr. Chopra asks, when you awaken to *the next state of consciousness*?

The dramatic and obvious answer is that you will look back upon the Waking state as being "only a dream." That is, as we progress into higher states of consciousness, we come to realize that the prior state of consciousness – although previously perceived as being "reality" – was merely an illusion. One of my main intentions in writing this book was to provide a means for people to awaken to that next level of consciousness, to awaken to the Transcendental state and thereby glimpse your soul. And then, upon awakening, to realize that *the Waking state level of consciousness is, in fact, only a dream*. I sought to make this point, and to provide a practical methodology for achieving it, from the perspectives of spirituality and science. As we've seen throughout this book, spirituality and science, normally oppositional, appear to be in complete agreement on at least this one point: our reality is an illusion, a dream-state of the mind. And, incredibly, both paradigms – science and spirituality – offer us a means to awaken out of this dream-state.

22.1 Paradigm Shift

The word "paradigm" refers to "the generally accepted perspective of a particular discipline at a given time." [373] For science, the dominant paradigm for the last three or four hundred years has been that of *materialism* – the notion that matter is the only reality and that all natural phenomena can be explained in terms of matter. This viewpoint has governed the thinking and direction of the sciences like a fearful and paranoid tyrant, neurotically suspicious of alternative views and jealously guarding its beliefs from all challengers. Now, however, thanks to a group of open-minded scientists, that restricted and restrictive mindset may be about to change.

In July of 2014 several scientists published a paper entitled, "Manifesto for a Post-Materialist Science" in which they outlined their case for a broadening of scientific thinking beyond the limits of the materialist view. In their paper they observe that the assumptions of scientific materialism and reductionism, while being very successful in extending our understanding of nature and in creating powerful technologies, have also severely limited the scope and development of scientific study. They note that, historically, science has evolved precisely because of, and in response to, phenomena that could not be explained by the prevailing scientific paradigm, in that the need to accommodate these phenomena prompted an expansion of the paradigm and thus the evolution of scientific thinking. Paradoxically, the current paradigm's insistence upon a compulsory adherence to the materialist view alone – as the only rational and acceptable avenue of scientific investigation – serves as an obstacle that thwarts the extension of scientific study into areas that clearly are not explainable by materialism alone. [374]

The authors refer to their proposed expansion of scientific thinking beyond the materialist view as the "post-materialist paradigm." Among this new paradigm's precepts – and of particular relevance to the theses I have presented in this book – they list the following:

- "There is a deep interconnectedness between mind and the physical world."

- "Mind (will/intention) can influence the state of the physical world…"

- "NDEs occurring in cardiac arrest, coupled with evidence from research mediums, further suggest the survival of consciousness, following bodily death, and the existence of other levels of reality that are non-physical."

- "Scientists should not be afraid to investigate spirituality and spiritual experiences since they represent a central aspect of human existence." [375]

If other scientists respond to this favorably, then I think we will be witnessing one of the most dramatic paradigm shifts in the history of science. This truly has the potential to be historic and, more importantly, to steer the human enterprise onto a course that is significantly more enlightened and nurturing than the dreadful course we are presently following. Dare we hope?

22.2 The Path to Awakening

In Chapter 2 I discussed the amazing transformative effects experienced by people who have had a near-death experience, and we learned that merely being *exposed to* the concepts and wisdom inherent in the near-death experience is sufficient to result in a transformation similar to that experienced by the NDEr herself. That is, by simply reading about or otherwise studying the NDE phenomenon and considering its content with an open mind, each one of us can have an opportunity to undergo a similarly life-transforming, life-enhancing metamorphosis. And, while I am not aware of any formal study exploring the possibility of people experiencing qualitative changes in their personality or world view as a result of reading LBL literature, I nevertheless wholeheartedly believe that such is the case: one reason, as I've stated before, is that I've experienced it myself. I can personally attest to the fact that reading about NDEs and LBL sessions has had a dramatic transformative effect on my life. When I later underwent LBL hypnosis I experienced further and deeper transformation.

In Chapters 2 and 9 I listed the more common life-enhancing aftereffects reported by NDErs, and which formal studies have demonstrated can be realized by merely *acquainting oneself* with the NDE literature. I also noted that many of these corresponded with information learned by LBL hypnosis subjects. Allow me to repeat that list one more time, as it has important relevance to my final observations.

Typical life-enhancing transformative effects experienced by NDErs include the following:

1. Diminished fear of death
2. Less judgmental/more tolerant and forgiving
3. Major changes in life situations (relationships, career)
4. Increased love and empathy for all life forms
5. Religious orientation replaced by spirituality
6. Increased appreciation for nature and ecological concerns
7. Less concerned with material possessions

8. Newfound interest in reincarnation, psychic phenomena, and the "new physics"
9. Increased zest for life
10. Increased happiness and optimism
11. Decreased stress and worry
12. Belief in God
13. Hunger for knowledge
14. Increased compassion and empathy for others
15. Importance of service-to-others

NDErs and LBL subjects are in full agreement that love and the acquisition of knowledge are of primary importance, and that *everything* is interconnected – All is One.

When I discussed the above listing of transformative effects in Chapter 9, I made a point of stressing that the ability to experience these changes by merely reading the NDE and LBL literature represented a *practical benefit* to be derived from these subjects – an opportunity to enhance and improve one's life experience *right now*. People do not usually connect so-called "airy-fairy" subjects with practical benefits; yet, as we've seen, in the case of the NDE and LBL, practical benefits can be easily obtained.

But now I'd like to take this "practical benefits" angle a giant step further. I ask you to consider the Dimensional Shift uncovered by Dolores Cannon (which was discussed in detail in Chapter 20) in light of the list above. It's obvious that each quality in this list is what would be called a "high frequency" or "high vibration" quality – qualities associated with one who is spiritually advanced and enlightened. Now recall that the Dimensional Shift described by Ms. Cannon involves the birth of a New Earth into a higher dimensional plane, and that those humans who are in spiritual resonance with the New Earth – that is, whose personal vibration/frequency is of a high enough level to be in sync with that of the New Earth – will make the transition to that new realm of existence. My point is this: *The qualities appearing in the list above are precisely the qualities one must develop in order to raise one's frequency to be in resonance with the Shift.* In other words, becoming familiar with the NDE and LBL literature would appear to provide a practical means to allow one to participate in the Shift. If the Shift is truly going to occur, then this is a critically important piece of information, a literal means to salvation.

But what if the Shift is not real? What if this business about humanity undergoing a spiritual evolutionary leap is just a fantasy created by frightened people desperately looking for some ray of hope in a world quickly falling into ruin? Well, in my humble opinion, that would not diminish the value of the qualities listed, nor would it diminish the desirability of having as many people as possible acquire and demonstrate those qualities.

22.3 Paradise Lost

The human race is clearly in trouble – *big* trouble; as I stated elsewhere, our world is broken. The utopian promise given to me in my childhood has turned out to be a dystopian nightmare: the promise of a long, healthy life-span has become the prospect of a cancer-plagued, prescription drug-saturated, expensive and prolonged stay in a "care" facility – even *children* are much sicker now than when I was a child; the promise of a shortened work week has now become massive unemployment, recession, economic instability, and evaporating pensions and health insurance; the promise that technology would ease our burdens has instead given us useless toys and pollution; art has degenerated; education has degenerated; the promise of world peace is now a grim reality of more wars, deadlier wars, and terrorism; life in general has become much more complicated and much less fun – people are joyless, morose and alarmingly apathetic. The promise of a paradise for humanity has yielded a paradise for about 3% of the population, and either literal or virtual slavery and hell for the rest of humanity.

Something, somewhere, has gone terribly, horribly awry. And, as Einstein said, we're not going to be able to fix it by using the same mindset that broke it. The systems that caused our problems are deeply entrenched in our society, they are in control of our society, and they are not going to willfully allow, nor participate in, their own restructuring. I believe that any hope for meaningful change can only come from, and must begin with, *us* – each one of us, on an individual level. In spite of a long-standing mythology that "one person can change the world," the truth is that the only thing most of us has the power to fundamentally change *is our self*. We must do what we can – *now* – to cleanse ourselves of attitudes, habits, and behaviors that are destructive and toxic; and we must simultaneously replace those negative mindsets and tendencies with healthy, life-affirming alternatives. I believe this can be accomplished if we actively strive to adopt the transformative effects experienced by NDErs; one way we can do that is by reading, studying, and contemplating the wisdom related in the NDE and LBL literature. If the forces of nature are not preparing some kind of mass species-wide planetary Shift for us, then we must effectuate that Shift ourselves. With each one of us working at it individually, we can accomplish it collectively.

Interestingly, when a new behavior or mindset is adopted by members of a population there is evidence that the spreading of that behavior can reach a point of critical mass wherein a major paradigm shift occurs throughout the population, resulting in a situation where, over time, the majority of the population has adopted the new behavior and made it the norm. This has become known as the "Hundredth Monkey Effect" and derives from observations made of monkeys on a Japanese island promulgating the practice of washing sweet potatoes before eating them. The process is often reported to be the result of a "spontaneous transmission of knowledge" that occurs rapidly and automatically via some subtle agency of communication akin to Rupert Sheldrake's concept of morphogenetic fields, while others claim that a more mundane process is responsible. [376] But whatever the case, the good news here is that *a shift in behavior, a shift in mindset, a shift in consciousness, can occur if enough members of a society adopt a new outlook.* Whether you believe in an impending Dimensional Shift from without, or a personally initiated Shift from within, the bottom line is the same: you cannot partake in the Shift until you have made specific, fundamental adjustments in your own attitudes. As Mahatma Gandhi said: "You must be the change that you wish to see in the world." The change so desperately needed now involves adopting the qualities contained in the list above, and one path to that change is through NDE- and LBL-derived wisdom.

One of the great and encouraging revelations to come out of the LBL literature is the acknowledgment that we humans possess *free will.* We have been given the right to make choices freely. This is a tremendous power, for once we make a choice and act upon it we are effecting reality. In much the same way that the collapse of a subatomic particle's quantum wave function transforms a cloud of probable quantum states into a specific, material state, so too do our personal choices transform a cloud of possible outcomes into a specific action with real-world consequences. *As above, so below.* We are living in a macro-world analog of the quantum uncertainty that exists at the subatomic level. When we exercise our free will and make choices, we are collapsing the macro-world wave functions … *we are creating reality out of possibility.* The ways in which we exercise our free will – the choices we make – directly determine the nature of our reality. How will we choose? How will *you* choose? *What world will you create?*

I have come to believe that each one of us is a song, and we are also the composer of that song. The song is a theme with variations: our eternal soul is the theme, and our many earthly incarnations are the variations on that theme. With each new variation that we compose we strive to refine our music, to perfect the harmony and melody until, eventually, we achieve a piece of music that is elevated to a state of such sublime purity and exquisite beauty that it transcends itself.

22.4 The Important Things

The shelves in the "Personal Growth" and "New Age" sections of bookstores are overflowing with tomes offering "how-to's" for achieving enlightenment, peace, and deliverance. And, trust me, I've read *a lot* of them. In my experience, most of them contain valuable wisdom and advice that can have a noticeable calming effect on the reader while simultaneously opening the reader's mind to new and stimulating ideas and views. Many such books have helped me in ways and to depths so profound that I can't even begin to express my gratitude to their authors. But a mass can become so voluminous that it is overwhelming, and a level of detail can become so over-refined that the original point is lost in the minutia. It is then that the enterprise becomes counterproductive.

After decades of research, personal exploration, and contemplation, I've come to realize that what is most vitally important, from a spiritual perspective, boils down to a rather simple collection of realizations.

Love

We must all develop within ourselves a genuine attitude of Love. Not the romantic or hormone-fueled feeling we've come to associate with love, but rather a deeper and more selfless emotion involving reverence, compassion, and kindness. Something akin to what a mother feels for her child: tenderness, devotion, warmth, and fundamental connection.

The primacy of Love on a list such as this would seem to be a no-brainer, yet I think that in our present-day society the importance of Love is often taken for granted, if not overlooked entirely. It is interesting to note that when asked (in Matthew 22: 36-40) by one of the Pharisees, "Teacher, which is the greatest commandment in the Law?" Jesus replied with two commandments, neither of which was one of the original ten commandments. Most important, Jesus said, was to love God; "And the second is like unto it: 'Love your neighbor as yourself.' Upon these two commandments hang all the Law and the Prophets."

To love others as you love yourself is also basic to the wisdom imparted by NDErs and LBL subjects, and it can most easily be understood in light of the fact that All is One – you and your neighbor are, in truth, one and the same.

All is One

We need to reach a point of understanding where we *know*, on an intuitive level, that *everything* in existence is fundamentally connected. We must come to understand that what we perceive as individual entities are, in fact, different manifestations of one singular plenum, *one entirety that is indivisible and indistinguishable*. This entails a complete and total abandonment of the illusions of distinctions, categorizations, individuality, and reductionism.

Forgiveness

We must, to the core of our being, be willing to forgive others for all transgressions, real or perceived, that we believe they have committed. There is abundant evidence that the harboring of grudges and ill will toward others can have a deleterious effect on the health and wellbeing of the person who is doing the harboring. [377] This does not mean one should accept all forms of behavior as "being OK," nor does it mean one must tolerate abuse; forgiveness involves how we choose to *respond*, within our own minds and hearts, to the hurtful acts and words of others. It is our choice whether or not to allow the cruelty of others to eat away at us from within. We may have only limited control over what others say and do, but we have a great deal of control over how we let their words and acts effect us psychologically and emotionally. As preacher Creflo Dollar has said, "Don't let other people rent space in your head."

My basic nature years ago was the complete antithesis of forgiveness – I doggedly held grudges and I resolutely believed that it was wrong and foolhardy not to perpetuate resentment overt slights inflicted by others. The value of forgiveness has been a basic theme in modern spirituality literature for decades, and thus, when I embarked on my spiritual journey, I became aware of the importance of adopting an attitude of forgiveness as a fundamental factor in spiritual growth. As such I struggled mightily to foster a forgiving mindset within myself, but despite my best efforts I made little progress. And the little progress I did make was a kind of forced forgiveness – I understood and accepted the essentialness of being a forgiving person, but it was so much against my basic grain that I could not assimilate it into my personality with any degree of genuineness. Then, after decades of strenuous but largely ineffective grappling with this matter, a miracle happened. A few days after my lengthy hypnosis session with Mira Kelley I realized that I no longer bore any resentments, grudges, or rancor. I had, astonishingly and inexplicably, forgiven everyone who had ever offended or harmed me. This forgiveness was real, sincere, and complete. And it just *happened*. Mira and I had not discussed my struggle for forgiveness, and it was not something that was addressed during the hypnosis session, yet it clearly was a byproduct of that session. The only thing I can attribute it to is the fact that, during that session, I had a very powerful experience of the Oneness of everything (see Chapter 21), and I suspect that that deep realization translated into an instant and utterly profound feeling of total forgiveness. It is probably the most important thing which I took away from that hypnosis session: Letting go of all that bitterness and resentment was so refreshing, so wonderfully unburdening, that I can't believe I allowed that poison to fester within me for so long. Believe me: forgiveness is a vital factor in personal spiritual growth.

Gratitude

We should develop a conscious sense of gratitude for the blessings we enjoy. There is a strong tendency in our society to concentrate on our problems and areas of lack, and we often do this to the exclusion of any recognition of the good things in our lives. This victim mentality has gotten so bad that self-perceived victims often seem to take a perverse pride in their victim status.

When I take walks, or before falling asleep at night, I run through a mental list of all the things in my life that I am thankful for. I am often astonished at how *many* things there are. More importantly, I am amazed at how *good* I feel after I devote a few minutes to contemplating gratitude. If we reflect back on the material covered in Chapter 18 regarding how our thoughts and emotions can affect our health, then the positive effects of pondering appreciation and thankfulness are really not so surprising after all. Imagine how I would feel if, alternatively, I spent my time bitterly bemoaning the "unfairness" and "lousy luck" of me having prostate cancer. Thinking about the good things in our lives not only makes us feel better emotionally and physically, it also helps to reset our mental attitude to a more positive and optimistic state; it neutralizes negative energies (with which we are incessantly bombarded by the media) and restores a sense of balance and objectivity.

Acquiring Knowledge

Many NDErs have returned from their experience with the message that the two most important things we should be doing in this life are *feeling love for all* and *acquiring knowledge*. When I first read this in the literature many years ago I was a bit taken aback: the "love" part was a no-brainer, but the business about "acquiring knowledge" was a surprise. Personally, I had a passion for acquiring knowledge and thus it was very important *to me*, but I was astonished to see it noted as one of the two most important things in life. Now, after many years of thinking on this and, hopefully, being wiser for my years, I've come to realize why the acquisition of knowledge would be deemed so critically important: knowledge leads to understanding, understanding to wisdom, and wisdom to insight. I've found, in my own life, that as my level of knowledge has increased I have experienced a corresponding increase in positive traits – kindness, consideration, understanding, generosity, humility, thoughtfulness, and a non-judgmental attitude – with a corresponding decrease in negative traits, such as prejudice, anger, selfishness, close-mindedness, and arrogance. Amazingly, it seems that many of the undesirable human qualities are the result of simple ignorance. And, of course, knowledge is the antidote for ignorance.

Living in the "Now"

In his wonderful book *The Power of Now* author Eckhart Tolle's simple yet profound message is that living in the present moment is vital to achieving peace, happiness and enlightenment. Most of us devote inordinate amounts of time dwelling on past events and worrying about what awaits us in our future. But, good or bad, the past is gone and there is nothing we can do to change it; similarly, the future is uncertain and dependent upon more variables than we could possibly ascertain, let alone control, so fretting over it unduly is counterproductive. The only time that is real for us is the present moment – right *now* – and we should not let this present moment go by unnoticed while we torture ourselves over past slights or future worries. Writer Allen Saunders famously said, "Life is what happens to you while you're busy making other plans." Life should not "happen to" us, it should be something we experience willfully, directly and consciously.

Meditation

Years ago I heard someone say, "Praying is talking to God, meditation is listening to God." Meditation is a practice that has been around for thousands of years, and for good reason: meditation is easy to do, costs nothing, and offers many positive health benefits. First and foremost, meditation reduces stress by inducing a state of deep relaxation and tranquility. [378] I have found that after meditating for thirty minutes I feel an odd mixture of calm serenity and abundant energy. Meditation revitalizes one emotionally, mentally, and physically. And these wonderful effects last for many, many hours after the meditation session ends. Considering the connections established between a wide variety of illnesses and stress, meditation (being a stress-reducer) offers the potential for many health benefits beyond mere relaxation, to include: lowering blood pressure, heightened immune function, improved heart rate, easing chronic pain, and reducing anxiety.[379]

When I was diagnosed with prostate cancer I decided to make guided imagery (discussed in Chapter 18) part of my healing process. Because getting into a meditative state greatly enhances the effectiveness of imagery, it was then that I began my practice of meditation. At first I found it difficult to do, as my mind seemed to be always buzzing and I had a hard time calming my thoughts. But with practice I found that getting into a meditative state became easier and easier; I later noticed that having undergone hypnosis has helped me to achieve a meditative state faster, and to go into a deeper state as well. I have been meditating for several years now, and I am still amazed at how good it makes me feel.

Being Non-Judgmental

Cultivating an attitude of being non-judgmental goes hand-in-hand, I believe, with Love and forgiveness, while its alternative – i.e., being judgmental – runs counter to the philosophy that All-is-One. Finding fault and being critical of others is, at the very least, unrealistic and egotistical, and, at its worst, cruel and malicious. It's easy to pass judgment on others when one is blind to one's own faults, but when one is honest with oneself then it is rather hard to criticize others. We're all struggling through this life, and we all experience hardships and challenges that we process in different ways. Life in this world is far from simple; situations, problems, and people are extremely complex. This complexity only increases when we view life from the enlightened perspective of the Afterlife Model, where we find that, to all the earth-based complexities, we must add the further complications of karma. If we are honest with ourselves, we realize that we cannot even begin to understand why people are in the situations they are in, or why they respond to situations the way they do. We pretend that the answers are simple – a homeless or unemployed person is "lazy" or an unsophisticated person is "stupid" – but the reality is that the reasons behind a person's situation in life are usually mind-bogglingly complex. Avoiding dangerous people is generally prudent, but judging them is misguided. Rather than passing judgment upon others, I think our time and effort would be better spent on assessing ourselves.

Releasing Fear

During a short-lived stint at a job I had over twenty years ago I found myself sitting at a lunch table with a co-worker with whom I had never before spoken. In the course of making small-talk to diffuse the awkwardness we discovered that we shared an interest in spiritual and new-age subjects. After that we purposely sat together for lunch every day and had many animated and fascinating conversations about our mutual interests. During one particular conversation this woman casually made a statement that, to me, was one of the most profound ideas I had ever heard: she said that each and every negative human emotion – greed, hate, envy, etc. – could be traced back to fear. The notion that fear is the primal and root emotion for all of the other negative emotions had never occurred to me before; indeed, I had never even considered the possibility that negative traits could be traced back to a single source. My colleague clearly considered the idea to be an undisputed fact, but for me it was a new and novel idea. I gave it much thought riding home on the subway that night, and for many days after, and it soon became clear to me that she was absolutely right: fear is the most destructive of the negative human emotions, and it is the source from which the other negative emotions spring forth.

I have since, and especially in recent years, seen this concept expressed repeatedly in many books dealing with spirituality, and even in books covering more mainstream topics. The idea that all of the undesirable human attributes and emotions have their origin in fear, and that fear is the baddest of the bunch, is quickly being taken as fact in an ever widening circle of writers and thinkers. Indeed, I have often seen it stated that fear is the polar opposite of Love. That notion is most dramatically expressed in a statement by Inelia Benz: "Fear is the biggest block a person can encounter when doing ascension work." [380] When one considers the degree to which we are bombarded by fear in our society today – fear of disease, fear of crime, fear of terrorism, fear of economic collapse, etc. – it immediately becomes apparent how desperately we need to adopt and practice an approach to life that is based in Love and that releases fear.

Controlling Ego

If it is true that all of the negative qualities arise out of fear, them I think that a strong case can be made that all of the positive qualities arise out of the philosophy that All-is-One. If we truly accept, as a fundamental truth, that everything in existence is interconnected in a single, cohesive whole, then hatred, greed, violence – all of the terrible things people do – will evaporate into nothingness; for how or why would something hate or harm itself? It is our falsely perceived sense of separateness, and the resulting competition we imagine to be necessary for survival or advancement, that breeds the fear which, in turn, breeds all the other awful acts and attitudes. And all of that – the sense of separateness, the need to compete, the desire for advancement and superiority – derives from ego. While the word "ego" is commonly used to denote a sense of inflated pride and superiority, its basic meaning is simply "a consciousness of your own identity." But that very "consciousness of your own identity" is the essence of the sense of separateness that pervades our society and that subverts the profound reality that All-is-One. In this way fear and ego go hand-in-hand and feed off of one another. Imagine the state of our world if I looked upon you, and you looked upon me, as "self" rather than as "other." Imagine living in a biological and societal paradigm of "cooperation" instead of "survival of the fittest." A mindset based upon competition has resulted in a situation where 16 percent of the world's population consumes almost 80 percent of its natural resources[381], where thousands of children starve to death while food rots in warehouses or is throw away. This is madness, and it is unforgiveable.

Because we live in a reality in which we perceive things as being separate we must, of necessity, employ an ego. But just because we perceive the world to be a certain way does not mean we have to *think* that way. In fact, to a large extent our thoughts influence our perceptions, so it behooves us to gain control of our egocentric mindset and tone it down several notches: for the sake of our own survival we must break free of the ego/fear cycle of self-destructive attitudes and behaviors and reset our thinking along the lines of unity, interconnectedness, and cooperation. Taming and moderating our egos is an essential step in that process.

Live a Healthy Lifestyle

Physical health is an important part of spiritual health. Our physical bodies are the vehicles our souls use while incarnating in this world. The healthier your body, the better equipped it is to get you through the challenges you will face. Unfortunately, it is usually not until we personally experience pain or limitation due to illness or injury that we truly appreciate the importance of good health. Alcohol and drugs dull the mind; in addition to the health problems they cause and the ensuing emotional and psychological distress, the net effect is one that is not conducive to spiritual growth – it's difficult to feel Love and gratitude, to release fear, and to acquire knowledge, when one is physically miserable. The healthier your body, the better you feel, and the better you feel, the healthier your outlook.

Thoughts are Things

In Chapter 6 I discussed how several books by Ruth Montgomery were the catalyst to opening my mind and setting me on a path of spiritual discovery. One of the key concepts she presented that particularly influenced me was the idea that "thoughts are things." In one sense we explored this notion in Chapter 18 where we saw how the mind can be used to influence reality, from healing through mental imagery or the placebo effect, to influencing events in external reality. Those examples exemplified the notion of "thoughts as things" in the sense that we can influence reality using the power of our minds. But there is another meaning to "thoughts are things," namely that everything done or created by humans has its origin in human thought. Inventions, ideologies, wars, problems, solutions to problems, … everything we humans make happen starts out as a thought in someone's mind. This realization places a huge importance on the thoughts we generate, since their future fruition could have dramatic consequences affecting large numbers of people. And *that* fact places a heavy responsibility upon us regarding the kinds of thoughts we allow to spring forth and evolve in our minds.

Once we understand the awesome potential for our seemingly innocent thoughts to manifest into reality we can appreciate the need to monitor our thoughts with greater care and discernment. We tend to think of our thoughts as self-contained, harmless, personal musings, and, as such, we believe that private thoughts are the one area where we can let loose with abandon. But the truth is that thoughts have much more power than we give them credit for, and they can make the transition from wisps of mental energy to manifestations in material reality without any conscious intention or awareness on our parts. Does an act of rape sometimes begin as an "innocent" sex fantasy? Does brutal dictatorship begin as an "innocent" power-trip fantasy? Does the creation of a violent movie or video game, originally intended as a source of entertainment, have unseen ramifications for society at large? I honestly think that we are obligated to be more attentive to the thoughts we have – and to think them through more thoroughly – before they have an opportunity to take form. Our material reality is born out of energy subjected to forms, and our minds appear to play a big role in shaping those forms. Our minds need to be tended to as one would a garden: flowers must be nurtured and weeds must be removed.

22.5 Reclaiming the Right to Think for Ourselves

Much of this book has dealt with theories about the origin and nature of reality. In modern society the two institutions that have separately laid claim to possessing the ultimate and exclusive truth in this area are science and religion. While mutually antagonistic, they do have one thing in common: both insist on doing the thinking for the rest of us. Religion tells us to stop thinking and accept its dogma on faith. Science, on the other hand, makes its dogma so complex that thinking about it is – for the average person – virtually impossible. Thus each institution has its appointed priest-class of specially trained experts standing ready to tell us how things are. Whatever their reasons, our two self-appointed arbiters of truth do not want us to think for ourselves – they happily take on the burden of interpreting obscure scriptural passages and incomprehensible formulas for the uninitiated masses. Thus we, the bulk of humanity, find ourselves living in a culture of imposed ignorance. It's disturbing to note that much of the slaughter and warfare throughout human history has been carried out in the name of *religion*, and that the weapons used to accomplish all that killing have been provided by *science*. Our two greatest institutions of wisdom have not been particularly successful in preserving, let alone improving, the quality of human life. Whether this is by design or the result of ineptitude is a topic for another book; what is of importance here is the realization that *the institutions of science and religion have failed us on a monumental scale, and they are the last two places we should be looking for guidance, wisdom, and answers*. It is imperative that we reclaim our minds from them and begin to think for ourselves.

22.6 Conclusion

I am firmly of the belief that the only conjectures that are conclusively provable are those of a mathematical nature; anything else must be assessed *a degree of acceptance* based upon the volume and quality of evidence that can be amassed in support of it. Even mainstream science cites "overwhelming supporting evidence" as grounds for accepting the "truth" of the Darwinian theory of evolution. But evidence isn't proof, and we must never lose sight of that distinction. Nevertheless, outside of the field of mathematics, amassed evidence is the best case we can make for the conditional acceptance of any theory. I honestly believe that the evidence presented throughout this book regarding the Afterlife, the Nature of Reality, and the Dimensional Shift, while far from conclusive, is dramatic and compelling. At the very least, it is worthy of serious consideration.

In the Introduction to this book I offered a list of theses I intended to develop and, hopefully, make convincing cases for. It is up to you now to judge whether or not I have succeeded. So, as a final summary of the important points made in this book, and as an aid in reviewing and reconsidering those points, I will close this book by reproducing that list below:

- There is an afterlife.
- Research has led to the establishment of a detailed model of the afterlife.
- The essential nature of human beings is spiritual and eternal.
- Karma and reincarnation are fundamental features of our spiritual existence.
- Our reality is not a physical reality.
- The true reality is an energy-information construct.
- Our reality is a perceived reality that is decoded by our senses and brain.
- We decode the energy-information construct into a holographic reality.
- The holographic illusion of reality serves as a school for spiritual growth.
- The Earth will soon undergo a dimensional shift.
- This dimensional shift will be accompanied by an evolutionary leap for humanity.

– END –

Notes

[1] Joseph Head and S. L. Cranston, <u>Reincarnation: The Phoenix Fire Mystery</u> (New York, NY: Warner Books, 1979) p. 8.

[2] Joseph M. Higgins and Chuck Bergman, <u>The Everything Guide to Evidence of the Afterlife</u> (Avon, MA: Adams Media, 2011) p. 29; <u>Many Mansions: The Edgar Cayce Story on Reincarnation</u> (New York, NY: Signet, 1999) p. 48.

[3] Discussions of the core components of the NDE can be found in virtually any book or web site that discusses basic near-death experiences, whether such sources are compendiums of the subject or detailed recountings of individual experiences. A simple web search on "near-death experience" will provide more examples than one could imagine. Here are just two of many: Daniel Neiman, "The Near Death 'Experience'" *NDERF*. Web. Accessed 4 Dec. 2014, <http://www.nderf.org/NDERF/Articles/ nde_general_info2.htm>; Dr. Bill Lansing, "NDE General Information" *NDERF*. Web. Accessed 4 Dec. 2014, <http://www.nderf.org/NDERF/Articles/NDE%20General%20Info.htm>.

[4] Michael Talbot, <u>The Holographic Universe</u> (New York, NY: HarperCollins, 1992) pp. 248-249; "Life review" *Wikipedia: The Free Encyclopedia*. Wikimedia Foundation, Inc. Web. 10 Oct. 2014. Accessed 20 Oct. 2014,. <http://en.wikipedia.org/wiki/Life_review>.

[5] "Pam Reynolds case" *Wikipedia: The Free Encyclopedia*. Wikimedia Foundation, Inc. 22 July 2004. Web. 9 Jul. 2014. Accessed 22 Oct., 2014, <http://en.wikipedia.org/wiki/Pam_Reynolds_case>.

[6] "BBC: PAM SEES GOD. NDE Pam Reynolds. Amazing! Full version! " [video file], *YouTube*. Web. 6 Apr 2009. Accessed 22 Oct. 2014, <http://www.youtube.com/watch?v=WNbdUEqDB-k>.

[7] Kenneth Ring, <u>Lessons from the Light</u> (Portsmouth, NH: Moment Point Press, Inc., 1998) pp. 64-66.

[8] Jeffrey Long and Paul Perry, <u>Evidence of the Afterlife: The Science of Near-Death Experiences</u> (New York, NY: HarperCollins, 2010) p. 44.

[9] Ibid., p. 141.

[10] Hurovitz, C., Dunn, S., Domhoff, G. W., & Fiss, H. (1999). The dreams of blind men and women: A replication and extension of previous findings. *Dreaming, 9*, 183-193.

[11] *op. cit.*, Long and Perry, p. 200.

[12] *op. cit.*, Higgins and Bergman, pp. 68-70.

[13] *op. cit.*, Long and Perry, p. 200.

[14] "Near-death experience." *Wikipedia: The Free Encyclopedia*. Wikimedia Foundation, Inc. 22 July 2004. Web. 10 Aug. 2004. <http://en.wikipedia.org/wiki/Near-death_experience>.

[15] "CONNECTICUT Q & A: KENNETH RING; 'You Never Recover Your Original Self'," The New York Times, 28 August 1988. <http://www.nytimes.com/1988/08/28/nyregion/connecticut-q-a-kenneth-ring-you-never-recover-your-original-self.html>

[16] Watchers 4, 81 min., Cinify, 2012, DVD.

[17] Eben Alexander, Proof of Heaven: A Neurosurgeon's Journey into the Afterlife (New York, NY: Simon & Schuster, Inc., 2012) p. 8.

[18] Ibid., p. 9.

[19] Ibid., p. 133.

[20] Ibid., p. 9.

[21] Cythia Logan, "Graduating from Kindergarten: Dr. Eben Alexander Speaks of Lessons Learned While 'Dead'," Atlantis Rising, Number 107 (September/October 2014): 64.

[22] Ibid., pp. 34-35.

[23] Ibid., p. 9.

[24] Ibid., page after p. 171, under title "Eternea."

[25] op. cit., Talbot, p. 268.

[26] op. cit., Ring, p. 5, 143, 181, 200; Op. Cit., Long and Perry, p. 193.

[27] Ibid., pp. 17-19, 30, 45-47, 49; Raymond A. Moody, Jr., Reflections on Life After Life (Stackpole Books) pp. 87-89.

[28] op. cit., Ring, p. 47.

[29] op. cit., Long and Perry, p. 174.

[30] op. cit., Ring, p. 5, 143, 181, 200; Op. Cit., Long and Perry, p. 193.

[31] op. cit., Ring, pp. 31-32, 124-128; Op. Cit., Long and Perry, pp. 145, 147, 174, 177-180, 193.

[32] "Near Death Experiences" AFTERLIFE EVIDENCE: Lawyer Victor Zammit on the scientific proof for Life after Death AND What happens when you die? Web. 19 Nov. 2013. Accessed 4 Dec. 2014, <http://www.victorzammit.com/evidence/nde.htm>.

[33] Calvin Conzelus Moore and John B. Williamson. "The Universal Fear of Death and the Cultural Response," <http://www.sagepub.com/upm-data/5233_Bryant_Sample_Article_Universal_Fear.pdf>

[34] op. cit., Head and Cranston, pp. 34-395; "Selections on Reincarnation in History," The Reincarnation Experiment, Accessed June 30, 2013, http://www.reincarnationexperiment.org/reincarnationhistory.html.

[35] Tristan Gulliford, "Terence McKenna's 'Alchemical Dream'," Reality Sandwich, Accessed June 30, 2013, <http://www.realitysandwich.com/alchemical_dream>.

[36] *op. cit.*, Head and Cranston, p. 1.

[37] "The Scole Phenomena," Afterlife 101, Accesssed June 30, 2013, <http://www.afterlife101.com/Scole_1.html>.

[38] Grant Solomon and Jane Solomon, The Scole Experiment: Scientific Evidence for Life After Death, (Campion Books, 2012) Author Update February 2006.

[39] Jim Tucker, Life Before Life: Children's Memories of Previous Lives (New York, NY: St. Martin's Press, 2005) pp. xiv, 17-22; Op. Cit., Head and Cranston, pp. 433-440; David Fontana, Is There An Afterlife?, (UK: O Books, 2005) pp. 438-440.; Op. Cit., Talbot, pp. 217-219; "Reincarnation research" *Wikipedia: The Free Encyclopedia.* Wikimedia Foundation, Inc. 22 July 2004. Web. 10 Aug. 2004. Accesssed July 4, 2013, <http://en.wikipedia.org/wiki/Reincarnation_ research>.

[40] *op. cit.*, Tucker, p. 20.

[41] *op. cit.*, Tucker, p. 20.

[42] *op. cit.*, Tucker, pp. 11-16; Op. Cit., Fontana, pp. 438-440; "Scientific Proof of Reincarnation Dr. Ian Stevenson's Life Work," The Reluctant Messenger, Accessed July 4, 2013, <http://reluctant-messenger.com/reincarnation-proof.htm>; "Reincarnation research" Wikipedia: The Free Encyclopedia. Wikimedia Foundation, Inc. 22 July 2004. Web. 10 Aug. 2004. Accessed July 4, 2013, <http://en.wikipedia.org/wiki/Reincarnation_research>.

[43] "Scientific Proof of Reincarnation Dr. Ian Stevenson's Life Work," The Reluctant Messenger, Accesssed July 4, 2013, <http://reluctant-messenger.com/reincarnation-proof.htm>.

[44] "Could a Little Boy Be Proof of Reincarnation?" Reverse Spins. Accessed July 4, 2013, <http://www.reversespins.com/proofofreincarnation.html>; Fox8 News [Video file]. Retrieved from http://www.youtube.com/watch?v=SF3KqGpxXvo. Accesssed July 4, 2013.

[45] *op. cit.*, Fontana, p. 429.

[46] *op. cit.*, Fontana, p. 430-431; Op. Cit., Talbot, pp. 295-296; Bruce Goldberg, Past Lives, Future Lives (New York, NY: Ballantine Books, 1991) pp. 61-62; "Brian Weiss" *Wikipedia: The Free Encyclopedia.* Wikimedia Foundation, Inc. 22 July 2004. Web. 10 Aug. 2004. Accesssed July 5, 2013, <https://en.wikipedia.org/wiki/Brian_Weiss>.

[47] *op. cit.*, Goldberg, pp. 57-58.

[48] Joel L. Whitton and Joe Fisher, Life Between Life (Garden City, NY: A Dolphin Book, 1986) p. 156; Op. Cit., Head and Cranston, pp. 402-403; Leonardo Vintini. "Xenoglossy: Evidence of Past Lives?" The Epoch Times. (Oct. 26, 2012), Accesssed July 5, 2013, <http://www.theepochtimes.com/n2/science/xenoglossy-cryptonesia-dr-stevenson-past-lives-4150.html>;

[49] "Unlearned Language: New Studies in Xenoglossy by Dr. Ian Stevenson, The University Press of Virginia, 1984" Afterlife101. Accessed July 5, 2013 <http://www.afterlife101.com/ Xenoglossy.html>.

[50] *op. cit.*, Fontana, pp. 432-434; Op. Cit., Talbot, p. 224; Op. Cit., Whitton and Fisher, p. 63.

[51] *op. cit.*, Fontana, p. 433-434; Op. Cit., Whitton and Fisher, p. 63.

[52] Ruth Montgomery, Here and Hereafter (New York, NY: Ballantine Books, 1985).

[53] Ruth Montgomery, A World Beyond (Greenwich, CT: Fawcett Crest Books, 1971).

[54] Michael Newton, Journey of Souls (St. Paul, MN: Llewellyn Publications, 2000) pp 3-5.

[55] Michael Newton, Journey of Souls (St. Paul, MN: Llewellyn Publications, 2000) p 193; Michael Newton, Destiny of Souls (St. Paul, MN: Llewellyn Publications, 2000) p 7.

[56] Dolores Cannon, Between Death and Life (Huntsville, AR: Ozark Mountain Publishers, 2001) pp 45, 61, 113-114,186-188; ; Joe H. Slate, Beyond Reincarnation: Experience Your Past Lives and Lives Between Lives (Woodbury, MN: Llewellyn Publications 2008) pp18-19, 25, 87-88; Robert Schwartz, Courageous Souls: Do We Plan Our Life Challenges Before Birth? (Whispering Winds Press, 2007) pp 29-31, 45, 92-93.

[57] Journey of Souls, *op. cit.*, pp 61, 203, 206; Between Death and Life, *op. cit.*, pp 181, 228; Beyond Reincarnation: Experience Your Past Lives and Lives Between Lives, *op. cit.*, pp 88, 96; Courageous Souls: Do We Plan Our Life Challenges Before Birth?, *op. cit.*, pp 21, 28-31, 101; From Birth to Rebirth: Gnostic Healing for the 21st Century, *op. cit.*, p 46.

[58] Journey of Souls, *op. cit.*, pp 213-214, 260; Destiny of Souls, *op. cit.*, pp 362, 371; Beyond Reincarnation: Experience Your Past Lives and Lives Between Lives, *op. cit.*, p 97; ; From Birth to Rebirth: Gnostic Healing for the 21st Century, *op. cit.*, p 51; Courageous Souls: Do We Plan Our Life Challenges Before Birth?, *op. cit.*, p 24.

[59] Journey of Souls, *op. cit.*, pp 77, 83-88,129,141-142,145; Destiny of Souls, *op. cit.*, pp 4, 191-194, 264-265, 275.; Between Death and Life, *op. cit.*, p 183; Beyond Reincarnation: Experience Your Past Lives and Lives Between Lives, *op. cit.*, pp 92-93; C.V. Tramont, From Birth to Rebirth: Gnostic Healing for the 21st Century (Columbus, NC: Swan-Raven & Co.,2009) pp 137, 222-223.

[60] Journey of Souls, *op. cit.*, pp 88, 115, 250; Destiny of Souls, *op. cit.*, pp 262-266; Courageous Souls: Do We Plan Our Life Challenges Before Birth?, *op. cit.*, p 194.

[61] Journey of Souls, *op. cit.*, pp 91-94; Destiny of Souls, *op. cit.*, pp 150-152, 157-169; Between Death and Life, *op. cit.*, pp 36-39, 47, 74-75.

[62] Journey of Souls, *op. cit.*, pp 107-110, 112, 115, 117, 119-121; Between Death and Life, *op. cit.*, pp 132-134, 182; Beyond Reincarnation: Experience Your Past Lives and Lives Between Lives, *op. cit.*, p 92; From Birth to Rebirth: Gnostic Healing for the 21st Century, *op. cit.*, pp 188, 195.

[63] Journey of Souls, *op. cit.*, pp 69-70, 85-86; Destiny of Souls, *op. cit.*, pp 8, 155, 201, 204-207, 210-216, 251-253; Between Death and Life, *op. cit.*, p 139; From Birth to Rebirth: Gnostic Healing for the 21st Century, *op. cit.*, pp 221-222, 232; Beyond Reincarnation: Experience Your Past Lives and Lives Between Lives, *op. cit.*, p 92.

[64] Journey of Souls, *op. cit.,* pp 203, 206-213, 216-217, 221, 226-227, 253-256; Destiny of Souls, *op. cit.,* pp 355-357, 362-363; ; Between Death and Life, *op. cit.,* p 228; Courageous Souls: Do We Plan Our Life Challenges Before Birth?, *op. cit.,* p 21.

[65] Journey of Souls, *op. cit.,* pp 100-103; Destiny of Souls, *op. cit.,* pp 5-6.

[66] Journey of Souls, *op. cit.,* p 38; Destiny of Souls, *op. cit.,* pp 211, 307; From Birth to Rebirth: Gnostic Healing for the 21st Century, *op. cit.,* pp 99, 221.

[67] Journey of Souls, *op. cit.,* pp 160, 195; Destiny of Souls, *op. cit.,* p 361; Between Death and Life, *op. cit.,* p 8; Courageous Souls: Do We Plan Our Life Challenges Before Birth?, *op. cit.,* p 69; From Birth to Rebirth: Gnostic Healing for the 21st Century, *op. cit.,* pp 39-40; Dying to be Me: My Journey from Cancer, to Near Death, to True Healing (Carlsbad, CA: Hay House, Inc., 2012) pp 67, 142.

[68] Journey of Souls, *op. cit.,* pp 189, 275; Destiny of Souls, *op. cit.,* pp 130-131, 243-244, 247-249.

[69] Journey of Souls, *op. cit.,* pp 9, 17.

[70] Journey of Souls, *op. cit.,* pp 19-24.

[71] Journey of Souls, *op. cit.,* pp 23-30.

[72] Journey of Souls, *op. cit.,* pp 34-35.

[73] Journey of Souls, *op. cit.,* pp 53-54.

[74] Journey of Souls, *op. cit.,* pp 55-70.

[75] Journey of Souls, *op. cit.,* pp 107-110, 112, 115, 117, 119-121.

[76] Journey of Souls, *op. cit.,* pp 69-70, 85-86; Destiny of Souls, *op. cit.,* pp 8, 155, 201, 204-207, 210-216, 251-253.

[77] Journey of Souls, *op. cit.,* pp 85-86; Destiny of Souls, *op. cit.,* p 204.

[78] Destiny of Souls, *op. cit.,* p 214.

[79] Journey of Souls, *op. cit.,* pp 91-94; Destiny of Souls, *op. cit.,* pp 150-152, 157-169.

[80] Journey of Souls, *op. cit.,* pp 162-168.

[81] Journey of Souls, *op. cit.,* pp 30, 59, 157, 190, 201, 263; Destiny of Souls, *op. cit.,* pp 252, 352, 371, 401.

[82] Journey of Souls, *op. cit.,* pp 204-205; Destiny of Souls, *op. cit.,* pp 211; Between Death and Life, *op. cit.,* pp 41, 89, 139; Beyond Reincarnation: Experience Your Past Lives and Lives Between Lives, *op. cit.,* p96.

[83] From Birth to Rebirth: Gnostic Healing for the 21st Century, *op. cit.,* p 232.

[84] Journey of Souls, *op. cit.*, pp 203, 206-207, 221-222, 226-227, 246; Between Death and Life, *op. cit.*, pp 228-233; Courageous Souls: Do We Plan Our Life Challenges Before Birth?, *op. cit.*, pp 21, 31, 45, 101.

[85] Journey of Souls, *op. cit.*, pp 207-213, 216-218; Destiny of Souls, *op. cit.*, pp 252, 355-360, 362-365.

[86] Journey of Souls, *op. cit.*, pp 253-256, 258-261; Destiny of Souls, *op. cit.*, p 274; Between Death and Life, *op. cit.*, p 181; Courageous Souls: Do We Plan Our Life Challenges Before Birth?, *op. cit.*, p 194.

[87] Journey of Souls, *op. cit.*, pp 67-68, 213; Destiny of Souls, *op. cit.*, pp 396-398; Courageous Souls: Do We Plan Our Life Challenges Before Birth?, *op. cit.*, p 22.

[88] Journey of Souls, *op. cit.*, p 263.

[89] Journey of Souls, *op. cit.*, p 272.

[90] Journey of Souls, *op. cit.*, pp 72, 122; Destiny of Souls, *op. cit.*, pp 130-131.

[91] Journey of Souls, *op. cit.*, p 189; Destiny of Souls, *op. cit.*, p 247.

[92] Journey of Souls, *op. cit.*, pp 193-194; Destiny of Souls, *op. cit.*, pp 247-248; Between Death and Life, *op. cit.*, pp 143-144, 147-148.

[93] Journey of Souls, *op. cit.*, p 275.

[94] Destiny of Souls, *op. cit.*, pp 243-248.

[95] Journey of Souls, *op. cit.*, p 49; Destiny of Souls, *op. cit.*, pp 74-76; Between Death and Life, *op. cit.*, pp 105-106; Is There An Afterlife?, *op. cit.*, p 464.

[96] Reflections on Life After Life, *op. cit.*, p 33.

[97] "Frightening and Hell-Like NDEs," Dr. Penny Sartori, July 26, 2011, accessed August 23, 2013, < http://drpennysartori.wordpress.com/2011/07/26/frightening-and-hell-like-ndes/>; "The NDE and Hell," accessed August 23, 2013, < http://www.near-death.com/experiences/research14.html>.

[98] Between Death and Life, *op. cit.*, p 106.

[99] Destiny of Souls, *op. cit.*, pp 74-76; A World Beyond, *op. cit.*, pp 64-65; Between Death and Life, *op. cit.*, pp 155-157.

[100] Journey of Souls, *op. cit.*, pp 46-52; Destiny of Souls, *op. cit.*, pp 93-95, 101-104; Between Death and Life, *op. cit.*, pp 58, 105, 156-157.

[101] Journey of Souls, *op. cit.*, p 49; Destiny of Souls, *op. cit.*, p 3.

[102] Journey of Souls, *op. cit.*, pp 30, 157, 190, 263; Destiny of Souls, *op. cit.*, pp 352, 371, 401.

[103] Journey of Souls, *op. cit.*, p 9; Between Death and Life, *op. cit.*, p 27.

[104] Note: In this section I will not repeat the footnote citations relating to NDEs (unless a new reference was used), as these references can be found in the notes for Chapter 2; instead I will only provide citations for the LBL content presented. Journey of Souls, op. cit., pp 160, 195; Destiny of Souls, op. cit., p 361; Between Death and Life, op. cit., p 8; Courageous Souls: Do We Plan Our Life Challenges Before Birth?, op. cit., p 69; From Birth to Rebirth: Gnostic Healing for the 21st Century, op. cit., pp 39-40; Dying to be Me: My Journey from Cancer, to Near Death, to True Healing (Carlsbad, CA: Hay House, Inc., 2012) pp 67, 142.

[105] Journey of Souls, op. cit., pp 30, 56, 59; Destiny of Souls, op. cit., pp 43-44, 252, 352, 371.

[106] Journey of Souls, op. cit., pp 3, 19, 56, 77 ; Destiny of Souls, op. cit., p 4, 401.

[107] Journey of Souls, op. cit., p 196; Destiny of Souls, op. cit., p 135.

[108] Destiny of Souls, op. cit., p 10; Between Death and Life, op. cit., pp 39, 60, 96, 110-111, 236; Beyond Reincarnation: Experience Your Past Lives and Lives Between Lives, op. cit., p 92; Courageous Souls: Do We Plan Our Life Challenges Before Birth?, op. cit., pp 31, 46, 103, 160, 201, 273, 309, 317; From Birth to Rebirth: Gnostic Healing for the 21st Century, op. cit., pp 46-47.

[109] Journey of Souls, op. cit., pp 67-68, 162, 181; Destiny of Souls, op. cit., pp 130, 396-398; Courageous Souls: Do We Plan Our Life Challenges Before Birth?, op. cit., pp 22, 125, 206.

[110] Journey of Souls, op. cit., pp 241-242, 266, 269-270; Destiny of Souls, op. cit., pp 8-9, 193, 198, 385, 387-394.

[111] Journey of Souls, op. cit., p 270; Destiny of Souls, op. cit., pp 391-393.

[112] Journey of Souls, op. cit., pp 77, 193 ; Destiny of Souls, op. cit., pp 6-7, 194.

[113] Journey of Souls, op. cit., p 30; Destiny of Souls, op. cit., p 43.

[114] Destiny of Souls, op. cit., p 43.

[115] Whitley Strieber, The Key: A True Encounter, (New York, NY: Penguin Group, 2011) pp 105, 188-189, 215.

[116] The Key: A True Encounter, op. cit., p 87.

[117] John Chambers, "Machines to Talk to the Dead: Thomas A. Edison, W.B. Yeats, and Instrumental Transcommunication," Atlantis Rising, Number 92 (March/April 2012): 41, 68-69.

[118] "Thomas Edison and the Ghost in the Machine," Paranormal-Encyclopedia.com, accessed Sep 4, 2013, < http://www.paranormal-encyclopedia.com/e/thomas-edison/>; Tim Woolworth, "Thomas Edison and his Mysterious Telephone to the Dead," ITC Voices, Feb. 6, 2011, accessed Sep 4, 2013, < http://itcvoices.org/thomas-edisons-telephone-to-the-dead-myth-or-fact/>.

[119] "List of Edison patents," Wikipedia: The Free Encyclopedia. Wikimedia Foundation, Inc. 22 July 2004. Web. March 18, 2013, accessed Sep 4, 2013, < http://en.wikipedia.org/wiki/List_of_Edison_patents>.

[120] Journey of Souls, *op. cit.,* p 115.

[121] Journey of Souls, *op. cit.,* p 115.

[122] Journey of Souls, *op. cit.,* p 203.

[123] Journey of Souls, *op. cit.,* p 202.

[124] "Materialism" *Wikipedia: The Free Encyclopedia.* Wikimedia Foundation, Inc. 22 July 2004. Web. 2 Sep. 2013. Accesssed Oct. 1, 2013, <http://en.wikipedia.org/wiki/Materialism>.

[125] *op. cit.,* Talbot, p. 163.

[126] "Brain's visual circuits edit what we see before we see it" *Kurzweil Accelerating Intelligence.* Web. 10 Dec. 2010. Accesssed Oct. 9, 2013, <http://www.kurzweilai.net/brain%E2%80%99s-visual-circuits-do-error-correction-on-the-flyerror-correction-on-the-fly>.

[127] *op. cit.,* Talbot, p. 163.

[128] "Paul Bach-y-Rita" *Wikipedia: The Free Encyclopedia.* Wikimedia Foundation, Inc. 22 July 2004. Web. 8 Apr. 2014. Accessed 21 June 2014. < http://en.wikipedia.org/wiki/Paul_Bach-y-Rita>; Michael Abrams, Dan Winters, "Can You See With Your Tongue? The brain is so adaptable, some researchers now think, that any of the five senses can be rewired" *Discover.* Web. 1 June 2003. Accessed 21 June 2014; J.T. Busnhell, "The Heart and the Eye: How Description Can Access Emotion" Poets and Writers, Jan/Feb 2013: 51-52.

[129] Marc Abrahams, "Experiments show we quickly adjust to seeing everything upside-down" *theguardian.* Web. 12 Nov. 2012. Accessed 12 Oct. 2013, < http://www.theguardian.com/education/2012/nov/12/improbable-research-seeing-upside-down>; George M. Stratton, "SOME PRELIMINARY EXPERIMENTS ON VISION WITHOUT INVERSION OF THE RETINAL IMAGE" *The Center for Neural Science at NYU.* Web. Accessed 12 Oct. 2013, < http://www.cns.nyu.edu/~nava/courses/psych_and_brain/pdfs/Stratton_1896.pdf; "Psychology: Inversion Goggles" [video file], *YouTube.* Web. 25 May 2012. Accessed 12 Oct. 2013, < http://www.youtube.com/watch?v=OkbunXhR1s4>; "BBC about upside down goggles" [video file], *YouTube.* Web. 30 Aug. 2012. Accessed 12 Oct. 2013, < http://www.youtube.com/watch?v=-kohUpQwZt8>.

[130] Adam Gopnik, "Music to Your Ears: The Quest for 3D Recording and Other Mysteries of Sound," The New Yorker, (January 28, 2013): 34.

[131] Ibid., p. 37.

[132] "Missing fundamental" *Wikipedia: The Free Encyclopedia.* Wikimedia Foundation, Inc. 22 July 2004. Web. 26 Jan. 2014. Accessed 02 Feb. 2014. < http://en.wikipedia.org/wiki/Missing_fundamental>.

[133] "Definitions of mathematics" *Wikipedia: The Free Encyclopedia.* Wikimedia Foundation, Inc. Web. 26 Oct. 2013. Accessed 14 Nov. 2013. <http://en.wikipedia.org/wiki/Definition_of_mathematics>.

[134] Clifford A. Pickover, The Math Book, (New York, NY: Sterling Publishing, 2009), p. 362; Suman Ganguli, "Gödel's Incompleteness Theorems: History, Proofs, Implications" *The Brooklyn Institute for Social Research.* Web. Accessed 10 Nov. 2013. < http://thebrooklyninstitute.com/

bisr_course/godels-incompleteness-theorems-history-proofs-implications/>; Mark Wakim, "Gödel, and his Incompleteness Theorem," *UCLA Dept of Mathematics*. Web. Accessed 10 Nov. 2013. < http://www.math.ucla.edu/~rfioresi/hc41/Goedel.html>; "Can someone explain Gödel's incompleteness theorems in layman terms?" *Mathematics Stack Exchange*. Web. 27 Jul. 2013. Accessed 10 Nov. 2013. < http://math.stackexchange.com/questions/453503/can-someone-explain-godels-incompleteness-theorems-in-layman-terms>.

[135] "Theory of Everything" *Wikipedia: The Free Encyclopedia*. Wikimedia Foundation, Inc. 22 July 2004. Web. 31 Oct. 2013. Accessed 11 Nov. 2013. < http://en.wikipedia.org/wiki/Theory_of_everything#G.C3.B6del.27s_incompleteness_theorem>.

[136] David Cassidy, "Quantum Mechanics: The Uncertainty Principle" *American Institute of Physics*. Web. Accessed 11 Nov. 2013. < http://www.aip.org/history/heisenberg/p08.htm>; James Schombert, "Uncertainty Principle" *Department of Physics, University of Oregon*. Web. Accessed 11 Nov. 2013. < http://abyss.uoregon.edu/~js/21st_century_science/lectures/lec14.html>.

[137] James Schombert, "Uncertainty Principle" *Department of Physics, University of Oregon*. Web. Accessed 11 Nov. 2013. <http://abyss.uoregon.edu/~js/21st_century_science/lectures/lec14.html>.

[138] *op. cit.*, McTaggart, pp. 19, 102; "Copenhagen interpretation" *Wikipedia: The Free Encyclopedia*. Wikimedia Foundation, Inc. 22 July 2004. Web. 11 Nov. 2013. Accessed 11 Nov. 2013. <http://en.wikipedia.org/wiki/Copenhagen_interpretation>.

[139] *Einstein's Relativity and the Quantum Revolution: Modern Physics for Non-Scientists, 2nd Edition*, taught by: Professor Richard Wolfson, Lecture 20: Particle or Wave? DVD. The Teaching Company, 2000.

[140] James Gleick, Chaos: Making a New Science, (New York, NY: Penguin Books, 1988) p. 6.

[141] "Chaos theory" *Wikipedia: The Free Encyclopedia*. Wikimedia Foundation, Inc. 22 July 2004. Web. 28 Dec. 2013. Accesssed 31 Dec. 2013, <http://en.wikipedia.org/wiki/Chaos_theory>.

[142] Ibid., p. 68.

[143] Ibid., p. 68.

[144] "Richard Feynman" *Wikipedia: The Free Encyclopedia*. Wikimedia Foundation, Inc. 22 July 2004. Web. 19 Nov. 2013. Accessed 20 Nov. 2013. <http://en.wikiquote.org/wiki/Richard_Feynman>.

[145] *op. cit.*, Pickover, p. 422; Dana Gaynor, " Physics and Mathematics on the Nature of Reality" *Dana Gaynor: Online. The Journal Of Psychospiritual Transformation, Issue 4, July 2003*. Web. Accessed 20 Nov. 2013. <http://www.danagaynor.com/JPT/issue%204/physics,%20inertia%20and%20chaos%20 theory.htm>.

[146] *op. cit.*,Pickover, p. 422; *op. cit.*, Gleick, pp. 21-23; *op. cit.*, Gaynor.

[147] *op. cit.*, Gleick, pp. 22-23, 44-45, 79.

[148] Heinz-Otto Peitgen, Hartmut Jurgens, and Dietmar Saupe, Chaos and Fractals: New Frontiers of Science (New York, NY: Springer, 1992) p 52.

[149] *op. cit.*,Pickover, p. 460; "Fractal" *Wikipedia: The Free Encyclopedia*. Wikimedia Foundation, Inc. 22 July 2004. Web. 25 Dec. 2013. Accessed 31 Dec. 2013. <http://en.wikipedia.org/wiki/Fractal>.

[150] *op. cit.*, Gleick, p. 98.

[151] "Self-similarity" *Wikipedia: The Free Encyclopedia*. Wikimedia Foundation, Inc. 22 July 2004. Web. 24 Dec. 2013. Accessed 30 Mar. 2014. < http://en.wikipedia.org/wiki/Self-similarity>.

[152] "Big Bang Theory - The Premise" *AllAboutScience.org*. Web. Accessed 2 Jan. 2014, <http://www.big-bang-theory.com/>; Jerry Coffey, "What is the Big Bang Theory" *Universe Today*. Web. 7 Feb. 2010. Accessed 2 Jan. 2014, <http://www.universetoday.com/54756/what-is-the-big-bang-theory/>; "Big Bang" *Wikipedia: The Free Encyclopedia*. Wikimedia Foundation, Inc. 22 July 2004. Web. 1 Jan. 2014. Accessed 2 Jan. 2014. <http://en.wikipedia.org/wiki/Big_Bang>.

[153] "Charles Darwin" *Wikipedia: The Free Encyclopedia*. Wikimedia Foundation, Inc. 22 July 2004. Web. 15 Jan. 2014. Accessed 22 Jan. 2014. <http://en.wikipedia.org/wiki/Charles_Darwin>.

[154] "Darwin's Theory of Evolution" *AllAboutScience.org*. Web. Accessed 22 Jan. 2014. <http://www.darwins-theory-of-evolution.com/>.

[155] Dr. Laurence Loewe, "Genetic Mutation" *Scitable by nature education*. Web. 2008. Accessed 26 Jan. 2014, < http://www.nature.com/scitable/topicpage/genetic-mutation-1127>.

[156] As quoted in: Richard William Nelson, Darwin, Then and Now: The Most Amazing Story in the History of Science, (Bloomington, IN: iUniverse: 2009) p. 183.

[157] "Cambrian Explosion" *Wikipedia: The Free Encyclopedia*. Wikimedia Foundation, Inc. 22 July 2004. Web. 26 Jan. 2014. Accessed 29 Jan. 2014. <http://en.wikipedia.org/wiki/Cambrian_explosion>; *Darwin's Dilemma*, DVD. Illustra Media, 2009.

[158] Michael J. Behe, Darwin's Black Box: The Biochemical Challenge to Evolution, (New York, NY: Touchstone, 1996) p. 39.

[159] Charles Darwin, On the Origin of Species, (Hazleton, PA: Electronic Classics Series, 2001-13) p. 173. [This is a pdf document, accessed from: http://www2.hn.psu.edu/faculty/jmanis/darwin/originspecies.pdf]

[160] Casey Luskin, "Molecular Machines in the Cell" *Center for Science and Culture*. Web. 11 Jun. 2010. Accessed 30 Jan. 2014., <http://www.discovery.org/a/14791>.

[161] *op. cit.*, Behe, pp. 4-5.

[162] Ibid., pp. 70-73.

[163] "Bacterial Flagellum" [video file], *YouTube*. Web. 20 Apr 2009. Accessed 30 Jan. 2014, < http://www.youtube.com/watch?v=Ey7Emmddf7Y>; Unlocking the Mystery of Life, 67 min., Illustra Media, 2003, DVD.

---

[164] Transcript of *Kitzmiller v. Dover* Trial, pm session, Nov. 3, 2005, p. 102. [transcript accessed in pdf format on the web: http://ncse.com/files/pub/legal/kitzmiller/trial_transcripts/2005_1103_day20_pm.pdf].

[165] Unlocking the Mystery of Life, 67 min., Illustra Media, 2003, DVD.

[166] *op. cit.*, Luskin: see the "Selected list of molecular machines" at the end of the article.

[167] Dr. John Ankerberg and Dr. John Weldon, " The Evolution of Life, Probability Considerations and Common Sense-Part 3" *The John Ankerberg Show*. Web. 2002. Accessed 31 Jan. 2014, <http://www.jashow.org/wiki/index.php?title=The_Evolution_of_Life,_Probability_Considerations_and_Common_Sense-Part_3>.

[168] " Statistical Probability of Evolution challenged" [video file], *YouTube*. Web. 29 Aug. 2009. Accessed 31 Jan. 2014, < http://www.youtube.com/watch?v=ai-DXFXZr8s>; David Berlinski, "Darwin and the Mathematicians" *Evolution News and Views*. Web. 7 Nov. 2009. Accessed 31 Jan. 2014, < http://www.evolutionnews.org/2009/11/darwin_and_the_mathematicians027911.html>

[169] John W. Oller, Jr., " Not According to Hoyle" *Institute for Creation Research*. Web. Accessed 31 Jan. 2014, < http://www.icr.org/article/243/>.

[170] Stuart A. Umpleby, "Physical Relationships Among Matter, Energy and Information," Systems Research and Behavioral Science, Vol. 24, No. 3 (2007): 369-372.

[171] Norbert Wiener as quoted in: "Norbert Wiener" *The Information Philosopher*. Web. Accessed 01 Feb. 2014, < http://www.informationphilosopher.com/solutions/scientists/wiener/>.

[172] Rene Fester Kratz, Molecular and Cell Biology for Dummies (Hoboken, NJ: Wiley Publishing, Inc. 2009) pp 267-268; "What is DNA?" *Genetics Home Reference*. Web. 3 Feb. 2014. Accessed 8 Feb. 2014, < http://ghr.nlm.nih.gov/handbook/basics/dna>; "What are proteins and what do they do?" *Genetics Home Reference*. Web. 3 Feb. 2014. Accessed 8 Feb. 2014, < http://ghr.nlm.nih.gov/handbook/ howgeneswork/protein>; Christian Nordqvist "What is a gene? What are genes?" *MNT (Medical News Today)*. Web. 2 Sep. 2013. Accessed 8 Feb. 2014, < http://www.medicalnewstoday.com/articles /120574.php>.

[173] Rene Fester Kratz, Molecular and Cell Biology for Dummies (Hoboken, NJ: Wiley Publishing, Inc. 2009) pp 267-274; " How do genes direct the production of proteins? " *Genetics Home Reference*. Web. 3 Feb. 2014. Accessed 9 Feb. 2014, < http://ghr.nlm.nih.gov/handbook/howgeneswork/makingprotein >; Sarah-Neena Koch, "DNA, the Brain, and Human Behavior " *MyBrainNotes.com*. Web. Accessed 9 Feb. 2014, < http://mybrainnotes.com/brain-dna-behavior.html >.

[174] Rene Fester Kratz, Molecular and Cell Biology for Dummies (Hoboken, NJ: Wiley Publishing, Inc. 2009) pp 328-329; "Noncoding DNA" *Wikipedia: The Free Encyclopedia*. Wikimedia Foundation, Inc. 22 July 2004. Web. 10 Feb. 2014. Accessed 10 Feb. 2014, <http://en.wikipedia.org/wiki/Noncoding_DNA>; "Junk DNA - What is Junk DNA?" *News Medical*. Web. Accessed 10 Feb. 2014. <http://www.news-medical.net/health/Junk-DNA-What-is-Junk-DNA.aspx>; "Susumu Ohno" *Wikipedia: The Free Encyclopedia*. Wikimedia Foundation, Inc. 22 July 2004. Web. 8 Feb. 2014. Accessed 10 Feb. 2014,

< http://en.wikipedia.org/wiki/Susumu_Ohno>.

[175] Karl S. Kruszelnicki, " Language in junk DNA" *ABC Science*. Web.04 Apr. 2001. Accesses 13 Feb. 2014, < http://www.abc.net.au/science/articles/2001/04/04/133634.htm>; R.N. Mantegna, et al, "Linguistic Features of Noncoding DNA Sequences", Physical Review Letters, vol 73 no 23 (5 Dec 1994): 3169-3172; Timothy G. Standish, "Rushing to Judgment: Functionality in Noncoding or 'Junk' DNA" *Geoscience Research Institute*. Web. 2002. Accesses 13 Feb. 2014. < http://www.grisda.org/origins/53007.pdf>.

[176] Timothy G. Standish, "Rushing to Judgment: Functionality in Noncoding or 'Junk' DNA" *Geoscience Research Institute*. Web. 2002. Accesses 13 Feb. 2014. < http://www.grisda.org/origins/53007.pdf>.

[177] April Cashin-Garbutt, " What are introns and exons?" *News Medical*. Web. Accessed 13 Feb. 2014, < http://www.news-medical.net/health/What-are-introns-and-exons.aspx>.

[178] Bruce Lipton, The Biology of Belief: Unleashing the Power of Consciousness, Matter and Miracles (Santa Rosa, CA: Mountain of Love/Elite Books, 2005) pp 22-23, 52, 60-61.

[179] Ibid., pp. 15, 26, 50-52.

[180] Ibid., pp. 67-73; "Epigenetics" *Wikipedia: The Free Encyclopedia*. Wikimedia Foundation, Inc. 22 July 2004. Web. 20 Feb. 2014. Accesssed 24 Feb. 2014, <http://en.wikipedia.org/wiki/Epigenetics>.

[181] Ibid., pp. 67-73.

[182] "Set (mathematics)" *Wikipedia: The Free Encyclopedia*. Wikimedia Foundation, Inc. 22 July 2004. Web. 6 Mar. 2014. Accessed 8 Mar. 2014, <http://en.wikipedia.org/wiki/Set_%28mathematics%29>.

[183] James R. Newman, The World of Mathematics, Volume One (Redmond, Washington: Tempus Books of Microsoft Press, 1956, 1988) pp 28-29.

[184] *op. cit*., Pickover, p. 124; "Applications of Imaginary Numbers" *The Math forum@Drexel: Ask Dr. Math*. 14 Oct. 1997. Accessed 10 Mar. 2014. <http://mathforum.org/library/drmath/view/53606.html>; "Using Imaginary Numbers" *The Math forum@Drexel: Ask Dr. Math*. 4 May 2001. Accessed 10 Mar. 2014. < http://mathforum.org/library/drmath/view/53879.html>.

[185] *op. cit*., Newman, p. 29.

[186] "A Visual, Intuitive Guide to Imaginary Numbers" *Better Explained*. Web. 21 Dec. 2007. Accessed 10 Mar. 2014. < http://betterexplained.com/articles/a-visual-intuitive-guide-to-imaginary-numbers/>.

[187] Ibid.

[188] Lloyd Motz, Jefferson Hane Weaver, The Story of Mathematics (New York, NY: Avon Books, 1993) pp. 73-74, 266-267.

[189] *op. cit*., Motz and Weaver, p. 266.

[190] *op. cit*., Motz and Weaver, pp. 264-266; *op. cit*., Pickover, p. 264.

[191] *op. cit.*, Pickover, p. 264.

[192] *op. cit.*, Motz and Weaver, pp. 266-268; *op. cit.*, Pickover, p. 264.

[193] *op. cit.*, Motz and Weaver, pp. 266-268; *op. cit.*, Pickover, p. 264.

[194] *op. cit.*, Newman, p. 501.

[195] W. Gellert, H. Kustner, M. Hellwich, H. Kastner, The VNR Concise Encyclopedia of Mathematics (New York, NY: Van Nostrand Reinhold Company, 1977) p. 675.

[196] Ibid., p. 675; *op. cit.*, Pickover, p. 234.

[197] *op. cit.*, Newman, p. 504; *op. cit.*, Pickover, p. 234.

[198] "James Lighthill" *Wikipedia: The Free Encyclopedia*. Wikimedia Foundation, Inc. 22 July 2004. Web. 9 Jan. 2014. Accesssed 21 Mar. 2014, <http://en.wikipedia.org/wiki/James_Lighthill>.

[199] Lokenath Debnath, as quoted in: Lokenath Debnath, "Sir James Lighthill And Modern Fluid Mechanics A Memorial Tribute" International Journal of Mathematics and Mathematical Sciences, Vol. 22, No. 4 (1999): 667–688, available here: <http://www.emis.de/journals/HOA/IJMMS/22/4667.pdf>

[200] Crystal Ives, "Human Beings as Chaotic Systems". Web. Accessed 24 Mar. 2014. < http://physics. oregonstate.edu/~stetza/ph407H/Chaos.pdf>.

[201] William Tucker, "Understanding E = mc2" *Energy Tribune*. Web. 21 Oct. 2009. Accessed 14 Oct. 2013, < http://www.energytribune.com/2771/understanding-e-mc2#sthash.kOfSlAl2.vbGO39Te.dpbs>.

[202] Lynne McTaggart, The Field: The Quest for the Secret Force of the Universe (New York, NY: Quill, 2003) p 33.

[203] Bernard Haisch, Alfonso Rueda & H.E. Puthoff, "BEYOND E=mc^2: A first glimpse of a postmodern physics, in which mass, inertia and gravity arise from underlying electromagnetic processes" published in THE SCIENCES, Vol. 34, No. 6, November / December 1994, pp. 26-31, New York Academy of Sciences, and posted on the Calphysics Institute web site < http://www.calphysics.org/haisch/sciences.html>. Accessed 14 Oct. 2013.

[204] Andrew Zimmerman Jones, "Matter" *About.com Physics*. Web. Accessed 14 Oct. 2013, < http://physics.about.com/od/glossary/g/Matter.htm>.

[205] Meinard Kuhlmann, "What is Real?", Scientific American, (August 2013): 45.

[206] "String Theory" *Wikipedia: The Free Encyclopedia*. Wikimedia Foundation, Inc. 22 July 2004. Web. 14 Oct. 2013. Accesssed 18 Oct. 2013, <http://en.wikipedia.org/wiki/String_theory>.

[207] "What is Consciousness?" [video file], *Deepak Chopra*. Web. 4 Sep. 2013. Accessed 20 Oct. 2013, < https://www.deepakchopra.com/video/view/440/the_rabbit_hole__what_is_consciousness%3F_%28animated_special%29 >.

[208] "The Holographic Universe Workshops" [video series] *The Holographic Universe.* Web. Accesssed 20 Oct. 2013, <http://www.holographicuniverseworkshops.com/>.

[209] "What is Reality? Kabbalah and the Perception of Reality" *Kabbalah.* Web. Accessed 25 Oct. 2013. <http://www.kabbalah.info/engkab/what_is_kabbalah/what_is_reality.htm>.

[210] David A. Cooper, God is a Verb: Kabbalah and the Practice of Mystical Judaism, (New York, NY: Riverhead Books, 1998) p. 11.

[211] Peter Russell, "The Illusion of Reality", *Peter Russell Spirit of Now.* Excerpt from Peter Russell's book FROM SCIENCE TO GOD: A Physicist's Journey Into the Mystery of Consciousness. Web. Accessed 26 Oct. 2013. < http://www.peterrussell.com/SG/ch4.php>.

[212] Paraphrase of Dr. Stuart Hameroff from "The Holographic Universe Workshops" [video series] *The Holographic Universe.* Web. Accesssed 20 Oct. 2013, <http://www.holographicuniverseworkshops.com/>.

[213] "Electron" *Wikipedia: The Free Encyclopedia.* Wikimedia Foundation, Inc. 22 July 2004. Web. 25 Oct. 2013. Accessed 26 Oct. 2013, <http://en.wikipedia.org/wiki/Electron#Quantum_mechanics>.

[214] *op. cit.*, Talbot, p. 33.

[215] Meinard Kuhlmann, "What is Real?", Scientific American, (August 2013): 44.

[216] "Young Two-Slit Experiment", *James Schombert v6.3 Department of Physics University of Oregon - 21st Century Science.* Web. Accessed 27 Oct. 2013. < http://abyss.uoregon.edu/~js/21st_century_science/lectures/lec13.html>; *op. cit.*, Talbot, p. 33-34; "Double-slit experiment" *Wikipedia: The Free Encyclopedia.* Wikimedia Foundation, Inc. 22 July 2004. Web. 27 Oct. 2013. Accessed 27 Oct. 2013, <http://en.wikipedia.org/wiki/Double-slit_experiment>.

[217] "Louis de Broglie" *Wikipedia: The Free Encyclopedia.* Wikimedia Foundation, Inc. 22 July 2004. Web. 22 Oct. 2013. Accessed 27 Oct. 2013, <http://en.wikipedia.org/wiki/Louis_de_Broglie>.

[218] *op. cit.*, Talbot, p. 22.

[219] *op. cit.*, Kuhlmann, p. 45.

[220] *op. cit.*, Talbot, p. 23.

[221] *op. cit.*, McTaggart, p. 19.

[222] Ibid., p. 23.

[223] Peter J. Oliver, "Fourier Series" *University of Minnesota School of Mathematics.* Web. 11 Dec. 2012. Accessed 2 Nov. 2013, < http://www.math.umn.edu/~olver/am_/fs.pdf >.

[224] *op. cit.*, Pickover, p. 210.

[225] Ibid., p. 210; *op. cit.*, Talbot, p. 27; *op. cit.*, McTaggart, p. 82-83.

[226] Alfred North Whitehead, <u>An Introduction to Mathematics,</u> (New York, NY: Oxford University Press, 1972) p. 142.

[227] *op. cit.*, Oliver; Shubing Wang, "Applications of Fourier Transform to Imaging Analysis" *University of Wisconsin-Madison, Department of Statistics*. Web. 23 May 2007. Accessed 2 Nov. 2013. <http://www. stat.wisc.edu/~mchung/teaching/MIA/projects/FT_complex.pdf>.

[228] *op. cit.*, McTaggart, pp. 82-83.

[229] "Louis de Broglie" *Wikipedia: The Free Encyclopedia*. Wikimedia Foundation, Inc. 22 July 2004. Web. 22 Oct. 2013. Accessed 4 Nov. 2013, <http://en.wikipedia.org/wiki/Louis_de_Broglie>.

[230] *op. cit.*, Talbot, pp. 27-28; *op. cit.*, McTaggart, p. 86; Karl Pribram, "Holonomic brain theory" *Scholarpedia: The Peer-Reviewed Open Access Encyclopedia*. Web. 2007. Accessed 4 Nov. 2013. < http://www.scholarpedia.org/article/Holonomic_brain_theory>.

[231] *op. cit.*, Talbot, p. 28.

[232] Karl Pribram, "Holonomic brain theory" *Scholarpedia: The Peer-Reviewed Open Access Encyclopedia*. Web. 2007. Accessed 4 Nov. 2013. < http://www.scholarpedia.org/article/Holonomic_brain_theory>.

[233] "Hun-tun" *Mythology Dictionary*. Web. Accessed 21 Dec 2014, <http://www.mythologydictionary.com/ hun-tun-mythology.html>.

[234] "Yin and yang" *Wikipedia: The Free Encyclopedia*. Wikimedia Foundation, Inc. 18 Dec. 2014. Accessed 22 Dec. 2014, <http://en.wikipedia.org/wiki/Yin_and_yang>.

[235] "Mathematical universe hypothesis" *Wikipedia: The Free Encyclopedia*. Wikimedia Foundation, Inc. 27 June 2013. Accessed 25 Nov. 2013, <http://en.wikipedia.org/wiki/Mathematical_universe_hypothesis>.

[236] *op. cit.*, Talbot, p. 1.

[237] "Holography" *Wikipedia: The Free Encyclopedia*. Wikimedia Foundation, Inc. 23 Mar. 2014. Accessed 28 Mar. 2014, <http://en.wikipedia.org/wiki/Holography>.

[238] Ibid; *op. cit.*, Talbot, pp. 14-18.

[239] *op. cit.*, Talbot, p. 25.

[240] Tracy V. Wilson, "How Holograms Work (p. 10)" *HowStuffWorks*. Accessed 3 Apr. 2014, <http://science.howstuffworks.com/hologram9.htm>.

[241] *op. cit.*, Talbot, pp. 12-14; David S. Walonick, "A Holographic View of Reality" *StatPac*. Web. 1993. Accessed 05 Apr. 2014, < http://www.statpac.org/walonick/reality.htm>.

[242] *op. cit.*, Talbot, pp. 18-20.

[243] *op. cit.*, Talbot, p. 26.

[244] Michael Talbot, "The Holographic Universe: Does Objective Reality Exist?" *Rense.com*. Web. Accessed 13 Apr. 2014, <http://www.rense.com/general69/holoff.htm>.

[245] *op. cit.*, Talbot, pp. 35-37; David S. Walonick, "A Holographic View of Reality" *StatPac*. Web. 1993. Accessed 05 Apr. 2014, < http://www.statpac.org/walonick/reality.htm>; "Quantum entanglement" *Wikipedia: The Free Encyclopedia*. Wikimedia Foundation, Inc. 5 Apr. 2014. Accessed 5 Apr. 2014, < http://en.wikipedia.org/wiki/Quantum_entanglement>; Timothy Ferris, "Quantum Weirdness". Web. 1997. Accessed 6 Apr. 2014. available at: < http://www.stanford.edu/dept/HPS/writingscience/Ferris.htm>.

[246] *op. cit.*, Talbot, pp. 37-39; David S. Walonick, "A Holographic View of Reality" *StatPac*. Web. 1993. Accessed 05 Apr. 2014, < http://www.statpac.org/walonick/reality.htm>.

[247] David Bohm, Wholeness and the Implicate Order, (New York, NY: Routledge, 1998) pp. x-xi, xv, 1-3, 7-9, 12, 16, 173.

[248] *op. cit.*, Bohm, pp. 173-175.

[249] *op. cit.*, Bohm, p. 176.

[250] *op. cit.*, Talbot, p. 39.

[251] *op. cit.*, Bohm, p. 177.

[252] *op. cit.*, Bohm, p. 149.

[253] *op. cit.*, Bohm, pp. 145-151; *op. cit.*, Talbot, pp. 46-47.

[254] "Theory of Forms" *Wikipedia: The Free Encyclopedia*. Wikimedia Foundation, Inc. 7 Feb. 2014. Accessed 11 Apr. 2014, <http://en.wikipedia.org/wiki/Theory_of_Forms>; "Plato" *Wikipedia: The Free Encyclopedia*. Wikimedia Foundation, Inc. 8 Apr. 2014. Accessed 11 Apr. 2014, <http://en.wikipedia.org/wiki/Plato>.

[255] David Banach, "Plato's Theory of Forms" 2006. Accessed 11 Apr. 2014. <http://www.anselm.edu / homepage/dbanach/platform.htm>.

[256] *op. cit.*, Talbot, pp. 286-291; Robert A.F. Thurman (translated by), The Tibetan Book of the Dead: Liberation Through understanding in the Between, (New York, NY: Bantam Books, 1994) pp. 16, 240-241; G.R.S. Mead (translated by), The Corpus Hermeticum: Initiation to Hermetics, (2008) pp. 23, 33, 38, 45.

[257] Alberto Güijosa, "What is String Theory?" 9 Sep. 2004. Accessed 12 Apr. 2014, < http://www.nuclecu. unam.mx/~alberto/physics/string.html>; Interview with George Musser, "The Complete Idiot's Guide to String theory" *Scientific American*. 16 Jul. 2008. Accessed 12 Apr. 2014, < http://www.scientificamerican.com/podcast/episode/ 29dc2da2-efd5-3d06-4d2e64931ba46d2d/>.

[258] "Cymatics" *Wikipedia: The Free Encyclopedia*. Wikimedia Foundation, Inc. 9 Mar. 2014. Accessed 12 Apr. 2014, < http://en.wikipedia.org/wiki/Cymatics>; TED Talk given by Evan Grant in 2009 - video available here: < http://www.cymatics.co.uk/intro-to-cymatics-ted-talk/>.

[259] Andrew Zimmerman Jones, "What is Bell's Theorem?" *About.com Physics*. Web. Accessed 14 Apr. 2014, < http://physics.about.com/od/quantuminterpretations/f/bellstheorem.htm>; "Bell's theorem" *Wikipedia: The Free Encyclopedia*. Web. Wikimedia Foundation, Inc. 3 Mar. 2014. Accessed 14 Apr. 2014, < http://en.wikipedia.org/wiki/Bell%27s_theorem>.

[260] Ibid.

[261] World Science Festival (2011, Sept. 2). "A Thin Sheet of Reality: The Universe as a Hologram". [Video file]. Retrieved from < http://www.worldsciencefestival.com/2011/09/a_thin_ sheet_of_reality_the_ universe_ as_a_hologram/ >. Accessed 6 June 2014.

[262] Ron Cowen, "Simulations back up theory that Universe is a hologram" *nature*. Web. 10 Dec. 2013. Accessed 2 June 2014, < http://www.nature.com/news/simulations-back-up-theory-that-universe-is-a-hologram-1.14328>; Ellie Zolfagharifard, "Are we living in a HOLOGRAM? Physicists believe our universe could just be a projection of another cosmos" *Mail Online*. Web. 12 Dec. 2013. Accessed 2 June 2014. < http://www.dailymail.co.uk/sciencetech/article-2522482/Is-universe-hologram-Physicists-believe-live-projection.html>.

[263] Sanjay Joshi, "Facts of Light" *Reefkeeping*. Web. Accessed 8 June 2014, <http://reefkeeping.com/issues/ 2006-03/sj/index.php>.

[264] Andrew Zimmerman Jones, "What is a Photon?" *About.com Physics*. Web. Accessed 8 June 2014.
< http://physics.about.com/od/lightoptics/f/photon.htm>.

[265] "Antiparticle" *Wikipedia: The Free Encyclopedia*. Wikimedia Foundation, Inc. 13 May 2014. Accessed 9 Jun. 2014, < http://en.wikipedia.org/wiki/Antiparticle>.

[266] "Speed of light" *Wikipedia: The Free Encyclopedia*. Wikimedia Foundation, Inc. 15 June 2014. Accessed 16 Jun. 2014, < http://en.wikipedia.org/wiki/Speed_of_light>.

[267] "Speed of light" *Wikipedia: The Free Encyclopedia*. Wikimedia Foundation, Inc. 15 June 2014. Accessed 16 Jun. 2014, < http://en.wikipedia.org/wiki/Speed_of_light>; "Ole Rømer " *Wikipedia: The Free Encyclopedia*. Wikimedia Foundation, Inc. 29 May 2014. Accessed 16 Jun. 2014, < http://en.wikipedia.org/wiki/Speed_of_light>; Alok Jha, "Why you can't travel at the speed of light: A short history of Einstein's theory of relativity" *The Guardian*. Web. 11 Jan. 2014. Accessed 16 June 2014, < http://www.theguardian.com/science/2014/jan/12/einstein-theory-of-relativity-speed-of-light>.

[268] Alok Jha, "Why you can't travel at the speed of light: A short history of Einstein's theory of relativity" *The Guardian*. Web. 11 Jan. 2014. Accessed 16 June 2014, < http://www.theguardian. com/science/2014/ jan/12/einstein-theory-of-relativity-speed-of-light>; Peter Russell, "The Mystery of Light" *Peter Russell Spirit of Now*. Web. Accessed 16 June 2014, < http://www. peterrussell.com/SG/Ch5.php>.

[269] *Einstein's Relativity and the Quantum Revolution: Modern Physics for Non-Scientists, 2nd Edition*, taught by: Professor Richard Wolfson, Lecture 22: The Particle Zoo. DVD. The Teaching Company, 2000; C. R. Nave, "Fundamental Forces: The Electromagnetic Force" *HyperPhysics*, Dept. of Physics and Astronomy, Georgia State University. Web. 2014. Accessed 16 June 2014. < http://hyperphysics.phy-astr.gsu.edu/hbase/forces/funfor.html>; "The Standard Model -

Electroweak Force" *Fermilab*. Web. 25 Apr. 2014. Accessed 16 June 2014. <http://www.fnal.gov/ pub/science/inquiring/matter/madeof/electroweakforce.html>.

[270] Judith Bluestone Polich, <u>Return of the Children of Light: Incan and Mayan Prophecies for a New World</u>, (Santa Fe, NM: Linkage Publications, 1999), p. 99.

[271] Sebastian Anthony, "Scientists work out how create matter from light, to finally prove Einstein's E=mc2" *Extreme Tech*. Web. 20 May 2014. Accessed 6 Dec. 2014, <http://www.extremetech.com/extreme/ 182701-scientists-work-out-how-create-matter-from-light-finally-proving-einsteins-emc2>; O. J. Pike, F. Mackenroth, E. G. Hill & S. J. Rose, "A photon–photon collider in a vacuum hohlraum" *nature photonics*. Web. 18 May 2014. Accessed 6 Dec. 2014, <http://www.nature.com/nphoton/journal/v8/n6/full/nphoton. 2014.95.html>; "Matter will be created from light within a year, claim scientists" *The Guardian*. Web. 26 Mar. 2014. Accessed 23 Dec. 2014, < http://www.theguardian.com/science/2014/may/18/matter-light-photons-electrons-positrons>.

[272] Rupert Sheldrake, <u>Science Set Free: 10 Paths to New Discovery</u>, (New York, NY: Deepak Chopra Books, 2012) pp 68-69, 82; "Dark Energy, Dark Matter" *NASA Science: Astrophysics*. Web. 14 May 2014. Accessed 31 Jul 2014, < http://science.nasa.gov/astrophysics/focus-areas/what-is-dark-energy/>; Robert Lamb, " What are dark matter and dark energy?" *HowStuffWorks*. 21 Apr 2010. Accessed 31 Jul 2014, <http://science.howstuffworks.com/ dictionary/astronomy-terms/dark-matter-dark-energy.htm>.

[273] "An Overview of the Human Genome Project" *genome.gov: National Human Genome Research Institute*. Web.8 Nov. 2012. Accessed 6 Aug. 2014, <http://www.genome.gov/ 12011238>.

[274] *op. cit.*, Lipton, pp. 62-64.

[275] "An Overview of the Human Genome Project" *genome.gov: National Human Genome Research Institute*. Web.8 Nov. 2012. Accessed 6 Aug. 2014, < http://www.genome.gov/ 12011238>.

[276] "Great chain of being" *Wikipedia: The Free Encyclopedia*. Wikimedia Foundation, Inc. 7 Apr. 2014. Accessed 9 Jul. 2014, < http://en.wikipedia.org/wiki/Great_chain_of_being>; Peter Suber, "The Great Chain of Being" *Peter Suber (*via *Earlham College* web site*)*. Web. Accessed 9 Jul. 2014, <http://legacy.earlham.edu/~peters/courses/re/chain.htm>.

[277] "The Great Chain of Being" *Herman Asarnow, Ph.D*. Web. Accessed 9 Jul. 2014, <http://faculty.up.edu /asarnow/greatchainofbeing.htm>.

[278] Terence McKenna Archive "Trialogue #24: The Heavens (Terence McKenna, R. Sheldrake, R. Abraham)". [Video file]. *YouTube*, 8 Jul. 2011. Accessed 9 Jul. 2014. < http://www.youtube.com /watch?v=yWqvY7CGaHw>.

[279] Miriam-Webster. Web. <http://www.merriam-webster.com/dictionary/solipsism>.

[280] "Law of attraction (New Thought)" *Wikipedia: The Free Encyclopedia*. Wikimedia Foundation, Inc. 2 Aug. 2014. Accessed 2 Aug. 2014, <http://en.wikipedia.org/wiki/Law_of_attraction_ %28New_ Thought%29>.

[281] Gregg Braden, <u>The Spontaneous Healing of Belief: Shattering the Paradigm of False Limits</u>, (Carlsbad, CA: Hay House, Inc., 2008) pp. 17-21.

[282] *op. cit.*, Lipton, pp. 137-138; "What Is the Placebo Effect?" *WebMD*. Web. Reviewed 10 Feb. 2014. Accessed 11 Aug. 2014, < http://www.webmd.com/pain-management/what-is-the-placebo-effect>; "Placebo" *Wikipedia: The Free Encyclopedia*. Wikimedia Foundation, Inc. 28 Jul. 2014. Accessed 11 Aug. 2014, < http://en.wikipedia.org/wiki/Placebo>.

[283] Bruce E. Wampold, Takuya Minami, Sandra Callen Tierney, Thomas W. Baskin, and Kuldhir S. Bhati, "The Placebo Is Powerful: Estimating Placebo Effects in Medicine and Psychotherapy From Randomized Clinical Trials" JOURNAL OF CLINICAL PSYCHOLOGY, Vol. 61(7), 835–854. Accessed 25 Dec. 2014 from <http://dm.education.wisc.edu/tminami/intellcont/Wampold_etal_JCP_2005-1.pdf>; *op. cit.*, Sheldrake, p. 274; Martin L. Rossman, M.D., <u>Fighting Cancer from Within: How to Use the Power of your Mind for Healing</u>, (New York, NY: Henry Holt and Company, 2003), p. 88; Sandra Blakeslee, "Placebos Prove So Powerful Even Experts Are Surprised; New Studies Explore the Brain's Triumph Over Reality" *The New York Times*. Web. 13 Oct. 1998. Accessed 25 Dec. 2014, < http://www.nytimes.com/1998/10/13/ science/placebos-prove-so-powerful-even-experts-are-surprised-new-studies-explore-brain.html? pagewanted=all&src=pm>.

[284] *op. cit.*, Sheldrake, pp. 270-274.

[285] Cara Feinberg, " The Placebo Phenomenon: An ingenious researcher finds the real ingredients of 'fake' medicine" *Harvard Magazine*. Web. Jan.-Feb. 2013. Accessed 13 Aug. 2014. <http://harvardmagazine.com /2013/01/the-placebo-phenomenon>.

[286] Ibid.

[287] "Nocebo" *Wikipedia: The Free Encyclopedia*. Wikimedia Foundation, Inc. 30 May 2014. Accessed 13 Aug. 2014, <http://en.wikipedia.org/wiki/Nocebo>.

[288] *op. cit.*, Talbot, p. 97.

[289] *op. cit.*, Sheldrake, pp. 270-272; "Irving Kirsch" *Wikipedia: The Free Encyclopedia*. Wikimedia Foundation, Inc. 30 Jul.. 2014. Accessed 13 Aug. 2014, <http://en.wikipedia.org/wiki/Irving_ Kirsch#Research_on_antidepressants>; *op. cit.*, Lipton, pp. 140-141.

[290] "Irving Kirsch" *Wikipedia: The Free Encyclopedia*. Wikimedia Foundation, Inc. 30 Jul.. 2014. Accessed 13 Aug. 2014, <http://en.wikipedia.org/wiki/Irving_Kirsch#Research_on_antidepressants>.

[291] Margaret Talbot, "The Placebo Prescription" *The New York Times (archives)*. Web. 9 Jan. 2000. Accessed 15 Aug. 2014, <http://www.nytimes.com/2000/01/09/magazine/the-placebo-prescription.html?src=pm&pagewanted=1>.

[292] Ibid.

[293] *op. cit.*, Rossman, p. 89.

[294] "Healing From Cancer: Mind-Over-Cancer Story of Mr. Wright" *walterorlowski.com*. Web. Accessed 14 Aug. 2014, < http://www.walterorlowski.com/healing-from-cancer.html>; *op. cit.*, Talbot, pp. 93-94; Lissa Rankin, M.D., "6 Stories That Will Make You Believe in the Power of

Your Mind to Heal" *Chopra Centered Lifestyle*. Web. Accessed 14 Aug. 2014, <http://www. chopra.com/ccl/6-stories-that-will-make-you-believe-in-the-power-of-your-mind-to-heal-you>; "The Power of Mind and the Promise of Placebo" *WRF: Healing Therapies Used Around the World*. Web. Accessed 14 Aug. 2014, <http://www.wrf.org/ alternative-therapies/power-of-mind-placebo.php>; Sandra Blakeslee, "Placebos Prove So Powerful Even Experts Are Surprised; New Studies Explore the Brain's Triumph Over Reality" *The New York Times*. Web. 13 Oct. 1998. Accessed 25 Dec. 2014, < http://www.nytimes.com/1998/10/13/ science/placebos-prove-so-powerful-even-experts-are-surprised-new-studies-explore-brain.html? pagewanted=all&src=pm>.

[295] Mosley JB, et al, "A controlled trial of arthroscopic surgery for osteoarthritis of the knee (abstract)" *PubMed*. (originally published in the *New England Journal of Medicine*, 2002 Jul 11;347(2):81-8). Web. Accessed 15 Aug. 2014. <http://www.ncbi.nlm.nih.gov/pubmed/ 12110735>.

[296] *op. cit.*, Lipton, pp. 139-140.

[297] *op. cit.*, Talbot, pp. 90-91; John Carey, with Amy Barrett, "Is Heart Surgery Worth It?" *Bloomberg Businessweek Magazine*. Web. 17 Jul. 2005. Accessed 15 Aug. 2014. <http://www.businessweek.com/ stories/2005-07-17/is-heart-surgery-worth-it>.

[298] Olly Bootle, "The remarkable power of the placebo: Patients who had FAKE surgery for a broken back recovered just as well, documentary reveals" *Mail Online*. Web. 13 Feb. 2014. Accessed 15 Aug. 2014. < http://www.dailymail.co.uk/health/article-2558438/ The-remarkable-power-PLACEBO-effect-Patients-FAKE-surgery-broken-recovered-just-documentary-reveals.html>; David H. Newman, M.D., "Placebo Surgery: More Effective Than You Think?" *Huffpost Healthy Living*. Web. 9 Mar. 2014. Accessed 15 Aug. 2014, < http://www. huffingtonpost.com/david-h-newman-md/placebo-surgery_b_4545071.html>.

[299] Dr. Christopher Kent, "Placebo surgery" *The Chiropractic Journal*. Web. Sep. 2002. Accessed 15 Aug. 2014, <http://www.chiro.org/research/FULL/Placebo_Surgery.html>.

[300] Ibid.

[301] Remy L Brim, Franklin G Miller, "The potential benefit of the placebo effect in sham-controlled trials: implications for risk-benefit assessments and informed consent" *Journal of Medical Ethics*. Web. 13 Dec. 2012. Accessed 15 Aug. 2014. <http://jme.bmj.com/content/ early/2012/12/12/medethics-2012-101045.full>.

[302] *op. cit.*, Rossman, pp. 84-87.

[303] "Guided Imagery - Topic Overview" *WebMD*. Web. 11 Jun. 2013. Accessed 16 Aug. 2014, <http://www.webmd.com/balance/stress-management/tc/guided-imagery-topic-overview>.

[304] Martin Brofman, <u>Anything Can be Healed</u>, (Findhorn, Scotland: Findhorn Press, 2003) pp. 10-14.

[305] "Guided Imagery Therapy" *WEIL: Andrew Weil, M.D.* Web. Accessed 17 Aug. 2014. <http://www.drweil.com/ drw/u/ART00468/Guided-Imagery-Therapy-Dr-Weil.html>.

[306] "What Evidence-Based Conditions Can Guided Imagery Help?" *Academy for Guided Imagery*. Web. Accessed 17 Aug. 2014. <http://acadgi.com/canimageryhelp/index.html>.

[307] Jane Hart, M.D. "Guided Imagery" MARY ANN LIEBERT, INC. • VOL. 14 NO. 6,

DECEMBER 2008, pp. 295-299. Accessed on 18 Aug. 2014 from *One Hour Drummer*. Web. <http://urbantaiko.com/Onehourdrummer/Wellness_Programs_files/Guided%20Imagery.pdf>; "Guided Imagery Therapy" *WEIL: Andrew Weil, M.D.* Web. Accessed 17 Aug. 2014, <http://www.drweil.com/ drw/u/ART00468/Guided-Imagery-Therapy-Dr-Weil.html>; Marian Sandmaier "Inside the Astonishing World of Guided Imagery" *Marian Sandmaier: Writer and Book Editor*. Web. Accessed 18 Aug. 2014, <http://www.mariansandmaier.com/downloads/ article_GuidedImagery.htm>.

[308] Mike Samuels, M.D. and Nancy Samuels, Seeing With the Mind's Eye: The History, Techniques and Uses of Visualization, (New York, NY: Random House, Inc., 1992) pp. 226-227.

[309] *Op. Cit.,* Talbot, p. 83.

[310] O. Carl Simonton, M.D., "Unproven Methods of Cancer Management" *CA-A Cancer Journal for Clinicians*, Vol. 32, No. 1, January/February 1982. Accessed on 19 Aug. 2014, from: <http://onlinelibrary. wiley.com/doi/10.3322/canjclin.32.1.58/pdf>.

[311] *op. cit.*, Sheldrake, p. 275.

[312] *Op. Cit.,* Samuels and Samuels, p. 222; S. Grant, "10 Amazing Examples of Mind Over Matter" *LISTVERSE*. Web. 21 May 2013. Accessed 21 Aug. 2014, < http://listverse.com/2013/05/21/10-amazing-examples-of-mind-over-matter/>.

[313] *Op. Cit.,* Talbot, pp. 132-138.

[314] *Op. Cit.,* McTaggart (The Field), pp. 35, 134; Vincent J. Daczynski, "Human Levitation! Yogi Pullavar - Self Levitation" *Amazing Abilities*. Web. 2004. Accessed 21 Aug. 2014, <http://www.amazingabilities.com/amaze8a.html>.

[315] *Op. Cit.,* Talbot, p. 88; *Op. Cit.,* McTaggart (The Intention Experiment), pp. 128-131; S. Grant, "10 Amazing Examples of Mind Over Matter" *LISTVERSE*. Web. 21 May 2013. Accessed 21 Aug. 2014, < http://listverse.com/2013/05/21/10-amazing-examples-of-mind-over-matter/>.

[316] D. T. Max, "Her Way: A Pianist of Strong Opinions," The New Yorker, (November 7, 2011): 62.

[317] *Op. Cit.,* McTaggart (The Intention Experiment), pp. 132-135; *Op. Cit.,* Samuels and Samuels, pp. 34, 66.

[318] Deepak Chopra, Ageless Body, Timeless Mind: The Quantum Alternative to Growing Old, (New York, NY: Harmony Books, 1993): pp. 92-95; Cara Feinberg, "The Mindfulness Chronicles: On 'the psychology of possibility'" *Harvard Magazine*. Web. September-October 2010. Accessed 25 Aug. 2014. <http://harvardmagazine.com/2010/09/the-mindfulness-chronicles>.

[319] *Op. Cit.,* Talbot, pp. 97-98; Daniel Goleman, "Probing the Enigma of Multiple Personality" *The New York Times (Archives)*. Web. Originally published 28 Jun. 1988. Accessed on web 18 Aug. 2014, <http://www.nytimes.com/1988/06/28/science/probing-the-enigma-of-multiple-personality.html?src=pm&pagewanted=1>; "Dissociative Identity Disorder - TWO FAMOUS CASES" *Psychology Encyclopedia*. Web. Accessed 18 Aug. 2014, <http://psychology.jrank.org/ pages/189/Dissociative-Identity-Disorder.html>.

320 *Op. Cit.,* Talbot, pp. 98-100.

321 *Op. Cit.,* Talbot, p. 98; *Op. Cit.,* Goleman (1988).

322 *Op. Cit.,* Talbot, pp. 97-99; Daniel Goleman, "NEW FOCUS ON MULTIPLE PERSONALITY" *The New York Times (Archives).* Web. Originally published 21 May 1985. Accessed on web 18 Aug. 2014, <http://www.nytimes.com/1985/05/21/science/new-focus-on-multiple-personality.html>.

323 *Op. Cit.,* Goleman (1988).

324 Rhonda Byrne, The Secret, (New York, NY: ATRIA Books, 2006) pp. 65, 89-91, 96-97, 115-116.

325 *Op. Cit.,*McTaggart (The Field), pp. 186-193; *Op. Cit.,* Rossman, pp. 227-228.

326 *Op. Cit.,*McTaggart (The Intention Experiment), pp. 182-184; Gregg Braden, The Divine Matrix: Bridging Time, Space, Miracles, and Belief, (Carlsbad, CA: Hay House, Inc., 2007) p. 94.

327 *Op. Cit.,* Braden (The Divine Matrix), pp. 118-121; Evolution Television "Cancer Cured in 3 Minutes - Awesome Presentation by Gregg Braden ". [Video file]. *YouTube*, 2 Sep. 2013. Accessed 30 Aug. 2014. <https://www.youtube.com/watch?v=VLPahLakP_Q>.

328 *Op. Cit.,* Talbot, pp. 141-142.

329 Annie Murphy Paul, "Your Brain on Fiction" *The New York Times Sunday Review| The Opinion Pages.* Web. 17 Mar. 2012. Accessed 28 Aug. 2014. < http://www.nytimes.com/2012/03/18/opinion/sunday/the-neuroscience-of-your-brain-on-fiction.html?pagewanted=all&_r=0>.

330 *Op. Cit.,* Talbot, p. 84.

331 *Op. Cit.,* Cooper, pp. 6, 35-37.

332 *Zohar* I:129a, as quoted in Cooper, p. 37.

333 Dolores Cannon, The Three Waves of Volunteers and the New Earth, (Huntsville, AR: Ozark Mountain Publishing, 2011) p. 451.

334 Ibid., pp. 9, 64, 68, 173, 311, 354, 408, 410, 446-447, 454, 462-466, 469-471, 500, 508-509, 513-517, 540-541, 546-547, 554-555.

335 Ibid., pp. 18, 64, 73, 173, 187, 311, 354, 364, 366, 368, 462-463, 465-466, 469-470, 508, 510-511, 513-516, 519-520, 526-529, 540-541, 554-555.

336 Ibid., pp. 187, 471, 500, 517, 519, 522, 526-529, 539-541, 543, 554.

337 Ibid., {see citations above}.

338 Ibid., p. 187.

339 *Op. Cit.,* Polich, pp. 101-102.

[340] "Human evolution" *Wikipedia: The Free Encyclopedia*. Wikimedia Foundation, Inc. 13 Sep. 2014. Accessed 13 Sep. 2014, <http://en.wikipedia.org/wiki/Human_evolution#Recent_and_current_human_evolution>; Robert W. Felix, <u>Magnetic Reversals and Evolutionary Leaps: The True Origin of Species</u>, (Bellevue, WA: Sugarhouse Publishing, 2009), p. 37.

[341] There are three schools of thought in the Christian community as to when the Rapture will occur in relation to the tribulation: before the tribulation ("pre-trib"), after the tribulation ("post-trib"), or somewhere in the middle ("mid-trib").

[342] "Terence McKenna - A Funny Idea" [Audio file]. *YouTube*, 27 Dec. 2010. Accessed 6 Feb. 2015. <https://www.youtube.com/watch?v=tL-33CuV5jo>.

[343] "Terence McKenna - A Forward Escape" [Audio file]. *YouTube*, 25 Sep. 2014. Accessed 6 Feb. 2015. <https://www.youtube.com/watch?v=srhjS6OOBjI>.

[344] P.M.H. Atwater, <u>Children of the Fifth World: A Guide to the Coming Changes in Human Consciousness</u>, (Rochester, VT: Bear & Company, 2012), pp. 10-13; *Op. Cit.*, Polich, pp. 84-87, 136; Alberto Villoldo, "Homo Luminous: The New Human" *Reality Sandwich*. Web. Accessed 16 Sep. 2014, <http://realitysandwich.com/1428/homo_luminous_the_new_human/>.

[345] Alberto Villoldo, "Homo Luminous: The New Human" *Reality Sandwich*. Web. Accessed 16 Sep. 2014, < http://realitysandwich.com/1428/homo_luminous_the_new_human/>; *Op. Cit.*, Polich, pp. 85-87, 136; *Op. Cit.*, Atwater, pp. 10-13.

[346] "Children of the New Earth: Frequently Asked Questions" *PlanetLightworker.com*. Web. Accessed 17 Sep. 2014, < http://www.planetlightworker.com/indigokids/faqs.htm>; "Indigo Children" *Namaste Café*. Web. Accessed 17 Sep. 2014, <http://www.namastecafe.com/evolution/indigo/>; *Op. Cit.*, Atwater, pp. 5, 7-8, 21,29; PMH Atwater, "The Fifth Root Race—In Ascendancy" *Edgar Cayce's A.R.E.* Web. 1 Feb. 2013. Accessed 17 Sep. 2014, <http://www.edgarcayce.org/are/blog.aspx?id=7926&blogid=445>.

[347] *Op. Cit.*, Cannon (<u>The Three Waves of Volunteers and the New Earth</u>), pp. 9-10, 17-20, 294-295, 318, 408, 436, 444-447, 534, 555.

[348] *Op. Cit.*, Cannon (<u>The Three Waves of Volunteers and the New Earth</u>), pp. 19-20.

[349] author designated as simply "Acolyte", "The CHANI Project: Computer-Interfaced Communication with Other Realms," <u>NEXUS Magazine</u>, (June-July 2011): 47-54, 70; original web forum thread available at <http://www.godlikeproductions.com/forum1/message520517/pg1>.

[350] Robert W. Felix, <u>Magnetic Reversals and Evolutionary Leaps: The True Origin of Species</u>, (Bellevue, WA: Sugarhouse Publishing, 2009), pp. xiv-xv.

[351] Ibid., pp. 21, 59.

[352] Ibid., p. 35.

[353] Ibid., pp. 39, 88-89, 99-104.

[354] Ibid., pp. 46-48, 51, 59-60, 73-74, 87-89, 98, 101.

[355] Alasdair Wilkins, "Earth's magnetic field just might be gearing up for a reversal" *io9*. Web. 15 Jul. 2012. Accessed 25 Sep. 2014, <http://io9.com/5926172/earths-magnetic-field-just-might-be-gearing-up-for-a-reversal>; Annie Sneed, "Earth's Impending Magnetic Flip: A geomagnetic reversal may happen sooner than expected" *Scientific American*. Web. 16 Sep. 2014. Accessed 25 Sep. 2014, <http://www. scientificamerican.com/article/earth-s-impending-magnetic-flip/>; *Op. Cit.*, Felix, pp. 92-93.

[356] Ibid., pp.51, 89-92, 153.

[357] Ibid., pp. 89-91; "The Precession of the Equinoxes" *The Ancient Wisdom Foundation*. Web. Accessed 24 Sep. 2014. <http://www.ancient-wisdom.co.uk/precession.htm#what%20is%20 precession>.

[358] Walter Cruttenden, Lost Star of Myth and Time, (Pittsburgh, PA: St. Lynn's Press, 2006), pp. 31, 34, 36-48; Giorgio De Santillana and Hertha Von Dechend, Hamlet's Mill: An Essay Investigating the Origin of Human Knowledge and Its Transmission Through Myth, (Jaffrey, New Hampshire: David R. Godine, Publisher, Inc., 1977), pp. 2-3, 58-59, 66-68, 140-147.

[359] Unexplained Universe "Atoms are mini black holes?" [Video file]. *YouTube*, 26 Aug. 2009. Accessed 2 Nov. 2014. < http://www.youtube.com/watch?v=8v0hcpeTCS4>.

[360] "Galactic Center" *Wikipedia: The Free Encyclopedia*. Wikimedia Foundation, Inc. 23 Sep. 2014. Accessed 27 Sep. 2014, < http://en.wikipedia.org/wiki/Galactic_Center#Supermassive _black_hole>.

[361] *Op. Cit.*, Alexander, pp. 47-48.

[362] Ibid., pp. 46-47.

[363] I originally transcribed this text from an audio file of a talk given my Mr. McKenna which I found on YouTube, but I have been unable to locate that file. The citation given here is a of an interview with Mr. McKenna in which he relates the same idea in similar terminology (he even refers to it as "the example I always use"): Gyrus & John Eden, "The Rollercoaster of Transcendence: An Interview with Terence McKenna" *Dreamflesh*. Web. Accessed 6 Feb. 2015. <http://dreamflesh.com/interviews/mckenna/>.

[364] David Derbyshire, "Is this how Eve spoke? Every human language evolved from 'single prehistoric African mother tongue'" *Mail Online*. Web. 16 Apr. 2011. Accessed 2 Oct. 2014, <http://www.dailymail. co.uk/sciencetech/article-1377150/Every-language-evolved-single-prehistoric-mother-tongue-spoken-Africa.html>.

[365] "How long have we been here?" *Natural History Museum*. Web. Accessed 2 Oct. 2014, <http://www. nhm.ac.uk/nature-online/life/human-origins/modern-human-evolution/when/index.html>.

[366] *The Queen of the Sciences: A History of Mathematics*, taught by: Professor David M. Bressoud, Lecture 3: Greek Mathematics – Thales to Euclid. DVD. The Teaching Company, 2008.

[367] "Logos" *Wikipedia: The Free Encyclopedia*. Wikimedia Foundation, Inc. 24 Sep. 2014. Accessed 5 Oct. 2014, < http://en.wikipedia.org/wiki/Logos>.

[368] "Fractal" *Wikipedia: The Free Encyclopedia*. Wikimedia Foundation, Inc. 5 Oct. 2014. Accessed 10 Oct. 2014, <http://en.wikipedia.org/wiki/Fractal#Natural_phenomena_with_fractal_features>.

[369] "RSA (cryptosystem)" *Wikipedia: The Free Encyclopedia*. Wikimedia Foundation, Inc. 11 Oct. 2014. Accessed 11 Oct. 2014, <http://en.wikipedia.org/wiki/RSA_%28cryptosystem%29>; *Op. Cit.* Pickover, p. 464.

[370] Marcus du Sautoy, The Music of the Primes: Searching to Solve the Greatest Mystery in Mathematics, (New York, NY: Perennial edition, HarperCollins Publishers, Inc., 2004), p. 5.

[371] Ibid., pp. 5-7; *Op. Cit.* Pickover, p. 292.

[372] *Op. Cit.* du Sautoy, pp. 9-11, 47-49; *Op. Cit.* Pickover, p.292; "Riemann hypothesis" *Wikipedia: The Free Encyclopedia*. Wikimedia Foundation, Inc. 28 Sep. 2014. Accessed 12 Oct. 2014, <http://en. wikipedia.org/wiki/Riemann_hypothesis#Distribution_of_prime_numbers>.

[373] The Sage English Dictionary and Thesaurus, version 5.1, release date 24 Jan. 2013. Software. A Sequence Publishing project. <http://www.sequencepublishing.com/thesage.html>.

[374] Mario Beauregard, PhD, Gary E. Schwartz, PhD, Lisa Miller, PhD, Larry Dossey, MD, Alexander Moreira-Almeida, MD, PhD, Marilyn Schlitz, PhD, Rupert Sheldrake, PhD, Charles Tart, PhD, "Manifesto for a Post-Materialist Science" *Explore: The Journal of Science and Healing*. Web. 2 Jul. 2014. Accessed 7 Dec. 2014. <http://www.explorejournal.com/article/S1550-8307%2814%2900116-5/fulltext>.

[375] Ibid.

[376] Elaine Myers, "The Hundredth Monkey Revisited: Going back to the original sources puts a new light on this popular story" *Context Institute: Whole-system pathways to a thriving sustainable future*. Web. 1985, 1997. Accessed 13 Oct. 2014. <http://www.context.org/iclib/ic09/myers/>; "Hundredth monkey effect" *Wikipedia: The Free Encyclopedia*. Wikimedia Foundation, Inc. 28 Jul. 2014. Accessed 13 Oct. 2014, <http://en.wikipedia.org/wiki/Hundredth_monkey_effect>; Ken Keyes, jr., "The Hundredth Monkey" *World Transformation*. Web. Accessed 13 Oct. 2014, <http://www.worldtrans.org/pos/monkey.html>.

[377] Dave Munger, "Is forgiving good for your health?" *ScienceBlogs*. Web. 12 Oct. 2005. Accessed 15 Oct. 2014, <http://scienceblogs.com/cognitivedaily/2005/10/12/is-forgiving-good-for-your-hea/>; "Holding a Grudge Can Be Bad for Your Health" *GoodTherapy.org*. Web. 10 Apr. 2012. Accessed 15 Oct. 2014, <http://www.goodtherapy.org/blog/holding-grudge-bad-for-health-0410122>.

[378] "Meditation: A simple, fast way to reduce stress" *Mayo Clinic*. Web. 19 Jul. 2014. Accessed 16 Oct. 2014, <http://www.mayoclinic.org/tests-procedures/meditation/in-depth/meditation/art-20045858?pg=1>.

[379] Jeanie Lerche Davis, "Meditation Balances the Body's Systems: The mind, heart, and body can improve with regular meditation" *WebMD*. Web. 1 Mar. 2006. Accessed 16 Oct. 2014, <http://www.webmd.com/ balance/features/transcendental-meditation>.

[380] Inelia Benz, <u>Personal and Global Ascension 2012: Volume One</u>, (Lulu Publishing, 2010), p. 105.

[381] Garrick Utley, "World's wealthiest 16 percent uses 80 percent of natural resources" *CNN.com*. Web. 12 Oct. 1999. Accessed 17 Oct. 2014, <http://www.cnn.com/US/9910/12/population.cosumption/>.

Index

F

G

H

I

J

About the author

John Mennella holds a B.S. degree with a major in mathematics from the City College of New York, and an M.S. degree in Computers in Education from Long Island University (Brooklyn). Motivated by a lifelong interest in mathematics, science, and the paranormal he began researching the afterlife and the nature of reality almost 40 years ago. A diagnosis of prostate cancer in 2003 spurred him to undergo hypnotic regression as a possible healing modality to supplement radiation treatments. This book is the result of his four decades of research and personal exploration.

To contact the author, to read articles and discussions regarding topics covered in this book, and to access free downloads of relevant materials, please visit the author's web site at:

www.reality-revealed.com

Made in the USA
San Bernardino, CA
19 November 2016